Developing Killer Web Apps *with* Dreamweaver MX *and* C#

Developing Killer Web Apps *with* Dreamweaver MX® *and* C#™

Chuck White

SYBEX

San Francisco · London

Associate Publisher: Joel Fugazzotto
Acquisitions Editor: Tom Cirtin
Developmental Editor: Brianne Agatep
Production Editor: Susan Berge
Technical Editor: Martin Reid
Compositor/Graphic Illustrator: Scott Benoit
Proofreaders: Darcey Maurer, Laurie O'Connell, Nancy Riddiough
Indexer: Ted Laux
Cover Designer: Caryl Gorska, Gorska Design
Cover Photographer: D. Normark/PhotoLink

Library of Congress Card Number: 2003115548

ISBN: 0-7821-4254-0

Manufactured in the United States of America

10 9 8 7 6 5 4 3 2 1

To India

Acknowledgments

This book wouldn't have been possible without the continued unwavering support and backing of Sybex's Tom Cirtin. The Sybex editorial, development, and production team put forth their usual stellar efforts. Special thanks to Brianne Agatep, Carol Henry, and Susan Berge for their patience and hard work. My technical editor, Martin Reid, provided invaluable insight, particularly in regards to my many SQL queries (no pun intended). In other words, this book was the result of hard work among many, many people. My sincerest thanks to all of them.

Contents at a Glance

Contents

Introduction

My first exposure to Macromedia's Dreamweaver was shortly after it was released. Unlike most WYSIWYG HTML editors of its time, Dreamweaver actually managed to output reliable HTML code, while providing a visual interface that graphic designers could relate to. Its success was pretty much instantaneous.

But it wasn't until I needed to develop a fairly complex Active Server Pages–based intranet involving a comprehensive invoicing system that I discovered how much Dreamweaver could help save both money and time. By then Dreamweaver had morphed into two different products: the simple, designer-based Dreamweaver, and a product geared toward data-driven websites called Dreamweaver UltraDev. On a job that otherwise would have cost me $80,000 to do, I estimate that Dreamweaver UltraDev probably saved me $40,000. The reason for this windfall was a visual interface that made creating a data-driven site very easy to do in a short amount of time. That was the good news.

The bad news was that I had to tweak a lot of code. It wasn't that Dreamweaver didn't write the code correctly. But if you look at how Dreamweaver handles the code generation process, it's clear that it simply writes out boilerplate code for you. Anyone who has done any substantial coding on a website knows that boilerplate code only takes you so far. There are a variety of situations in a production environment that boilerplate code cannot accommodate.

Nevertheless, I charged full-speed ahead, knowing how much money I was saving my company by creating the core of the application in Dreamweaver. The code tweaking was pretty much a piece of cake. Dreamweaver saved me hours of time and resources, and paid for itself in the first day of its use.

When Microsoft introduced ASP.NET and I was presented with my first opportunity to build a website using .NET, I blindly downloaded Microsoft's Visual Studio, the company's IDE (Integrated Development Environment) for .NET. Make no mistake: Visual Studio is a fantastic IDE. But you don't need it. In fact, the first thing I want to impress upon you is to not make the same mistake I made on my first ASP.NET project. I spent countless hours grappling with fundamental ASP.NET chores that, had I used the new Macromedia Dreamweaver MX 2004, could have been avoided. The amazing thing was, I already owned the product (actually, I owned Dreamweaver MX, the predecessor to Dreamweaver MX 2004). A time-saving machine was sitting on my desktop and I had no clue.

Dreamweaver MX is a very deceptive product. It contains remarkable functionality that is almost hidden from view. Its support for ASP.NET is impressive, and once I discovered the full scope of its capabilities I was once again stunned by the amount of time and money I could save developing a complex, data-driven site using ASP.NET.

If only I'd had a book like this, I could have saved even more money and time. Luckily, now, you do have a book like this.

This book isn't merely a step-by-step tutorial about how to use Dreamweaver MX with ASP.NET, although there are certainly plenty of those kinds of lessons inside. This book takes the examination of Dreamweaver MX and ASP.NET a step further and explores what is happening under the hood as Dreamweaver generates code for you. And it explores ways to develop your own scripts to either work with Dreamweaver-generated code or even sidestep that code altogether on those rare occasions you need to.

Is This Book for You?

If you want to learn ASP.NET, the fastest way to get there is to crank out some pages using Dreamweaver MX. Nothing can teach you faster than seeing how other people code, and although Dreamweaver MX isn't a person, it's a great teacher. But you'll need help interpreting what is going on, and this book will help you get there. The book also features a short but easy-to-follow tutorial on C#, the language you'll be developing with in this book.

If you're an accomplished ASP.NET coder already, you'll get a lot from this book, too. Dreamweaver works through a custom control that you'll want to get to know well. This custom control is a DLL that allows you to invoke a number of data-driven custom elements. Many of Dreamweaver's best features, such as working with stored procedures, are undocumented or poorly documented. Combining the power of stored procedures with Macromedia's nearly instant code-generation capabilities will save you hours of development time.

Although there are some books on the market that do what a basic manual for Dreamweaver should do (the manual that comes with the program is quite limited), few, if any, books cover Dreamweaver in its role as a developer's IDE for .NET. What few books there are don't have a good grasp of situations as they develop in the real world. They touch on fundamentals but rarely provide examinations of the runtime issues that always afflict deployments.

This book explores Dreamweaver as a real-world rapid development IDE for developing next-generation websites or, more accurately, web applications. It provides insight on production, configuration, and deployment issues. It also explores Dreamweaver's code "under the hood." This will give developers the power to troubleshoot coding issues that can develop when using Dreamweaver's visual interface, and guidance for manually tweaking the code when the output isn't quite right.

How This Book Is Organized

This book covers the intricacies of working with ASP.NET using Dreamweaver MX. It details the user interface of Dreamweaver as it pertains to .NET controls. It explores Dreamweaver's custom user control for .NET, which comes in the form of the Dreamweaver Control DLL (`DreamweaverCtrl.DLL`). When the DLL is placed in the `bin` directory of a .NET web application, a large library of special elements for working with databases is exposed to the developer.

From a developer's perspective, the key to using Dreamweaver MX is in understanding how it works under the hood. This book explains in detail what happens when the Dreamweaver user inserts, for example, a .NET DataSet using the Dreamweaver Insert ➤ DataSet command.

The book shows how these kinds of commands are invoked from the user interface; explains the options available in the various dialog boxes that are used to manipulate the controls; and most importantly in my view, describes what is happening under the hood by looking at the code that Dreamweaver outputs.

The book consists of nine chapters of progressively complex topics. You'll start off with basic ASP.NET configuration issues. By the second chapter, you'll be diving into the meat of what makes Dreamweaver such a great IDE as you learn how to work with SQL, the query language for databases that plays such a key role in your data-driven applications. In Chapter 3 you'll apply this knowledge as you build SQL-based pages using Dreamweaver's visual interface.

The next three chapters (Chapters 4 through 6) explore ASP.NET server components and how to leverage Dreamweaver's powerful visual interface to create these components rapidly, and how to handle problems that can arise along the way.

Chapter 7 takes a look at some advanced coding techniques and demonstrates how to do things such as compile C# programs using the ASP.NET compilers. Chapter 8 is an introduction to the Web Services technology and how you can use Dreamweaver to rapidly develop your own services. Finally, Chapter 9 takes you on a tour of a rather extensive web application named Realtor designed for real estate agents that forms the heart of most of the book examples. You can download the file for this chapter, named `Realtor.zip`, from this book's catalog page at `www.sybex.com`.

Additionally, two bonus chapters are available at `www.sybex.com`. Bonus Chapter 1, "Developing a Workflow," walks you through the process of developing a workflow for your website. Bonus Chapter 2, "Working with XML," offers a brief, basic tutorial on XML and explains how XML is used with ASP.NET and Dreamweaver.

Conventions Used in This Book

This book uses several distinct conventions to help you find the information you need as quickly as possible. Tips, Notes, and Warnings, shown here, are used to highlight important topics:

TIP   Here you'll find insider tips, shortcuts, and interesting bits of information that will aid you in your ASP.NET and Dreamweaver development. Warnings indicate that extra caution should be used, or that a specific problem could crop up that may force you to reconsider your life as a developer.

NOTE   A Note represents details I want to bring to your attention.

WARNING   Warnings indicate that extra caution should be used, or that a specific problem could crop up that might force you to reconsider your life as a developer.

Sidebars

Interesting but somewhat tangential information that deserves more than a note will appear as a sidebar. In this type of box you might find details on some code I'm explaining that is not necessarily directly relevant to the topic but is useful information anyway, a historical perspective on the subject at hand, or some other ancillary information.

When a small snippet of code is used, I generally refer to it as a code fragment, which appears in the book like this:

```
<script runat="server">
void getCityb_click(Object Src, EventArgs E)
{
}
</script>
```

The book text also uses a monospace font to illustrate the use of specific elements and attributes, and their contents or properties, methods, and functions. For example, when discussing the following element and its runat="server" attribute/value pair:

```
<script runat="server">
void getCityb_click(Object Src, EventArgs E)
{
}
</script>
```

the element will be referred to as script, the attribute as runat, and the element content as some content. I don't enclose string (text) values with quotes. If I am referring to string content, I simply use a monospace font like this.

Much of the source code for this book has been edited or truncated to save space. You can download all the source code listings from www.sybex.com. The source-file listings there contain the unedited versions of the source code.

In code listings, a continuation arrow (➥) indicates that the printed line of code wraps to the next line and that the transformation or script could fail if you break the line of code in a real environment.

Why C#?

This book uses C# as its language of choice. One reason for this was simply to save space. There is no reason you can't use VB.NET instead. The fundamentals of what goes on under the hood don't change at all.

Because of its strong datatyping, VB.NET is very different from the old VBScript, which means you no longer will be working with the old variant datatype. In fact, VB.NET resembles C# more than it resembles VBScript. C# and VB.NET both require use of object classes from the .NET Framework, so the important thing in both languages is to understand how to discover information about the massive object model library within the .NET framework. What language you actually use is not as important as understanding the class library. This book will help you understand how to get the information you need about the various class objects in the .NET Framework.

If you want to convert a page written in C# to VB.NET and vice versa, try the following website. It offers instructions on how to port your pages for both languages.

    http://www.4guysfromrolla.com/webtech/012702-1.shtml

Have Some Fun

Dreamweaver MX can make your application programming quite a bit of fun. But it's a lot more fun when you know what's going on. If you simply rely on Dreamweaver's substantial capabilities to generate all your data-driven code, you'll be in the dark all the time, and it will be very difficult to troubleshoot problems. In my mind, there is simply no substitute for understanding how Dreamweaver does what it does.

This book will help you learn how to develop ASP.NET applications in Dreamweaver whether you're an accomplished coder or a novice. It may even help you develop the next eye-opening website. If it does, I do have a Pay Pal account if you wish to share your new fortune.

Good luck, and have fun. Questions? Comments? E-mail me at chuck@tumeric.net.

CHAPTER 1

Configuring Dreamweaver for ASP.NET

- Defining a site

- Setting up your IIS environment for production

- Configuring Dreamweaver MX for use in versioning software

- Managing the `Web.config` file

Before you do anything with Dreamweaver MX, you'll need to figure out how it works at the site level. In other words, how can you configure it to build and deploy your website? Besides the normal configuration issues you'll encounter when working with Dreamweaver MX, such as the site definitions that all users need to learn, you'll want to get familiar with some of the intricacies of .NET and how they relate to decisions you make as your projects get underway.

.NET serves pages by compiling them at runtime into an intermediary language. Sometimes, some or all of the compilation takes place before runtime, such as when you develop what is called a *code-behind page*, but I'll save the intricacies of that for Chapter 9, "Advanced Coding with Dreamweaver MX." This intermediary language I'm talking about is basically machine code that is generated by ASP.NET from any number of sources written in languages such as C#, VB.NET, or even JavaScript. This is why you find so many different ways to work with .NET. Whatever language is being used, the pages ultimately get converted into machine code that tells the application server how to render your HTML.

All your code resides in either the code-behind page I just mentioned, or, more frequently for the purposes of this book because of the way Dreamweaver outputs ASP.NET pages, within special `script` tags. These tags have a `runat="server"` attribute value pair that is read exclusively by the server. The server interprets the script between the `script` tags and processes any functions you've defined within those tags. By including `runat="server"` in the `script` element, you prevent the contents of that tag from being interpreted by the browser, because ASP.NET compiles the page and returns HTML based on the instructions on the ASP.NET page you created.

One of the chief advantages of .NET is this compilation scheme, because it allows you or your loved ones to create custom controls in your favorite language and compile them as DLLs. Then, when you slip one of these DLLs into the `bin` directory of your .NET-based web application, .NET can use it to generate pages according to the functions it contains.

This is where Dreamweaver MX comes in. The good folks at Macromedia have already written a killer custom control for you, and it's where all the magic happens. With Dreamweaver MX, you can simply choose commands from the Dreamweaver interface to generate database-driven code. Dreamweaver generates special ASP.NET tags that tell ASP.NET how to interact with the Dreamweaver custom control. The amount of hand-coding time you can save is almost astonishing, and you'll save even more when you start your application development efforts with proper configuration settings. This chapter explores all these configuration issues, to get you off to the best possible start.

Defining a Site

Your first activity when you launch Dreamweaver MX, unless you're just looking at it to gain familiarity, will probably involve setting up a site using the Site menu to define your website. This will include telling Dreamweaver MX what language you want to use to create your .NET applications, and the specifics about accessing your site. This is a necessary step to take, since you need access to a server that can process .NET applications.

There are two ways to set up a site in Dreamweaver: Use a wizard, or choose the Advanced tab of the Site Definition panel. When the program is first launched after installation, it defaults to the wizard. However, if you choose the Advanced tab to define your site, the next time you start a new site definition the program will default to Advanced tab setup. To change it back to the wizard, click the Basic tab at the top of the Site Definition panel.

Using the Site Definition Wizard

Start off by choosing Site ➤ Manage Sites. A dialog box labeled Manage Sites will appear. Click the New… button. When you do this, you'll see two options appear: Site, and FTP & RDS Server. Choose Site. A new, larger dialog box named Site Definition will appear. Click the tab labeled Basic. You'll see a Site Definition dialog box that looks similar to that in Figure 1.1.

FIGURE 1.1:

The Site Definition wizard

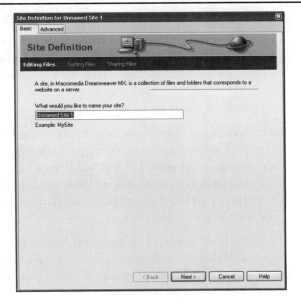

Here are the steps for completing the wizard:

1. The wizard asks you what you'd like to name your site. Give the site a descriptive name, and click the Next button.

2. The wizard next asks you if you want to work with a server technology such as ColdFusion, ASP.NET, ASP, JSP, or PHP. Under the question are two radio buttons. Choose the second one, "Yes, I want to use a server technology." When you click that, another question appears along with a drop-down list of choices. In this book we're using ASP.NET C#, so choose that from the list.

3. The next page asks you, "How do you want to work with your files during development?" Four radio buttons below that question reveal the following choices:

   Edit and test locally (my testing server is on this computer)   This means you want to edit and test from the same directory on your machine. If your computer has IIS (Microsoft's Web Server, Internet Information Services), Dreamweaver MX should know about it and will display a message indicating so at the bottom of the wizard. "Edit and test locally" is the default selection because most people like to test and develop locally, then deploy to the production site. In this dialog box you will need to choose where to store your files. Enter that information into the text field "Where on your computer do you want to store your files?" The wizard will suggest a folder for you, but you can override that choice with your own.

   Edit locally, then upload to remote testing server   This means you want to edit local files on your hard drive, then upload them to a server for testing. The testing server is not your production server. Enter the location for storing your files into the text field "Where on your computer do you want to store your files?" You can accept the default choice or select your own folder.

   Edit directly on remote testing server using local network   This means you want to set up a directory on your local machine that also serves as the root source for a local testing server using HTTP. You'll need to have a web server configured in order for this to work because the wizard will ask you for a testing server URL. This is usually `http://localhost` but can also be `http://127.0.0.1` (which is the same thing as `localhost`).

   To find out if your server is running, type either of these locations into your web browser. If the server is running and you haven't performed any custom configurations, your browser will generally display a page like that shown in Figure 1.2. Once you're certain your server is running, fill in the text field "Where are your files on the network?" You'll also choose this if you are in a workgroup working on a networked server. Either way, access is provided through a LAN, and you need to have access to a live server.

FIGURE 1.2:

When you type in
`http://localhost`,
your browser will show
an IIS page similar
to this.

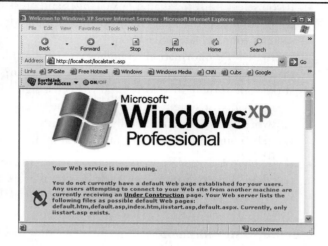

Edit directly on remote testing server using FTP or RDS   Clicking this option reveals a bit more information about your editing choice, informing you that Dreamweaver will need to download files from an FTP site. So the wizard asks you, "Where on your computer do you want Dreamweaver to store local copies of your files?" You can browse to the location or input the path directly into the text field. This is where Dreamweaver will store local copies of files downloaded from the FTP site. It's a reasonable choice if you are working with a remote hosting service and you're worried that testing on your own server won't be a true gauge of your site's performance.

TIP   You can set up a sandbox on your remote site by creating a directory within the root of your domain and calling it something like "test_root". Then you can mirror your site and copy everything onto your production server exactly as mapped out in your test directory.

4. The next wizard page will depend on your choice from Step 3. Let's do an "if … then" routine to map out your options:

Edit and test locally   If you chose this option, the next page contains a dialog box with a text field "What URL would you use to browse to the root of your site?" An example of what you might enter in this field might be something like **http://localhost/mySite/**.

Edit locally, then upload to remote testing server   If you chose this option, you'll be presented with a screen with a drop-down list at the top, labeled "How do you connect to your testing server?" The four options available are "I'll set this up later," FTP, Local/Network, and RDS. Forget about RDS since that's specific to ColdFusion.

- You can choose "I'll set this up later," and move to the next page.

- If you select FTP, the dialog box changes and presents options for filling in your FTP connection information. The hostname or FTP address of your server should be the same as your website, unless your host provider or system administrator has given you alternate FTP information. Whether you need to fill in the text field "What folder on the testing server do you want to store your files in?" depends on whether the site is at the root of the FTP address you've been assigned. If you don't know, contact your host provider or system administrator to be sure. You'll also need your username and password in order to successfully connect to your FTP service. These, too, are provided by your host provider or network administrator.

- If you choose Local/Network, choose a folder the test files should be stored in in the text field "Where do you copy your files to in order to test them?" You can click the small folder icon next to the text field to browse to the folder that should store your test files.

Edit directly on remote testing server using local network   If you chose this option, the next wizard page asks, "What URL would you use to browse to the root of the site?" The answer to this will vary, and it's important to get it right, so if you're not administering your own site, be sure to check with your system administrator to be sure you enter the correct information. Dreamweaver manages links based on a correctly mapped mirror between the root of your testing site and the root of your deployed site, so if the root doesn't properly map to subfolders or directories, your links may not work when you go live. After you've entered URL information in the field (or browsed to your files), click the Test URL button to see if you have established a connection. If the test is unsuccessful, a number of things could be wrong. Check Appendix A in the section titled "Common Configuration and Deployment Errors" for details.

TIP   When you're done setting up your site, you may need to go into the Advanced tab in the Site Definition panel and choose Passive FTP in order to create a successful FTP connection, especially if you are working behind a firewall. The unnamed alternative to Passive FTP is called Active FTP and is the default, but it relies on the client's listening for FTP connections, which doesn't work well with firewalls.

Using the Advanced Tab to Define a Site

I shy away from wizards whenever I can, because they often make assumptions about my choices that I might later regret. So as quickly as possible, I try to figure out what everything means and understand the options available to me when I'm configuring something on a

Windows machine—whether I'm using Windows itself or an application configuration tool such as Dreamweaver MX's Site Definition panel.

So let's hit the Advanced tab in the Site Definition panel and take a closer look at our options (refer again to Figure 1.1 to see where the Advanced tab is). To do this, start the process of going to the Site Definition Wizard outlined at the top of this section immediately under the heading "Using the Site Definition Wizard," but this time, choose the Advanced tab rather than Basic. Instead of invoking a wizard, you'll be setting your configuration manually (Site Files ➤ Edit Sites).

So start the process once again by going to Site Files ➤ Edit Sites. In the Edit Sites dialog box, you can choose a current site to edit or you can create a new one. Let's create a new site and give it whatever name you like. This is where, instead of going into the Basic tab, you should click the Advanced tab. There you'll see categories on the left, grouped as a column in a tall text box. We've covered a lot of these options in the preceding section on using the Site Definition Wizard, so let's focus here on some details not visible to you when using the wizard.

Local Info

The Local Info category manages the settings pertaining to the machine on which you're running Dreamweaver. You will normally want to keep images and media in separate directories. This option helps Dreamweaver keep track of them in the File panel's Assets tab and tends to improve the efficiency of image downloads. (When you use the wizard, you'll not see a dialog box asking you where to store images.)

Remote Info

This category lets you choose between several options just as the wizard did, except that here you can override what you originally entered into the wizard.

This is where you can choose Passive FTP, as discussed in the earlier Tip. Passive FTP allows the client to initiate FTP connections rather than simply listening for them. For a more technical discussion on this, see the section "The Nefarious 'Waiting For Server' Message" in this book's appendix, "Troubleshooting Web Applications Using Dreamweaver." You are also presented with an option to automatically upload files when you save the site definition.

Testing Server (and Server Model Language)

Most of the Testing Server options are covered in the section on using the wizard, but here we'll touch a little more on the significance of choosing your *server model language*.

Since you're using .NET, this part is pretty easy. I chose to use C# for the examples throughout the majority of this book, but generally the code I use is portable to VB.NET or J#, with some minor tweaking. (This code is available on the Sybex website, at www.sybex.com, by the way.)

When you choose a server model language, you're basically setting your preferences in such a way that when you click File ≻ New and choose Dynamic Page from the Category window, Dreamweaver MX automatically goes into ASP.NET mode. When you save your first file, Dreamweaver will automatically append the .aspx extension onto the end of your filename, unless you manually override this option.

More importantly, Dreamweaver inserts the correct type of code into your Dreamweaver page when you issue, for example, a Record Insertion Form command from the Dreamweaver menu (Insert ≻ Application Objects ≻ Record Insertion Form), as in this example:

```
<MM:Insert
runat="server"
CommandText='<%# "INSERT INTO chuckwh.AdCopy (AdAutoNumber,
➥    AdTimeStamp, AdDate, AdIO_ID, AdTextCopy, AdTextCopyN, AdImage)
➥    VALUES (@AdAutoNumber, @AdTimeStamp, @AdDate, @AdIO_ID,
➥    @AdTextCopy, @AdTextCopyN, @AdImage)" %>'
ConnectionString='<%# System.Configuration.ConfigurationSettings.AppSettings
➥    ["MM_CONNECTION_STRING_Tumeric"] %>'
DatabaseType='<%# System.Configuration.ConfigurationSettings.AppSettings
➥    ["MM_CONNECTION_DATABASETYPE_Tumeric"] %>'
Expression='<%# Request.Form["MM_insert"] == "form1" %>'
CreateDataSet="false"
Debug="true"
>
  <Parameters>
    <Parameter Name="@AdAutoNumber" Value='<%#
➥    ((Request.Form["AdAutoNumber"] != null) &&
➥    (Request.Form["AdAutoNumber"].Length > 0)) ?
➥    Request.Form["AdAutoNumber"] : "" %>' Type="Int" />
<!- SNIP ->
  </Parameters>
</MM:Insert>
<MM:PageBind runat="server" PostBackBind="true" />
```

The real work here is performed in a compiled binary object called the DreamweaverCntrls .dll, and the MM:Insert element is used for interacting with the compiled object and passing parameters to it. This is why Dreamweaver MX can provide a visual interface to robust application server technology. (If you chose VB.NET as your server language, Dreamweaver would output VB.NET code instead.)

NOTE   For more on the `DreamweaverCntrls.dll`, see the last section of this chapter, "Deploying the Dreamweaver Control," and Chapter 5, "Working with Components."

There are a number of additional options in the Testing Server panel designed to help you with site management.

Cloaking

Cloaking lets you hide files from Dreamweaver's file-uploading services. You provide extensions for the files you don't want Dreamweaver to upload, such as the native Flash extension, `.fla`, or PSD (Photoshop) files that you may have saved into your Images directory while building site images.

Design Notes

You can pass information to team members using Design Notes, which let you make highly customized notes and add levels of attention for project management purposes. There are two check boxes:

- Maintain Design Notes. Enable this to tell Dreamweaver to maintain Design Notes.
- Upload Design Notes for Sharing. Enable this if you want to have Design Notes uploaded with the associated file.

Site Map Layout

You can view the structure of your website and the relationship between various site documents using the Site Map Layout tool. In order to use it, you'll need to choose your home page so that the tool can reveal broken or orphaned links within your site; this is a common feature found in many site management tools.

You can customize the tool by adjusting the number of columns and column width, designating whether icons will contain descriptive text, and choosing whether to display hidden or dependent files.

File View Columns

If you've worked with previous versions of Dreamweaver, you might really miss the way the program used to display site files. The old view provided lots of information, such as any associated notes, the date a file was modified and/or checked out, and size. This view is still there, but it's hidden away in the Site/File panel. When you click the last icon the Site/File panel (Figure 1.3), the panel expands and covers the entire Dreamweaver interface to reveal the "old style" Dreamweaver Site Management window (Figure 1.4).

FIGURE 1.3:

FIGURE 1.3:

The Site
Management icon

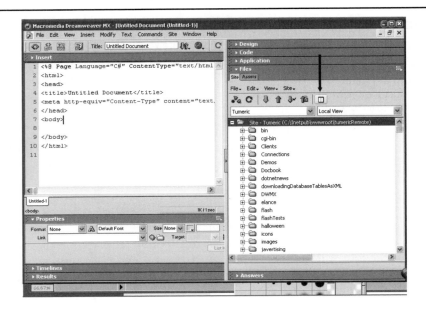

FIGURE 1.4:

The "old-style" Site
Management window
look of the File panel

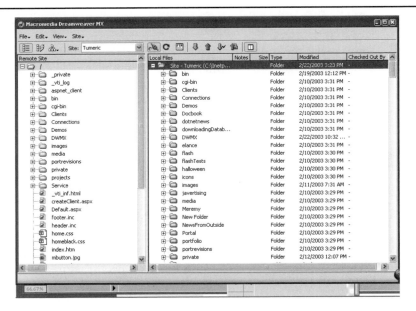

You can customize the look of the old-style view by selecting the next-to-last category in
the Advanced tab of the Site Definition panel, File View Columns. By clicking one of the

Options check boxes at the bottom of the File View Columns panel, you can designate whether to hide or show the highlighted feature in the view (Figure 1.5).

FIGURE 1.5:

Highlight a feature
and select the Show
checkbox to include
the item in the
old-style File view

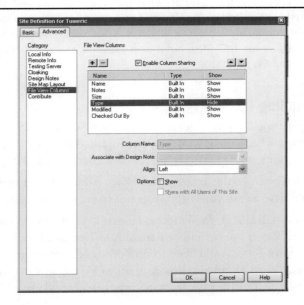

Setting Up the IIS Environment for Development

To use ASP.NET with Dreamweaver MX, you will need access to the .NET Framework. Even though .NET Framework is a new technology, it doesn't require an upgrade of Internet Information Services (IIS), which is the Microsoft web server that comes with Windows 2000 and Windows XP. You only need to download the .NET Framework (or get it on CD). You can download it free from Microsoft at http://www.microsoft.com/net/.

You also need IIS, which comes with Windows Server operating systems, including Windows 2000 and Windows XP. To test and see if it is already installed, type http://localhost into your browser. If you get a "Cannot Find Server" error, you probably need to install IIS. Double-check by opening your Administrative Tools control panel and look for the Internet Information Services component. If you see it, right-click the website you are using by expanding the computer icon in IIS (see Figure 1.6, which shows a highlighted computer within IIS) and then the Web Sites folder. Choose the website you are using and right-click the site. If you're running Windows XP or something other than Windows Professional Server, you will only be licensed for one site, named Default Web Site, so choose that. You'll see a series of options in a context menu. Choose Start. If the website is running, the menu option will say Stop, which means you should actually be seeing the website when you type in http://localhost into your browser.

TIP   If you are running XP Home, you'll find that it doesn't install either IIS or Personal Web Server (PWS), the latter of which is a small-footprint web server Microsoft distributed previously with Windows 9x. However, you can go to www.asp.net/webmatrix/default.aspx? and download WebMatrix, which is a free open-source offering by Microsoft. WebMatrix is an editor for .NET files, but it also includes a server that XP Home users can use in lieu of IIS and PWS.

Installing IIS

It's very possible that Internet Information Services (IIS) did not come as part of the installation package when you or someone else installed Windows 2000 or Windows XP Professional on your computer. If that's the case, you'll need to install it.

That's easy to do, assuming you have Administrator rights on your computer. If you don't, you'll have to ask your Administrator to set up your system for you.

To install IIS, go to Windows Control Panel and choose Add/Remove Programs. In Windows XP, this option will be named Add/Remove Programs and Windows Components. In Windows 2000, you'll need to drill down one more time to Add/Remove Windows Components. When Windows displays a list of Windows components that can be installed, check the box next to Internet Information Services and click Next to install IIS.

The IIS snap-in will appear in your Administrative Tools Control Panel. If you're running Windows XP and not viewing your Control Panel in classic view, you'll need to click the Performance and Maintenance section of your Control Panel. When you double-click Internet Information Services, you'll see a snap-in expand into a window like the one in Figure 1.6.

FIGURE 1.6:

The IIS snap-in

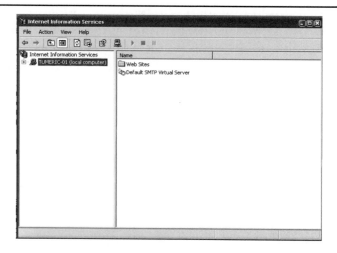

Configuring IIS

The IIS snap-in works similarly to any other Microsoft Management Console (MMC) window. MMC is a hosting environment that presents a common interface for multiple applications such as IIS and Index Server. This makes it easier for users to use what really amounts to a number of fairly complex Windows components, without needing to figure out the nuances of the assortment of interfaces for those components. Even if you've never used an MMC-based component, it's easy to learn because it looks so much like Windows Explorer.

At the top of the IIS MMC window is an icon and the name Internet Information Services. Under that is your computer name, and next to that is a little plus sign, just like Windows Explorer. When you click the plus sign, the computer expands to reveal the components of your computer that are relevant to IIS. One of those will be a folder named Web Sites. Expand Web Sites and you'll see your Default Web Site. If you have Windows 2000 Server, you can add additional sites. If you have what amounts to personal editions of Windows 2000, such as Windows 2000 Professional or Windows XP, you won't be able to add additional websites and you'll have to use the Default Web Site because that's all you're licensed for.

You're actually ready to go, but chances are you'll want to break your web applications down into separate directories. This means you need to make a *virtual directory*. A virtual directory is a mapped directory interface to a physical directory on the web server's computer. By creating a virtual directory, you can have a directory located at

```
C:/documents/docs/moredocs/yetmoredocs/docs/xdocs/ydocs/vdocs/
```

accessed via the server at

```
localhost/vdocs
```

This is because you tell the web server that the physical path should point to the virtual directory mapping you provide.

To try it out, right-click the Default Web Site in IIS and navigate to New/Virtual Directory. The New Virtual Directory Wizard will appear. The first thing you'll have to do is name your virtual directory by entering it into the Alias text field. The name you give is the name of your web application. You can have more than one web application in a website. In fact, you can have zero web applications in your website and run everything from the root (and still have subdirectories), but that's not a terribly efficient way to do things.

The next page asks you to locate the physical folder that stores the files to be used by the virtual directory. It's important to realize at this point that the Virtual Directory doesn't actually store any files, or even copy them anywhere, even though it will look like it does when you're finished with the wizard. The Virtual Directory is an application that runs by implementing code it finds in the physical directory you name on this page of the wizard. The nice thing about this is that, even if you serve an HTML page from a directory that is not involved in any way with your virtual directory, you can refer to the virtual directory in any code on your site like this (assuming our current example):

```
<a href = "/vdocs/foo.html">A link</a>
```

Notice where the first solidus (/) character is on the path. Using that character as the first character on a path tells IIS to look for a virtual directory named by whatever lies between the first and second solidus characters. So in the preceding line of code, the link points to a virtual directory named vdocs that would resolve to the domain name followed by vdocs, or

```
http://www.domainname.com/vdocs
```

Another advantage to using virtual directories is that you can make them resolve to sub-domains like this:

```
http://services.domainname.com/vdocs
```

where vdocs resolves to the subdomain services.

The last page of the wizard asks you which Access Permissions you want for your Virtual Directory. For our purposes here, you will generally not need anything more than the Read and Run Scripts permissions. Exceptions to this will be noted during the course of the book. Always make Read and Run Scripts your choice as your instinctive reaction (rule of thumb) to this page. You can always change things later.

NOTE   The configuration described in this section was tested on Windows XP Professional. Your IIS configuration windows may differ slightly but will be basically the same.

Configuring Dreamweaver MX for Use in Versioning Software

Versioning software, also referred to as *source control* or *content management systems software*, is software that locks files when a team member checks them out for editing so that team members can't edit the same files simultaneously. Among such software, Dreamweaver MX provides direct support only for Microsoft's Visual SourceSafe and Macromedia's SiteSpring. SiteSpring is being left to die on the vine by Macromedia; they have released their last version of the product.

Before I introduce you to specific source control systems, let's have a brief look at team workflow as practiced within the Dreamweaver environment.

Checking In and Checking Out

The basic tenet of Dreamweaver's Check In/Check Out system is based on one thing: Don't use the Get or Put commands, ever, if you are using Check In/Check Out. Get and Put are

FTP commands that get files from the server and put files onto the server, respectively. Of course, there might be exceptions to this if you are using, for example, Perforce, which is a third-party source control system, but that's because Perforce has its own checking-in-and-out workflow that bypasses Dreamweaver's. (There's more about configuring Dreamweaver MX for Perforce in a later section.)

> **NOTE** To use Check In/Check Out, each team member must be using Dreamweaver, which can be a drawback if you have programmers who resist using it. This is one of the reasons it's sometimes best to develop using a third-party source control system. If every team member is using Dreamweaver MX, Check In/Check Out can be a good option for version control, but keep in mind that it doesn't lock files as true source control software does.

Team Workflow

To use Check In/Check Out, each team member defines a local root folder on his or her development machine. If you're an administrator, configure a common remote sharing server. Otherwise, your administrator will do that for you. Make sure that in your Site Definition panel, under Remote Server in the Advanced tab, you check the Enable File Check In and Check Out box. Then, to retrieve a file, instead of using the Get command, you use the Check Out command. All team members access files this way; so when a file is checked out, it's critical that you do not check it out. You can tell by viewing the icons in the File panel that indicate whether or not files are checked out (refer again to Figure 1.4).

The bad news about Check In/Check Out is that the system doesn't lock the files in the same way as industrial-strength source control systems, so it's actually possible to check out a file even if it has already been checked out, and then overwrite someone else's changes when you check the file back in. This can also happen if you use the Get and Put commands—a good reason never to do this when you're using Check In/Check Out. Users attempting to retrieve files that were checked out by someone else will get a confirmation message asking if they really want to go through with it. Even knowledgeable users, however, can make mistakes and accidentally hit the OK button, especially when they're distracted.

If it sounds like I'm arguing that workgroups should design a better system, one that really locks files when they're checked out, I am. Nevertheless, Check/In Check Out is available in Dreamweaver, and there may be some instances where you might use it. So let's take a quick look at how to set it up.

Setting Up Check In/Check Out

You must first define a site and select certain options in the Site Definition panel to activate Check In/Check Out:

Setting up the local site Each team member defines a site, designating a folder on their computer's hard drive as the local root folder. You already know how to do this from the section titled "Defining a Site" earlier in the chapter.

Setting up the remote site In the Site Definition dialog panel, in the Advanced Tab's Remote Info category, specify a server folder (Host Directory for FTP access) or a remote folder (for local/network access) as shown in the section titled "Defining a Site" earlier in the chapter.

Enabling Check In/Check Out In the Remote Info category, select the Enable Check In/Check Out check box. Two more text fields appear beneath that check box. Fill in a name and your e-mail address in the two fields provided. After these options have been activated, the Check In and Check Out icons appear in the File panel.

Configuring for Concurrent Versions System (CVS)

Concurrent Versions System (CVS) is a reliable old workhorse among long-time developers. On Windows the most commonly used implementation is WinCVS. On the Mac, you can get a CVS implementation called MacCVS. WinCVS has proven frustrating for most Dreamweaver developers in production environments, but there are two options to consider to make it a viable solution for versioning.

The first is a SourceForge Dreamweaver/CVS project that is in its earliest stages for integrating Dreamweaver with WinCVS. You'll find it at `http://dwcvs.sourceforge.net/`.

NOTE	As this book was being written, the SourceForge project was in its earliest stages, and the developers had not yet posted any files. That may have changed by the time you read this.

A better bet, because it gets good reviews for stability and ease of use and is in fact available, is another SourceForge project named TortoiseCVS. There isn't any specific module for integration with Dreamweaver, but as a general versioning control system, it's worth a try: `http://www.tortoisecvs.org/download.shtml`. And MacCVS is available at SourceForge at `http://www.maccvs.org/`.

You'll have to use TortoiseCVS and MacCVS outside of Dreamweaver because direct integration with them isn't supported.

Configuring for Perforce

Perforce is a versioning system that has a loyal following in many large-scale development shops. You can configure Dreamweaver to work with Perforce's storage units (called depots) and access them in Dreamweaver using FTP. The following instructions assume a basic knowledge of Perforce.

There are three Perforce directory areas to be aware of:

- The client workspace is an area of working storage on the computer where P4FTP, the Perforce FTP tool, runs. This workspace must not overlap the local root.

- The local root is the directory where Dreamweaver stores its working copies of the website files for editing.

- The host directory is the Perforce depot location where your website files live. The remote host directory must be the path to your Perforce ftp- client workspace, plus any additional directories that you need in order to get you to the files you're working on.

For example, suppose you're running Dreamweaver on a Windows computer, P4FTP on a Unix computer named ftpserver, and the Perforce server on a Unix computer. You would use the following Perforce configuration:

Host: ftpserver

Client root: /usr/team/userName

Client view: //depot/... //ftp-userName/...

The Dreamweaver configuration for a website named mySite would be as follows:

Local root: c:\dwroot\mySite

Host directory: /usr/team/userName/main/mySite/

Creating Websites

To use Dreamweaver to create a website that resides in a Perforce depot, follow these steps:

1. Choose ➤ New Site. The Site Definition dialog box is displayed. Click the Advanced Tab.

2. Create a folder on your computer where you want Dreamweaver to store the local copies of your website files, making sure you specify an existing directory that does not live in your client root.

3. In the Category pane, click Remote Info. The Remote Info pane is displayed.

4. From the Access list, choosing FTP reveals the following fields:

   FTP Host   Enter the name of the computer where P4FTP is running and the port on which it is listening for FTP requests. For example: **myftphost:1234**.

   Host Directory   This is the location in the Perforce depot to upload and download website files using the Put and Get FTP commands. If you're running in a mixed OS environment, the name of this directory should be based on the conventions of the operating system that is running P4FTP. This must be an existing directory, so if one doesn't exist, create one first using Perforce or through an FTP client with a command-line interface.

Login and Password   Enter your Perforce login and password.

WARNING   Do *not* check the box Enable File Check In and Check Out.

The next step is to create the Perforce depot location in your client workspace. Copy any existing website files to the client workspace location that corresponds to the depot location of the website you defined with the Site Definition panel. Use the Perforce p4 Add command to add files to the depot.

Configuring for Visual SourceSafe

Dreamweaver MX provides direct support for Visual SourceSafe. You can connect directly to SourceSafe through the Remote Info category in the Advanced tab of the Site Definition panel. When you choose SourceSafe Database from the Access drop-down list, a Settings button appears to the right of the drop-down list. Click that button to display a dialog box with the settings you need to configure for connecting to the desired Visual SourceSafe database (see Figure 1.7). After you complete these entries, you can connect to the SourceSafe database and check files in and out.

FIGURE 1.7:

The Settings input for connecting to Visual SourceSafe

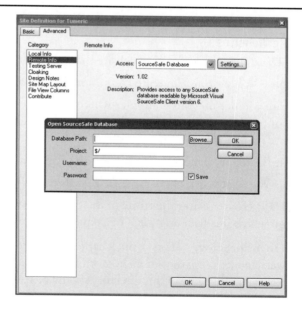

It's possible that the site administrator won't want direct connections to the Visual Source-Safe database, in which case you'll have to work on your site locally and check files in and out of Visual SourceSafe using your Working folder in SourceSafe. Details on this will depend on how your administrator has set up the SourceSafe environment, so be sure to check with your site administrator for details.

NOTE   Unfortunately, up to this point, my experience with WebDAV in Dreamweaver has not been very positive. In fact, every time I have attempted to use it, the application has crashed, and this has been the case on multiple versions of Dreamweaver MX and Dreamweaver MX 2004.

The Art of Managing the *Web.config* File

Anytime you're working with component-based architecture, and .NET as deployed from Dreamweaver certainly qualifies, it's best to think about how many problems can be solved globally. By this I don't mean solving the world's problems, but rather how many of your web development tasks can be resolved on a global level, so that you can drill down and add specificity on a granular level.

To see what I mean, pay special attention to this section, because the more you can manage configuration outside of your actual application code, the better. In ASP.NET, you can control a number of your web application's configuration properties through an XML file named `Web.config`.

When you store a `Web.config` file in your domain's root directory, all the files throughout the rest of your site inherit the properties that are in the configuration file. If there is no `Web.config` file, the application acts as if you have one in the root anyway, and everything is defaulted to ASP.NET's settings that the Framework adopted when it was originally installed.

The settings of the `Web.config` file, whether they're placed by you or are the .NET default settings, can be overridden by adding a configuration file named `Web.config` to the directory that contains the application you want to influence. Looking at Figure 1.8, if you want to make some application configurations in the directory named `Sub1` different from the rest of your site, you would add a `Web.config` file to `Sub1`. The web applications in `Sub2`, since it is a child of `Sub1`, would then inherit the configurations deployed in `Sub1`. So if you wanted them to be like the rest of the site, you'd need to either provide that directory with its own `Web.config` file, or set up different `system.web` elements for each directory within the root directory's `Web.config` file.

FIGURE 1.8:

Directories inherit
Web.config
properties from
their parents

Listing 1.1 shows what a typical structure for a Web.config file might look like.

Listing 1.1   **Typical structure for a** Web.config **file**

```
<configuration>
    <appSettings />
    <system.web>
        <authentication>
            <forms>
                <credentials>
            <passport>
        <authorization>
            <allow>
            <deny>
        <browserCaps>
            <result>
            <use>
            <filter>
                <case>
        <clientTarget>
            <add>
            <remove>
            <clear>
        <compilation>
            <compilers>
                <compiler>
            <assemblies>
                <add>
                <remove>
                <clear>
        <customErrors>
            <error>
        <globalization>
        <httpHandlers>
            <add>
            <remove>
            <clear>
        <httpModules>
            <add>
            <remove>
```

```
        <clear>
    <httpRuntime>
    <identity>
    <machineKey>
    <pages>
    <processModel>
    <securityPolicy>
        <trustLevel>
    <sessionState>
    <trace>
    <trust>
    <webServices>
        <protocols>
            <add>
            <remove>
            <clear>
        <serviceDescriptionFormatExtensionTypes>
            <add>
            <remove>
            <clear>
        <soapExtensionTypes>
            <add>
        <soapExtensionReflectorTypes>
            <add>
        <soapExtensionImporterTypes>
            <add>
        <WsdlHelpGenerator>
    </webServices>
  </system.web>
</configuration>
```

You may want to configure everything in one root directory, however. It certainly will be easier to maintain, because you won't have to remember to update various Web.config files as your site grows. Instead, you just need to remember to alter the root Web.config file.

For example, you might want to create particular configurations for different languages. In that case, you wrap each system.web element in a location element, like so:

```
<location path="EnglishPages">
  <system.web>
    <globalization
      requestEncoding="iso-8859-1"
      responseEncoding="iso-8859-1"
    />
  </system.web>
</location>
```

```
<location path="JapanesePages">
  <system.web>
    <globalization
      requestEncoding="Shift-JIS"
      responseEncoding="Shift-JIS"
    />
  </system.web>
</location>
```

Here, a different `system.web` configuration element is used for Japanese and English pages. All files in the `EnglishPages` directory will use the iso-8859-1 encoding, and all files living in the `JapanesePages` directory will use Shift-JIS encoding. You can also use any of the other `system.web` child elements that you'll be visiting in the next section.

Web.config Elements and Attributes

It doesn't do much good to have this nifty XML-based configuration document if you don't know what its elements and attributes mean. This section provides a look into the properties of the one file you're likely to encounter the most while working with Dreamweaver. We're not providing a detailed analysis of every element and attribute available to this file, because, like so many Microsoft object models, the underlying schema that defines these elements is substantial and there just isn't enough space in this book to justify the deforestation such detailed analysis would trigger. Instead, I've focused on areas that will be of particular interest to Dreamweaver MX .NET developers. You can get more information from the .NET Framework SDK at

```
http://msdn.microsoft.com/library/default.asp?url=/library/en-us/cpgenref/html
➡    /gngrfaspnetconfigurationsectionschema.asp
```

appSettings

One of the main reasons for using Dreamweaver MX in the first place is to take advantage of its rapid application development (RAD) capabilities, especially when you're working with databases. If you look at your site's `Web.config` file after you set up your database, you'll find something like this:

```
<appSettings>
    <add key="MM_CONNECTION_HANDLER_MyConnection" value="sqlserver.htm" />
    <add key="MM_CONNECTION_STRING_ MyConnection" value=
      "Persist Security Info=False;Data Source=11.11.1.1;
      Initial Catalog=mydb;User ID=user;Password=somepass" />
```

```
        <add key="MM_CONNECTION_DATABASETYPE_ MyConnection" value="SQLServer" />
        <add key="MM_CONNECTION_SCHEMA_ MyConnection" value="" />
        <add key="MM_CONNECTION_CATALOG_Tumeric" value="" />
    </appSettings>
```

These settings are created by Dreamweaver and inserted into your root directory's `Web.config` file when you set up your first database connection. The settings, of course, will depend on exactly what settings you choose when you create your database connection string to connect to your database. The process is driven by the `appSettings` element, which can have three child elements:

The `add` element, which is the one you'll see used most often, has two attributes, `key` and `value`. The `key` is simply the name of the application setting that will be accessed by .NET during runtime, and the `value` is the value sent to .NET to process the component. For example, when you create a dataset in Dreamweaver MX, Dreamweaver inserts a custom .NET control element named `MM:DataSet` into your web page. One of the attributes for this element is the `ConnectionString` attribute. In Figure 1.9 you can see there is a direct connection between the `MM:DataSet` element's `ConnectionString` attribute and the `Web.config` file's element's `appSettings` element. The `ConnectionString` calls the key named `MM_CONNECTION_STRING_Tumeric`, and that key is the value of the connection string. Therefore, this:

```
ConnectionString='<%# System.Configuration.ConfigurationSettings.AppSettings
➥ ["MM_CONNECTION_STRING_MyConnection"] %>'
```

could have been written like this directly in an `.aspx` page, instead:

```
ConnectionString="Persist Security Info=False;Data Source=11.11.1.1;
➥    Initial Catalog=mydb;User ID=user;Password=somepass"
```

This form, however, forces us to edit the connection string in the `.aspx` page that is using it. And we don't want to do this, because if we end up with numerous such pages we'd have to go into each page in order to edit the connection string. It's much easier to define the connection string within the `appSettings` element and refer to it repeatedly in other pages. That way, if we want to change it later, we easily can by simply updating the `Web.config` file.

The `remove` element of `appSettings` can be used to remove a configuration setting deployed further up in the configuration hierarchy.

The `clear` element removes all settings defined further up in the hierarchy.

MM:DataSet element

```
<MM:DataSet
id="clientDS"
runat="Server"
IsStoredProcedure="false"
ConnectionString='<%#
System.Configuration.ConfigurationSettings.AppSettings["MM_CONNECT
ION_STRING_myConnection"] %>'
DatabaseType='<%#
System.Configuration.ConfigurationSettings.AppSettings["MM_CONNECT
ION_DATABASETYPE_myConnection"] %>'
CommandText='<%# "SELECT Client_ID  FROM ClientInfo WHERE CEMail =
@CEMail" %>'
Debug="true"
>
```

appSetting element in Web.config file

```
<appSettings>
        <add key="MM_CONNECTION_HANDLER_myConnection"
value="sqlserver.htm" />
        <add key="MM_CONNECTION_STRING_myConnection" value="Persist
Security Info=False;Data Source=11.111.1.11;Initial Catalog=myDB;User
ID=uid;Password=yourpassword" />
        <add key="MM_CONNECTION_DATABASETYPE_myConnection"
value="SQLServer" />
        <add key="MM_CONNECTION_SCHEMA_myConnection" value="" />
        <add key="MM_CONNECTION_CATALOG_myConnection" value="" />
</appSettings>
```

authentication

The authentication element configures ASP.NET authentication support. This is one of the more important elements when you are building Dreamweaver .NET apps, because it makes it easy to develop password-protected areas and redirection routines. Authentication can be handled in one of four ways, as represented by the mode attribute:

- Through Windows authentication
- Through forms
- Through Microsoft's proprietary Passport system
- None (there is no authentication)

The syntax for this element looks like this:

```
<authentication mode="Windows|Forms|Passport|None">
<forms name="name"
       loginUrl="url"
       protection="All|None|Encryption|Validation"
       timeout="30" path="/" >
   <credentials passwordFormat="Clear|SHA1|MD5">
      <user name="username" password="password" />
   </credentials>
</forms>
<passport redirectUrl="internal"/>
</authentication>
```

The `authentication` element has some child elements that are worth looking at. These all help you develop robust authentication routines for directories, virtual directories and applications.

The *forms* Element

The `forms` child element has nothing to do with the HTML `form` element we've all grown to love and nurture. Rather, this is used for the .NET authentication process. Consider this element as the key to the city for your users. Let's say you set up a virtual directory or web application named `catalog` that is accessed when a user types `www.mydomain.com/catalog` into their browser. You use the `forms` element to handle the users' routing so that everyone, if you want, goes to the same page. This means if someone has a part of this directory bookmarked, let's say `www.mydomain.com/catalog/profile.aspx`, they can only get there if they are an authenticated user. You use the `forms` element to manage this routing apparatus.

There are a number of attributes to the `forms` element you might want to get familiar with, so let's have a look:

name   This attribute specifies the HTTP cookie to use for authentication. By default, the value of `name` is `.ASPXAUTH`. When more than one application is running on a single server and each application requires a unique cookie, each application must have its own cookie name in each application's `Web.config` file.

loginUrl   When a user attempts to visit a page on a site that has been configured for authentication, the user will first get redirected to the page specified by the `loginUrl` attribute if no valid authentication cookie is found; this happens even if the page is bookmarked. The default value is `default.aspx`, but you can change it to any name you wish. The page to which you redirect the users should have a login form, or, at a bare minimum, a link to a login form, since the page really acts as the gateway to the rest of the directory configured for authentication.

protection   This attribute specifies what kind of encryption to use. There are four possible values for this attribute:

- All: The default and recommended value; this means the application uses both data validation and encryption to protect the cookie.

- None: Although it makes authentication less challenging to system resources, Microsoft recommends against using the none protection value because both encryption and validation are disabled.

- Encryption: Specifies that the cookie is encrypted using Triple-DES or DES (for more information on encryption schemes, go to http://csrc.nist.gov/cryptval/des.htm), but data validation is not performed on the cookie. According to Microsoft, cookies used in this way might be subject to chosen plaintext attacks.

- Validation: This is a validation confirmation technique for preventing cookie data tampering while the data is transported over the network. This attribute value tells .NET to create a cookie by concatenating (adding one string value to another to form a new string) a validation key with cookie data, computing a message authentication code, and appending the message authentication code to the outgoing cookie.

timeout   This specifies the amount of time, in integer minutes, after which the cookie expires. The default value is 30.

path   Use the path attribute to specify the path for cookies generated by your application. It's best to keep the path at the default value, which is a backslash (\), because most browsers are case-sensitive and will not send cookies back if there is a case mismatch in the path.

The forms child element itself has an optional child element named credentials, consisting of a mandatory attribute named passwordFormat that you use to indicate how you want to encrypt the password. You have three options: Clear, which provides no encryption, and which you obviously want to avoid unless you want hackers to have access to your users' passwords; MD5, for the MD5 hash algorithm; and SHA1, for the SHA1 hash algorithm.

The credentials element, too, has a child element named user, which can be used to store a username and password directly in the Web.config file.

Take a look at the following Web.config file snippet, a form that authenticates against an application named logon.aspx. This form is the gateway, so to speak, for all who attempt to access a file in the directory. If users try to access a file but hasn't yet logged on, they are automatically re-directed to logon.aspx.

```
<authentication mode="Forms">
    <forms name=".ASPXAUTH "
    loginUrl="logon.aspx"
    protection="All" path="/" timeout="30" />
</authentication>
```

Listing 1.2 is an example of the script that drives logon.aspx. When a user tries to get into another page in the same directory, if they haven't logged in, they'll get bounced back to logon.aspx. This is true even if they know the query string that would take them to their profile page and try to type that into their browser.

Listing 1.2   A login script for logon.aspx

```
<script runat="server">
        bool ValidateUser(string uid, string passwd)
    {
        SqlConnection cnn;
        SqlCommand cmd;
        SqlDataReader dr;
        cnn = new SqlConnection(ConfigurationSettings.AppSettings
        ➥ ["MM_CONNECTION_STRING_Tumeric"]);
        cmd = new SqlCommand("SELECT Client_ID, CPassword, ClientName,
➥ CFirstName,
        ➥    CLastName FROM ClientInfo where CEMail='" + uid + "'",cnn);
        cnn.Open();
        dr = cmd.ExecuteReader();
        try {
        while (dr.Read())
        {
            if (string.Compare(dr["CPassword"].ToString(),passwd,false)==0)
            {
                cnn.Close();
                return true;
            }
        }
        }
        catch (Exception e)
        {
        lblMsg.Text = "An application error has occurred. Please call us
        ➥    at 415-553-8857 for further assistance.";
        }
        cnn.Close();
        return false;
    }

        void Page_Load(object sender, System.EventArgs e)
    {
      if (Page.IsPostBack)
      {
      if (ValidateUser(txtUserName.Value,txtUserPass.Value) )
      {
            FormsAuthenticationTicket tkt;
            string cookiestr;
            HttpCookie ck;
            tkt = new FormsAuthenticationTicket(1, txtUserName.Value,
➥ DateTime.Now,
            ➥    DateTime.Now.AddMinutes(30), chkPersistCookie.Checked,
```

```
➥     "your custom data");
cookiestr = FormsAuthentication.Encrypt(tkt);
ck = new HttpCookie(FormsAuthentication.FormsCookieName, cookiestr);
if (chkPersistCookie.Checked)
    ck.Expires=tkt.Expiration;
Response.Cookies.Add(ck);

string strRedirect;
strRedirect = Request["ReturnUrl"];
if (strRedirect==null)
    strRedirect = "client2.aspx?CEMail=" + txtUserName.Value;
Response.Redirect(strRedirect, true);
        }
        else
            lblMsg.Text = "You have provided an invalid user name or password.
➥        Please try again";

        }
    }
```

You'll learn how to build this kind of form authentication in Chapter 4, "Working with Databases."

authorization

You can also allow users entry into a directory or application through the authorization element and its child allow and deny elements, which define who gets in and who doesn't.

```
<authorization>
    <allow users="comma-separated list of users"
           roles="comma-separated list of roles"
           verbs="comma-separated list of verbs" />

    <deny users="comma-separated list of users"
           roles="comma-separated list of roles"
           verbs="comma-separated list of verbs" />
</authorization>
```

When defining who gets in and who doesn't, a question mark (?) allows anonymous users; an asterisk (*) indicates that all users are accepted, as in this next example. It allows access to all members of the Admin role and denies access to everyone else by blocking out all users using an asterisk.

```
<configuration>
    <system.web>
        <authorization>
            <allow roles="Admins" />
            <deny users="*" />
        </authorization>
    </system.web>
</configuration>
```

In authorization code, users and roles may be obvious to you, but what about verbs? This attribute is a comma-separated list of HTTP methods granted access to the resource. Possible values are GET, HEAD, POST, and DEBUG.

browserCaps

The browserCaps exposes ASP.NET's browser capabilities component to help you better handle various incoming browsers. This lets you write code to make your web application behave differently depending on the browser type accessing your site. This process is called *browser sniffing*, often done in the past using client-side JavaScript. The browserCaps element structure looks like this:

```
<browserCaps>
    <result type="class" />
    <use var="HTTP_USER_AGENT" />
        browser=Unknown
        version=0.0
        majorver=0
        minorver=0
        frames=false
        tables=false
    <filter>
        <case match="Windows 98|Win98">
            platform=Win98
        </case>
    <case match="Windows NT|WinNT">
        platform=WinNT
    </case>
    </filter>
    <filter match="Unknown" with="%(browser)">
        <filter match="Win95" with="%(platform)">
        </filter>
    </filter>
</browserCaps>
```

The filter element's with attribute uses regular expressions, the nuances of which are beyond the scope of this chapter, but generally you won't need to alter the default capabilities of ASP.NET's browser-sniffing. You can use .NET's HttpBrowserCapabilities class to manage the web application behavior based on the kind of browser attempting to access the page.

Back in the days of the browser wars, redirecting users using different browsers was one way, if an expensive one, to manage browser capabilities. Generally, today's developers shy away from expensive browser-sniffing routines because most modern browsers interpret standard HTML in a reliable way, and you can use Cascading Style Sheets (CSS) to enhance visual layouts. Browsers that don't support CSS won't display CSS-based visual enhancements, but if the coding is done correctly, these browsers will still display the page reasonably well because they understand the basic HTML elements that to render the pages.

Nevertheless, you may find yourself wanting or even needing to do some browser sniffing, especially if you're on a corporate intranet and you want to take advantage of, for example, IE6's extensive Dynamic HTML model. To make procedural decisions based on browser make and version, you can do something like this:

```
if(Request.Browser.Browser.Equals("IE") && Request.Browser.MajorVersion >= 5)
    Response.Write("Good, you are using IE 5 or higher");
```

clientTarget

.NET contains a collection of user agent aliases, which bind arbitrary names (for example, "ie5") to user agent information. You can add to this collection using your own aliases. Use whatever name you want in the alias attribute, but the userAgent attribute to which you bind the name needs to be recognizable by .NET, such as

```
Mozilla/4.0 (compatible; MSIE 5.5; Windows NT 4.0)
```

Here's an example of clientTarget code:

```
<clientTarget>
    <add alias="alias name to use"
        userAgent="identification of user agent" />
    <remove alias="alias name to remove" />
    <clear />
</clientTarget>
```

compilation

This is an element that contains all the compilation settings used by ASP.NET:

```
<compilation debug="true|false"
             batch="true|false"
             batchTimeout="number of seconds"
             defaultLanguage="language"
             explicit="true|false"
             maxBatchSize="maximim number of pages per
                          batched compilation"
             maxBatchGeneratedFileSize="maximum combined size
(in KB) of the generated source file per batched compilation"
             numRecompilesBeforeAppRestart="number"
             strict="true|false"
             tempDirectory="directory under which the ASP.NET temporary
               files are created" >
    <compilers>
        <compiler language="language"
                extension="ext"
                type=".NET Type"
                warningLevel="number"
                compilerOptions="options" />
    </compilers>
```

customErrors

This element defines custom error messages for an ASP.NET application:

```
<customErrors defaultRedirect="url"
             mode="On|Off|RemoteOnly">
    <error statusCode="statuscode"
          redirect="url"/>
</customErrors>
```

If you wanted to redirect a user who was receiving a 404 File Not Found error, you could do something like this:

```
<customErrors defaultRedirect="generr.htm"
    mode="RemoteOnly">
    <error statusCode="404"
        redirect="FNF.htm"/>
</customErrors>
```

You should turn custom errors on by making the mode value On when you are in development, and turn them off when you are ready to go live by making the mode value RemoteOnly. Actually, RemoteOnly doesn't turn them off; it redirects the user to a custom error page so that they don't see the ASP.NET errors that are of benefit to you as a Web developer.

globalization

You encountered this element when introduced to the Web.config element earlier in the chapter. The globalization element configures the globalization settings of an application:

```
<globalization requestEncoding="any valid encoding string"
               responseEncoding="any valid encoding string"
               fileEncoding="any valid encoding string"
               culture="any valid culture string"
               uiCulture="any valid culture string" />
```

You might be wondering what the culture-related strings do. They provide ways to automatically handle things like regional-specific date data-types. Dates in the United States are typically structured as "August 11, 2003," whereas dates in some other countries are typically structured as "11 August 2003." In addition, .NET sets the default currency to euro (instead of the dollar) for cultures that use the euro.

httpHandlers

This element maps incoming URL requests to IHttpHandler classes:

```
<httpHandlers>
    <add verb="verb list"
        path="path/wildcard"
        type="type,assemblyname"
        validate="" />
```

```
  <remove verb="verb list"
          path="path/wildcard" />
  <clear />
</httpHandlers>
```

Handlers accept requests and produce responses and manage them through page-handler classes. One area where you might see this `httpHandlers` element used frequently is Web Services, which allows a site to expose programmatic functionality via the Internet by accepting messages and sending replies, and running complex functions based on this communication.

When the .NET runtime environment sees a request for a file with an `.aspx` extension, the handler that is registered to handle `.aspx` files is called, which by default is the `System.Web.UI` `.PageHandlerFactory` class. However, when an `.asmx` file is detected, Web Services are invoked through a different class, the `System.Web.Services.Protocols.WebServiceHandlerFactory`. By customizing this process through the `Web.config` file, you can determine which HTTP requests are handled by using the `verb` attribute of the `add` child element of `httphandlers`.

```
<httphandlers>
<add verb="GET" path="*.asmx"
type="System.Web.Services.Protocols.WebServiceHandlerFactory,
System.Web.Services" validate="false" />
</httphandlers>
```

This code designates that for all `GET` requests, if the file being requested is an `.asmx`, the system should create an instance of the `WebServiceHandlerFactory`, which lives in the `System.Web.Services.dll` assembly. If you want the handler to accept all HTTP verbs, you would change the verb value to `"*"`. This makes it possible to generate an HTML page that describes a Web Service.

httpModules

The `httpModules` element adds, removes, or clears HTTP modules within an application. Most of the processes you encounter using Dreamweaver .NET have everything you need in the default settings. The `httpModules` element has three subelements: `add`, `remove`, and `clear`. The add subelement has one attribute, `type`, which is the assembly and class name of the handler you wish to include:

```
<httpModules>
    <add type="classname,assemblyname" name="modulename" />
    <remove name="modulename" />
    <clear />
</httpModules>
```

httpRuntime

This element configures ASP.NET HTTP runtime settings. This section can be declared at the machine, site, application, or subdirectory level:

```
<httpRuntime useFullyQualifiedRedirectUrl="true|false"
        maxRequestLength="size in kbytes"
        executionTimeout="seconds"
        minFreeThreads="number of threads"
        minFreeLocalRequestFreeThreads="number of threads"
        appRequestQueueLimit="number of requests" />
```

identity

Normally, all ASP.NET application operations are performed by a user named ASPNET. This user is created automatically when you install the .NET Framework. Then, you have to be sure the virtual directory (your web application) has been granted user privileges to ASP.NET. Sometimes you'll want to "impersonate" a user, which means that instead of using the ASPNET user account, you'll name another account for running the web application. The identity element controls this process with some fairly self-explanatory attributes:

```
<identity impersonate="true|false"
        userName="username"
        password="password"/>
```

machineKey

This element configures keys to use for encryption and decryption of a form's authentication cookie data and can be declared at the machine, site, or application levels, but not at the sub-directory level:

```
<machineKey validationKey="autogenerate|value"
        decryptionKey="autogenerate|value"
        validation="SHA1|MD5|3DES" />
```

pages

The page element identifies page-specific configuration settings such as session state and page buffering:

```
<pages buffer="true|false"
      enableSessionState="true|false|ReadOnly"
      enableViewState="true|false"
      enableViewStateMac="true|false"
      autoEventWireup="true|false"
      smartNavigation="true|false"
      pageBaseType="typename, assembly"
      userControlBaseType="typename" />
```

processModel

The `processModel` element configures the ASP.NET process model settings on Internet Information Services (IIS) web server systems:

```
<processModel enable="true|false"
              timeout="mins"
              idleTimeout="mins"
              shutdownTimeout="hrs:mins:secs"
              requestLimit="num"
              requestQueueLimit="Infinite|num"
              restartQueueLimit="Infinite|num"
              memoryLimit="percent"
              cpuMask="num"
              webGarden="true|false"
              userName="username"
              password="password"
              logLevel="All|None|Errors"
              clientConnectedCheck="HH:MM:SS"
              comAuthenticationLevel="Default|None|Connect|Call|
                                      Pkt|PktIntegrity|PktPrivacy"
              comImpersonationLevel="Default|Anonymous|Identify|
                                     Impersonate|Delegate"
              maxWorkerThreads="num"
              maxIoThreads="num" />
```

securityPolicy

This element manages security policy:

```
<securityPolicy>
   <trustLevel name="value" policyFile="value" />
</securityPolicy>
```

sessionState

This element handles and directs session-state issues:

```
<sessionState mode="Off|Inproc|StateServer|SQLServer"
              cookieless="true|false"
              timeout="number of minutes"
              stateConnectionString="tcpip=server:port"
              sqlConnectionString="sql connection string" />
```

trace

This element configures the ASP.NET trace service:

```
<trace autoflush="true|false"
       indentsize="indent value"/>
```

trust

The `trust` element indicates the access security permission of an application:

```
<trust level="Full|High|Low|None" originUrl="url" />
```

webServices

This element controls the settings of XML Web services created using ASP.NET:

```
<webServices>
   <protocols>
      <add name="protocol name" />
   </protocols>
   <serviceDescriptionFormatExtensionTypes>
   </serviceDescriptionFormatExtensionTypes>
   <soapExtensionTypes>
      <add type="type" />
   </soapExtensionTypes>
   <soapExtensionReflectorTypes>
      <add type="type" />
   </soapExtensionReflectorTypes>
   <soapExtensionImporterTypes>
      <add type="type" />
   </soapExtensionImporterTypes>
   <wsdlHelpGenerator href="help generator file"/>
</webServices>
```

Deploying the Dreamweaver Control

Perhaps the most important thing you'll do when developing a .NET application in Dreamweaver MX will occur when you deploy the Dreamweaver Control. The Dreamweaver Control is a DLL developed by Macromedia specifically for use with Dreamweaver MX. This custom control is analogous to having hundreds of lines of code within a server script tag, right in your web page. The difference is that in the case of Dreamweaver Control, the code for the script lives in a different file (a source file called `DreamweaverCtrls.cs`, available in the Macromedia directory that is installed when you install the program, at `DreamweaverMX\Configuration\ServerBehaviors\Shared\ASP.Net\Scripts\Source`. This script was compiled "at the factory." Macromedia used the .NET compiler to compile the code into the DLL, which turned it into a binary executable that .NET can access anytime the control is called from within Dreamweaver.

Whenever you use Dreamweaver MX to create, for example, a `DataSet` (Insert ➢ Application Objects ➢ DataSet), you'll see that the Dreamweaver's code output contains special tags such as `MM:DataSet`. The definitions for these kinds of tags are made available through the `DreamweaverCtrls.dll`. We'll be covering the hows and whys of this methodology in Chapter 5.

When you create a .NET-driven data behavior, you'll need to deploy the Dreamweaver Control in order for .NET to recognize the Dreamweaver tags. To do this, go to Site ➢ Advanced ➢ Deploy Supporting Files. You'll see a dialog box that asks you how you access your site and to which directory you want to deploy (see Figure 1.10). Always deploy to the bin directory of your application. This is Dreamweaver's default. If the directory doesn't exist, Dreamweaver will create one for you.

FIGURE 1.10:

Deploying the DreamweaverCtrls.dll

Wrapping Up

If you want to start building applications properly from the ground up, configuring Dreamweaver MX to work with .NET involves more than simply setting up your site definition.

Think of your website as a top-down process from the very beginning. Everything inherits from the top down. In other words, if the top level of your configuration indicates that your pages should be rendered in U.S. English, then all of them will be rendered in that language until ASP.NET encounters a directory in your site that overrides this settings. Moreover, this is how ASP.NET handles *all* object inheritance when code is involved, so it's a concept you'll want to remember as you dive into application development in future chapters.

There are two steps to take in order to begin your site:

1. Define a site.

2. Set up your IIS environment for production.

Technically, the additional configuration options are optional. You'll be able to serve pages without them, but your efficiency will be compromised—so we strongly recommend that you also configure the following as quickly as possible:

- Dreamweaver MX for use in versioning software

- The Web.config file, or at least the debugging elements it uses

The next chapter will look at the critical concept of workflow, examining how a web development team moves across a project from inception to final production using Dreamweaver MX.

CHAPTER 2

SQL and Dreamweaver Web Applications

- Learning about SQL

- The fastest primer ever on relational databases

- Creating tables

- A crash course in data manipulation

- Stored procedures

SQL is a language used for querying and manipulating data, and for creating databases and tables and other objects for those databases. Understanding SQL is important if you want to do any serious interaction with Dreamweaver's data manipulation behaviors. Although it is true that you can use Dreamweaver's Simple mode (for example, Insert ➤ Application Objects ➤ DataSet) for creating data queries, inserts, and updates, these simple statements are quite limiting. The real power comes from creating your own SQL statements in the Advanced mode. And figuring out how to work with form values, when to pass parameters, and so forth, is very difficult when your familiarity with SQL is limited or nonexistent.

NOTE   This chapter takes a very fundamental approach to learning SQL. If you already know SQL, you can skip this chapter.

Learning About SQL

SQL consists of a large number of statements that any robust relational database understands, and offshoots of the standard have been implemented by Oracle and Microsoft and other large commercial database vendors. Oracle provides support for SQL, as well as a procedural language extension to SQL called PL/SQL. Microsoft's version of SQL is called Transact-SQL, which is also used by Sybase (although there are some differences between the Microsoft and Sybase versions).

Luckily, most of the SQL statements you will use to manipulate data in Dreamweaver MX are part of all the versions of SQL you'll find out there. Most of the differences in the language relate to the way it is used to manipulate the database itself. Generally, these differences shouldn't have much bearing on what you do via Dreamweaver to create and work with dynamic web applications.

There are two major subsets of SQL. One, a Data Definition Language (DDL), is used to create tables and databases. If you're part of a large team you won't be encountering this part of the language very often, because the job of developing databases will rightly be handled by a different team or team member. If you're part of a smaller web development shop or are a one-person operation, you'll need to know how to set up a database and therefore will use DDL. Most of your SQL development in Dreamweaver will focus on the other subset, the Data Manipulation Language (DML), which defines how to query, update and delete data.

This chapter can't begin to cover the intricacies of SQL, of course. What it can give you is a good introduction to get you started, and that certainly should be sufficient for all but the most complex Dreamweaver tasks. I'll be adding to the concepts presented in this chapter as we move forward through the many data development capabilities provided by Dreamweaver, and most of the database-related problems you will tackle will be covered.

There are many good books available on SQL, and at least as many ways to set up a database poorly. Smart database development requires a level of expertise that I can't offer in one small portion of a chapter. So if you really want to explore SQL thoroughly, buy a good book on it, like Transact-SQL Programming by Lee Gould, Andrew Zanevsky, and Kevin Kline (O'Reilly & Associates, 1999).

A Word about Database Management Systems

In this book I'm using SQL Server as my main data provider, but you can use a free database management system (DBMS) if you wish. One such option is MySQL, or even Microsoft's SQL Server in the form of the MSDE distributable—it's basically a free version of SQL Server with limited concurrent processing threads, which means that the more connections you have, the slower it gets. Another drawback is that there is no user interface. The MSDE distributable is available as part of Microsoft Office.

The reason I don't use Microsoft Access is that it isn't an enterprise-level database manager, and is not designed for the Web. I can't in good conscience write a book on .NET development and even hint that it is okay to work with Access if you're anticipating several thousand users accessing the database.

If you have Office, install MSDE, which is available with Office. Access is a fine system, perfect for many things (in fact, it's a wonderful client for SQL Server). It is not, however, designed to handle lots of users concurrently. After you grow past a few hundred users, you should think seriously about moving to a more robust DBMS.

You can launch the MSDE installation wizard from the Office 2000 CD-ROM by double-clicking on the `\Sql\x86\Setup\Setupsql.exe` file.

The Fastest Primer Ever on Relational Databases

A *database* is a way to store data. A shopping list is a database.

A *relational database* is a set of tables that bear some relation to each other. In a typical database, one table may be a kind of client table that holds information about your clients. The reason relational data works so well is that when you enter information about, say, an order of widgets, it's important to keep the data about your widgets separate from the data about the customers ordering the widgets. In addition, you will probably have yet another table containing orders. How you maintain the relationship among these three tables is one of the principles of relational database management.

Relational databases are, in many ways, very simple to understand. At a higher level, they can become wildly complex. Luckily, for most of our purposes here, you will rarely need to venture that far. When you're ready and willing, you can look into deeper levels of complexity discussed by fellows such as C. J. Date (*An Introduction to Database Systems*, Addison-Wesley, 2003) and E. F. Codd (*The Relational Model for Database Management: Version 2*, Addison-Wesley, 1990). These experts present classic works on databases, geared toward professional database administrators (DBAs).

I'm going to eschew some of the more intricate theory on databases involving such things as normalization, tuples, and so on, and dive right into the specifics of what you need to know for your Dreamweaver work.

Tables: The Building Blocks of Databases

Tables, consisting of columns and rows, are the principal components of databases. Each row is an individual record of data consisting of one field of data per column. Here is a table of clients with four rows of data:

```
First Name              Last Name               Title
-------------           ----------------        -----
John                    Johnson                 Owner
Exelon                  McCoy                   Expert
Tester                  McTester                Tester
John                    Doe                     CEO
```

The results of a database search can come in the form of a grid, as well, like that in Figure 2.1. You can have many more columns than shown in this example, of course, and you can also have thousands or even millions of rows.

FIGURE 2.1:

Database results in a grid format

Creating Relationships with Keys

The relational aspect to databases comes in when you want to build a relationship between one table and another table. In this case, let's say we want to build a relationship between a table with client info and another table with real-estate listings. The Clients table will possess a column with a unique identifier, which means the value of that column is unique and won't be found in more than one row of that column. So given our earlier example of a client table, we might have something like this:

ID	First Name	Last Name	Title
1	John	Johnson	Owner
2	Exelon	McCoy	Expert
3	Tester	McTester	Tester
5	John	Doe	CEO

The first column is the unique identifier, which can be generated automatically in SQL Server. The unique identifier is generated when you create a column that has an *identity constraint*. This is known as the *primary key*. You'll see how to do this in the next section on creating tables.

Now, consider a real estate office. When a Listings table is created, it will contain a column called ClientID or something like it, and the column value when the table receives inserts (new records) will always come from the Clients table. So you might have a partial real-estate listing that looks something like this:

MLS Number	Description	Client Name
52335	Rose Street Beauty	John Johnson

Does that client name, John Johnson, come from the Listings table? Absolutely not. That would be bad database design, because when you needed to update the client's info, you'd have to go through all the Listings rows and fix the affected records one by one. Yikes. Relational databases allow you to link one table to another. They do this by establishing links using common data in each table.

When data is entered into the Listings table, you can set it up so that the database requires one column of data to come from the Clients table (let's call this the ClientInfo table). That column's data comes from, in this case, the ClientInfo table's Client_ID column. When the database user enters a client ID into the Listings table, all the data associated with that client ID in the ClientInfo table can be made available to the Listings table. This is known as establishing a *foreign key*.

The data itself isn't physically stored in the Listings table; it's only made available. You have to write a SQL query to actually get at the data, but it still amounts to this: When you enter the Client_ID number 1 (for example) into the Listings table, you are "almost" actually entering all of the following information into that Listings table:

ID	First Name	Last Name	Title
1	John	Johnson	Owner

Look at Figure 2.2 to see the relationship between these two tables. Remember when I mentioned the unique identifier in the `ClientInfo` table? This is made available to other tables through a link between the `Listings` table and the `ClientInfo` table based on the foreign key value from the `ClientInfo` table. Each client can have many real-estate listings. For each, in addition to the listing data you will also store its related client ID, which enables you to link the listing back to its associated client record.

FIGURE 2.2:

The relationship between the Clients table and the Listings table

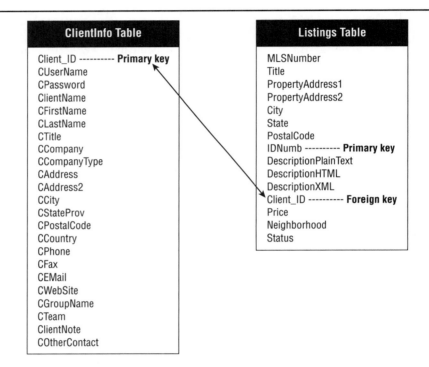

ClientInfo Table	Listings Table
Client_ID ---------- **Primary key**	MLSNumber
CUserName	Title
CPassword	PropertyAddress1
ClientName	PropertyAddress2
CFirstName	City
CLastName	State
CTitle	PostalCode
CCompany	IDNumb ---------- **Primary key**
CCompanyType	DescriptionPlainText
CAddress	DescriptionHTML
CAddress2	DescriptionXML
CCity	Client_ID ---------- **Foreign key**
CStateProv	Price
CPostalCode	Neighborhood
CCountry	Status
CPhone	
CFax	
CEMail	
CWebSite	
CGroupName	
CTeam	
ClientNote	
COtherContact	

Primary Keys

A primary key is an attribute that uniquely identifies a record to the database. None of the values can be null because a primary key must always have a value (a null means the value is unknown). An *index* is a separate table specified when you select a clustered index in SQL Server. The index orders the table in the way we want, so that a search is more efficient when we have thousands of rows of data. With an index, the database doesn't have to scan the entire table for a specific row of data, which would be time-consuming because the data is not entered in any specific order.

One simple and obvious way to order (index) data is by the primary key, which in our example is simply an ordered list of unique sequential integers. Most database gurus will create tables with indexes defined upon creation that go beyond primary keys. For example, a likely index for our example would be based on the column `lastName` in the `ClientInfo` table, because many searches are likely to be performed on the client's last name.

A table column that consists of unique identifiers doesn't *have* to be a primary key, but a primary key does need to be a unique identifier. Suppose you made another column your primary key, let's say a column of e-mail addresses; that would be one way to guarantee nobody entered an e-mail address that was already stored in the table, because the database would force a *constraint* on the data.

By constraint, I am referring to a process that the database uses to force certain conditions on data input. In the case of our e-mail address column, the database knows that you've defined the e-mail address column as a primary key, and so each e-mail address entered into the system must be unique. So if one instance of chuck@myemail.com is entered, nobody else can enter it, or the database will complain that a constraint was violated. You'd see a message like this:

```
Violation of PRIMARY KEY constraint 'PK_myDBTable'.
  Cannot insert duplicate key in object 'myDBTable'.
```

The only way to correct this error is to enter data that doesn't already exist in the column.

Foreign Keys

Now take another look at Figure 2.2, and notice the column in the `Listings` table marked "Foreign Key." This is the column that must receive data that exists in the `ClientInfo` table. The data in this column is the same as the data in the `ClientInfo` table's `Client_ID` column. The names of both columns in this case are the same, but they don't have to be. The foreign key assignment forces the constraint that the data is the same, and the actual names of the columns are irrelevant.

Consider the following table of client information in the table named `ClientInfo`:

ID	First Name	Last Name	Title
1	John	Johnson	Owner
2	Exelon	McCoy	Expert
3	Tester	McTester	Tester
5	John	Doe	CEO

Let's assume for now that this is *all* of the data that exists in the `ClientInfo` table. Now, let's assume another `Listings` table, just like the one we diagrammed in Figure 2.2. Let's assume this is *all* of the data we have in the `Listings` table:

MLS Number	Description	Client Name
52335	Rose Street Beauty	John Johnson

Now we want to enter a new real-estate listing. A client named Bill Gates has just listed his home for $300 million. We have not yet entered him into the `ClientInfo` table, but somehow we know that he will be client number 6. So we go ahead and enter it into SQL Server using Enterprise Manager, as shown in Figure 2.3. We end up with a message like this:

```
INSERT statement conflicted with COLUMN FOREIGN KEY constraint
   'FK_Listings_ClientInfo'. The conflict occurred in database 'Realtor',
   table 'ClientInfo', column 'Client_ID'.
The statement has been terminated.
```

The reason for this conflict isn't particularly obvious from the error message. It occurs because the data doesn't exist in the `ClientInfo` table's `Client_ID` column, because we created a relationship between the primary key `Client_ID` in the `ClientInfo` table and the `Client_ID` column in the `Listings` table (the foreign key).

FIGURE 2.3:

Entering a new client via a web page

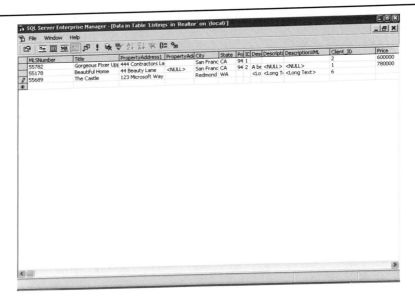

Determining Whether a Table Contains Keys

How do we know whether a table contains primary or foreign keys? And who made them? This is not an issue if it's you who made them, but what if you're manipulating a database designed by a DBA or some other team member? The fast answer if you're using SQL Server is to use a metadata view obtained using this SQL syntax:

```
SELECT * FROM
databaseName.INFORMATION_SCHEMA.CONSTRAINT_COLUMN_USAGE
```

This will provide a view into all the constraints used in the database you name (databaseName).

For example, in the database I am using for this chapter, named Realtor, about which you'll find more discussion soon, the following SQL statement will give you the results shown in Table 2.1:

```
SELECT * FROM
Realtor.INFORMATION_SCHEMA.CONSTRAINT_COLUMN_USAGE
```

NOTE   SQL syntax is not case sensitive. For consistency throughout this book I use uppercase for statements such as SELECT and INSERT. You don't have to do that, but be aware that using all caps for keywords has become a convention among SQL developers.

TABLE 2.1: Retrieving Primary and Foreign Key Information

*T_C	*T_S	*T_N	*C_N	*C_C	*C_S	CONSTRAINT_NAME
Realtor	dbo	admin	uid	Realtor	dbo	PK_admin
Realtor	**dbo**	**ClientInfo**	**Client_ID**	**Realtor**	**dbo**	**PK_ClientInfo**
Realtor	dbo	dtproperties	id	Realtor	dbo	pk_dtproperties
Realtor	dbo	dtproperties	property	Realtor	dbo	pk_dtproperties
Realtor	dbo	Images	img_pk	Realtor	dbo	PK_Images
Realtor	dbo	Images	MLSNumber	Realtor	dbo	FK_Images_Listings
Realtor	**dbo**	**Listings**	**Client_ID**	**Realtor**	**dbo**	**FK_Listings_ClientInfo**
Realtor	dbo	Listings	MLSNumber	Realtor	dbo	PK_Listings
Realtor	dbo	News	NewsID	Realtor	dbo	PK_News
Realtor	dbo	users	uid	Realtor	dbo	PK_users

*T_C=TABLE_CATALOG, *T_S=TABLE_SCHEMA, *T_N=TABLE_NAME, *C_N=COLUMN_NAME,
*C_C=CONSTRAINT_CATALOG, *C_S=CONSTRAINNT_SCHEMA

As you can see, SQL Server gives primary and foreign keys' names. The ones we're interested in are the primary keys in the ClientInfo table, and the foreign key in the Listings table.

In the next chapter I'll show you how to use obtain a list of primary and foreign keys from within Dreamweaver's visual interface.

NOTE   You may have noticed that the tables diagrammed in Figure 2.2 contain many more columns of data than what I'm showing in this discussion. To show all those columns would be impossible on a printed page in this book, so I am only using a few columns of data. You'll be doing this all the time with SQL anyway, as you'll soon find out. Because you often want and need only a few columns of data, you can write a query requesting only that data.

If you're using MySQL, inquiring into a table's keys can be done using the SHOW or DESCRIBE keyword, and the name of the table about which you are inquiring:

```
SHOW COLUMNS FROM ClientInfo
```

This will return all the names of the columns and their datatype, plus the existence of any key.

> **NOTE**   As an aside, but an important one, I should mention that if you're not familiar with databases, there's an awful lot of new jargon to learn. To get comfortable, start with the jargon that is particular to the relationship model, and the terms and concepts associated with primary and foreign keys.

The Importance of Keys

If you come away from this discussion with nothing else, keep in mind the relationship between two or more columns in two different tables. The linkages between the two are what make it possible to maintain the integrity of your data.

In the preceding examples, you can't update client information in the Listings table. You can change the Client_ID of a client associated with a particular listing (which means you will be referring to a different client), but not unless that ID is in the ClientInfo table. And you certainly can't change any of the information related to that client, even the client's name, from within the Listings table. You can "peer into" the ClientInfo table from the Listings table (although that's not exactly what you're doing when you're viewing data from both tables) and find out information about the client associated with a particular ID. However, to actually update that client information, you must go into the ClientInfo table.

You can't delete a client from the ClientInfo table if you are referencing that client in the Listings table, because you will violate the foreign key restraint. In the same way the database expects you to insert existing Client_ID data into the Listings table, it also expects it to stay there. So you would have to delete the listing before you delete the client.

> **NOTE**   Actually, there *is* a way to delete the client from the ClientInfo table when there is a reference to that client in the Listings table—by setting up a cascading trigger. But if you know that much about database operations, you've probably only read this far into the chapter because you're looking to nail me on something.

Creating Tables

Most modern databases come with a visual interface (GUI) that you can use to create tables. This is the route chosen by most people who are just beginning to get comfortable with database technology, although it isn't necessarily the best one. After you become more familiar with database technology and SQL in particular, you'll likely opt for hand-coding for table creation, because it gives you more control over table creation options. In fact, I would go so far as to say that if you're just starting out now with SQL, forget the GUI and go straight to your text editor and/or command line. (SQL Server has a very nice SQL editor called Query Analyzer, which is a text editor for hand coding but offers views of the database in an Explorer-like panel to the left of the text editor. From there you can view field names and datatype information, which makes it easier to write your SQL.)

Despite the benefits of hand-coding tables, some of us simply prefer the GUI, so I'm going to demonstrate table creation techniques in this section using both a GUI and a text editor.

NOTE   The demonstration code in this chapter is written and tested for a SQL Server 2000 platform.

TIP   Although SQL Server itself is expensive, you can usually find a website hosting plan that incorporates SQL Server for a very reasonable fee. This kind of site rents out a database for you, allowing you to run a data-driven site for as little as $25 U.S. per month. There are limitations, of course, the most severe being that you are usually limited to one database per subscription. You can also use a combination of MSDE and Access (see the sidebar "A Word about Database Management Systems").

Determining Datatypes

Before we begin defining and creating tables, you should know something about what *type* of data you can include in your tables. This covers quite a wide range, but it's important to determine what kind of data will be used in each column before you actually define the table.

TIP   Planning for table data is something that should be part of the web application plan, as discussed in Bonus Chapter 1 on Sybex's website. I haven't covered any specifics here about a requirements document for a database, but you should draw one up if you are responsible for creating the database. It can be as simple as a series of charts indicating the scheme of your database, with tables mapped out on paper, specifying the columns of each table and the type of data they should contain. Like other aspects of a web application, the more time you spend designing the database, the better it will be, and the better any web application built on that database will be.

The general types of data, or *datatypes*, fall within several general categories. My focus here is on SQL Server datatypes, but other databases follow the same general scheme.

Binary Data

Binary data consists of hexadecimal numbers and is stored using the `binary`, `varbinary`, and `image` datatypes in SQL Server.

Character Data

Character data consists of any combination of letters, symbols, and numeric characters and is stored using the `char`, `varchar`, and `text` datatypes.

- Use `varchar` when the entries in a column vary in the number of characters they contain, but the length of any entry does not exceed 8K.

- Use `char` when every entry for a column has the same fixed length (up to 8K).

- Columns of text data can be used to store ASCII characters longer than 8K.

A good candidate for the text datatype is an HTML or XML document (many database management systems now provide support to store XML directly within the database), because they'll usually be longer than 8K. When defining table columns using `char` or `varchar`, you need to include the maximum number of characters allowed in the case of `varchar`, and the exact number of characters allowed in the case of `char`. So `myColumn varchar(50)` means the column can store up to 50 characters, whereas `myColumn char(50)` means the column *must* store 50 characters of data.

International character data and/or Unicode data are stored using `nchar`, `nvarchar`, and `ntext` datatypes. Unicode is a standardized set of character set tables, such as Basic Latin, or ISO 8859-1, and Cyrillic, or ISO 8859-5 (there are hundreds of others). Used by XML and Java, Unicode makes it possible to work with characters in just about every language on earth. For Unicode-based data consisting of 4,000 or more characters, use `ntext`.

Date and Time Data

Date and time data consists of valid date or time combinations using the `datetime` and `smalldatetime` datatypes.

The `timestamp` is a special SQL Server datatype used for generating binary numbers upon row changes, and shouldn't be confused with the SQL-92's standard timestamp, which is actually more in line with SQL Server's `datetime` datatype.

NOTE   ANSI SQL-92 is the SQL language standard. Not all relational databases maintain absolutely perfect adherence to the standard, but most well-known databases have reliable conformance to all of the common SQL statements.

Numeric Data

Numeric data consists of positive and negative numbers, decimals and fractions, and integers (whole numbers).

- An integer (the `int` datatype) stores 4 bytes of information and can range from –2,147,483,648 to 2,147,483,648.

- The `smallint` stores 2 bytes of information and can range from –32,768 to 32,768.

- The `tinyint` stores 1 byte of information ranging from 0 to 255.

- The mother of all integer types is the `bigint`, which can store numbers ranging from –2^63 (–9223372036854775808) through 2^63–1 (9223372036854775807). The storage size for this type is 8 bytes.

- You can also use a `decimal` datatype, which stores numbers to the least significant digit. Its storage size depends on the total number of digits for the data, and the number of decimal digits to the right of the decimal point. This means that more bytes are required to store the value 111111.1111 than to store the value 1.1.

Monetary Data

Monetary data using the `money` and `smallmoney` datatypes can be stored to an accuracy of four decimal places. I usually find that for working with application server technology like .NET, at least through Dreamweaver, it's easier to use `decimal` datatypes, because Dreamweaver's data conversion functions work better with the `decimal` datatype than `money` or `smallmoney`.

bit

A `bit` datatype consists of either a 1 or a 0. This is the obvious choice for Boolean statements (true or false and yes or no).

uniqueidentifier

A `uniqueidentifier` is a 16-byte hexadecimal, globally unique identifier (GUID). This unique value is possible because the last 6 bits of information on the number are drawn from the machine on which SQL Server is running. (It comes from the network card if the machine has one, or is otherwise generated as a random 48-bit number.)

sql_variant

These are typically used in user-defined functions to store data whose size or even actual type might be uncertain, especially when passing parameters in and out of SQL Server. (*Parameters* are values assigned by, often, other systems and passed into the SQL engine.)

This datatype can't be used with values of `text`, `ntext`, `timestamp`, `image`, and `sql_variant`.

table

This is used to store temporary data as a table-based result set and is only available within the scope of a local variable or as the return value of a user-defined function.

User Defined

You can also define your own datatypes based on existing SQL Server datatypes. You might want to do this when you require consistency in a specific type of column across datatypes. To accomplish this, you use a special stored procedure named `sp_addtype`. This is a SQL Server system stored procedure that takes three parameters. The first is the name of your new datatype, the second is the type of datatype it is based on, and the third indicates whether or not it can ever be null:

```
USE Master
EXEC sp_addtype MLSNumber, char(5), 'NOT NULL'
```

Then, when you define a table, you can use `MLSNumber` as a datatype instead of `char(5)`. SQL Server will then treat it as a `char` datatype.

Creating a Table Using a GUI

If you have ever used a GUI such as SQL Server's Enterprise Manager to create database tables, then you've used SQL, even if you didn't know it. This is because everything you do in a database management system, from administrative tasks to creating tables and inserting data into them, is performed through SQL.

When you use Enterprise Manager, you get a window similar to Figure 2.4. You can create a new table by simply navigating to the database you want the table to appear in. To do that, expand the appropriate server group in the left-hand panel, and then expand your database to reveal the tables in the right-hand pane. Right-click Tables in the left panel to get the context menu (also shown in Figure 2.4). Click New to create a new table.

NOTE   If you don't have SQL Server or Enterprise Manager, read along anyway, because a database tool with a visual interface uses SQL under the hood to create tables. As you may have guessed, I'm trying to talk you out of relying on visual interface tools in general—with the obvious exception of Dreamweaver MX. They can be quite useful for rapid development, but you will inevitably, someday, need to tweak code. To lead a happier, more productive developer's existence, it's best to learn about what is happening underneath it all. Dreamweaver will save you hours of development time, but it's important to understand the code it generates for you.

FIGURE 2.4:

Creating a new table
in Enterprise Manager

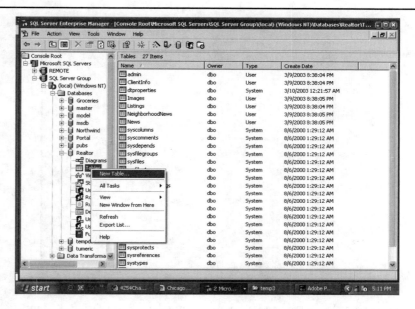

The visual interface for designing the columns and rows of a new table is shown in Figure 2.5. First you enter a name, then the datatype (int, varchar, etc.), then the maximum length of data, and whether the column you are creating will accept null values or not. If you're following along on your computer, go ahead and start creating this table; enter the following data:

MLSNumber	varchar	50	0
Title	varchar	50	1
PropertyAddress1	varchar	50	1
PropertyAddress2	varchar	50	1
City	varchar	50	1
State	varchar	50	1
PostalCode	varchar	50	1
IDNumb	int	4	0
DescriptionPlainText	text	16	1
DescriptionHTML	text	16	1
DescriptionXML	text	16	1
Client_ID	int	4	1
Price	int	4	1
Neighborhood	varchar	50	1
Status	varchar	50	1

FIGURE 2.5:

The table designer in Enterprise Manager

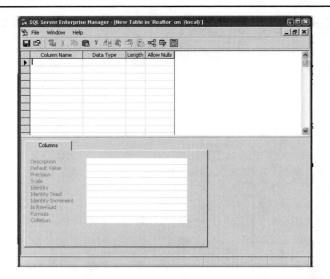

When you're working on a real-world database, you don't need to have varchar lengths as long as what I've suggested here, unless you have international clients (which can result in some long names for certain things). I made the lengths consistent because I wanted to simplify your typing.

NOTE   It's important to remember that a null value doesn't mean zero. It means that the value for a specific row in a column is not known.

If you expect to search a column's data frequently, it's a good idea to set up an index. In the table designer, right-click anywhere in the fields and select Indexes/Keys from the context menu. A window labeled Properties will pop up. Select the Indexes/Keys tab as shown in Figure 2.6 if it is not already selected and click the New button. A default name for a new index will appear in the Index Name field. Choose the column you want for the index and then designate the index to be sorted in ascending or descending order. There are a number of good indexing candidates in this table, including PropertyAddress1, City, and State. When you are done creating your index, click the Close button to return to the table designer window.

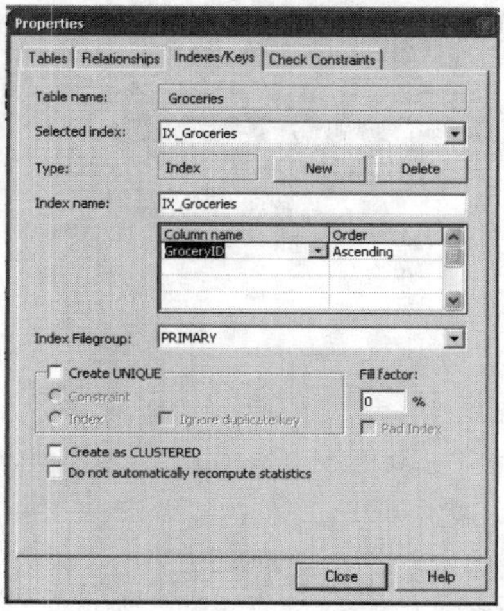

FIGURE 2.6:

Choosing the
Indexes/Keys tab in
the Table Properties
pop-up window

You can also set a primary key by clicking on the key icon in the menu bar of the table designer window. If you want the primary key to be an identity, click on Identity in the column properties at the lower-left of the window. Setting the Identity property of the column to Yes tells the database to insert a value automatically whenever an insert is made into the table.

WARNING   Be sure, when creating INSERT statements, not to insert into a column with the Identity property enabled. Generally, the database will insert unique values, but this uniqueness isn't guaranteed. To guarantee uniqueness, you need to declare a UNIQUE or PRIMARY key on that column.

When you are done, click the Save icon at the top of the window, and when Enterprise Manager asks for a table name, call it Listings. When you return to the Enterprise Manager, right-click on the Listings table and navigate to All Tasks ➤ Generate SQL Script. Click Preview in the Generate SQL Scripts window (see Figure 2.7). You should see code that looks similar to Listing 2.1.

FIGURE 2.7:

You can preview table-creation SQL script in Enterprise Manager

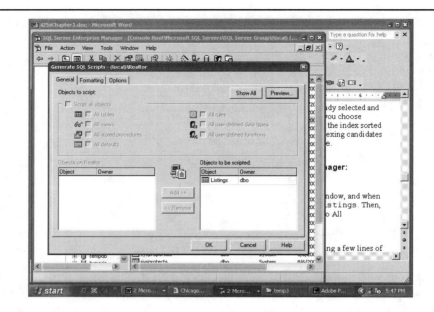

Listing 2.1   **Enterprise Manager-generated SQL code for a table**

```
if exists (select * from dbo.sysobjects where id =
object_id(N'[dbo].[Listings]') and OBJECTPROPERTY(id, N'IsUserTable') = 1)
drop table [dbo].[Listings]
GO

CREATE TABLE [dbo].[Listings] (
    [MLSNumber] [varchar] (50) COLLATE SQL_Latin1_General_CP1_CI_AS NOT NULL ,
    [Title] [varchar] (50) COLLATE SQL_Latin1_General_CP1_CI_AS NULL ,
    [PropertyAddress1] [varchar] (50) COLLATE SQL_Latin1_General_CP1_CI_AS NULL ,
    [PropertyAddress2] [varchar] (50) COLLATE SQL_Latin1_General_CP1_CI_AS NULL ,
    [City] [varchar] (50) COLLATE SQL_Latin1_General_CP1_CI_AS NULL ,
    [State] [varchar] (50) COLLATE SQL_Latin1_General_CP1_CI_AS NULL ,
    [PostalCode] [varchar] (50) COLLATE SQL_Latin1_General_CP1_CI_AS NULL ,
    [IDNumb] [int] IDENTITY (1, 1) NOT NULL ,
    [DescriptionPlainText] [text] COLLATE SQL_Latin1_General_CP1_CI_AS NULL ,
    [DescriptionHTML] [text] COLLATE SQL_Latin1_General_CP1_CI_AS NULL ,
    [DescriptionXML] [text] COLLATE SQL_Latin1_General_CP1_CI_AS NULL ,
    [Client_ID] [int] NULL ,
    [Price] [int] NULL ,
    [Neighborhood] [varchar] (50) COLLATE SQL_Latin1_General_CP1_CI_AS NULL ,
    [Status] [varchar] (50) COLLATE SQL_Latin1_General_CP1_CI_AS NULL
) ON [PRIMARY] TEXTIMAGE_ON [PRIMARY]
GO
```

The important part for you to observe right now is the code in brackets, because those are your column names and their datatypes. So the Client_ID column is an integer and is also a primary key.

The other thing of note is that you could have done all this yourself using SQL, without the help of a visual tool. Many professional DBAs shun visual interfaces because they like full control over the setup of their tables. Regardless of your preference, you should know how to create tables using SQL, and we'll look at that next.

Creating a Table Using SQL

At its most basic, the process of creating a table is as simple as writing a few lines of code:

```
CREATE TABLE myTable
    (
    myNumber INT,
    myFirstName VARCHAR(40) NULL,
    myPhrase VARCHAR(50) NULL
)
GO
```

Of course, a table like this contains no optimizations whatsoever, but it does show how simple SQL can be at the fundamental level. You can start at this easy-to-learn stage and graduate to higher levels of complexity as you become comfortable with the language.

Let's go back to our sample Listings database table and create it with SQL instead of a GUI. Incidentally, if you did follow along with the steps of the preceding section and created a table called Listings using the GUI, you will want to "drop" that table before continuing with this exercise. Simply right-click on the Listings table in Enterprise Manager and choosing Delete.

Listing 2.2 shows our first attempt at creating the Listings table.

Listing 2.2	Creating the Listings table with SQL

```
CREATE TABLE Listings (
     MLSNumber varchar (50)   NOT NULL ,
     Title varchar (50)   NULL ,
     PropertyAddress varchar (50)   NULL ,
     PropertyAddress2 varchar (50)   NULL ,
     City varchar (50)   NULL ,
     State varchar (50)   NULL ,
     PostalCode varchar (50)   NULL ,
     IDNumb int IDENTITY (1, 1) NOT NULL ,
     DescriptionPlainText text   NULL ,
     DescriptionHTML text   NULL ,
     DescriptionXML text   NULL ,
     Client_ID int NULL ,
     Price int NULL ,
```

```
Neighborhood varchar (50)    NULL ,
Status varchar (50)    NULL,
CONSTRAINT  pk_MLSNumber PRIMARY KEY NONCLUSTERED
(MLSNumber)
WITH FILLFACTOR = 50 -,
-- uncomment the comma above
-- and the next two lines if
-- you have already built the ClientInfo table
-- with a Client_ID primary key.
--CONSTRAINT fk_Client_ID FOREIGN KEY (Client_ID)
--REFERENCES ClientInfo(Client_ID)

)
GO
```

The process for writing out the code in Listing 2.2 is very similar to using the GUI. You need to designate names for the columns, their datatype, and the storage size.

Note the use of -- characters to designate comments within the code. At the end of the WITH FILLFACTOR line, I commented out a comma, which you'll need to uncomment if you use the two lines I commented out (in bold in the listing). Those two lines must be commented out because, if you haven't built your ClientInfo table yet and you created a primary key on that table's Client_ID column, you'll get an error like this:

```
Server: Msg 1776, Level 16, State 1, Line 1
There are no primary or candidate keys in the referenced table 'ClientInfo'
   that match the referencing column list in the foreign key 'fk_Client_ID'.
Server: Msg 1750, Level 16, State 1, Line 1
Could not create constraint.
```

Using the *CREATE* Keyword

The magic all starts with the CREATE keyword. After your CREATE TABLE keywords, you name the table that you want to create. I like to name tables without any spaces in them, for interoperability reasons. After the table name, you add parentheses, and in between the parentheses you create your table definitions. In this case the table definitions consist of column definitions, separated by commas, and two constraint definitions, also separated by a comma.

Let's look at the two constraints named in the table we just created: a primary key constraint and a foreign key constraint. By now you probably know what they're for. You can create many other kinds of constraints, and you'll run into some of these in later chapters, but let's keep things simple for now.

A Word about Clustered Indexes

Notice that when I declared the primary key, I used the keyword NONCLUSTERED (although normally you'll probably choose CLUSTERED). When you create indexes that are clustered, it means you are dictating the physical ordering of the index on disk. You can only have one clustered index for each table (and remember that primary keys are a form of indexing). So it's best to save your opportunity for clustered indexes for later, since you may decide you want to use another column for clustered indexes. Why? A frequently accessed column that has a clustered index will perform better. You won't notice it much when you don't have a lot of data, but it's still good to get into the habit of forming clustered indexes. Indeed, this kind of thinking may help you trick your DBA into handing you a better set of keys to the database in the form of increased privileges (but don't count on it—these keys are often guarded by vicious attack dogs). Furthermore, keep in mind that by default, SQL Server will cluster primary keys unless you specifically tell it not to. Check out *Mastering SQL Server 2000* by Mike Gunderloy and Joseph L. Jorden (Sybex, 2000) for more on this topic.

A Crash Course in Data Manipulation

You might wonder why I spent so much time with the Data Definition Language aspect of SQL after claiming you won't need it often if you're working with Dreamweaver. It's because understanding how the data originated in the first place, and particularly the relationships of tables to each other, is vital to understanding data manipulation.

NOTE   You will encounter numerous examples of SQL data-manipulation code in action through-out this book, so if you feel that the coverage in this section isn't enough, keep in mind there's much more to come.

SQL data manipulation (sometimes called DML) is accomplished with a number of statements used to massage data. The most common you will encounter are SELECT, INSERT, UPDATE, and DELETE. There are others, but I'm going to keep the focus on these for now.

The *SELECT* Statement

The most fundamental data-manipulation statement is the SELECT statement. This does what you would expect it to do. It selects data. How much data it selects is determined by how you write the statement. You can select all the data in the ClientInfo table, for instance, by using this simple SELECT statement:

```
SELECT *
FROM ClientInfo
```

More typically, you'll want to select only some of a table's data columns. (In fact, using SELECT * is actually a serious no-no unless you for some reason really do need all the columns.) This is because there's no reason to incur all the memory and processor overhead retrieving this data will incur if you're not going to even use it. For example, if we only want the first and last name of each registered user in our table, we would explicitly name those columns like this:

```
SELECT CFirstName, CLastName
FROM ClientInfo
```

This code will generate the following more-specific result, instead of all the data from the table:

```
CFirstName              CLastName
--------                ---------

John                    Johnson
Exelon                  McCoy
Tester                  McTester
Another                 Test
John                    Doe

(5 row(s) affected)
```

Selecting from More Than One Table

I've given you a taste of how important keys and relationships are, but one of the best ways to really understand their significance is to see them in action. Thus far, you've seen the ClientInfo and Listings database tables in various stages of development. Let's take a look at how we might get some data out of each table to create a separate result set (or *dataset*, in .NET parlance). The following SELECT statement may look a little odd at first glance, but it's not complicated:

```
SELECT
  "MLS Number" = l.MLSNumber, "Description" = l.Title,
     "Client"= c.CFirstName + SPACE(1) + c.CLastName
From Listings l
INNER JOIN ClientInfo c ON l.Client_ID = c.Client_ID
```

This statement will result in the following:

```
MLS Number              Description              Client
--------                ---------                -----

55782                   Gorgeous Fixer Upper     Exelon McCoy
55178                   Beautiful Home           John Johnson

(1 row(s) affected)
```

The client's name is retrieved from the information in the ClientInfo table. We can do this because the ClientInfo table contains a Client_ID, and we use that to find out the name of the client associated with this listing. To see how this works, let's break the statement into several parts.

First, consider that I am using a text-based query tool called Query Analyzer, which returns the column names as they actually exist in the table. I want to name the columns differently. To do this using SQL, I write out the name I want to use and wrap it in quotes, then assign that name to the column I am renaming. Normally it would look something like this:

```
SELECT
  "MLS Number" = MLSNumber
```

In this example, `"MLS Number"` is a column alias that acts as the column name as we wish it to appear in the results table, and `MLSNumber` is the column name in the actual table from which we retrieve the records. Note that we aren't actually changing the name of the column in the table, we are only giving the column a different name in the results set. It is for presentation purposes only. It has no long-standing status, and the next time we select data, if we don't want the results column to be named `MLSNumber`, we'll have to assign a different name again.

There's something else that is different about this `SELECT` statement that may have taken you by surprise. Did you notice the use of the `l` before `MLSNumber`? This is called a *table alias*, and it's designed to promote shorter code. The alias is actually assigned in a part of the statement that appears later:

```
From Listings l
```

Making a table alias is somewhat akin to assigning a variable name and value. If you're wondering how the code can refer to the `l` alias before the assignment takes place, keep in mind that SQL isn't a procedural language; it's a declarative one. So SQL code isn't interpreted in the order of its appearance (unless you're using the procedural add-ons that vendors such as Microsoft and Oracle make available).

Let's interpret the full statement. If it were to speak to us like a human, it would say, "**Select** the `MLSNumber` column and call it 'MLS Number,' then **select** the `Title` column, and call it 'Description'. Also, **select** the *concatenation* (combination) of the `CFirstName` column, a space (using the SQL `Space()` function), and the `CLastName` column, and call the combination of these columns 'Client.' **Select** this data from the `Listings` table. I want to **join** this data with data from the `ClientInfo` table, **on** the `Client_ID` column, so that you present me with each listing associated with each client. In other words, if there's a client with a listing, show me that listing, and ignore all the others."

The *FROM* and *JOIN* Keywords

At its simplest, the `FROM` keyword selects data *from* an object, such as a table. But `FROM` can get much more complex than that.

In our example so far, there is a common column shared between the `Listings` and `ClientInfo` tables. This column is a common key called `Client_ID` that is handled by the

PK_ClientInfo primary key I showed you in Table 2.1. It's a primary key in the ClientInfo table, and a foreign key in the Listings table, and it acts as the "key" to unlock data from both tables. Use the FROM keyword to name the initial table you are retrieving data from, in this case the Listings table. Then you'll also want to perform some additional work within the entire FROM clause, to specify information regarding exactly which listings you want to retrieve.

This is where the JOIN keyword comes in. JOIN allows you to "join" data from one table with the data of another table, typically pivoting on a key (although a key isn't absolutely necessary as long as the columns being joined are of the exact same datatype and length). There are several kinds of join statements, but most of the time you'll use INNER JOIN, which is the default whenever you use the JOIN keyword by itself (JOIN means the same thing as INNER JOIN).

INNER JOIN Statements

INNER JOIN statements retrieve only the rows that share common data in primary and foreign key columns. In the example I presented in "Selecting from More Than One Table," I used this clause to help filter the data I wanted to retrieve:

```
INNER JOIN ClientInfo c ON l.Client_ID = c.Client_ID
```

As mentioned, you don't have to use the INNER keyword, because a join is an inner join by default if no other modifying keyword is used (such as INNER, LEFT, or CROSS).

This INNER JOIN statement presents only data in which the column Client_ID in the Listings table and Client_ID in the ClientInfo table share identical data. From those rows, all of the data in the row in each corresponding table is returned, and presented as one row of results. To get a better understanding of this, think about what would happen if we chose only the listings information from the Listings table, without the join to the ClientInfo table, using a query like this:

```
SELECT
  * From Listings
```

We would get this:

```
MLSNumber    Client_ID   Price     Neighborhood
-------      -------     ---       ------
55782        1           600000    Noe Valley
55178        2           780000    Noe Valley
```

I didn't include most of the actual listing data here because of the constraints of the printed page, but you can view the results file online by downloading the AllListingsReport.rpt file from www.sybex.com.

The point here is that the only actual client data available with our query was the client ID number, which is not very much information. The way to make that useful is through the

INNER JOIN. Similarly, if we create a query like the following to retrieve all the client information, we'll get all the client information we want but none of the listing information at all:

```
SELECT
  * From ClientInfo
```

We won't even get a listing number (MLSNumber) because there is no such column in the ClientInfo table.

You can see precisely which data we'll get by download the ALLClientsReport.rpt file.

CROSS JOIN Statements

The CROSS JOIN creates a cross-product of two tables; it returns all the data from the second table in the statement for each row in the first table. The syntax looks like this:

```
SELECT
  'MLS'=MLSNumber, 'Address'=l.PropertyAddress, l.Neighborhood,
    'Client_ID'= l.Client_ID, 'Client Name' = c.CfirstName
    + SPACE(1) + c.CLastName From Listings l

CROSS JOIN ClientInfo c
```

If you look at the following results of this cross join, you'll see a lot of redundant data retrieved in a way that isn't very useful. It's doubtful you'll encounter a need for this set of info, unless you want to create some bulk test data, perhaps.

MLS	Address	Neighborhood	ClientID	Client Name
55782	444 Contractors Lane	Noe Valley	2	John Johnson
55782	444 Contractors Lane	Noe Valley	2	Exelon McCoy
55782	444 Contractors Lane	Noe Valley	2	Tester McTester
55782	444 Contractors Lane	Noe Valley	2	John Doe
55178	44 Beauty Lane	Noe Valley	1	John Johnson
55178	44 Beauty Lane	Noe Valley	1	Exelon McCoy
55178	44 Beauty Lane	Noe Valley	1	Tester McTester
55178	44 Beauty Lane	Noe Valley	1	John Doe

LEFT and RIGHT JOIN Statements

The LEFT JOIN statement returns all data on the left side of the join regardless of whether the table on the right side of the join has matching data based on a key match. A RIGHT JOIN does the opposite, returning all data on the right side of the join regardless of a match. This means you'll get null values for the empty row sets for which there are no matches. To see the implications of these joins, it's best to look at a simple result. Consider the following RIGHT JOIN:

```
SELECT
  * From Listings l
RIGHT JOIN ClientInfo c ON l.Client_ID = c.Client_ID
```

You can see that null values were created for the MLSNumber column, in which there were clients, but no listings related to those clients:

```
MLS     Address                Neighborhood  Client ID   Client
55178   44 Beauty Lane         Noe Valley    1           John Johnson
55782   444 Contractors Lane   Noe Valley    2           Exelon McCoy
NULL    NULL                   NULL          3           Tester McTester
NULL    NULL                   NULL          5           John Doe
```

The *FULL JOIN* Statement

The FULL JOIN retrieves all rows from both tables, but unlike the CROSS JOIN it keys on a specific shared column of data.

```
SELECT
  "MLS" = l.MLSNumber, "Description" = l.Title,
    "Client"= c.CFirstName + SPACE(1) + c.CLastName
From Listings l
FULL JOIN ClientInfo c ON l.Client_ID = c.Client_ID
```

The shared column (Client_ID) is the same as in the statements I've used throughout this chapter. This time the data makes a little more sense. This join fills the MLS numbers for those clients who don't have listings with null values, but it's still useful information:

```
MLS     Description           Client
55178   Beautiful Home        John Johnson
55782   Gorgeous Fixer Upper  Exelon McCoy
NULL    NULL                  Tester McTester
NULL    NULL                  John Doe
```

You can see that the listings associated with each client are retrieved, in addition to those clients who don't have listings, with null values returned for information drawn from the Listings table. We could have queried additional columns from the ClientInfo table and retrieved more information about each client.

The *WHERE* Statement

One of the keywords you'll encounter most frequently while working with Dreamweaver MX and .NET is the WHERE statement. This is because you'll often have situations where you're trying to get some data based on a query string from a form or some other form of user input. So you need to be able to create statements like this one:

```
SELECT x from y WHERE xColumn = yFormField.
```

Acquiring user input values is accomplished by declaring a parameter and assigning it some value.

Normally, you would assign the value from a web form, but since we're not working with a web interface yet, we'll hard-code it right into the SQL. This is a good exercise because you can see exactly where the value from the form gets fed into the SQL engine. It will be useful information when you're thinking about the relationship of web forms and SQL. In the following code, I've highlighted the parameter and the parameter value assignment in bold:

```
DECLARE
@pField int
SELECT @pField = 1
SELECT
"Client ID" = c.Client_ID, "MLS Number" = l.MLSNumber,
    "Description" = l.Title, "Client"= c.CFirstName + SPACE(1) + c.CLastName
From Listings l
INNER JOIN ClientInfo c ON l.Client_ID = c.Client_ID
WHERE c.Client_ID = @pField
```

In a web application, you would not include that second bold line of SQL, SELECT @pField = 1, because you'll name a parameter value in your web form. All that's said in this SELECT statement is to select some columns of data keyed on the Client_ID column, where the Client_ID column is equal to 1.

You'll be encountering the WHERE statement frequently, and I'll show you how to pass a parameter value when we cover databases and web controls in Chapter 3, "Working with Databases: An Introduction," and Chapter 4, "Working with the Dreamweaver Custom Control."

The *INSERT* Statement

An INSERT statement inserts data into the database. Like SELECT statements, building a basic INSERT statement is very easy, but the complexity can increase significantly. INSERT statements are often used with parameters.

Fundamental *INSERT* Statements

Here is a basic INSERT statement:

```
INSERT INTO
ClientInfo (CPassword, ClientName, CFirstName, CLastName, CTitle,
    CCompany, CCompanyType, CAddress, CAddress2, CCity, CStateProv,
    CPostalCode, CCountry, CPhone, CFax, CEMail, CWebSite, ClientNote,
    COtherContact)
VALUES
 ('12de34', 'Trevor Mills', 'Trevor', 'Mills', 'President',
    'International Confections', 'Manufacturer', '111 Laurel', '',
    'San Francisco', 'CA', '94112', 'USA', '415-555-5555', '415-555-5555',
'trevor@tumeric.net', '', '', '')
```

This is a pretty intuitive statement that simply says, "Insert into the ClientInfo table's columns that are named in the parentheses, the values that are named in the next set of parentheses." String values must be surrounded with single quotes. Numbers, such as integers, should not be in quotes. The values must correspond to the column names in sequential order. So the following would generate a SQL error:

```
INSERT INTO
   myTable (myNumber, myFirstName, myPhrase)
VALUES
   ('John', 11, 'Foo phrase')
```

Can you see why? One problem is that the first column expects a number. Of course, you can't know that from just looking at this sample code, but you can make the inference from the name of the first column, myNumber, which is the first clue that the SQL code is written incorrectly. Look at the Clients_ table I created at the beginning of this chapter; you'll see I defined the first column as an integer. So when executing the preceding INSERT statement, you'll get this error as your result:

```
Syntax error converting the varchar value 'John' to a column of data type int.
```

The other problem with our INSERT statement is even more fundamental: The sequential order in the first half of the code doesn't match the order of the columns in the second half of the code. So even apart from the potential data-typing problem, the data wouldn't be entered into the system correctly. The myNumber column would have 'John', the myFirstName column would have '11', and the myPhrase column would be the only correct one with 'Foo phrase'. This is because each named column of the table must have a corresponding value in the same position as the value you are inserting.

If you are at all confused about this, type the following into Notepad or another text editor, and save the file as **inserts.csv**:

```
myNumber,myFirstName,myPhrase
11,John,Foo Phrase
```

Next, open the file in Excel or another spreadsheet program. Notice how the first row falls into column heads and the next row fills in values in the correct columns? Now, add one more value to the second line, like this:

```
11,John,Foo Phrase,test
```

Then save the file and reopen it in your spreadsheet program. You'll see that there is no column heading over the value test. This isn't a problem in a spreadsheet program because a spreadsheet program doesn't do anything to regulate the integrity of your data. However, the following would be fatal in a database insert:

```
INSERT INTO myTable (myNumber,myFirstName,myPhrase)
VALUES (11,'John', 'Foo Phrase', 'test')
```

This code will result in yet another kind of error in SQL Server:

```
There are fewer columns in the INSERT statement than values
   specified in the VALUES clause. The number of values in the
   VALUES clause must match the number of columns specified in
   the INSERT statement.
```

If you don't have an identity defined, you'll get a message like the following, because of the no-null-value constraint:

```
Cannot insert the value NULL into column 'Client_ID',
    table 'tumeric.dbo.ClientInfo'; column does not allow nulls.
    INSERT fails.
The statement has been terminated.
```

However, it will be a rare occasion that your primary key column isn't also an identity column, in which case the database inserts the values automatically.

Using Parameters to Place *INSERT* Values

You'll rarely use an INSERT statement like those I've described so far. In fact, you may never have use for this kind of statement at all, because it is unlikely you'd ever hard-code INSERT values into your SQL code. Instead, these values will be provided by a user in some way. So the question becomes, how do we set up our INSERT values to receive those values from the user?

As you work with Dreamweaver MX databases, you'll become very familiar with the notion of parameters, because they are what open the door to inserting values into your databases. You'll find parameters everywhere. You'll find them in INSERT and UPDATE statements, as well as stored procedures (discussed later in this chapter). As a result, you'll also find them used extensively by Dreamweaver MX when it generates code from the various data-insertion commands available from the visual interface.

Listing 2.3 shows how to use variables to insert values into a table.

Listing 2.3   Using variables to insert values

```
DECLARE @number int,
@firstName varchar(40),
@myPhrase varchar(50)
SELECT @number = 1, @firstName='John', @myPhrase='Hello'
INSERT INTO myTable (myNumber,myFirstName,myPhrase)

VALUES (@number, @firstName, @myPhrase)
```

When you access the data you just inserted using a SELECT * FROM myTable statement (replacing myTable with a valid table name, of course), this is what your results will look like:

```
myNumber      myFirstName      myPhrase
------        ------           -----
1             John             Hello

(1 row(s) affected)
```

Note how each result corresponds to the variable assignments made in the SELECT statement in Listing 2.3.

You can also assign a variable value using the SET keyword, instead:

```
SET @number = 32
SET @firstName='Boris'
SET @myPhrase='Menchin'
```

Notice, though, that you have to use SET each time you assign a value, and get rid of the commas. So SELECT is often more convenient for assigning variables.

The *UPDATE* Statement

UPDATE works similarly to INSERT. As in the INSERT statement, generally you'll use parameter values to insert actual data. In the code that follows, the parameter value assignments are made using the SELECT statement, which will be discarded in favor of assignments within your .NET code when working with web applications. Here's an UPDATE statement that updates the myTable table using parameter values:

```
DECLARE @number int,
@firstName varchar(40),
@myPhrase varchar(50)
SELECT @number = 3, @firstName='Ralph', @myPhrase='Goodbye'
UPDATE myTable
SET myNumber = @number,myFirstName=@firstName,myPhrase=@myPhrase
```

As with INSERT, you can simply hard-code the values directly in the UPDATE statement, but you'll rarely need to do that.

The *DELETE* Statement

The DELETE statement does just what you'd expect—it deletes specified data from the database. One catch: Using DELETE without a WHERE will delete all the data from the named table.

WARNING   Remember that using DELETE is very easy. Too easy. To avoid accidentally deleting *all* the data in the table your DELETE statement operates on, always check to see if there is a WHERE statement before you execute the DELETE command. It's also good practice to run a SELECT first, to confirm the data you're looking at is the data you want to delete. Then you can simply change SELECT to DELETE.

Just as you do with INSERT and UPDATE, you'll often find yourself using parameters when giving users a chance to delete data. Here's how a basic DELETE statement might look using a parameter to look for a Client_ID column:

```
DECLARE @Client_ID int
SET @Client_ID = 1
DELETE FROM ClientInfo WHERE
Client_ID=@Client_ID
```

This time, I declared the variable and then set its value using the SET keyword rather than SELECT, only to show another variation on how to set a variable's value.

By the way, if you actually tried the preceding DELETE statement you'd get an error message like the following, unless you first deleted the listing that is associated with Client 1:

```
DELETE statement conflicted with COLUMN REFERENCE constraint 'fk_Client_ID'.
    The conflict occurred in database 'Realtor', table 'Listings',
    column 'Client_ID'.
The statement has been terminated.
```

The database protects itself from goof-ups when we use keys, which is the main reason I've been emphasizing the importance of learning how they work.

Stored Procedures

Stored procedures are particularly lovely tools. They're often found in major databases because they're compiled once when accessed for the first time and then are basically ready to roll for other users. With a stored procedure, the server doesn't have to recompile, for example, a SELECT statement every time a user hits a web page that brings in data, which it does have to do when you simply write out SELECT statements in your web page. Stored procedures are so fast that database-based web pages that seem to hang will suddenly snap up when you convert them to stored procedure–based pages. Not only that, but security-conscious developers can write stored procedures to access tables that are secured away from your users. The users don't need permissions on a table if they have permission to run the stored procedure that is run against the table.

The bottom line on stored procedures is, put them to work wherever you can.

Anything you've seen in this chapter can be done as a stored procedure, including INSERT and UPDATE statements. For example, you can create the following stored procedure named selectProc using a SELECT statement that we built earlier in the chapter:

```
CREATE PROCEDURE selectProc
AS
SELECT
  "MLS Number" = l.MLSNumber, "Description" = l.Title,
    "Client"= c.CFirstName + SPACE(1) + c.CLastName
From Listings l
INNER JOIN ClientInfo c ON l.Client_ID = c.Client_ID
```

To create the stored procedure, simply add the additional code in bold to the previously developed SQL SELECT statement.

There are some serious tricks to using stored procedures and setting them up well to work with Dreamweaver and .NET. Luckily, the Dreamweaver custom control includes pretty decent support for stored procedures, as you'll discover in the next chapter. I'll be covering these tricks throughout the book, as we encounter more opportunities to work with stored procedures.

Wrapping Up

This chapter is certainly not an exhaustive study of SQL. It can't be, because that would require a whole book. Here, I have focused only on one small part of SQL, but it's the part that will matter to most to you as a Dreamweaver MX .NET developer. The focus on the relational database model, and understanding how it works, will have a direct effect on your ability to use Dreamweaver to rapidly build data-driven applications.

Remember that the key is database design, and one of the keys to database design is keys. Using them competently, and knowing how to access them within the scope of the tables you manipulate, is an important skill to develop.

On a certain level, SQL can be very easy because many of its statements and keywords are intuitive. SELECT selects data, UPDATE updates data, and DELETE deletes it. FROM tells the database from where to do the data manipulation.

Remember, too, that Dreamweaver MX is a great teacher. When you create DataSets in Dreamweaver, experiment with the DataSet dialog box, which you'll learn about in the next chapter, by starting work in Simple mode and then clicking on the Advanced tab to look at the code Dreamweaver writes.

Of course, as your skills develop you'll find that SQL can become remarkably complex, but it will always remain fairly intuitive. The complexity comes from its power and the SQL statements you write that harness that power. In the next chapter we're going to do just that, as we explore Dreamweaver MX and its ability to build data-driven pages in .NET.

CHAPTER 3

Working with Databases: An Introduction

- How to build connection strings

- Creating DataSets

- Building dynamic tables

- Accessing data in stored procedure

Dreamweaver MX is a very powerful IDE that allows you to rapidly create data-driven sites in a fraction of the time it would take with traditional sources. Dreamweaver builds on its tradition of a powerful graphical interface to quickly put together key .NET components. Unfortunately, using many of these tools is not intuitive, and if you're not a database expert the experience can quickly become frustrating.

This chapter describes how to access various forms of data from a database using Dreamweaver MX and .NET. When you're done reading this chapter, you should be able to at least connect to a database and write simple queries against it using web pages developed in Dreamweaver. The chapter is an introduction to database connectivity and data manipulation through web forms. As the book progresses, you'll draw upon the concepts presented here and build on what you learn.

> **NOTE**   You'll work with two databases in this chapter: Realtor.mdb and Publications.mdb. I strongly recommend that you upsize these databases to SQL Server using the Microsoft Access Upsizing Tools, if you have it available. However, you *can* use these databases as is if it's easier for you to do so.

How to Build Connection Strings

Most common database scenarios will ultimately involve a high-end database manager such as SQL Server or MySQL. If you want to build front-end interfaces that manipulate data, you'll need to know how to connect to your server. The easiest way to do it is to build a *connection string*, because it allows you to centralize your data access services through Dreamweaver. You can also use a data source name (DSN), which is similar but more machine-specific.

A connection string is sort of an "edit once, apply everywhere" tool, which makes your data-driven sites more portable. Because the connection string is stored in the `Web.config` file, you only need to make a change there, instead of seeking out all the web pages that might have the affected information. For example, you can create a Realtor site that you can then tweak and sell to real estate agencies. Or, if you're working for a large company, you can build administrative modules that can be reused across departments.

> **NOTE**   In this day and age, does it surprise you to find out there is an excellent web resource on connection strings at `www.connectionstrings.com`?

One way to build a connection string in Dreamweaver is using the Databases tab in the Application panel (Figure 3.1). From there, you have two options for creating a connection string, as shown in Figure 3.1: an OLE DB Connection or a SQL Server Connection. If you click on OLE DB Connection, you'll be presented with a dialog box like that in Figure 3.2.

NOTE   The Application panel is where the action is whenever you want to create links to databases and insert server behaviors. A *server behavior* in Dreamweaver MX is a script that operates or is executed on the server and is accessible through the Application panel.

FIGURE 3.1:

The Application panel holds the key to the city when it comes to databases in Dreamweaver MX.

FIGURE 3.2:

The OLE DB Connection dialog box allows you to build a connection string in a number of ways.

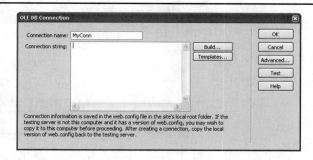

As you can see from Figure 3.2, there's a text field for choosing a name for your connection, and a larger text field for building your actual string. This roomy field is a good thing, since you'll often have this information handy (maybe your database administrator or web host provider e-mailed it to you), in which case you can just paste it in.

The second way to build a string is by using a number of templates that Dreamweaver MX provides. Clicking on the Templates button reveals a dialog box like that in Figure 3.3.

FIGURE 3.3:

Dreamweaver MX
comes preconfigured
with several
connection string
templates.

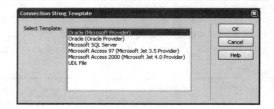

When you choose a connection string template, Dreamweaver MX inserts a code fragment like the code shown just below and in Figure 3.4. This particular example is the code that would be inserted if we chose the first template, Oracle (Microsoft Provider):

```
Provider=MSDAORA;
Data Source=[OracleServiceName];
User ID=[username];
Password=[password];
```

Your job is to simply replace the placeholders with real information—one thing that the minds of Macromedia have not figured out how to help you with. They can't plug in your own user information and data source, but they do manage to cover a very important piece of work for you here: If you don't know the syntax for the connection string you're building, you needn't look it up. You can just click a button and there it is.

FIGURE 3.4:

You can choose from
several connection
string templates.

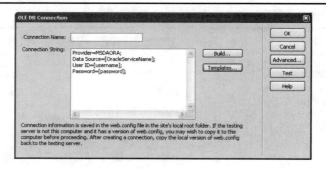

If you're building a SQL Server connection, as we'll be doing in this chapter, you can click the SQL Server template. The following code will appear in the OLE DB Connection dialog box:

```
Provider=SQLOLEDB.1;
Persist Security Info=False;
Data Source=[serverName];
Initial Catalog=[databaseName];
User ID=[username];
Password=[password];
```

For this discussion, however, we're going to focus on the other option that is available to us for building connection strings, using the Application panel's Database tab (Figure 3.1). We're going to choose SQL Server Connection and accept the default code that the program drops in for us:

```
Persist Security Info=False;
Data Source=[serverName];
Initial Catalog=[databaseName];
User ID=[username];
Password=[password];
```

To turn this into a valid connection string, we need to provide some customized information:

Our database source   In this case, the database source is a local server, which means it's the copy of SQL Server that resides on my hard drive. If your database is provided by a host provider, you will usually enter an IP address as the database source.

The initial catalog   This is the name of the database that serves as the "home" for all your connections. That way, when you attempt to access a table, you don't need to specify which database the table belongs to, because your initial catalog is the "starting point" for all your data operations.

The user ID   This is the user ID to which you want to give access. If you're the DBA (database administrator), you already know what to do here. If you have been given a username by your DBA, this is where it goes.

The password   This is the password for the user, which you assign through the ASP.NET page that accesses your database tables. Note that, in terms of the connection, this is the user's password to SQL Server—not a password of the ASP.NET page.

Listing 3.1 shows how we'll build our connection string. This connection string can be used throughout the website because the information resides in the Web.config file described in Chapter 1, "Configuring Dreamweaver for ASP.NET," as soon as you click the last OK button. (Of course, your own information will be different because your database will have its own ID and password information.)

Listing 3.1   **A typical connection string**

```
"Persist Security Info=False;
Data Source=(local);
Initial Catalog=Realtor;
User ID=sybex;
Password=dreamweavermx"
```

Notice the quotes in Listing 3.1, which are required when inputting the information in the SQL Server Connection dialog box. Also, note the parentheses around `local`. You need to include these if you are accessing a local SQL Server database. If you are using an IP address, do not use the parentheses. Here's how it looks in the `Web.config` file:

```
<appSettings>
    <add key="MM_CONNECTION_HANDLER_mdriscollString" value="sqlserver.htm" />
    <add key="MM_CONNECTION_STRING_mdriscollString"
    value="Persist Security Info=False;Data
    ➥Source=(local);Initial Catalog=Realtor;User ID=sybex;Password=dreamweavermx"
    />
    <add key="MM_CONNECTION_DATABASETYPE_mdriscollString" value="SQLServer" />
        <add key="MM_CONNECTION_SCHEMA_mdriscollString" value="" />
        <add key="MM_CONNECTION_CATALOG_mdriscollString" value="" />
    </appSettings>>
```

Another Way to Make a Connection String

There are other ways to make connection strings, which you may want to consider if you can't find the appropriate template. This is a good trick to know, anyway, and helps you get familiar with the various ways to set up a connection. This method revolves around the creation of a text file that you then convert to a Database Connection Wizard file. Let's get a better feel for this by just doing it instead of talking about it. Just follow these brief instructions, and you'll be able to create a connection string in no time:

WARNING   This method was not completely reliable on all Windows operating systems, particularly Windows 2003 Server, at the time of this writing. If you have trouble, before giving up, try making sure the folder options are set to display filename extensions.

1. From your desktop, right-click and choose New ➢ Microsoft Data Link; if this option isn't available, choose New ➢ Text Document.

2. If you make a new text file, change the filename extension from .txt to .udl.

3. Double-click on the new text file. This opens the Microsoft Connection Wizard in a window named Data Link Properties (Figure 3.5).

The Data Link
Properties window's
Connection tab

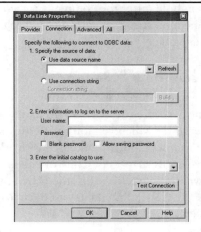

4. Choose your database driver and connection properties (Figure 3.6).

Choosing a database
driver from the Data
Link Properties
window

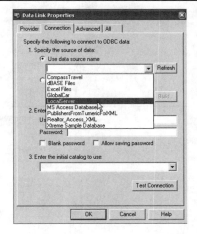

5. Click the Test Connection button to test the connection. When everything is working, choose OK to save the file.

6. Now, just change the extension on the .udl filename back to .txt, and double-click the newly named file. You'll get a text file with contents similar to the following, with the variance depending on which data source you chose:

```
[oledb]
; Everything after this line is an OLE DB initstring
Provider=MSDASQL.1;Persist Security Info=False;
User ID= sybex ;Data Source=Realtor_Access_XML
```

7. The lines in bold (after the comment ; `Everything after this line is ...`) are your ADO connection string, which you can use in Dreamweaver's Database OLE DB Connection dialog box (Figure 3.2).

Creating a New Data Source

You may have to create a new data source, which you can then access using the procedures outlined in the preceding section. To do that, you need to find your ODBC control panel. Its location depends on which version of Windows you're using, but it's usually available from among the Windows Control Panel icons. In Windows XP and Windows 2000, it's in the Administrative Tools snap-in of Control Panel. Open that up and you'll see a group of icons like that shown in Figure 3.7. Click the Data Sources (ODBC) icon, and you'll see the dialog box in Figure 3.8. Generally, you'll want to choose the User DSN or System DSN tab (System DSN if on a server).

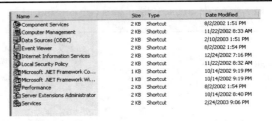

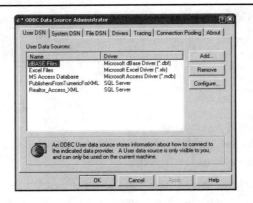

The Data Source Administrator is a handy device if you're connecting through multiple interfaces. I like to use Microsoft Access as a front-end to SQL Server database tables, so DSNs are a nice way to manage that, and then I can use that same connection for a website that I'm testing on my server. I like to use the same master connection string on everything I test with, because it's so easy to change them later thanks to Dreamweaver's centralized way of handling connection strings.

> **NOTE** In Microsoft terms, the term *ODBC* is "dead." *OLEDB* is the preferred method for connections particularly using SQL Server and .NET, since the connection is specifically optimized for working with SQL Server. OLEDB is also faster than DSNs, though not as easy to reconfigure.

Assuming you're going to make a User DSN (remember that a User DSN is only visible on the machine being used), click that tab. You'll see a list of available drivers.

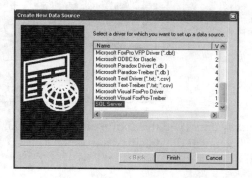

For our purposes, we'll choose SQL Server at the bottom of the list. When you click Finish, you're not really finished. The next screen to appear is the one shown in Figure 3.9. Fill in the three text fields. The last one can get a little tricky depending on your Windows version. It makes sense that you'd want to click on the arrow to reveal a list of available SQL Servers (your machine may already "know about" several). My experience has not been very positive with this, however, so I like to manually input my server information name. In this case, I would type in (local).

FIGURE 3.9:

Creating a new data source to SQL Server

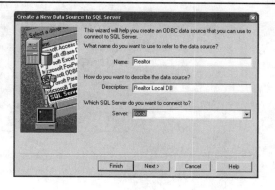

Next up is the dialog box shown in Figure 3.10, asking how you want to connect. You can choose your NT connection service, which is really your Windows account, or go through the database. Generally, you'll choose the database, but check with your systems administrator if there is any doubt.

FIGURE 3.10:

Choosing information for login to your data source

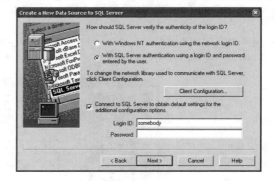

The next window offers you the option of changing your default database. As you can see in Figure 3.11, I changed the default database by selecting the one named Realtor in the drop-down list.

WARNING   At this point in the data source creation process, you need to be really careful with SQL Server, because you could use the model or master databases by mistake. You don't want to do this, because these databases provide core functionality to SQL Server; changing them could corrupt your database.

FIGURE 3.11:

You can change your default database.

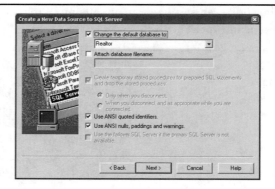

Click Next and then Finish, and you'll arrive at the dialog box shown in Figure 3.12. Now you can test your connection by clicking Test Data Source at the bottom.

FIGURE 3.12:

From here, you can test your connection by clicking the Test Data Source button.

You can now access your new data source using the process described earlier, in which you create a new text file on your desktop, change the extension to .udl, and use the Data Link Properties window's Connection tab to connect to the data source.

Now that you've made a connection, Dreamweaver MX gives you a sneak view into your database. Look at the Application panel in Dreamweaver and open the Database tab. Here you can browse your database and view various database objects.

Creating DataSets

In the old days of ASP, a set of rows resulting from a SQL query was referred to as a record set. Today, in .NET, we call it a *dataset*. In the days of ASP, we needed to pay a lot of attention, from a programming standpoint, to where the cursor was at any given time, so we had to know which row was being pointed to. Now most of this is handled by ASP.NET, through what are called *paging properties*, which comprise a number of built-in classes that manage this process for you. Most of what isn't managed for you by .NET is taken over by Dreamweaver.

Unless you're using a stored procedure, building a DataSet in Dreamweaver is an important initial task if you want to query or update data in any way. As I'll be pointing out whenever I get the chance, stored procedures are the most efficient way to manage relational database resources. That said, there's nothing wrong with using Dreamweaver's built-in facilities for managing data, if only as a way to learn more about web page interaction with databases.

One of the first steps in working with your database and establishing a DataSet is becoming familiar with the database you're accessing, especially if you didn't develop it. You can simply browse the tables and other database objects using the Application panel, as mentioned earlier. Another way is to get familiar with the key relationships in the database, so you can more effectively develop joins and use other SQL statements that bring in data from multiple tables.

Checking for Primary and Foreign Keys

Before building a DataSet, it's a good idea to familiarize yourself with the database tables you are working with. You'll want to know not only what the table columns look like, but what your primary and foreign keys are so that you can properly join the tables when you query them. In Chapter 2, "SQL and Dreamweaver Web Applications," I showed you how to check for primary and foreign keys using SQL Server. You can also check for them using Dreamweaver (as long as your database is a SQL Server database).

In Dreamweaver, you create a new DataSet and click on the Advanced tab (you'll examine this process more closely later in the chapter). In the DataSet dialog box, type the following into the SQL text box:

```
SELECT * FROM
tumeric.INFORMATION_SCHEMA.CONSTRAINT_COLUMN_USAGE
```

Then, click Test (replacing `tumeric` with the name of your database). The results will be displayed in the Test SQL Statement pane (see Figure 3.13).

You can do the same thing if you're working with MySQL rather than SQL Server. When you type the SELECT * FROM statement into the SQL text box, replace INFORMATION_SCHEMA.CONSTRAINT_COLUMN_USAGE with SHOW CREATE TABLE tablename.

The Test SQL
Statement window
after looking for keys

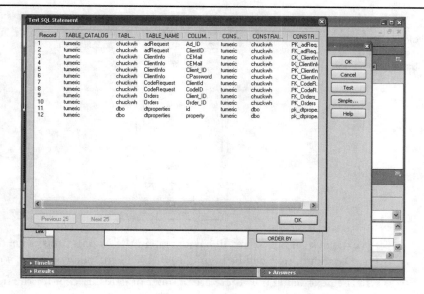

Building the DataSet

The hardest part to building a DataSet in Dreamweaver, if you've already built your database, has already been done. If not, you can download any of the SQL files that I used to build some database tables. These are located at www.sybex.com. Alternatively, you can download the Realtor.mdb file, a Microsoft Access database, which you can then convert to a SQL Server database using the Upsizing Wizard in Access under Tools ➢ Upsizing Wizard. The advantage of using the Realtor.mdb file is that it already contains some data, so you won't have to input anything. You can also find this database at www.sybex.com.

You use a visual interface to create DataSets in Dreamweaver. The interface is launched when you click on the Application panel's Server Behaviors tab and choose DataSet; then you fill in the dialog box with the appropriate information. When you're done, you can reuse the DataSet in your web page for a variety of different things, primarily queries and updates, but also if you need to insert data from another table.

Starting with the Basics: Using Simple Mode

To start building your first DataSet, create a new page by choosing File ➢ New, and then select Dynamic Page and ASP.NET C# from the New Document dialog box (see Figure 3.14). There are many options to choose from—in this case we're building a dynamic page using C#.

FIGURE 3.14:

Building a dynamic
page in the New
Document dialog box

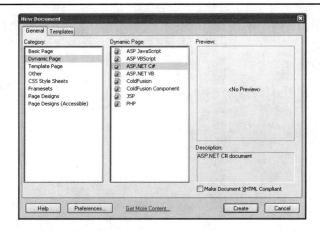

Next, click on the Server Behaviors tab in the Applications panel of Dreamweaver MX. The DataSet option will be highlighted. That's the one you want, so go ahead and choose it.

In the next dialog box, there are number of fields. Except for the field labeled "Name", none of them is a *free form* text field, in which you can pretty much enter anything you want; these fields all provide options from which you must choose. The first thing you'll want to designate is your connection. If you've made any, they should be available in the Connection drop-down list. Choose the connection that you made. Your dialog box will morph from a bunch of empty fields to a dialog box containing a drop-down list labeled Table consisting of the database tables that you have access to through your connection (Figure 3.15). The dialog box automatically chooses the first table Dreamweaver encounters from this drop-down list. These tables appear in alphabetical order. Figure 3.15 shows how the dialog box will look if you choose the ClientInfo table from the Table drop-down list.

FIGURE 3.15:

The DataSet dialog
box in Simple mode

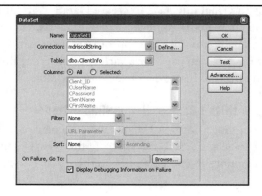

Choose the database table you want. In this case, we're accessing a table named `ClientInfo`, which contains the kind of data you'd expect to find in such a beast, such as a client's name, address, and so forth. Just accept all the default values for now. To do this, click the All radio button, and then click the Test button to make sure your web page is pulling the dataset you want. Rarely will you need something as simple as this, but it happens, so go ahead and click OK in the DataSet dialog box and see what results from your efforts. If you left in the default name for the DataSet, you'll see that the Application panel's Server Behavior tab now has a DataSet named `DataSet1`.

Now, select the Bindings tab in the Application panel. Click on the + button next to the DataSet appearing in the window (Figure 3.16), and you'll expand the DataSet to reveal all the columns accessed by *your SQL code*. Your what? Oh, wait, you don't remember writing any SQL code, do you? Well, you did, sort of. Actually, Dreamweaver MX did it for you when you created your DataSet. The Bindings tab doesn't reveal all the columns in the relevant table; it shows only those called for by your SQL code as established in the DataSet dialog box.

FIGURE 3.16:

The Bindings tab reveals columns made available through SQL Server code written by Dreamweaver for your DataSet.

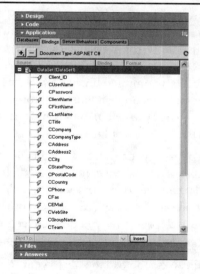

But Dreamweaver does much more than that. It generates an element into your web page, called the `MM:DataSet` element. This element consists of the SQL code that was created when you waltzed through that dialog box, happily accepting all those defaults. Listing 3.2 shows you what Dreamweaver MX wrote when you did that, and the SQL code is highlighted.

Listing 3.2   **Code generated when you create the DataSet**

```
<MM:DataSet
id="DataSet1"
runat="Server"
IsStoredProcedure="false"
ConnectionString='<%# System.Configuration.ConfigurationSettings.AppSettings
➥["MM_CONNECTION_STRING_mdriscollString"] %>'
DatabaseType='<%# System.Configuration.ConfigurationSettings.AppSettings
➥["MM_CONNECTION_DATABASETYPE_mdriscollString"] %>'
CommandText='<%# "SELECT * FROM dbo.ClientInfo" %>'
Debug="true"
> </MM:DataSet>
```

You'll be exploring the deeper meaning of some the attributes of MM:DataSet in the next chapter. Becoming familiar with these elements will make you a much better Dreamweaver MX .NET developer, because sometimes you'll want to tweak these elements in order to either troubleshoot a problem or make your application run more smoothly.

What you're seeing in Listing 3.2 is a .NET *custom control*. The .NET Framework contains of a lot of built-in controls, most of which you'll get to know in Chapter 4, "Working with the Dreamweaver Custom Control." This custom control is defined in the DreamweaverCtrls.dll that ships with Dreamweaver MX. You can't see this definition because a DLL is a compiled binary, which means it executes very similarly to the way a software program executes on your desktop machine. You could conceivably create your own DLL with your own element definitions, to do all kinds of fancy stuff, and that's exactly what the creators of Dreamweaver MX did.

Now that you have your DataSet, it's time to play. From the Bindings tab, make sure your DataSet is expanded to reveal columns of data from the table, as shown in Figure 3.16. Now, drag one of the columns onto your web page. Make sure you drag it to someplace within the body element on the page. Let's say you choose the ClastName column; the following would appear in your web page after you drag the column and let go of your mouse:

```
<%# DataSet1.FieldValue("CLastName", Container) %>
```

Save your file. Next, upload the file to your server. The easiest way is to simply click the convenient Get/Put arrow button at the top of the application window; it displays a drop-down menu as shown in Figure 3.17.

FIGURE 3.17:

Use the Get/Put arrow button to upload the file to your server.

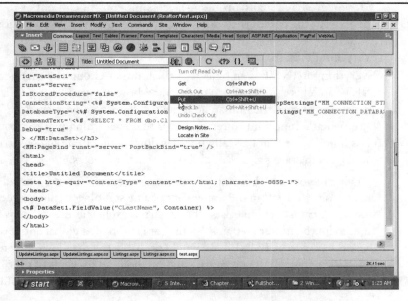

Now, go to your page. If you don't have a test site on your server, you can mimic mine. I created a virtual directory on my machine called `Realtor`, so my test page is reached by entering `http://localhost/Realtor/test.aspx` into my browser. You should get a window like the one in Figure 3.18. All it reveals is the last name of your client (or whatever other data you used). The magic all occurs courtesy of the following code fragment that you created by dragging and dropping from the Application panel.

```
<%# DataSet1.FieldValue("CLastName", Container) %>
```

FIGURE 3.18:

The browser window displaying your data

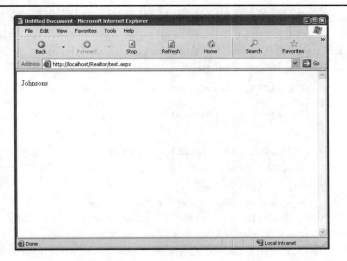

If you are having any problems accessing your document at this stage, check out the appendix at the end of the book, "Troubleshooting Web Applications Using Dreamweaver."

Everything's an Object

Everything in .NET is an object. Well, almost—enough so that getting a good grasp on the .NET model is a good way to understand how it works. .NET relies on a huge object model that seems to rival the human genome database, so obviously there's no way to cover it all here. What's important to remember is that everything works through a system of object and class inheritance that basically bubbles down a hierarchy of chained events, which in turn act on objects that are parents or children of other objects.

Think of your car's heating system. It's distinct from the car, and all the little heater doodads are encapsulated within the framework of a master object called, I guess, the heater. Its relationship to the car is there; it exists—but it isn't as explicit as the relationship of all the properties and "methods" the heater contains. So the car is more of a global entity of sorts, which contains all these other objects. In .NET we would probably call the global car entity a namespace, because it would contain all the properties and methods and objects of everything that makes the car work, and allows for a hierarchical structure to organize the underlying architecture.

Returning to the heater, when you press its buttons or turn its dial, it gets hotter or cooler through methods named `heat()` and `cool()`—well, at least that would be true if cars were computers. The heater would probably be a class, most likely a public class just in case other things needed to access it, such as a web page (or the car's driver). The buttons or dial might be a public object of some defined datatype. Since that datatype can't really be an integer or a string, we won't worry too much about it and will instead jump back to the matter at hand: this piece of code that Dreamweaver MX dropped in when we dragged our column of data into the web page:

```
<%# DataSet1.FieldValue("CLastName", Container) %>
```

Here, the public object is a string named `FieldValue`, which was defined in the `DreamweaverCtrls.dll`. You won't see this because it's defined in the DLL, but the definition looks like this:

```
public string FieldValue(string FieldName, System.Web.UI.Control Container)
{
    return FieldValueAtIndex(0, FieldName, Container);
}
```

Of course, the return value has yet another dependency, and the chain goes on and on if you look at the source code for the `DreamweaverCtrls.dll`, which you can do by navigating to the following directory:

```
C:\Program Files\Macromedia\DreamweaverMX
\Configuration\ServerBehaviors\Shared\ASP.Net\Scripts
```

There, you'll find a script called `DreamweaverCtrls.cs`. This is, of course, assuming your installation is in the `C:\Program Files\Macromedia` directory. It very well may not be, so you should change the part of the path shown in bold just above to be what is appropriate to your machine.

WARNING   Whatever you do, don't change the source code in this file without making a backup first, and then don't bother unless you're a major C# whiz.

As you move forward through the file, look closely at the code you encounter and try to find relationships between objects and their properties and methods. Generally, the syntax looks like this: `object.property`. The keyword on the left side of the dot notation (period) is the object, and the keyword on the right is a property or method. You can recognize a method because it has parentheses. If there are no parentheses next to the keyword on the right, then it's a property, not a method.

Understanding Form Variables and the Process of Passing Them

Our initial DataSet was pretty lame and won't actually generate any worthwhile data, because it will give us every row in the DataSet. We may want that, but we probably won't. If we don't, we need to process some *form variables* to filter our data. First, let's get a very brief primer on form variables.

Whenever you reach a website, you do so by sending a request to a server in the form of a URL. The base part of a URL, the part that simply requests a web page, stops at the point where it contains a question mark (?). The following URL will return a page with no specific instructions about what data to retrieve from a database, if there is one:

```
http://www.tumeric.net/Service/client.aspx
```

Even if this URL accesses a database, it can't access any specific data that is customized for the user. It might access a table through a SQL command built into the page, but that data is the same for everyone.

In order to create a request specific to a user, you need to add a question mark followed by an attribute/value pair. Let's say I want to retrieve my personal profile from a website. I could type a URL that looks like this into my browser (and I happen to know what the needed form variables are because I wrote the page, of course):

```
http://www.tumeric.net/Service/client.aspx?CEMail=chuck@tumeric.net
```

This tells the web page to retrieve the row of information containing the personal profile (we're assuming that's the core functionality of `client.aspx`) from the database of the individual where the `CEMail` column contains the data `chuck@tumeric.net`. If nobody with that e-mail address exists in the database, no data will be returned.

Note that this works when you are using the `method="get"` attribute/value pair in your form definition. When you're using `method="post"`, form variables are hidden from view. You can't just type them into your browser's address window because the variables are sent in the body of the HTTP message that is sent to the web server, With `method="get"`, on the other hand, the variables are encoded into the URL that is sent. This doesn't belie my point, though; one way or another, you still need those attribute/value pairs to be sent.

The `get` method is very useful for troubleshooting, by the way. See the sidebar "Differences between `post` and `get`" for advice on when you should use each method.

Differences between *post* and *get*

If you use `method="post"` in your form element definition, the attribute/value pairs are hidden from view. So for the tumeric website example in this chapter, the URL in your window would remain `http://www.tumeric.net/Service/client.aspx`. However, the attribute/value pairs do still get sent in the body of the HTTP request. You should use the `post` method whenever there are any side operations resulting from a form's being submitted (such as an update to the database or recording of submitted credit card info). You should use `get` when there are no effects.

The reasons for this specification of `post` and `get` roles go far beyond the traditional view that the `post` method is good because it hides the character strings (and, thus, the attribute/value pairs) that are used in form processing. It has to do with cached pages. When the `post` method is used, a user who is *revisiting* the page to which the form variables are passed will very likely see a page from their history stack (or a cached page). You've probably seen, after hitting your Back button during the form submittal process, messages that tell you a page has expired. This happens whenever a form uses a `post` method. This message is supposed to be a warning that something negative could result in the processing of your data when you click that Back button and then reload the page. But if your site contains the `post` method on pages where reloading doesn't matter (such as a simple query into the database with no updates), then you're like the boy who cried wolf. Eventually, your users won't believe anything bad can ever happen and they'll always reload. If, on the other hand, the message is rarely encountered, users are more apt to heed the warning.

Of course, as you advance in your .NET programming, you'll code your pages in such a way that it won't matter how many times users hit their Back buttons—they'll never corrupt *your* data. Nevertheless, it can be annoying to get those messages, so you should expose users to such messages only when you have to. Additionally, many times you'll be passing information to the database, such as primary keys, that you don't want seen in a URL. The less data you show to hackers, the better

Managing Form Variables in Dreamweaver

Often when working with forms, you'll need some refinement to what our previous `tumeric` example delivers. This is particularly true if the web page your users are accessing has different entry points. Let's assume that's the case here, and we want to key in on two different form variables that will provide entrance to our client profile page. We'll keep the first variable, the client e-mail address, but we'll add another, the client's ID. For this we must get out of the Simple mode in the DataSet dialog box and use the Advanced tab. When you click the Advanced tab, the dialog box that opens provides access to a SQL editing field into which you can put SQL code directly, as shown in Figure 3.19. Here is an example:

FIGURE 3.19:

The DataSet dialog box in Advanced mode

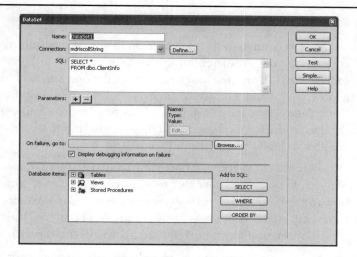

```
SELECT * FROM dbo.ClientInfo
WHERE CEMail = @CEMail OR Client_ID=@ClientID
```

If it hadn't been for that last WHERE statement, we could have kept it "simple," but the WHERE statement contains more than one filter, and the Simple mode accommodates only one. You can have the DataSet dialog box help you anyway, and that's not a bad policy to follow if you're unsure of how to put together a form variable (either through Dreamweaver or by hand-coding it yourself). To see what I mean, enter the SELECT * FROM statement shown just above, into the SQL Editor in Advanced mode. Make sure you leave out the WHERE statement; then click the Simple button to return to another DataSet dialog box (Figure 3.20).

FIGURE 3.20:

Creating SQL filters
with the DataSet
dialog box

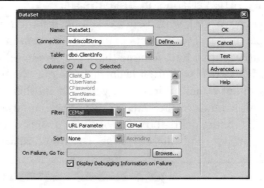

Choose a column of data to use from the Filter drop-down menu. These are the various columns in your database. In this example, as shown in Figure 3.20, I've chosen a column called CEMail. Leave the = sign selected as the operator in the adjacent drop-down list. Next, choose URL Parameter (the default) from the drop-down list underneath the first Filter list. Enter CEMail into the free-form text box next to that. This will be the name of the form field that passes the form value entered by your user to the server. Your completed DataSet dialog box should look like the one in Figure 3.20.

Now, click the Advanced button. The advantage to doing this should be immediately obvious. Even if you know how to hand-code all sorts of form variables, you may not know how to work through Dreamweaver's various dialog boxes for this process, so it helps to get some help along the way. As you can see from Figure 3.21, that help comes in the form of some important information entered for you in the DataSet/Advanced dialog box.

FIGURE 3.21:

You can learn a lot
about Advanced mode
by setting values in
Simple mode first and
then switching back to
Advanced mode.

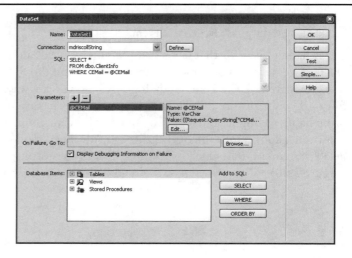

Notice that Dreamweaver updates the SQL by adding the following WHERE clause:

```
SELECT *
FROM dbo.ClientInfo
WHERE CEMail = @CEMail
```

This tells the database that you want selected columns of data where (when) the CEMail column equals a certain value. That value will be different for every visitor to your website. The value is sent through a form field—either an asp:textbox (a server-side control that acts like an HTML text field on steroids and runs from the server instead of on the client, about which you'll learn in Chapter 4), some other ASP.NET form control, or through a more traditional HTML input element. The form field must have a name or id attribute assigned to it, but since we haven't created the form yet, let's assume we plan to keep things consistent and name it CEMail.

TIP   Naming form fields is where one of those nice little diagrams described in Bonus Chapter 1, "Developing a Workflow," comes in handy. You have to create either your SQL queries first or your form first; either way, one references the other, and it can be hard to track without a hard-copy reference to your architecture. It's handy to have that document you've created, to map out the flow of your web application and assist you in maintaining name consistency.

Adding Parameters Using Dreamweaver

Look again at Figure 3.21, and notice the Parameters input fields right under the SQL text box. The little + and – buttons tell you that you can add additional parameters if you want. Parameters accept the form values and end up as part of the SQL code. They allow you to "communicate" to the web server. You'll notice that Dreamweaver has done some initial editing for you in the box on the right. You can click the Edit button to bring up the Edit Parameters dialog box and take a closer look (see Figure 3.22).

FIGURE 3.22:

Perusing the Edit Parameters dialog box

A URL parameter is appended to a URL and begins with a question mark (?) followed by a series of name/value pairs. Generally these name/value pairs are associated with form fields (the name of each field) and their values (the value of each field), and take the form name=value. If more than one URL parameter exists, each name/value pair is separated by an ampersand (&). The following example shows a URL parameter with two name/value pairs (with the URL parameters in bold):

```
http://localhost/directory/document?name1=value1&name2=value2
```

When a server receives a request that includes parameters in the URL of the request, the server reads those parameters and passes them to the data source with which the page is interacting.

All of the form values that come streaming into the web server from a form come as a sort of list or, in Microsoft parlance, a *collection*. So if you have a form containing 50 fields, you'd have a collection of 50 form attribute/value pairs. This is handled by the `QueryString` collection. (There are other, similar collections, such as the `Form` collection.) The `QueryString` collection is like an array. It's available to you at any time. Collections are all available either through indexing, which means you can count each one in the series in the order of its appearance in the form, or by name, as in our example in the Edit Parameter dialog box:

```
((Request.QueryString["CEMail"] != null) &&
(Request.QueryString["CEMail"].Length > 0)) ? Request.QueryString["CEMail"] : ""
```

In this case, Dreamweaver references a specific item in the collection by name by referencing the form item named CEMail. Also, Dreamweaver checks to make sure it isn't a null value and that there is actually something in the collection (the `Length>0` bit of code is a Boolean test). It doesn't matter whether this form item is from a text box or some other type of form input (although it can't be a drop-down box; that requires some special handling you'll learn about in Chapter 5, "Using Web Server Controls"). What is critical is that there actually be a form input of some kind named CEMail. If there isn't, your form will generate errors when it runs.

Choosing between form variables and URL parameters is basically a choice between using the `QueryString` collection or the `Form` collection. Generally, when using a GET command with a form, you use the `QueryString` collection, and with a POST command you use the `Form` collection. That's because with GET, name/value pairs are passed as part of the URL, whereas with POST they are passed as form data after the HTTP header. If you have no clue about which to use, you can use the `Params` collection, which is a union of the `ServerVariables`, `QueryString`, `Forms`, and `Cookies` collections. In other words, you can write this:

```
Request.Params("someValue")
```

and ASP.NET will retrieve and use the appropriate collection.

If you're worried about sensitive data, you won't want the queries to be seen in the URL, so in those cases you'll want to avoid the `QueryString` collection.

You might have noticed in the Edit Parameter dialog box (Figure 3.22) a field named Type. Dreamweaver communicates directly with your database, so generally it can determine the datatype of the column your parameter is referencing. Notice also that Dreamweaver applies the proper syntax to the parameter name by placing an @ character in front of it, which tells the database that it's about to deal with a parameter.

Working with Parameters in the MM:DataSet Element

Now, close out of all the dialog boxes you've been exploring, by accepting all the input so far, Let's have a look at what Dreamweaver has created for us, which is shown in Listing 3.4.

Listing 3.4   **A Dreamweaver-built element containing a SQL query and all the required parameters**

```
<MM:DataSet
id="DataSet1"
runat="Server"
IsStoredProcedure="false"
ConnectionString='<%# System.Configuration.ConfigurationSettings.AppSettings
➥["MM_CONNECTION_STRING_mdriscollString"] %>'
DatabaseType='<%# System.Configuration.ConfigurationSettings.AppSettings
➥["MM_CONNECTION_DATABASETYPE_mdriscollString"] %>'
CommandText='<%# "SELECT  *  FROM dbo.ClientInfo  WHERE
➥CEMail = @CEMail" %>'
Debug="true"
>
    <Parameters>
      <Parameter  Name="@CEMail"  Value='<%# ((Request.QueryString["CEMail"] !=
null) && (Request.QueryString["CEMail"].Length > 0)) ?
Request.QueryString["CEMail"] : "" %>'  Type="VarChar" />
    </Parameters>
  </MM:DataSet>
```

The MM:DataSet element, as you can see, is packed with all kinds of information. You're going to be taking a much deeper look into this element in the next chapter, but for now let's see what happens when we add one more parameter to the mix. This would be done in the Advanced mode, but now that we've seen how Dreamweaver does it, we can mimic that and hand-code it. Listing 3.5 shows the same code as Listing 3.4, with some additions in bold.

NOTE   Keep in mind that SELECT * is bad coding practice and should only be done by book authors looking to save space on the printed page. SELECT * is bad practice because you don't want to bring in fields of data you don't need.

Listing 3.5   **Adding a parameter to the SQL code from Listing 3.4**

```
<MM:DataSet
id="DataSet1"
runat="Server"
```

```
IsStoredProcedure="false"
ConnectionString='<%# System.Configuration.ConfigurationSettings.
➥AppSettings["MM_CONNECTION_STRING_mdriscollString"] %>'DatabaseType='<%#
System.Configuration.ConfigurationSettings.
➥AppSettings["MM_CONNECTION_DATABASETYPE_mdriscollString"] %>'CommandText='<%#
"SELECT *  FROM dbo.ClientInfo  WHERE
➥CEMail = @CEMail OR Client_ID=@Client_ID" %>'
Debug="true"
>
<Parameters>
      <Parameter  Name="@CEMail"  Value='<%# ((Request.QueryString["CEMail"] !=
null) && (Request.QueryString["CEMail"].Length > 0)) ?
Request.QueryString["CEMail"] : "" %>' Type="VarChar"   />
      <Parameter  Name="@Client_ID"  Value='<%#
((Request.QueryString["Client_ID"] != null) &&
(Request.QueryString["Client_ID"].Length > 0)) ?
Request.QueryString["Client_ID"] : "" %>' Type="Int"   />
      </Parameters>
   </MM:DataSet>
```

You can use the Edit Parameter dialog box (Figure 3.22) to accomplish this, but you're really doing the same thing: hand coding. I prefer working right in Dreamweaver's Code view for these kinds of edits—although one advantage to using the Edit Parameters dialog box is that it reminds you to name your datatype. When you're working in Code view, if you copy and paste one parameter to create another, you might forget to give the second parameter the proper datatype. For instance, if you left Client_ID as a varchar, the form would generate a SQL error.

Remember that you can look up a datatype by clicking on the Databases tab in the Application panel and expanding the table you're working on to view information about each column.

Accessing a DataSet Through Form Variables

Now that we've seen the fundamentals of putting together a DataSet that works with form variables, let's create a simple form that will work with our DataSet. Listing 3.6 shows our form, which contains two simple fields.

Make sure when you build your own form in Dreamweaver that the name of a field matches the name of the QueryString named in the Parameter element associated with that field. In our example, the form fields need to have names that match these two query strings (in bold):

```
Request.QueryString["CEMail"]
```
and
```
Request.QueryString["Client_ID"]
```

Listing 3.6   **Building a form to send parameters to the database**

```
<form name="form1" method="get" action="L0306.aspx">
  <p>Email
    <input name="CEMail" type="text">
  </p>
  <p>Client ID number:
    <input name="Client_ID" type="text" id="Client_ID">
  </p>
  <p>
    <input type="submit" name="Submit" value="Submit">
  </p>
</form>
```

If you used this form within the same file you built your initial query, your final code should look like that in Listing 3.7 and should render in a browser as illustrated in Figure 3.23.

FIGURE 3.23:

The final form rendered in a browser

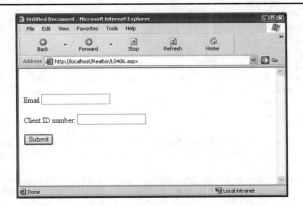

Listing 3.7   **The final form, including the DataSet**

```
<%@ Page Language="C#" ContentType="text/html" ResponseEncoding="iso-8859-1" %>
<%@ Register TagPrefix="MM"
Namespace="DreamweaverCtrls"Assembly="DreamweaverCtrls,version=1.0.0.0,publicKey
Token=
➥836f606ede05d46a,culture=neutral" %>
<h3>
  <MM:DataSet
id="DataSet1"
runat="Server"
IsStoredProcedure="false"
```

```
ConnectionString='<%# System.Configuration.ConfigurationSettings.AppSettings
➥["MM_CONNECTION_STRING_mdriscollString"] %>'
DatabaseType='<%#
➥System.Configuration.ConfigurationSettings.AppSettings
➥["MM_CONNECTION_DATABASETYPE_mdriscollString"] %>'
➥CommandText='<%# "SELECT  *   FROM dbo.ClientInfo  WHERE
➥CEMail = @CEMail OR Client_ID=@Client_ID" %>'
Debug="true"
>
<Parameters>
      <Parameter  Name="@CEMail"  Value='<%#
➥((Request.QueryString["CEMail"] != null) &&
➥(Request.QueryString["CEMail"].Length > 0)) ?
➥ Request.QueryString["CEMail"] : ""  %>' Type="VarChar" />
      <Parameter  Name="@Client_ID"  Value='<%#
➥((Request.QueryString["Client_ID"] != null) &&
➥ (Request.QueryString["Client_ID"].Length > 0)) ?
➥ Request.QueryString["Client_ID"] : ""  %>' Type="Int" />
    </Parameters>
  </MM:DataSet>
</h3>
<MM:PageBind runat="server" PostBackBind="true" />
<html>
<head>
<title>Untitled Document</title>
<meta http-equiv="Content-Type" content="text/html;
charset=iso-8859-1">
</head>
<body>
<p>
  <%# DataSet1.FieldValue("CFirstName", Container) %>
  <%# DataSet1.FieldValue("CLastName", Container) %>
</p>
<form name="form1" method="get" action="L0306.aspx">
  <p>Email
    <input name="CEMail" type="text">
  </p>
  <p>Client ID number:
    <input name="Client_ID" type="text" id="Client_ID">
  </p>
  <p>
    <input type="submit" name="Submit" value="Submit">
  </p>
</form>
<p><br>
</p>
</body>
</html>
```

Notice how the parameter name defined in each `Parameter` element has a matching operand in the SQL code (see Figure 3.24):

```
WHERE CEMail = @CEMail OR Client_ID=@Client_ID"
```

There is a parameter named `@CEMail` and a parameter named `@Client_ID`. If you had additional filters, you would need to have additional `Parameter` elements within the `Parameters` element, which in turn lives in the `MM:DataSet` element.

FIGURE 3.24:

There is a matching parameter value for each database column used in the filtering operation.

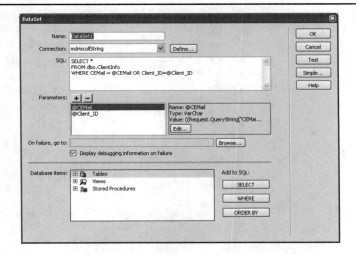

NOTE   Chapter 4 provides some reference material about each element and attribute for each control, including the `MM:DataSet` element that is defined by the `DreamweaverCntrls.dll` library.

I've also added an additional data binding, also in bold, so that the form will return a full name.

When you create your form, use the `get` method in your form method attribute because we're using query strings. If you were using the `post` method, you'd want to use the `Form` collection, but this is a simple query and using the `get` method is fine. Plus, using `get` lets you use the browser address bar to see what form variables are getting passed.

Building Dynamic Tables

Everyone who has developed web pages has worked with tables, and most of us have worked with dynamic, data-driven tables. Those who haven't can consider themselves lucky that they will be introduced, through .NET, to a process that makes the creation of data-intensive tables a breeze. And you won't have to write miles of spaghetti code to do it. With a surprisingly small amount of code, you can insert a table and include in that table a wide range of characteristics. Such a table can page through a large number of records via a navigation system like that shown in Figure 3.25.

FIGURE 3.25:

Navigating through a record set

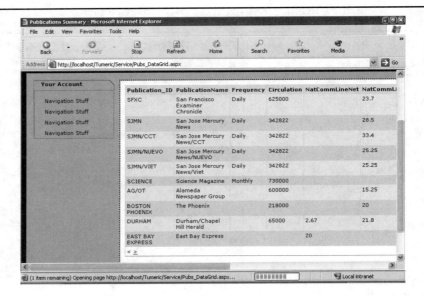

There are a number of ways to get data into a web page using Dreamweaver MX and .NET. I've already shown you the easiest way, which is to simply drag a data binding onto your web page. That won't go far enough, however, if you want to repeat the data within the page (like the data shown in Figure 3.25). In .NET, three controls are used for dealing with repeated data. Because they are bound, or linked, to specific data, these controls are said to be *data bound* controls. Each control is progressively more complex. From the simplest to the most complex, here they are:

- `asp:Repeater`
- `asp:DataList`
- `asp:DataGrid`

We'll explore each one, but first we'll to cover some general principles that apply to all of these.

Introducing Templates

Templates are ASP.NET elements that define the content and display of .NET data controls such as DataLists, DataGrids, and Repeater controls. They contain information about how the data should be presented. When you use any of these controls, you also use templates, which consist of a number of elements that can exist within each of the controls. Eligible elements depend on the data control you are working with. Table 3.1 describes the purpose of each template element and lists the data controls that use it.

TABLE 3.1: Template Elements in .NET Data Controls

Template Name	Description	Controls
AlternatingItemTemplate	An optional element that determines the content and layout of alternating items. If not defined, ItemTemplate is used.	DataList, Repeater
BoundColumn	Controls the order of data binding, and rendering of the columns.	DataGrid
ButtonColumn	Bubbles a user command from within a row to an event handler on the grid. The user command is then handled by an event-handling function in your script (see Chapter 7).	DataGrid
EditCommandColumn	Displays Edit, Update, and Cancel links in response to changes in the DataGrid control's EditItemIndex property.	DataGrid
EditItemTemplate	An optional element that determines the content and layout of the item being edited. If not defined, the ItemTemplate, AlternatingItemTemplate, or SelectedItemTemplate element is used, depending on the circumstances.	DataList
FooterTemplate	An optional element that determines the content and layout of the list footer. If not defined, there is no footer.	DataList, Repeater
HeaderTemplate	An optional element that determines the content and layout of the list header. If not defined, no header is rendered.	DataList, Repeater
HyperLinkColumn	Presents bound data in HyperLink controls.	DataGrid
ItemTemplate	Defines the content and layout of items within the control. This is a required element in the DataList and Repeater controls.	DataList, Repeater

Continued on next page

TABLE 3.1 CONTINUED: Template Elements in .NET Data Controls

Template Name	Description	Controls
SelectedItemTemplate	An optional element that determines the content and layout of the selected item. If not defined, either ItemTemplate or AlternatingItemTemplate is used, depending on whether the item is an alternating one.	DataList
SeparatorTemplate	An optional element that is rendered between items and alternating items. If not defined, no separator is rendered.	DataList, Repeater
TemplateColumn	Lets you designate which controls are rendered in the column.	DataGrid

Each data control has its own advantages in particular situations. The Repeater element might be an option when you have a full list of data that doesn't need any paging (where there is a subset of data on your page and a navigation link that lets you advance to the next subset of data in the order called for in the DataSet's SQL code). If you want a somewhat more robust display, you can try the DataList; and for data requiring a strict grid or table structure and/or paging, you can use a DataGrid.

Table 3.2 compares these elements. Since each is progressively more complex to code, we'll start with the easiest one first, the Repeater control; in examining the Repeater, you'll see how to work with templates.

TABLE 3.2: Comparing the Functionality of Data-Bound Controls

Functionality	Repeater	DataList	DataGrid
Columns	No	Yes	Only as part of a table
Flow layouts	Yes	Yes	No
Paging	Not built into the control itself, but you can create paging programmatically	Yes	
Selecting, editing, deleting data	No	Yes	Yes
Sorting	No	No	Yes
Styling	No	Yes	Yes
Table layout	No	No	Yes
Templates	Yes	Yes	Optional

Working with Repeating Regions

The simplest kind of data control is the `asp:Repeater` element. This element can contain a number of additional elements, which you can discern from Table 3.1. You can use Dreamweaver to create a Repeater control by clicking the Repeat Region Command in the Server Behaviors tab in the Application panel. If you try to do this without selecting any code while in Code view, you'll get an error message from Dreamweaver instructing you to first select an item before using this behavior. This is because Dreamweaver wants to know what data you wish to repeat. You'll also need to be sure you've set up a data source if you're experimenting with a new file.

We're going to work with a particular data source for this file, but you can use one of your own if you prefer. If you wish to use the one set up for this chapter, you can download `Publications.mdb` from this book's page at the `www.sybex.com` site. Then you can either create a SQL Server database from that `.mdb` file using the Microsoft Access Upsize Wizard, or simply create a data source for the `.mdb` file and use that file locally on your machine. If you use the Publications database, create a new DataSet named `Pubs` using the `PubSummary` table. If you're using your own data, call it whatever you like; just remember that I'll be referring to the DataSet as `Pubs` in this discussion.

Since we'll need to select some code to create our Repeater control (of course, you can always hand-code it in Code view instead), we might as well create some content we want to repeat. We can start off with a data binding, which can be found in the Bindings tab. Drag one of the bindings from the `Pubs` DataSet (or one that you created) over to the page in a sensible place. Assuming the page is empty, just make sure it's within the body element. For this example I'm dragging the `PublicationName` column from the Bindings tab to my web page (Figure 3.26).

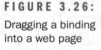

FIGURE 3.26:

Dragging a binding into a web page

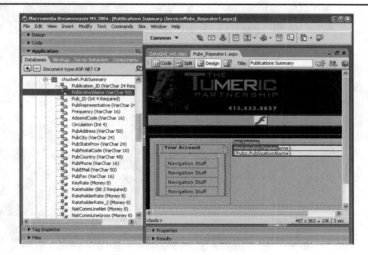

If you test the page at this point, you'll get all the Publication Names in the table, but they'll be all splattered together like one big run-on sentence. That's because each instance of the data repeats, but there's nothing in the Repeater control to separate the repeating instances. We need to devise some HTML for that, and that's where templates come in.

Before we see how to do this by hand, which is an important skill to have, let's see how you can crank one out using Dreamweaver in just a minute or two.

In Design view, click on the first cell in the row of data and hold down the left mouse button as you drag the mouse pointer across the entire row. (You can also go into Code view and select the entire row.) After you've made your selection, go into the Server Behaviors tab again and select Repeat Region.

In the Repeat Region dialog box, choose your DataSet and the number of records you wish to display. If you choose not to display all records, you'll need to add DataSet Paging to the DataSet. To do that, choose DataSet Paging from the Applications panel and click the type of paging you want (see Figure 3.27). The options are self-explanatory. Each page corresponds to a set of records totaling the number of records you designated in the Repeat Region dialog box.

FIGURE 3.27:

Selecting a DataSet Paging option

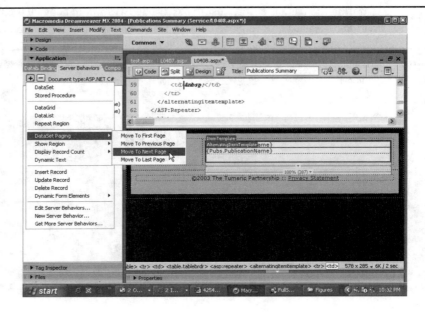

In this case, I chose the Move To Next Page option for paging. In the next dialog box, we simply choose the DataSet to be paged. Since we only have one DataSet this is pretty easy, and we choose Pubs.

The other item in the paging dialog box specifies how to establish your link. The default is "Next", which Dreamweaver will add to the page. The DataSet Paging server behavior then becomes attached to that link, like this:

```
<a href="<%# Request.ServerVariables["SCRIPT_NAME"]
➥%>?Pubs_currentPage=<%# Math.Min(Pubs.CurrentPage + 1,
➥Pubs.LastPage) %>">Next</a>
```

You can also create a graphic and highlight that graphic before you insert a DataSet Paging behavior. If you do, that graphic will appear in the drop-down menu. When you click OK, the new link appears on the page where you had your cursor at the time you inserted the server behavior.

WARNING Be sure to put your Paging server behavior *outside* of the Repeater control, because a Repeater can't contain HTML elements unless they're inside a template.

Listing 3.8 shows one version of our final Repeater control. The ItemTemplate element acts as a container for all the things you want repeated. So we'll add table tags outside of the Repeater control, since we don't want hundreds of tables but rather to repeat table rows within one table.

Listing 3.8   **Repeating rows of data using the Repeater control**

```
<table width="100%" border="0" cellpadding="0" cellspacing="0"
bgcolor="#FFFFFF" class="tablebrdr">
  <ASP:Repeater runat="server"
   DataSource='<%# Pubs.DefaultView %>'>
    <ItemTemplate>
        <tr>
           <td valign="top">
<%# Pubs.FieldValue("PublicationName", Container) %>
           </td>
        </tr>
    </ItemTemplate>
    <alternatingitemtemplate>
      <tr bgcolor="#00FF99">
```

```
          <td>
<%# Pubs.FieldValue("PublicationName", Container) %>
          </td></tr>
       </alternatingitemtemplate>
     </ASP:Repeater>
   </table>
   <p><a href="<%# Request.ServerVariables["SCRIPT_NAME"]
➥%>?Pubs_currentPage=<%# Math.Min(Pubs.CurrentPage + 1,
➥Pubs.LastPage) %>">Next</a></p>
```

The Repeater control's definition is now set up so that there are two templates. One, for every repeating item, is called the `ItemTemplate` element and contains all the content we want to repeat. I want each table row to repeat, and I want each table row to contain a table cell consisting of the data from the database. I only need to write one actual HTML table row. ASP.NET will interpret the Repeater control and the content within, and generate multiple table rows based on my design. Another template, called the `AlternatingItemTemplate`, is used exactly the same way and tells the server to generate a new row in between each `ItemTemplate` item. By creating new HTML table rows within each item and alternating item template, we can vary the colors of each row. If you include a data source within the `AlternatingItemTemplate` definition, then the rows of data maintain their sequence between the `ItemTemplate` and the `AlternatingItemTemplate`. The final product should look something like Figure 3.28.

FIGURE 3.28:

A Repeater control rendering publication names in alternating colors into a browser

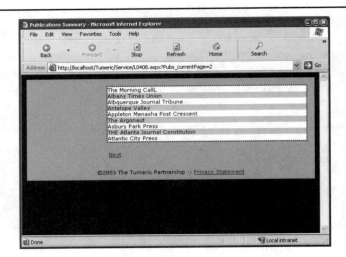

TIP   Dreamweaver's Code Editor contains a syntax helper, shown in Figure 3.29, that informs you of what kind of content can go inside a .NET control.

FIGURE 3.29:

You can use a built-in syntax helper in Dreamweaver MX to build ASP.NET controls.

Another thing we'll want to do is have away of navigating through the records. The easiest way to do this is with Dreamweaver's built-in DataSet Paging facility as discussed earlier, found in the Application Panel under Server Behaviors. I only used one of these for this example, but of course you can install as many of these paging behaviors as you want in your application. I chose Move to Next; when I inserted it, this is the code I got:

```
<a href="<%# Request.ServerVariables["SCRIPT_NAME"] %>
➥?Pubs_currentPage=<%# Pubs.CurrentPage + 1 %>">Next</a>
```

Keep in mind that it matters very much where you put this code, as Listing 3.9 demonstrates. You can see in Figure 3.30 that we have a bit of a mess on our hands that we'll need to clean up. The data source plays a pivotal role in this "problem" because the elements within the ItemTemplate element are repeated for each row of data in the DataSet.

FIGURE 3.30:

The "Next" link repeats for every row of data from the DataSource. We don't want that.

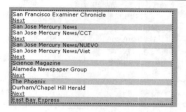

Listing 3.9   A Repeater control that doesn't quite work

```
<table width="100%" border="0" cellpadding="10" cellspacing="0"
bgcolor="#FFFFFF" class="tablebrdr">
  <ASP:Repeater runat="server"
DataSource='<%# Pubs.DefaultView %>'>
  <ItemTemplate>
    <tr>
      <td valign="top">
        <%# Pubs.FieldValue("PublicationName", Container) %>
      </td>
    </tr>
    <tr>
      <td>
```

```
        <a href="<%# Request.ServerVariables["SCRIPT_NAME"]
➡ %>?Pubs_currentPage=<%# Pubs.CurrentPage + 1 %>">
➡Next</a>
          </td>
        </tr>
      </ItemTemplate>
      </ASP:Repeater>
      </table>
```

The key is to use the Move To Next Page element *outside* of the Repeater control, because the Repeater will do just what its name implies. It will repeat whatever contents exist inside it for *each* record in the dataset (see Figure 3.31). So for anything you put within the Repeater control's `ItemTemplate` element, you'd better be sure you want it repeated as many times as there are records.

FIGURE 3.31:

Oops—everything in the ItemTemplate gets repeated

Everything between here gets repeated for each row of data from the data source.

```
<ASP:Repeater runat="server" DataSource='<%# Pubs.DefaultView %>'>
        <ItemTemplate>
    <tr>
        <td valign="top">
    <%# Pubs.FieldValue("PublicationName", Container) %>
    </td>
        </tr>
        <tr>
        <td>
        <a href="<%# Request.ServerVariables... %>">Next</a>
                </td>
                </tr>
        </ItemTemplate>
        </ASP:Repeater>
```

Using DataLists

The Repeater control is somewhat limiting because it forces you to list in a straight row downward, like you will see in a typical table of data, but the asp:DataList element can render its items horizontally or vertically. This means you can control the number of "columns" that are rendered through the `RepeatColumns` attribute.

With the asp:DataList element's `RepeatDirection` attribute at `Horizontal` and `Repeat-Columns` at 5, the items are rendered in rows containing five columns:

```
1 2 3 4 5
6 7 8 9 10
11 12 13 14
```

With the `RepeatDirection` attribute set as `Vertical`, and `RepeatColumns` as 5, the items are rendered in five columns, each equal in length to the total number of items divided by five:

```
1 4 7 10 13
2 5 8 11
3 6 9 12
```

This technique is especially useful when you're working with lots of textual data. Let's say we have a database table that contains newsletter stories. Instead of displaying one row, then another row, we might want to achieve the columnar feel of a magazine or newspaper by displaying a row of data with a lot of text right next to another row of data. Figure 3.32 shows a real estate agent's newsletter containing two rows of table data, or, in other words, one story after another. If you rendered this using the Repeater control, the stories would be stacked. The reader would have to scroll all the way past the end of the first story to get to the next. Using a DataList control, however, you can create two (or more) columns of data. Those columns each represent a new row of data in the database table.

FIGURE 3.32:

You can have two rows of data next to each other instead of on top of each other when you use the DataList control.

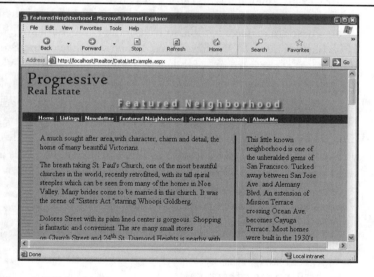

You'll need a DataSet established before you can create a DataList control, so if you don't have one, create one now. (If you want to use the same data I used for this example, create a DataSet that selects all the data from the NeighborhoodNews table in the `Realtor` database.) Then click the plus button in the Server Behavior tab and choose DataList. You'll get the DataList dialog box that lets you set various DataList attributes (Figure 3.33).

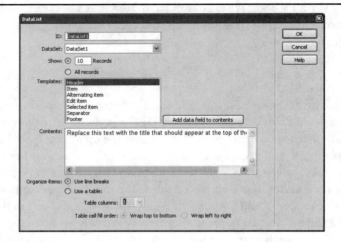

Once again, you'll use templates to display your data in a way that's right for you. In this case, much of our data's appearance depends on some of the global attributes for the DataList control itself. These are managed at the bottom of the DataList dialog box (Figure 3.33). Look at the radio buttons next to Organize Items. When you select Line Breaks, Dreamweaver changes the RepeatLayout attribute of the DataList element to Flow. When you select Use a Table, Dreamweaver changes the RepeatLayout attribute to Table.

The Table Cell Order radio buttons control the RepeatDirection attribute. Wrap Left To Right tells Dreamweaver to give the RepeatDirection attribute a value of Horizontal. Wrap Top To Bottom tells Dreamweaver to give the attribute a value of Vertical, which is the one you want if you want two adjacent columns in the layout. This is how the beginning of a typical DataList control might look like in Code view:

```
<asp:DataList  CellPadding="10"
SeparatorStyle-VerticalAlign="top"
AlternatingItemStyle-VerticalAlign="top"
ItemStyle-VerticalAlign="top" id="DataList1"
runat="server"
RepeatColumns="2"
RepeatDirection="Vertical"
RepeatLayout="Table"
```

The DataList control contains many styling elements for each template. (Refer back to Table 3.1 to see which template elements you can use inside a DataList control.) For each template you can use, there is also a global styling element. This element can be accessed as an attribute of the DataList element. Don't worry about memorizing all these elements; all you need to know is that each template has an attribute that you can use for determining the look of each template.

After you've set this style element, you simply click on the `asp:DataList` element in Code view, making sure the cursor is right next to the end of the tag name. When you advance the cursor in the text editor with your spacebar, a small context menu presents the attribute choices, as shown in Figure 3.34. You can deduce which element to pick for styling a particular element by choosing from the list. For example, if I choose the `ItemStyle-BackColor` attribute, I know that the color I choose will affect the `ItemTemplate` element. The `ItemTemplate` element will render as an HTML `td` element, so `ItemStyle-BackColor="black"` will translate to `<td bgcolor="black">` when .NET renders the page.

TIP　　Right-clicking next to an element name usually results in a context menu whose first item is Edit Tag. Choosing Edit Tag gets you a rich dialog box, making it easy to take full advantage of .NET control elements. This method is described further in the next section on DataGrids.

FIGURE 3.34:

Which attribute to use for styling a template? Choose from Dreamweaver's list and use your intuition.

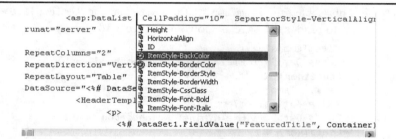

Once you've decided on global layout properties, you'll focus on your templates. Dreamweaver presents a number of options in the Templates list box of the DataList dialog box, some of which you'll never use because they aren't relevant to the DataList control. Here are the Templates options you'll be interested in:

Header　This maps out to the `HeaderTemplate` element in Code view. Use this for providing information about what your data does.

Item　This maps out to the `ItemTemplate` element in Code view. It contains the content of your DataList and will usually have at least one data binding.

Alternating item　This maps out to the `AlternatingItemTemplate` element in Code view. It usually contains the same content as the `ItemTemplate`, but you might want to change the style to differentiate rows. If, for example, your DataList repeats horizontally, it will look like a traditional table if your `RepeatLayout` is set as `Table`. In a table with a lot of records, the rows in the table won't have anything between them to help the user distinguish them (such as a rule between table rows, or alternating background colors). To fix this, change a style property in this element to differentiate it from table rows created by `ItemTemplate` elements.

Separator   This maps out to the `SeparatorTemplate` element in Code view. You can use this to add things like horizontal rules. This element can be overkill in tables, since the `AlternatingItemTemplate` element does essentially the same thing, but the Separator is helpful when you have a more free-flowing data display rather than a table.

Footer   This maps out to the `FooterTemplate` element in Code view. This is like the Header, except that in the Footer you add ancillary information such as copyright information or a privacy statement.

When creating your DataList, the most important element is the `ItemTemplate` element and its sibling, the `AlternatingItemTemplate` element, because these will hold your data. Think of the `ItemTemplate` element as an HTML `td` cell. Anything you can put into a `td` cell, you can put into an `ItemTemplate` element—a table, paragraphs, links, etc. Just remember that the data will repeat for every row of data that exists in the DataSet used by your DataList control.

This is what the `ItemTemplate` and `AlternatingItemTemplate` elements look like in Code view, to render the page as shown in Figure 3.30:

```
<ItemTemplate>
  <%# DataSet1.FieldValue("NeighborhoodNews",
➥Container) %>
  </ItemTemplate>
  <AlternatingItemTemplate>
    <%# DataSet1.FieldValue("NeighborhoodNews",
➥Container) %>
  </AlternatingItemTemplate>
```

To add a data field like those shown here in bold, you click the Add Data Field To Contents button (see Figure 3.33).

Listing 3.10 shows how this entire DataList control looks in Code view. (You can download the complete source code at www.sybex.com.)

Listing 3.10   A finished DataList control

```
<asp:DataList CellPadding="10"  SeparatorStyle-VerticalAlign="top"
AlternatingItemStyle-VerticalAlign="top"
ItemStyle-VerticalAlign="top" id="DataList1"
   runat="server" RepeatColumns="2"
   RepeatDirection="Vertical" RepeatLayout="Table"
   DataSource="<%# DataSet1.DefaultView %>" >
    <HeaderTemplate>
      <p>
      <%# DataSet1.FieldValue("FeaturedTitle", Container) %>
```

```
    </p>
  </HeaderTemplate>
  <ItemTemplate>
    <%# DataSet1.FieldValue("NeighborhoodNews", Container) %>
  </ItemTemplate>
  <AlternatingItemTemplate>
    <%# DataSet1.FieldValue("NeighborhoodNews", Container) %>
  </AlternatingItemTemplate>
   <SeparatorTemplate>
     <table>
     <tr bgcolor="#000099">
        <td width="1" valign="top">
           <img src="shim.gif" width="1" height="250">
        </td>
     </tr>
     </table>
  </SeparatorTemplate>
  </asp:DataList>
```

Notice, also, in Figure 3.35 that in Dreamweaver's visual interface you can see the control's templates. Click the – button to reveal the template detail, shown in Figure 3.36. (I assume this – button is a bug in Dreamweaver, since unexpanded items normally have a + button.)

FIGURE 3.35:

The control templates in a DataList, viewed in Design mode

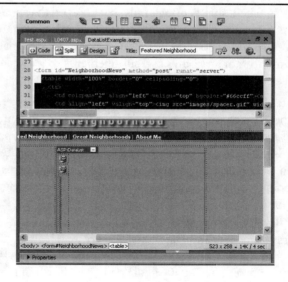

FIGURE 3.36:

Expanded DataList
control in Design
mode reveals
template details.

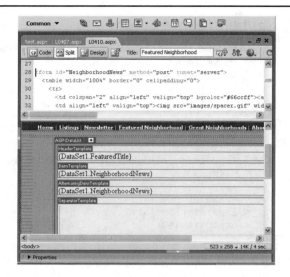

Using DataGrids

The concept of data grids has been around for quite awhile in traditional ASP web development. In fact, a small cottage industry grew up that marketed data grid controls for creating robust, table-based data manipulation controls very quickly. Microsoft must have noticed the trend and has come up with a DataGrid control that is immensely flexible, with a very large number of attributes and sub-elements to let you control the way your grid looks and behaves.

DataGrid controls are like DataList controls, except DataGrids are limited to table layouts and there is built-in paging support for them. Paging means you can display a chosen number of records on one page, and provide a link on that page that advances to the next set of records. You can also use the DataGrid control to create editable rows of data for your users. When they click a link within a row table, the row turns into a set of text fields with the data still bound to them, and the user can change the data and update the database.

Creating a Simple DataGrid

As with Repeaters and DataLists, you create a DataGrid control from the Server Behaviors tab of the Application panel. Again, as is the case with DataLists, be sure you have established a DataSet first. The DataGrid dialog box is shown in Figure 3.37.

FIGURE 3.37:

Creating a DataGrid
control

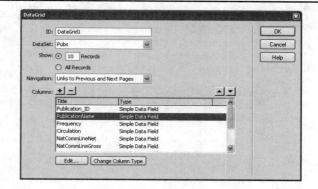

FIGURE 3.37:

Creating a DataGrid
control

For this example I'm using the PubSummary table introduced earlier in the chapter. Remember that we're keeping things very simple in this chapter and will explore more complex styling capabilities in Chapter 4. For now, we're mostly interested in how the DataGrid control interacts with the database.

Listing 3.11 shows how the DataGrid looks if we accept the default choices in the dialog box and then go into the code to make a few stylistic changes.

Listing 3.11   A simple DataGrid control

```
<asp:DataGrid id="DataGrid1"
runat="server"
AllowSorting="False"
AutoGenerateColumns="false"
CellPadding="3"
CellSpacing="0"
ShowFooter="false"
ShowHeader="true"
DataSource="<%# Pubs.DefaultView %>"
PagerStyle-Mode="NextPrev"
AllowPaging="true"
AllowCustomPaging="true"
PageSize="<%# Pubs.PageSize %>"
VirtualItemCount="<%# Pubs.RecordCount %>"
OnPageIndexChanged="Pubs.OnDataGridPageIndexChanged">
<HeaderStyle HorizontalAlign="center" BackColor="#E8EBFD"
ForeColor="#3D3DB6" Font-Name="Verdana, Arial, Helvetica, sans
  serif" Font-Bold="true" Font-Size="smaller" />
<ItemStyle BackColor="#F2F2F2" Font-Name="Verdana, Arial,
  Helvetica, sans-serif" Font-Size="smaller" />
 <AlternatingItemStyle BackColor="#E5E5E5" Font-Name="Verdana,
```

```
 Arial, Helvetica, sans-serif" Font-Size="smaller" />
 <FooterStyle HorizontalAlign="center" BackColor="#E8EBFD"
  ForeColor="#3D3DB6" Font-Name="Verdana, Arial, Helvetica,
  sans-serif" Font-Bold="true" Font-Size="smaller" />
 <PagerStyle BackColor="white" Font-Name="Verdana, Arial
 Helvetica, sans-serif" Font-Size="smaller" />
 <Columns>
   <asp:BoundColumn DataField="Publication_ID"
       HeaderText="Publication_ID"
       ReadOnly="true"
       Visible="True"/>
   <asp:BoundColumn DataField="PublicationName"
       HeaderText="PublicationName"
       ReadOnly="true"
       Visible="True"/>
    <!- More bound columns here ->    </Columns>
</asp:DataGrid>
```

There's quite a bit going on within this small amount of code. For one thing, it introduces a new property called PageSize, which stores the number of pages of data the table holds. Dreamweaver intervenes directly here and tells the DataGrid that the PageSize should be determined by evaluating this statement: <%# Pubs.PageSize %>, instead of giving some literal number of pages, such as PageSize="10".

Notice the Show radio buttons in the DataGrid dialog box. These two buttons include a Records text field where you can enter exactly how many records you want to show (the default is 10); the other option is All Records. When you select the top radio button and declare a specific number of records (say, 10), look at your MM:DataSet element in Code view and you'll see that Dreamweaver added an attribute/value pair to that element, PageSize="10". In this example, the MM:DataSet has an ID attribute whose value is Pubs. So when Dreamweaver inserts <%# Pubs.PageSize %> as the DataGrid's PageSize value, what it's doing is referring to the Pubs element and accessing its property named PageSize. Remember that each attribute in any .NET element is accessible as a scriptable property.

Customizing a DataGrid

So far you've been introduced to the fundamental process of working with Repeater, DataList, and DataGrid controls. Unless you jumped ahead and did some research or some serious experimentation on your own, however, it's doubtful you were able to fully grasp just how much customization you can do with the DataGrid control. Now is a good time to do that.

You can begin your exploration by simply clicking on a DataGrid you've already started in Dreamweaver's Design view. If you don't have one handy, you can start with Listing 3.12, which is downloadable as `L0301.aspx` in the online code supplied for this book at `www.sybex.com`.

A DataGrid is replete with formatting properties in the form of `asp:DataGrid` element attributes. Here's a list of some of the formatting properties available to the various style elements that can be contained within a DataGrid:

`BackColor`   Specifies the background color.

`Font`   Specifies font family, point size, bold, italicized, and other font information.

`CellPadding`   Defines the cell padding for the HTML table.

`CellSpacing`   Gives the cell spacing for the HTML table.

`Width`   Specifies the width of the HTML table in pixels, percentages, etc.

`HorizontalAlign`   Tells .NET how the table should be aligned horizontally (Left, Right, Center, NotSet).

Luckily, you don't need to write all this code by hand. In typical Dreamweaver fashion, there's a nice dialog box that you can fill in. If you're using Dreamweaver MX 2004, you can simply click the control in Design view and right-click to reveal a context menu that says "Edit Tag." You also have access to the Tag panel containing all the DataGrid attributes (and any other element you're using). The Tag panel is in the same group with the Application, Files, Code, and Design panels. (If you don't see these, look in Dreamweaver's main menu under Window ➤ Show Panels.)

If you're running Dreamweaver MX instead of Dreamweaver MX 2004, you need to jump through a couple of hoops. You might think that you should get to the tag editor from Design view, but you can't, because it's not an HTML element. Instead, you have to go into Code view and click on the specific element you want to edit. Then right-click to get a context menu next to your cursor in the window. Figure 3.38 shows how this looks when you click next to the HeaderStyle element in Code view.

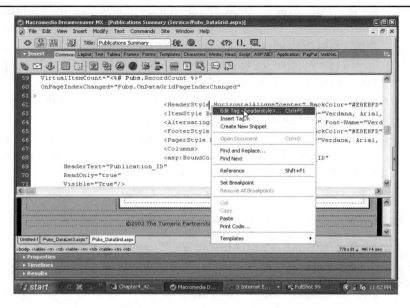

In the context menu, the Edit Tag item also shows you which element you're trying to edit. Select Edit Tag to see the dialog box for editing the element. As you can see in Figure 3.39, most of the HeaderStyle attributes are optional.

When you change the style properties, .NET will render the table in the best way possible for the browser that calls the page. If a browser has good support for CSS, .NET will know it by reading information about the user agent (the browser) and will spit out CSS properties rather than older styling elements like the font element. And if an older browser calls forth a page, .NET will spit out font tags instead of CSS. Of course, you can control this completely if you want to, by using the CSSClass attribute and defining your own styles in the header of your page using Dreamweaver's excellent CSS editor.

You have to repeat the same procedure for all of the style-related elements of the DataGrid control, such as the ItemStyle, AlternatingItemStyle, FooterStyle, and PagerStyle. However, you can also dictate the style of the DataGrid on a global level by giving value to the asp:DataGrid's style attributes. There is a group of asp:DataGrid attributes for each style element, so instead of changing styles element by element, you can control the entire DataGrid at the top level by changing its style attributes. To change all the AlternatingItemStyle elements, for instance, you simply change each of the relevant asp:DataGrid style attributes:

```
asp:DataGrid AlternatingItemStyle-BackColor="#CCCC99"
id="FileList" runat="server" BorderColor="orange"
BorderWidth="2" CellPadding="4" AutoGenerateColumns="false"
ShowHeader="true" ItemStyle-VerticalAlign="Top" ItemStyle
HorizontalAlign="Left">
```

The attributes shown here will then affect the entire DataGrid unless a style element overrides one of them. Table 3.3 describes the style elements available.

TIP   If you're trying to make your final HTML output XHTML-compliant, you should use the CSS Class to add all the styling properties.

TABLE 3.3: DataGrid Style Elements

Style Element	DataGrid Item Affected by the Style
AlternatingItemStyle	Alternating items in the control
EditItemStyle	Current item being edited
FooterStyle	Footer section
HeaderStyle	Header section
ItemStyle	Items in the control
PagerStyle	Page selection section
SelectedItemStyle	Selected item in the control

Listing 3.12 shows how some of these can be used. However, the best way to become familiar with them is to simply work with them in Dreamweaver's convenient interface. Just

fill in the fields in the Tag Editor or Tag Inspector and let Dreamweaver do the rest of the work for you.

Listing 3.12   **A customized DataGrid (`ViewClients_NotCodeBehind2.aspx`)**

```
<asp:DataGrid id="FileList"
 DataSource="<%# ClientQuerySP.DefaultView %>"
 runat="server"
 BorderColor="orange" BorderWidth="2"
 CellPadding="4" AutoGenerateColumns="false"
 ShowHeader="true" ItemStyle-VerticalAlign="Top"
 ItemStyle-HorizontalAlign="Left">
   <HeaderStyle BorderColor="White" BackColor="black"
    ForeColor="White" Font-Bold="True" Font-Name="Arial"
    Font-Size="9" HorizontalAlign="Center" />
   <Columns>
      <asp:HyperLinkColumn HeaderText="Delete"
        DataTextFormatString="Delete"
        DataNavigateUrlField="Client_ID"
        DataNavigateUrlFormatString="DeleteClient.aspx?
      ➥Client_ID={0}" DataTextField="Client_ID"
        ItemStyle-VerticalAlign="Top"
        ItemStyle-HorizontalAlign="Left"
        HeaderStyle-HorizontalAlign="Left"
        HeaderStyle-VerticalAlign="Top"></asp:HyperLinkColumn>
      <asp:HyperLinkColumn HeaderText="Details"
        DataTextFormatString="Details"
        DataNavigateUrlField="Client_ID"
        DataNavigateUrlFormatString="ClientDetails.aspx?
      ➥Client_ID={0}" DataTextField="Client_ID"
        ItemStyle-VerticalAlign="Top"
        ItemStyle-HorizontalAlign="Left"
        HeaderStyle-HorizontalAlign="Left"
        HeaderStyle-VerticalAlign="Top">
      </asp:HyperLinkColumn>
      <asp:TemplateColumn HeaderText="Client"
        ItemStyle-HorizontalAlign="Left"
        ItemStyle-VerticalAlign="Top">
     <ItemTemplate>
       <%# ClientQuerySP.FieldValue("CFirstName",
         ➥Container) %> <%#
         ➥ClientQuerySP.FieldValue("CLastName",
         ➥Container) %> </ItemTemplate>
      </asp:TemplateColumn>
      <asp:TemplateColumn HeaderText="Address"
        HeaderStyle-VerticalAlign=Top
        ItemStyle-VerticalAlign=Top>
     <ItemTemplate>
     <table width="200" border="0" bgcolor="#99CCFF">
      <tr>
```

```
            <td>
            <%# ClientQuerySP.FieldValue("CAddress", Container) %>
            </td>
         </tr>
         <tr>
            <td><%# ClientQuerySP.FieldValue("CAddress2",
             ➥Container) %></td>
         </tr>
         <tr>
            <td><%# ClientQuerySP.FieldValue("CCity",
             ➥Container) %>, <%# ClientQuerySP.FieldValue
             ➥("CStateProv", Container) %>  
             ➥<%# ClientQuerySP.FieldValue
             ➥("CPostalCode", Container) %>
            </td>
         </tr>
      </table>
   </ItemTemplate>
 </asp:TemplateColumn>
 <asp:HyperLinkColumn HeaderText="Update"
  DataNavigateUrlField="Client_ID"
  DataNavigateUrlFormatString="UpdateClients.aspx?
  ➥Client_ID={0}" DataTextField="Client_ID"
  DataTextFormatString="Update"
  ItemStyle-VerticalAlign="Top"
  ItemStyle-HorizontalAlign="Left"
  HeaderStyle-HorizontalAlign="Left"
  HeaderStyle-VerticalAlign="Top">
 </asp:HyperLinkColumn>
 </Columns>
</asp:DataGrid>
```

TIP   Sometimes when you right-click in the `asp:hyperlink` tag in Design view, the Edit Tag context menu will be deflected to a parent tag. The workaround: right-click from within the tag in Source view.

Listing 3.12 was appropriate for presenting the data through a DataGrid because we don't have to show everything using a strict tablelike or gridlike interface. We can opt to show all the relevant address, city, state, and postal code info in one table cell, even though they all come from separate fields of data in the table they come from. One of the most powerful aspects of the DataGrid control, however, is the ability to quickly create a DataGrid that can be edited by a user. In other words, with a small amount of effort using Dreamweaver, you can create a DataGrid that changes with the click of a button from display mode to editing mode for the developer. You'll see how that is accomplished in Chapter 4, when you learn about the MM:DataSet element's Parameter child element.

Accessing Data in Stored Procedures

One of the most important aspects of any decently designed relational DBMS is the use of stored procedures. They can make the difference between a website that hangs a bit when a user interacts with the site's database, and a site that snaps its pages up quickly even when encountering heavy database traffic. A stored procedure stores a group of SQL statements directly in the database as a precompiled object that can be executed whenever a client requests data services. Stored procedures offer such advantages as better security, reduced processing time on the server, and a convenient way to manage and change queries.

Even if precompiling didn't offer a huge boost in optimization and speed, you can imagine how much better a heavily trafficked database will perform if it only has to accept a simple, short "exec such_and_such" procedure command, as opposed to a long SQL Select query consisting of 20 or 30 lines of code.

Any SQL code you write using the DataSet dialog box in Advanced mode can be converted to a stored procedure. Do so, and watch your database smoke! Consider the boldfaced SQL code in Listing 3.13. You *could* have written all this code out in the SQL text field in the DataSet dialog box, but as long as you're writing that much code, why not create a stored procedure? That way, if the code needs to change, you change it in the stored procedure—much less of a hassle than going into all the web pages that may be using this query.

In this section, we'll take a look at how the stored procedure in Listing 3.13 does its work.

Listing 3.13   Stored procedure for accessing client listings

```
CREATE PROCEDURE ListingQueryImagesAndClientsWithParams
- this is for querying Listings
@MLSNumber varchar(50)
AS
BEGIN
SELECT
   dbo.Listings.MLSNumber,
    dbo.Listings.Title,
    dbo.Listings.PropertyAddress1,
    dbo.Listings.PropertyAddress2,
    dbo.Listings.StreetOrAve,
    dbo.Listings.City,
    dbo.Listings.State,
    dbo.Listings.PostalCode,
    dbo.Listings.IDNumb,
    dbo.Listings.DescriptionPlainText,
    dbo.Listings.DescriptionHTML,
    dbo.Listings.Client_ID,
```

```
      dbo.Listings.Price,
      dbo.Listings.Neighborhood,
      dbo.Listings.Status,
      dbo.Images.img_pk,
      dbo.Images.img_name,
      dbo.Images.img_data,
      dbo.Images.img_contenttype,
   dbo.ClientInfo.Client_ID,
   dbo.ClientInfo.CFirstName,
   dbo.ClientInfo.CLastName
FROM dbo.Listings LEFT JOIN dbo.Images  ON dbo.Images.MLSNumber =
dbo.Listings.MLSNumber
INNER JOIN dbo.ClientInfo ON dbo.ClientInfo.Client_ID = dbo.Listings.Client_ID
WHERE @MLSNumber = dbo.Listings.MLSNumber
   END

GO
```

To convert this code into a stored procedure, you need to access a SQL Editor that is connected to your database. A stored procedure is created using the CREATE PROCEDURE keywords, followed by the name of the procedure. (You won't ordinarily choose a name as long as the one I used in Listing 3.13—in this case I wanted the name to describe exactly what the stored procedure was doing.)

Your stored procedure might receive a value from a web form field of some kind. If that's the case, you'll need to declare a parameter that can accept the input. This kind of SQL variable is called an *input variable*. You can also create output parameters that return values, but for now we'll stick to input parameters. Remember that a parameter needs to have the @ character in front of it for SQL Server to recognize it as a parameter. This parameter must be declared before you do anything else. In this case, we're going to be designing a web page that retrieves listings based on an incoming MLSNumber, so our parameter will be declared based on that. You must declare the datatype with your parameter declaration.

The next important keyword is AS. Don't omit it, or your stored procedure won't compile.

The rest of the stored procedure is basically a standard SQL statement. Now let's see how to access the stored procedure through Dreamweaver.

At its most basic, accessing a stored procedure is very simple using Dreamweaver MX. You just go to the Application panel, open the Server Behaviors tab, and choose Stored Procedure. A Stored Procedure dialog box will pop up (Figure 3.40). Give your stored procedure a name. I like to use names ending in Proc to help me remember that I'm referring to a stored procedure in the code.

FIGURE 3.40:

Working with the
Stored Procedure
dialog box

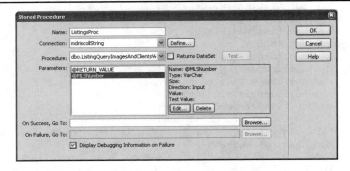

Choose your connection string, then choose the stored procedure you wish to access. In this case, we access the one we just made. Notice how the parameters show up. If you click each parameter, its definition shows up in the box to the right. When you click OK, Dreamweaver generates a DataSet control that looks something like this:

```
<MM:DATASET id=ListingsProc
Debug="true"
CommandText="ListingQueryImagesAndClientsWithParams"
...
</MM:DATASET>
```

Unfortunately, if you click OK after accepting the defaults for all the parameters, you'll get an error message that says:

```
"Missing run-time value for variable: @MLSNumber
Please enter a test value for the parameter @MLSNumber
```

It's as if the program just assumes we know what we're doing. So let's figure out what we're doing.

The first place we see a parameter is at the top of the stored procedure in Listing 3.13:

```
@MLSNumber varchar(50)
```

Next, we see it at the end of the stored procedure, in a WHERE clause:

```
WHERE @MLSNumber = dbo.Listings.MLSNumber
```

You can see how parameters work by just replacing @MLSNumber with a real number (get one from the database by doing a SELECT * FROM Listings statement). In fact, a good way to design a stored procedure, especially a simple one like this, is to build the SQL statements in whatever you're using as a query editor, and test the results there. You don't have to go to your database's query editor, however—you can just use Dreamweaver to test some things, which is handy when you're trying to bang out web pages on a deadline. To do this, I go to the Application Panel and define a new DataSet. Often I'll do this from a new file, called something like temp.aspx. Then I'll just proceed as if I were creating a new DataSet.

Now select the appropriate connection from the Connection drop-down list and, if necessary, switch the DataSet dialog box to Advanced mode. Then, just test your SQL code by entering it into the SQL text field and clicking Test. In our current example, you can input all of the bolded code (except the WHERE statement) to retrieve an MLSNumber value to test, as shown in Figure 3.41.

FIGURE 3.41:

Using the DataSet dialog box in Advanced mode to test some SQL code

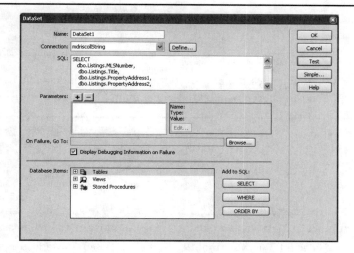

Add a WHERE SQL statement and replace the @MLSNumber parameter with one of the MLSNumber values you just retrieved from the database. So this:

```
WHERE @MLSNumber = dbo.Listings.MLSNumber
```

becomes this:

```
WHERE 250433 = dbo.Listings.MLSNumber
```

Note that you don't need any double or single quotes around the number because it isn't a string; it's an integer.

This code should return one listing to the test window.

Now let's go back to that "Missing run-time value…" error message we got earlier. We have to build "runtime" values for the parameter because Dreamweaver needs them for the testing server. Luckily, there's a little button hidden away that helps you build these values. To get to it, in the Stored Procedure dialog box click the parameter that needs to be edited. Then click the Edit button in the window to the right of the parameter list. In this example, we're going to click @MLSNumber.

The next dialog box is labeled Edit Parameter, as shown in Figure 3.42. This is where you'll see the Build button.

FIGURE 3.42:

The Edit Parameter
dialog box

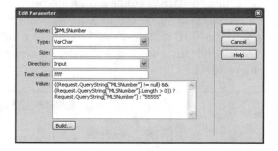

When you click the Build... button, another window like that shown in Figure 3.43 pops up. You can choose which kind of parameter to choose from.

FIGURE 3.43:

The Build Value
dialog box

In this case, choose URL Parameter. For Default Value, enter 1 (this is just an arbitrary number). Click OK, and Dreamweaver builds the following as the value for the parameter:

```
((Request.QueryString["MLSNumber"] != null) &amp;&amp;
(Request.QueryString["MLSNumber"].Length > 0)) ?
Request.QueryString["MLSNumber"] : ""
```

This value, when generated in Dreamweaver, is added to the `Parameters` element in the `MM:DataSet` element, similarly to what I described earlier in this chapter's section "Accessing a DataSet Through Form Variables":

```
<Parameters>
    <Parameter  Name="@RETURN_VALUE"   Type="Int"
    Direction="ReturnValue" />
    <Parameter  Name="@MLSNumber"
    Value='<%# ((Request.QueryString["MLSNumber"]
 ➥ != null) &amp;&amp;
 ➥(Request.QueryString["MLSNumber"].Length > 0))
 ➥? Request.QueryString["MLSNumber"] : ""  %>'
 ➥Type="VarChar"   Direction="Input" />
</Parameters>
```

The value is generated by a .NET C# script that checks to see if there is actually a variable getting passed into the database; if so, the script reads the variable and stores it as the `Parameter` value that should be checked in the database. If the user submits an `MLSNumber` that the database is aware of, a web page containing the records for that `MLSNumber` is returned.

We're going to dig a little deeper in the next chapter, into this last bit on parameters and stored procedures as well as many of the concepts you've been introduced to in this chapter—so if you don't feel like you've absorbed everything, don't worry. There are still some details you need to absorb in order to really get your arms around some of this stuff. So let's get ready to do just that.

Wrapping Up

This chapter gives you the opportunity to get familiar with the basics of database integration and .NET through the Dreamweaver interface. Most of the hard work is handled by Dreamweaver, which is a good thing—there is a lot that Dreamweaver hides from you. Having Dreamweaver in control makes coding much less laborious than if you had to rely strictly on hand-coding.

The best way to get comfortable with the way Dreamweaver builds data-driven web pages, especially if you're not comfortable or familiar with SQL, is to start off building some simple DataSets and looking at the code Dreamweaver produces. There's a lot to be said for this less-than-sophisticated method of teaching yourself how to write code! As you become more comfortable with SQL and .NET, your code-writing skills will grow, and your SQL is sure to get better as time goes on.

Now let's move on to Chapter 4, which will take the concepts introduced here and get into the nitty-gritty details. You'll find out more about how to blend these components with SQL, pick them apart, and then blend them again.

CHAPTER 4

Working with the Dreamweaver Custom Control

- Using .NET controls

- Introducing .NET custom tags

- Working with Dreamweaver custom tags

- Elements of the Dreamweaver control

The most important control a .NET developer will use is the Dreamweaver control, which is a custom control created by Macromedia to manage the rendering of data-bound web pages. In the context of Dreamweaver, getting a good grasp on this control is almost more essential than understanding the other .NET controls, because it plays a fundamental role in everything you do.

The truth is, you can get by without knowing the intricacies of this control, because everything is handled by Dreamweaver's GUI. But plenty of experience digging into the control's code has shown me the value of understanding how it works.

What makes the Dreamweaver control special is that, as a precompiled control, it eliminates hours of coding time. On one project, by putting core application together using Dreamweaver, I estimated that I saved $40,000 in development costs over hand-coding everything in a text-based editor or even Visual Studio.

In this chapter we'll find out why `DreamweaverCtrls.dll` is such a valuable part of the Dreamweaver experience.

Using .NET Controls

In Chapter 3, "Working with Databases: An Introduction," you received a pretty intense indoctrination into the notion of data-driven .NET controls. But by diving right into them you may have been left wondering how exactly these things work.

Bonus Chapter 1, "Developing a Workflow," (on the Sybex website) defined the three types of controls that can be used in a .NET environment: HTML controls, web server controls (also known simply as web controls), and custom controls. Each type serves its own purpose, and each interacts directly with the server. All of them require a `runat="server"` attribute/value pair in order to work properly. A web control or custom control without a `runat="server"` attribute/value pair will generate an error. An HTML control without the attribute/value pair will be treated as any other HTML element. The difference between these three controls lies in the actual classes that control them.

The classes underlying .NET controls are derived from a main class of objects that is a *superclass* of all objects in the .NET hierarchy. Every other object in ASP.NET is ultimately derived from this one class, the `System.object` class, which contains a few public methods that can be used by any of `System.object` class's "children." A class is an object definition, so each derived class comprises a set of definitions, all of which are inherited from the `System.object` class. (It is for this reason that Microsoft refers to these classes as *derived classes*.)

To appreciate the vastness of the .NET framework, all one has to do is visit the web page showing the "children" (the derived classes):

```
http://msdn.microsoft.com/library/en-us/cpref/html
/frlrfsystemobjectclasshierarchy.asp
```

You'll see hundreds of classes, but scroll down to the System.Web classes to find those you'll be interested in as an ASP.NET developer. You can also see the class hierarchy illustrated in Figure 4.1.

FIGURE 4.1:

Following the .NET class hierarchy helps you understand the derivation of an object's properties and methods.

```
- System.Object
    + Microsoft.CSharp.Compiler
    + Microsoft.CSharp.CompilerError
    + Microsoft.Win32.Registry
    + Microsoft.Win32.SystemEvents
    + System.Activator
    + many more additional classes...
    - System.Web.UI.Control
        + System.Web.UI.BasePartialCachingControl
        + System.Web.UI.DataBoundLiteralControl
        + System.Web.UI.HtmlControls.HtmlControl
        - System.Web.UI.HtmlControls.HtmlControl
            - System.Web.UI.HtmlControls.HtmlContainerControl
                System.Web.UI.HtmlControls.HtmlAnchor
                System.Web.UI.HtmlControls.HtmlButton
                System.Web.UI.HtmlControls.HtmlForm
                System.Web.UI.HtmlControls.HtmlGenericControl
                System.Web.UI.HtmlControls.HtmlSelect
                System.Web.UI.HtmlControls.HtmlTable
                System.Web.UI.HtmlControls.HtmlTableCell
                System.Web.UI.HtmlControls.HtmlTableRow
                System.Web.UI.HtmlControls.HtmlTextArea
        + System.Web.UI.LiteralControl
        + System.Web.UI.TemplateControl
        + System.Web.UI.WebControls.Literal
        + System.Web.UI.WebControls.PlaceHolder
        + System.Web.UI.WebControls.Repeater
        + System.Web.UI.WebControls.RepeaterItem
        - System.Web.UI.WebControls.WebControl
                System.Web.UI.WebControls.AdRotator
                System.Web.UI.WebControls.BaseDataList
                System.Web.UI.WebControls.Button
                System.Web.UI.WebControls.Calendar
                System.Web.UI.WebControls.CheckBox
                System.Web.UI.WebControls.DataListItem
                System.Web.UI.WebControls.HyperLink
                System.Web.UI.WebControls.Image
                System.Web.UI.WebControls.Label
                System.Web.UI.WebControls.LinkButton
                System.Web.UI.WebControls.ListControl
                System.Web.UI.WebControls.Panel
                System.Web.UI.WebControls.Table
                System.Web.UI.WebControls.TableCell
                System.Web.UI.WebControls.TableRow
                System.Web.UI.WebControls.TextBox
                System.Web.UI.WebControls.ValidationSummary
        + System.Web.UI.WebControls.Xml
```

For our discussion, you'll mostly be interested in the System.Web.UI.Control classes, whose derived classes consist of both HTML and web controls. If you drill down farther by clicking on the link at the Microsoft website for this class, you'll see several more classes. Look at Figure 4.1 and you can see the plus signs that are used to expand the parent class of each layer in the hierarchy. After the top-level class, `System.object`, come hundreds of direct descendants of this class of objects. Among these is the group we're interested in: the `System.Web.UI.Control` class and its direct descendants.

Each group of parent classes consists of a large number of properties and methods that make an instance of each class "work," or do its job, in your application. The magic of encapsulation, discussed in Bonus Chapter 1, occurs from inheritance of these properties and methods. An `asp:Image` control, which is derived from the WebControl class, inherits not only all the properties and methods from the WebControl class, but from the parent class of the WebControl class, as well.

This concept holds true for all .NET classes, although some properties and methods are "overridden." This means there could be an alteration in the way a base class's public properties or methods work on a lower-level object, because that lower-level object's class definition includes a same-named property or method with a different definition that is more suitable for that lower-level object. Think in terms of an oven. An `oven` superclass would have a `heat()` method that accepts electrical current as input. However, a `gas_range` element or oven, which would be a child of the `oven` class, might have a `heat()` method that overrides the parent's `heat()` method, to specifically define gas as the input.

HTML Controls

The simplest kind of .NET control is an HTML control. An HTML control is simply a good old-fashioned HTML element, such as an `input` element, that interacts directly with a .NET-enabled application server, such as IIS 5.0 with the .NET Framework installed, or IIS 6.0 with native .NET support. Figure 4.2 shows such a control in Dreamweaver.

FIGURE 4.2:

A text input control in Dreamweaver's Design view and Code view panels

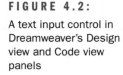

Turning an HTML element into an HTML control for .NET is easy. You just use the `runat="server"` attribute/value pair I described earlier:

```
<input name="text1" type="text" runat="server" id="text1">
```

You have programmatic access in any server-side script to any HTML server controls you use. In terms of the preceding code fragment, you would access the control by referring to its ID, `text1`, as indicated by the `id="text1"` attribute/value pair, which is the standard way to access any control. Dreamweaver even has a little area at the bottom-left of its Design view panel (refer again to Figure 4.2) where you can see the name of an object. It looks like this (Figure 4.3):

FIGURE 4.3:

Identifying tags in Dreamweaver's Design View

HTML controls are managed by, for the most part, the `HtmlGenericControl` class, which is a member of the `System.Web.UI.HtmlControls.HtmlContainerControl` class, which in turn is a member of the `System.Web.UI.HtmlControls.HtmlControl` class. That class, in turn, is a member of the `System.Web.UI.Control` class. Follow the class hierarchy like a tree, and follow the inheritance scheme, and your coding will become a natural part of your existence as a developer.

Web Controls

A web control is a special control native to the .NET framework. A number of them add a high degree of functionality without requiring you to do a lot of programming. For example, the following `asp:textbox` web control has similar functionality to the HTML input control (see also Figure 4.4):

```
<asp:TextBox ID="text1" runat="server" TextMode="SingleLine" />
```

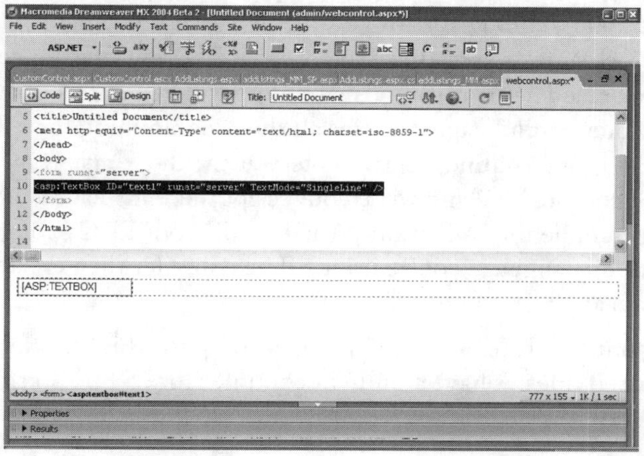

FIGURE 4.4:

An `asp:textbox` control in Dreamweaver's Design view and Code view

Web controls are managed by the `System.Web.UI.WebControls.WebControl` class. This class itself doesn't do anything because it's an abstract class from which other classes are derived. Other classes "borrow" the properties and methods of this class, and have some of their own. You can see a list of web controls made available through the WebControl class in Figure 4.1.

You'll find out more about many of these web controls in Chapter 5, "Using Web Server Controls."

Custom Controls

The third type of control, the custom control, is a control you create yourself. This is, in fact, exactly what Macromedia did when they created the Dreamweaver control, which is a pre-compiled Dynamic Link Library (DLL) that gets deployed into a `bin` directory when you create database-driven ASP.NET web pages using Dreamweaver.

The custom controls you create are derived from the same class that HTML and web server controls are derived from: the `System.Web.UI.Control` class. This is accomplished by overriding that class's `render()` method. We'll take a closer look at it a bit later in the chapter. You may never actually create a control of your own, since the more complex they are, the harder it is to program them. Nevertheless, it's important to understand how they're used in a web page because there are a plethora of custom controls available, many of which are free.

Introducing .NET Custom Tags

One limitation in Dreamweaver is that you can't use code-behind very easily. *Code-behind* is the default technique used by Microsoft Visual Studio .NET for generating web pages that use any kind of web controls.

Here's what happens: When creating a web page using Visual Studio .NET, the application generates a code-behind page for your main ASPX file. That code-behind page generally takes the same name as your ASPX file, with a different filename extension. So if you have a web page named `hello.aspx`, Visual Studio will generate a code-behind page named `hello.cs`. The code-behind page contains all the programming for `hello.aspx`. So instead of adding your scripting routines to script elements with a `runat="server"` attribute/value pair, you use the code-behind and write your script there instead. When you're done programming, you compile the code using Visual Studio .NET's C# compiler (or VB.NET compiler if that's the language you're using). The compiler then creates a `.dll` file that you put into your web application's `bin` directory.

You can get your hands on a compiler and accomplish this with Dreamweaver, but Dreamweaver itself doesn't have a built-in compiler for .NET. So this isn't a terribly convenient solution, since compiling it without the assistance of Visual Studio can be a pain. A nice workaround is to create custom web controls (or use other developers' custom controls). That way, you can continue to encapsulate your code and run your web application more efficiently, because compiled code runs faster than code embedded in `script` elements.

NOTE   It may be a bit of a pain to compile without Visual Studio, but I'll show you how anyway, in Chapter 7, "Advanced Coding with Dreamweaver MX."

The most efficient way to work with custom controls is to compile them into DLLs that you then place into the `bin` directory of your application. But you don't have to do that. You can just create a custom control with embedded script tags, just as we do in most of the examples throughout the book. Either way, you refer to your custom control by registering it on your ASPX page.

Let's see what a simple control might look like, then access it in an ASPX page. Take a look at Listing 4.1.

Listing 4.1   **Building a very simple custom control**

```
<%@ Control Language="C#" %>
<script runat="server">
private string sString;

public string overdue
{
get
{
return sString;
}
set
{
sString = value;
}
}
protected void Page_Load(Object Src, EventArgs E)
{
pLabel.Text = sString;
}
</script>
<asp:Label id="pLabel" Runat="server" />
```

Listing 4.1 is saved using the `.ascx` filename extension, which is the extension you always use when creating and saving a custom control.

Making Sure You Can Work in Design View

You may need to configure Dreamweaver to recognize the `.ascx` extension so that you can see the page in Design view. The product should ship with the correct configuration, but it's good to know how to add a filename extension, anyway, so that files can be seen in Design view. Go into the Macromedia directory on your hard drive and find a file named `MMDocumentTypes.xml`, which should be located in a path similar to this:

```
C:\Program Files\Macromedia\Dreamweaver MX 2004\Configuration\DocumentTypes
```

Then look for the correct `documenttype` element by checking the `servermodel` attributes until you find one for, in this example, ASP.NET C#. Next, look for an attribute within that element named `winfileextension`. It should read

```
winfileextension="aspx,ascx,asmx"
```

If `ascx` is missing from this element, you can add it. (There is a similar `macfileextension` attribute.) When you're done editing the file, save it. Naturally, it's a good idea to make a backup of this document before you tinker with it.

You access a custom control by creating custom tags in your ASPX page based on a namespace binding, like this:

```
<%@ Register TagPrefix="CC" TagName="Prop"
```

The `TagPrefix` attribute in this Register directive, which appears at the top of your ASPX page, dictates what the prefix for your custom tag should look like:

```
<CC:Prop broken="false" overdue="true"
Runat="server"/>
```

The tag itself is defined with the `TagName` attribute.

Listing 4.2 defines two tags, just so you're clear on how custom controls are called. When you run the application, the browser window will print the words "true false."

Listing 4.2   **Accessing a user control in an ASPX page**

```
<%@ Register TagPrefix="CC" TagName="Prop"
Src="CustomControl.ascx" %>
<%@ Register TagPrefix="CC" TagName="Prop2"
Src="CustomControl.ascx" %>
<html><head><title>Demo user control</title></head>
<body><p>
<CC:Prop overdue="true"
Runat="server"/>
<CC:Prop2 overdue="false"
Runat="server"/>
</p>
</body></html>
```

An alternative to the method shown in Listing 4.2 is to call a control through the namespace attribute in the Register directive. In this scenario, you need to do more than just save the control as an ASCX file. You compile the control into a DLL, and then deploy that DLL into the `bin` directory of your application. You'll see how to compile code in Chapter 7. The next section will show you how to deploy a compiled control, by introducing you to the all-important Dreamweaver control.

Working with Dreamweaver Custom Tags

The mother of all custom controls, at least as far as Dreamweaver users are concerned, is the Dreamweaver control, `DreaweaverCtrls.dll`. This custom control was created by Macromedia for the specific purpose of working with SQL-based databases. It is many, many orders of magnitude more complex than the simple example I used to begin this discussion of custom controls.

The Dreamweaver Control

The main difference between the Dreamweaver control and the simple custom control we made earlier is that the Dreamweaver control is precompiled. Whenever you make a web page involving one of the Dreamweaver data manipulation commands, Dreamweaver creates a set of custom tags that draws on the built-in capabilities of the Dreamweaver control.

An example of this occurs when you create a DataSet using the Dreamweaver interface. When you do this, you have the option of creating a new DataSet from the Bindings panel or with the Insert command (Insert ➤ Application Objects ➤ DataSet). You saw how to do this in Chapter 3. But what goes on behind the scenes when Dreamweaver does this for you?

For one thing, Dreamweaver knows you want a .NET DataSet and not a record set for, say, PHP, because your server model was defined when you defined your site. Hopefully, you designated ASP.NET as your server model. This book assumes your choice to be ASP.NET C#, but you could also choose ASP.NET VB. When you create your DataSet by filling out the Dreamweaver dialog boxes, Dreamweaver creates an element named `MM:DataSet`. The same thing happens when you choose the Insert Record command from the Insert menu (Insert ➤ Application Objects ➤ Insert Record). In this case, Dreamweaver cooks up an `MM:Insert` element.

All of this makes for rapid development of ASP.NET applications, because a lot of coding is made unnecessary. The more-difficult coding tasks are handled by the precompiled Dreamweaver control. All you have to do is designate a few parameters that the Dreamweaver control needs to do its thing. To take full advantage of the control's capabilities, however, it's a good idea to understand some of its inner workings.

You can find the source code for the Dreamweaver control in the following directory, or something very much like it if you're running a slightly different version of Dreamweaver than what was used in this book. The file is named `DreamweaverCtrls.cs`, and the code is at

```
C:\Program Files\Macromedia\Dreamweaver MX 2004\Configuration\ServerBehaviors\
Shared\ASP.Net\Scripts\Source
```

> **WARNING** If you change the source code and recompile it, Dreamweaver's ASP.NET capabilities will likely break unless you know exactly what you are doing. So before you make an attempt to change the file, be sure to keep a backup of the original control somewhere safe so that you can put it back if your alterations mess things up. It doesn't hurt, anyway, to drag a copy of the original source code into another directory to view it for educational reasons, because it contains a number of classes directly relating to the elements the control uses.

In the following sections, we'll explore some of the attributes and methods associated with the various elements available through the Dreamweaver control. Remember that a custom control consists of custom elements and attributes. The Dreamweaver control has several of these.

`DreamweaverCtrls.dll` consists of the following elements:

MM:DataSet   Used to access and manipulate .NET DataSet objects.

MM:Insert   Used to create SQL INSERT statements when you're not using a stored procedure to do so.

MM:Update   Used to create SQL UPDATE statements when you're not using a stored procedure to do so.

MM:Delete   Used to create SQL DELETE statements when you're not using a stored procedure to do so.

MM:PageBind   Used to manage page binding, giving you a chance to control when page binding takes place.

MM:If   Used for processing conditional business logic.

An element attribute becomes an object property at runtime, which means all the attributes available to an element are available as properties. In other words, the following:

```
MM:DataSet id="myDS" SuccessURL="http://www.tumeric.net/places/success.aspx"
```

translates to:

```
myDS.SuccessURL="http://www.tumeric.net/places/success.aspx"
```

when viewed from within script.

This means you can change just about any of the properties of a Dreamweaver control at runtime.

The *MM:DataSet* Element

The MM:DataSet element is used to create a .NET DataSet object using .NET's DataSet class. A DataSet is an in-memory cache of data that can actually come from a number of different sources, but in the case of the MM:DataSet element relies exclusively on SQL-based data sources.

Dreamweaver generates this element when you create a DataSet through either the Application panel's Server Behavior tab (Figure 4.5) or by selecting Insert ➤ Application Objects ➤ DataSet from the main menu. All it's actually doing is inserting an ASP.NET control, albeit a custom one, into the code window based on a public class named DataSet defined in the DreamweaverCtrl.cs file (and of course made available through the compiled DLL). If you were to examine the source document for the Dreamweaver control, you'd find the following code, which defines the attributes for the DataSet element:

```
public string CommandText = "";
public string DatabaseType = "OleDb";
public Boolean IsStoredProcedure = false;
public string ConnectionString = "";
public string SuccessURL = "";
public string FailureURL = "";
public Boolean Expression = true;
public Boolean Debug = false;
public Boolean ProcessOnPostBack = true;
public Boolean CreateDataSet = true;
public int PageSize = 0;
public int CurrentPage = 0;
public Boolean GetRecordCount = true;
protected int _recordCount = 0;
```

FIGURE 4.5:

Clicking the + button in the Application panel's Server Behaviors tab reveals the Insert DataSet option.

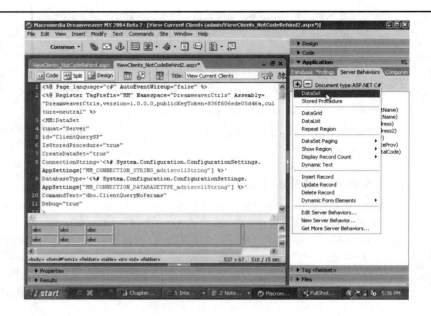

Attributes Used by *MM:DataSet*

Like HTML and ASP.NET elements, Dreamweaver control elements have attributes that can be used to customize your control. What follows is a description of attributes available to the MM:DataSet element. Unless I explicitly mention that an attribute of the MM:DataSet tag is required, you can assume the attribute is optional. Although many of these attributes are handled for you when Dreamweaver generates a DataSet, as your ASP.NET knowledge grows you'll find that knowing what these properties do will enhance your troubleshooting skills. There will also be occasions where you'll have to customize the code yourself, because Dreamweaver will simply not give you the options you need through the visual interface.

NOTE   These attributes are also used by the MM:Insert, MM:Update, and MM:Delete elements, which are also used by the Dreamweaver control to manage SQL-based data manipulations.

ConnectionString   This required attribute is a string that specifies the connection string to use for connecting to the database. The default value is "".

CommandText   This required attribute is a string for specifying a SQL statement or stored procedure. The default value is "". If IsStoredProcedure="false", this attribute is used to specify the SQL statement to execute. If IsStoredProcedure="true", the attribute is used to specify the name of the stored procedure to execute. SQL statements can be parameterized by using question marks (?) as placeholders.

runat Any tag running on a .NET server, whether it's a custom tag such as `MM:DataSet` or one of the built-in .NET web or HTML server controls, must specify `runat="server"`.

ProcessOnPostBack Changing this Boolean from its default of false to true is usually not necessary, and in fact this option doesn't appear in the list of attribute options for this element in the Tags panel or when you click next to the element in Code view and press the spacebar to trigger the code editor's syntax helper. `ProcessOnPostBack` is used when, during the page initialization process, you want to override the default action of not doing any processing. (Note that page *initialization* is different from page *loading*.)

CreateDataSet This indicates whether, when using `CommandText` to manage SQL statements or stored procedures, the resulting DataSet should be preserved. Macromedia recommends leaving this value at true, its default, unless you're using `INSERT`, `UPDATE`, or `DELETE` SQL statements (in which case the value should be `false`).

Expression This is a performance enhancement tool that controls when the action specified by the `CommandText` attribute is executed by the server. You can use this in your code when you want to improve performance by limiting exactly when SQL statements using the `CommandText` attribute are run. `Expression` takes a Boolean true or false.

The `CommandText` attribute can also be used to perform actions such as inserting, updating, or deleting records from a database. You use the `Expression` attribute to denote when it is appropriate to perform these actions. To do so, you typically set `Expression` to `false`, check to make sure the server has all the information it needs to perform the action (for example, by validating a form), and then set the attribute to `true`.

IsStoredProcedure This Boolean indicates that the command used via the `CommandText` attribute involves a stored procedure. When you insert a stored procedure using Dreamweaver, Dreamweaver changes this attribute automatically for you, from false (the default) to true. Actually, when creating a DataSet using Dreamweaver, you won't even see this attribute unless you're using a stored procedure, since the absence of the attribute means the same as the default value.

TableName This attribute is used to refer to records, as in

`(myDataSet.theDS["myTableName"].DefaultView)`

You'll rarely need to use this attribute because the default value is adequate, and because you usually need to refer directly to the `theDS` attribute when referring to records. (`theDS`, described shortly, is an `MM:DataSet` property that refers to a DataSet object created when the `CreateDataSet` attribute is set to true.) The `TableName` attribute is provided by Macromedia for those developers who want to hook into the low-level data behind this tag.

Debug   This Boolean is a debugging tool. Before you go live, use this to troubleshoot problems with your DataSet by setting the value to true to get more information when the MM:DataSet element's use throws an exception. If Debug="true", then the FailureURL attribute is ignored.

FailureURL   This is a string that specifies a URL to which the user's browser is redirected if an exception is thrown while executing the CommandText action or if the given attributes conflict. FailureURL attribute is ignored if Debug="true".

SuccessURL   This string specifies the URL to which the browser should be redirected if the CommandText action executes with no exceptions thrown.

CurrentPage   CurrentPage is an integer used with PageSize to control the number of records and specify which records appear on a page. If PageSize is set to 0, it means no records appear; if it is set to 10, it means 10 records appear on one page; and so on. CurrentPage indicates a specific page, which is found from the collection of records that exists in the DataSet through an indexed value. This index is zero based, meaning the index of the first page is zero.

PageSize   This attribute consists of an integer value that indicates how many records are displayed per page. You can also use MaxRecords, but if you use both, .NET will rely on the PageSize attribute and ignore MaxRecords.

MaxRecords   This attribute is an integer indicating the maximum number of records that should be displayed on the page.

StartRecord   This attribute is used in conjunction with CreateDataSet="true" to specify from which point in the DataSet you wish to begin displaying records. If StartRecord="0", the records are displayed beginning with the first record. The value is an integer, and the default is 0, which is the same as saying the page should display records beginning with the first record. If PageSize is greater than 0, then StartRecord is calculated automatically as (PageSize * CurrentPage).

GetRecordCount   This attribute is used to stop the record counting process, so you'll only use it when you are manipulating the DataSet programmatically. This attribute takes a Boolean true or false, but in fact you'll really only use it when you want to stop counting records, in which case you'll set it to false (the default value is true). Using PageSize can negatively impact performance because of the toll it takes to count records, so GetRecordCount can be used to stop the record-counting process.

RecordCountCommandText   This can be used to improve performance when using the PageSize attribute (when it's greater than 0) and GetRecordCount="true", because the algorithms used to obtain RecordCount values can be slow. This attribute specifies a string value that represents an explicit SQL statement to obtain the count, such as SELECT COUNT(*) FROM.... The statement can include WHERE clauses but should not be parameterized (that is, should not use question marks as placeholders). This way, you hand the work of records counting to the database, instead of to the application server (.NET).

DefaultView   This is a read-only attribute that accesses .NET's DataView object, which is a built-in class in .NET that provides you with a way to look at the data in a DataSet. If you look at the code Dreamweaver generates when you create a DataGrid with a DataSet as its source, you'll see an attribute/value pair similar to the following in the `asp:DataGrid` element:

```
DataSource="<%# someDS.DefaultView %>"
```

Whenever you're troubleshooting DataGrids, that is often the first place you'll want to look. Does your DataSource look right? Is it even there?

EndRecord   This attribute is an integer that represents the minimum of

```
(CurrentPage + 1) * PageSize  and
RecordCount
```

LastPage   This attribute is an integer calculated when `PageSize` and `GetRecordCount="true"` are used. The calculated value is the last page of the zero-based index based on `PageSize` and `RecordCount`.

RecordCount   This attribute is used in conjunction with `CreateDataSet="true"` and `GetRecordCount="true"`. `RecordCount` is an integer that represents the total number of records corresponding to the `CommandText` attribute.

theDS   This attribute returns a .NET DataSet for storing records obtained by setting `CreateDataSet` to `"true"`.

Methods Used by *MM:DataSet*

A number of methods are available for customizing the DataSet on-the-fly. Dreamweaver provides a direct interface for the most important one (`FieldValue()`).

FieldValue(string FieldName, System.Web.UI.Control Container)

This important method is used to retrieve the value of a specific field (column) of data in the DataSet. Generally you don't need to write any code from this. You can simply drag a field from a DataSet expanded in the Bindings tab (as shown in Figure 4.6).

To do this, click on the appropriate DataSet and expand it (if it isn't already). Make sure you are working with both Design view and Code view open so you can watch what happens with the code as it gets created. Then click the field you wish to display on your web page and drag it into an appropriate spot in the Design view panel. In Figure 4.6 we've dragged it into an `ItemTemplate` within an expanded DataGrid.

After you're done, when you click on the new binding you've just created in the Design view you'll see it highlighted in Code view. It should look something like this:

```
<%# ClientQuerySP.FieldValue("CCity", Container) %>,
```

Look at the Bindings tab, and you'll see the field you dragged is still highlighted. If you choose another field and drag that over, the same thing will happen. When you click the first binding you created, the appropriate code will be highlighted in Code view, as will the field in the Bindings tab.

NOTE   If you're the kind who gets frustrated with GUIs, you can always hard-code this stuff yourself. But one clear advantage of using Dreamweaver to do it is that you won't have to worry about misspellings, and drag-dropping fields from the Bindings tab to a spot in your layout using Design view is awfully easy.

FIGURE 4.6:

Dragging a field from the Bindings tab into Design view generates a `FieldValue()` method in your Dreamweaver code.

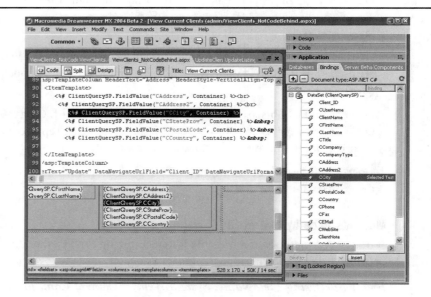

FieldValueAtIndex(int Index, string FieldName, System.Web.UI.Control Container)
This method does the same thing as the `FieldValue()` method, except in this case you can specify the field by citing the row's position in the DataSet. This is a zero-based index, which means the counting begins at 0, not 1, so if you're trying to get at the first record you would write something like this:

```
The first client in the database is: <%# ClientQuerySP.FieldValueAtIndex
➡(0, "ClientName", Container) %>
```

ParameterValue(string ParameterName)

You can retrieve the value of a DataSet's parameter programmatically by using the `ParameterValue()` method. All you need to do is name the parameter you want to retrieve:

```
Client Number: <%# ClientQuerySP.ParameterValue("@Client_ID") %>
```

This would retrieve the value of a stored procedure parameter named `@Client_ID` and return its value as a string.

Child Elements of *MM:DataSet*

When your users are interacting with your data-driven website, they'll often do things such as submitting a request for data, which requires you to know the row of data they're requesting. This is usually discovered through a form submission of some kind. When a row can be identified by equating it to a form field, that row of data is returned to the user's browser. For example, a user registered with your site will probably have a unique ID. You can track that unique ID in some way; and when, for example, a hidden form field with that ID is submitted, a web page will return a row of data corresponding to that ID.

If you look at the code of a DataSet, you'll generally find a number of child elements. These elements help you further refine the values retrieved from a database. They focus on the `Parameters` and `Parameter` elements, which are used to manage DataSet parameters. You might use them to retrieve something like the client ID described just above, or maybe some detailed information from a large set of data.

Using the *Parameters* Element

The `Parameters` element is sort of the envelope around the set of individual `Parameter` elements you use. Actual parameter values are defined within `Parameter` elements, but a `Parameter` element must be contained within a `Parameters` element.

Using the *Parameter* Element

A `Parameter` element, which defines an actual parameter value, must be contained within a `Parameters` element.

To see what parameters are about, let's look at a truncated example from a longer listing you'll see later in the chapter. In the chuck of code that follows, we create a stored procedure for inserting data into a Listings table. We want to pass data into the stored procedure from a form field. In order to do that, we need a device in the stored procedure for collecting form field values; this device is a parameter. A parameter in SQL Server is declared using the @ symbol before the name of the parameter, and the @ becomes part of the name; so a parameter name is `@MLSNumber`, not `MLSNumber`. Here, the parameters are highlighted in bold:

```
CREATE PROCEDURE ListingInsertionsShort
@MLSNumber int,
```

```
@Client_ID int
AS
INSERT INTO Listings
    (
      MLSNumber,
      @Client_ID
      )
VALUES
    (
@MLSNumber,
@Client_ID
      )
GO
```

When you develop your web application, you'll need to bind the parameter names to form fields. In this example, your stored procedure will expect to receive form field values for the MLSNumber and Title parameters. When they're received the stored procedure will pass the values into the MLSNumber and Title columns of the database. It's important that when you write a stored procedure like this, the parameters are in the same order as the columns in the INSERT statement.

The Dreamweaver control's Parameter element consists of several attributes that help you pass the form field values to the parameters in the stored procedure (or simply to a simpler DataSet).

Parameters aren't used only with stored procedures, though; they can also be used with any DataSet object. The following Parameter element is used to retrieve values from a QueryString:

```
<Parameter  Name="@Client_ID"  Value='<%# ((Request.QueryString["Client_ID"] !=
null) && (Request.QueryString["Client_ID"].Length > 0)) ?
Request.QueryString["Client_ID"] : "1"   %>' Type="Int"  Direction="Input" />
```

Wow. How are you going to start writing code like that if you're new to programming or new to .NET? Luckily, you won't have to. But if you build your Parameter element using Dreamweaver's interface while you're in Code view and Design view simultaneously, you can learn a lot about the code structure, so that if you need to write it yourself at some point, you can.

Let's see how this is done with a real example. Listing 4.3 shows a stored procedure like the one I just talked about, except this one (for the Realtor database) is more complete.

Listing 4.3   **A stored procedure for insertions into a database**

```
CREATE PROCEDURE ListingInsertions
- this is for adding Listings
@MLSNumber int,
@Title varchar(50),
@PropertyAddress1 varchar(50),
@PropertyAddress2 varchar(50),
```

```
@StreetOrAve varchar(50),
@City varchar(50),
@State varchar(50),
@PostalCode varchar(50),
@DescriptionPlainText text,
@DescriptionHTML text,
@DescriptionXML text,
@Client_ID int,
@Price int,
@Neighborhood varchar(50),
@Status varchar(50)
AS
BEGIN
    SET NOCOUNT ON
    DECLARE @IDNumb int
INSERT INTO Listings
    (
    MLSNumber,
    Title,
    PropertyAddress1,
    PropertyAddress2,
    StreetOrAve,
    City,
    State,
    PostalCode,
    DescriptionPlainText,
    DescriptionHTML,
    DescriptionXML,
    Client_ID,
    Price,
    Neighborhood,
    Status
    )
VALUES
    (
@MLSNumber,
@Title,
@PropertyAddress1,
@PropertyAddress2,
@StreetOrAve,
@City,
@State,
@PostalCode,
@DescriptionPlainText,
@DescriptionHTML,
@DescriptionXML,
@Client_ID,
@Price,
@Neighborhood,
@Status
    )
- is there an error, and if so, display it
```

```
if @@error <> 0
return @@error
else
- if no error, set a variable to return the Listings Id as a unique identifier
- NOTE: The column named IDNumb is the identity seed
SELECT @IDNumb = @@IDENTITY
    END
GO
```

Now we need to go into Dreamweaver's Server Behaviors tab in the Application panel and create a stored procedure. Click the plus button, or choose Stored Procedure from the Insert ≻ Application Objects menu. You'll get a Stored Procedure dialog box like that shown in Figure 4.7.

FIGURE 4.7:

Adding a stored procedure

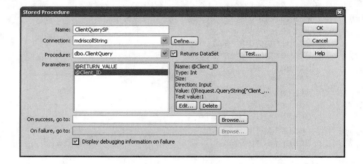

This isn't one of the most intuitive dialog boxes in the Dreamweaver arsenal. On first glance, it looks like you're going to really have to know all the ins and outs of creating code for handling the parameters in the stored procedure. So you take it slow, and do the obvious things first. You give the procedure a helpful name, because your code will refer to it later. This name becomes the ID attribute of the resulting MM:DataSet element. You're going to check the Returns DataSet box for this example because this stored procedure is querying a clients table and returning records.

NOTE   In real production environments, it's unlikely that a web developer would create a stored procedure on the server. Typically a DBA or SQL developer will perform this task.

Next you have to choose your connection. (Hopefully you've already built one, but if you haven't, go back to Chapter 3 to see how.) Once you've chosen your connection, a list of available procedures should be accessible from the Procedure list box. Choose the one you want—or use Listing 4.3 if you are using the Realtor database. The name of the procedure is always the same as that indicated in bold in Listing 4.3 immediately following the word CREATE. So in this case, the name of the procedure that will show up in the list is `ListingInsertions` (*not* `ListingInsertions.sql`, which is simply a filename and a way to save text that you want to run later in your database). If a stored procedure has been altered, instead of `CREATE procedure ListingInsertions`, the first line of Listing 4.4 would be ALTER procedure `ListingInsertions`.

If it doesn't show up in the list box, be sure to check the permissions on the stored procedure and make sure that you have permission to execute it (you'll need to check with your DBA if you don't have administrative privileges).

Look at Figure 4.7—you'll see a text window named Parameters. All the parameters that are used by the stored procedure are in that window.

A stored procedure can have either output or input parameters. In this case, we're only worried about input parameters, which are "incoming" parameters waiting to accept a value from an outside source. The outside source can be any number of things, but in our case it's form fields from a website. The outside source could even be a command-line program if you wanted it to be. (If you're curious, output parameters are used in case you want to output values from your stored procedure.)

When you click one of the parameters in the Parameters window, you'll see some information in the adjacent gray window, along with Edit and Delete buttons, as shown in Figure 4.7.

Click the Edit button and the Edit Parameter dialog box pops up (Figure 4.8). We'll go through the dialog box and examine the attributes of the `Parameter` element simultaneously.

FIGURE 4.8:

The Edit Parameter dialog box

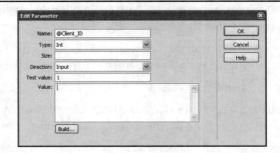

Name The first text field in the Edit Parameter box is easy; it's just the name of the parameter. For parameterized SQL statements, the name can be anything, but it's best to associate it with its actual meaning, and Dreamweaver will associate it to similarly named fields in SQL statements that the program reads when it generates `Parameter` elements. An example in this case is the `@Client_ID` name, which begins with the `@` character. The order in which `Parameter` elements appear must correspond to the order of any question-mark placeholders in a SQL statement. Since the name is optional in this case, you can omit it. In that case, the name will be set to `parameter_` plus the 1-based index of the parameter within the list of parameters provided.

For stored procedures, all names must match any parameters appearing in the stored procedure (for example, @Client_ID). Any parameters of type ReturnValue must occur before any other Parameter element.

Type   Dreamweaver can read database info, so the next text field in the Edit Parameter dialog box is easy, too. When you pass values to database parameters, you usually need to identify the datatype as well. If what you choose doesn't match the datatype in the stored procedure, you'll get a database error. Luckily, because Dreamweaver can read the tables, it should choose the correct datatype for you. Otherwise, you have to go to the database and determine the datatype, if you don't already know it by heart.

The possible attribute values of the Type attribute are as follows: Boolean, Decimal, Double, Numeric, Single, Integer, UnsignedInt, SmallInt, UnsignedSmallInt, TinyInt, UnsignedTinyInt, BigInt, UnsignedBigInt, Char, WChar, VarChar, LongVarChar, VarWChar, LongVarWChar, VarNumeric, Currency, Date, DBDate, DBTime, DBTimeStamp, Filetime, BSTR.

If you're using the Managed Provider for SQL Server, you can use any of these instead of one of the preceding values: Int, SmallInt, TinyInt, BigInt, Decimal, Float, Char, NChar, VarChar, NVarChar, Text, NText, Real, Money, SmallMoney, TimeStamp, DateTime, SmallDateTime, Bit.

Size   The next field corresponds to the Parameter element's Size attribute, which specifies the size of the parameter's value. This is also known as the "width of the column." If not provided, Dreamweaver will try to determine the value of this attribute based on what it sees in the Type and Value attributes. It's better, in the case of such variable-sized datatypes as VarChar, to name the value yourself. If you are using datatypes whose sizes never vary, such as an integer or bit, you can omit the size.

Direction   Selecting the appropriate value from the Direction drop-down list will output that value into the Parameter element's Direction attribute. The choices are as follows:

- Input, when a database parameter expects a value from a form or other source.
- InputOutput, when a database parameter either may be expecting a value from another source or when the database uses a parameter to return a value to the web application.
- Output, when the database returns a value to the web application.
- ReturnValue, when a specific value is returned by the database.

Value   Here's where things get tricky. If you look at the bottom field of the Edit Parameter dialog box, you'll see it asks for the value of the parameter. The first thought that entered my head when I first saw this was, "How am I supposed to know?" But guess what happens when you click the Build button? Suddenly, your life changes before your eyes as Dreamweaver asks you to choose the source for your parameter value in the Build Value dialog box (Figure 4.9). Remember, this is the value that is going to go from your web application to your stored procedure.

In this case we'll choose a query string, so we select URL Parameter from the Source drop-down list. For the name, I chose Client_ID, so that when a query string Client_ID=x is passed from the browser, the stored procedure will pass the form value into the correct table column during the insert procedure. You also need to enter a test value into the Test Value field. You can put in anything you want, but it's best to specify a value you can actually test when clicking the Test button to see if everything is working. In this case, I entered 1, which will retrieve the first client.

When you click the OK button in the Build Value dialog box, you'll suddenly see the full parameter value you need in the Value field of the Edit Parameter dialog box (see Figure 4.10).

FIGURE 4.9:

The Build Value dialog box

The code you get will look something like this in your MM:DataSet element:

```
<Parameter Name="@Client_ID" Value='<%#
((Request.QueryString["Client_ID"] != null) &&
(Request.QueryString["Client_ID"].Length > 0)) ?
Request.QueryString["Client_ID"] : "1"  %>' Type="Int"  Direction="Input" />
```

FIGURE 4.10:

The Value field is completed after you fill in the Build Value dialog box

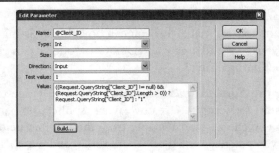

The "1" you see at the end of the Value attribute is the test value you entered in the Build Value dialog box. This also acts as a default value. If you don't want a default value, you can change "1" to an empty string ("")—but if you do, Dreamweaver will yell at you when you double-click the stored procedure in the Server Behaviors tab, go back to the Edit Parameters dialog box, then attempt to close it by clicking OK with no test value. Dreamweaver wants that test value. In other words, Dreamweaver won't let you set up the parameters without a test value. So if you really don't want one, you'll have to keep adding a test value and removing it. You can also combat Dreamweaver's error message by using a test value that you know will never be in the field.

The `Value` attribute specifies the value to be assigned to a parameter when the `Direction` attribute is set to `Input` or `InputOutput`. The `Value` attribute is cast to an appropriate datatype before being passed to the database. *Casting* is the act of converting one datatype into another, such as an integer into a string, so that, for example, 1 becomes `"1"`. This casting is determined when .NET reads in the `Type` attribute.

When the `Direction` attribute is set to `Output`, `InputOutput`, or `ReturnValue`, the `Value` attribute will be set after the `CommandText` is executed.

Creating Editable DataGrids Using *EditOps*

In Chapter 3 you were introduced to DataGrids. DataGrids are not simply nice data display tools, but they can also be used for editing data. When a user clicks an Edit button or hyperlink on your DataGrid, the DataGrid transforms into a grid with editable fields. Traditional ASP.NET requires a fair amount of coding to make this happen, but with Dreamweaver it's a simple matter of clicking a few buttons.

Let's access the same table you used in Chapter 3, `ClientInfo`, but this time we're going to change our DataGrid because there's no way to easily create editable fields from free-form templates (described in Chapter 3). So we'll create a DataGrid with simple data fields.

Listing 4.4 shows a portion of our new DataGrid. I've taken out some of the repeating elements to save space, but you can download Listing 4.4 from this book's catalog page at `www.sybex.com`. To create the DataGrid, once again you'll need to be sure you've got a DataSet defined first.

Using the *EditOpsTable* Element to Set the Table to Be Edited

Let's start by going to Dreamweaver's Application panel and creating a new DataGrid. When you choose your DataSet from the DataSet field, the columns will basically all load. However, you need to do one more thing, and that's add a new column by clicking the plus button next to Columns. Choose "Edit, update, cancel buttons" from the list that drops down, as shown in Figure 4.11.

FIGURE 4.11:

Choose the Edit, update, cancel buttons item in the Add Columns menu to create an editable DataGrid

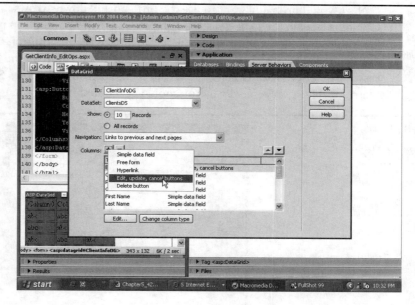

Click the resulting Edit button to make sure your database table is selected. Another dialog box appears, labeled Edit, Update, Cancel Button Column. Dreamweaver should know what the Primary Key is, and the appropriate field should show up in the dialog box's Primary Key drop-down list. If for some reason it doesn't, you can choose it yourself from the list. You can also use this dialog box to choose whether or not you want a button or a hyperlink to be the item that tells users they can do some editing.

Before we go any further, by now you may be wondering, "Hey, what happened to that EditOps element you were talking about?" Little did you know that you're creating it right now. Once we're done, you'll see that you can also hand-code it. Click OK in the Edit, Update, Cancel Button Column dialog box, and let's proceed.

The EditOps element is really just a container for other elements. One of those is the EditOpsTable element. When you used Dreamweaver's interface to create Edit buttons, Dreamweaver generated an EditOps element and some child elements:

```
<EditOps>
    <EditOpsTable Name="dbo.ClientInfo" />
    <Parameter Name="Client_ID" Type="Int" IsPrimary="true" />
</EditOps>
```

Next, you'll probably want to use the little up and down arrows on the right side of the Columns label in the DataGrid dialog box to move the Edit button up in the list of columns. Continue clicking the up arrow until you've moved the Edit button all the way to the top of the window. This makes sure the Edit link is the first column on the left of the grid and thus easy for the user to see. Then click OK in the DataGrid dialog box. Save your file as an ASPX file; then view it on your server. You should get something like what you see in Figure 4.12.

FIGURE 4.12:

An editable DataGrid? Almost…

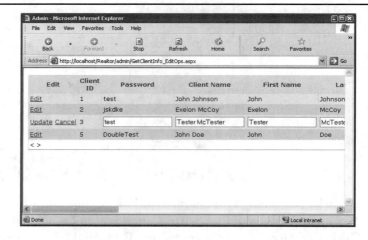

If you want to customize the DataGrid, you can look at Listing 4.5 to get started. Read through the listing so you can see where some of the properties of the MM:DataSet element live in the code. Remember that the MM:DataSet is accessed programmatically by its ID attribute, the value of which is ClientsDS. I've highlighted the relevant code in bold. If you don't have a DataSet handy, you can download Listing 4.4 (L0404.aspx) from www.sybex.com.

Listing 4.4   **Creating an editable DataGrid using simple data fields**

```
<asp:DataGrid id="ClientInfoDG"
  runat="server"
  AllowSorting="False"
  AutoGenerateColumns="false"
  CellPadding="3"
  CellSpacing="0"
  ShowFooter="false"
  ShowHeader="true"
  DataSource="<%# ClientsDS.DefaultView %>"
  PagerStyle-Mode="NextPrev"
  AllowPaging="true"
  AllowCustomPaging="true"
```

```
    PageSize="<%# ClientsDS.PageSize %>"
    VirtualItemCount="<%# ClientsDS.RecordCount %>"
    OnPageIndexChanged="ClientsDS.OnDataGridPageIndexChanged"
        DataKeyField="Client_ID"
    onCancelCommand="ClientsDS.OnDataGridCancel"
    onEditCommand="ClientsDS.OnDataGridEdit"
    onUpdateCommand="ClientsDS.OnDataGridUpdate"
    onItemDataBound="ClientsDS.OnDataGridItemDataBound"
    onDeleteCommand="ClientsDS.OnDataGridDelete"
>
    <HeaderStyle HorizontalAlign="center" BackColor="#E8EBFD"
ForeColor="#3D3DB6" Font-Name="Verdana, Arial, Helvetica, sans-serif" Font-
Bold="true" Font-Size="smaller" />
    <ItemStyle BackColor="#F2F2F2" Font-Name="Verdana, Arial, Helvetica, sans-
serif" Font-Size="smaller" />
    <AlternatingItemStyle BackColor="#E5E5E5" Font-Name="Verdana, Arial,
Helvetica, sans-serif" Font-Size="smaller" />
    <FooterStyle HorizontalAlign="center" BackColor="#E8EBFD"
ForeColor="#3D3DB6" Font-Name="Verdana, Arial, Helvetica, sans-serif" Font-
Bold="true" Font-Size="smaller" />
    <PagerStyle BackColor="white" Font-Name="Verdana, Arial, Helvetica, sans-
serif" Font-Size="smaller" />
    <Columns>
      <asp:EditCommandColumn
        ButtonType="LinkButton"
        CancelText="Cancel"
        EditText="Edit"
        HeaderText="Edit"
        UpdateText="Update"
        Visible="True"> </asp:EditCommandColumn>
      <asp:BoundColumn DataField="Client_ID"
        HeaderText="Client ID"
        ReadOnly="true"
        Visible="True"/>
      <asp:BoundColumn DataField="CPassword"
        HeaderText="Password"
        ReadOnly="false"
        Visible="True"/>
      <asp:BoundColumn DataField="ClientName"
        HeaderText="Client Name"
        ReadOnly="false"
        Visible="True"/>
<!-- Additional Bound colunns are not shown in
This code listing, but the full listing can be
downloaded. -->

      <asp:BoundColumn DataField="CEMail"
        HeaderText="CEMail"
        ReadOnly="false"
        Visible="True"/>
```

```
<asp:ButtonColumn
        ButtonType="LinkButton"
        CommandName="Delete"
        HeaderText="Delete"
        Text="Delete"
        Visible="True"/>
</Columns>
</asp:DataGrid>
```

Using the *EditOps* Element's *Parameter* Elements to Manage DataGrid Edits

Try to load the page we just built (Listing 4.4) into your browser (but remember to do it through your server). Click Edit, and although you see an Update and Cancel button, there aren't any editable fields. This is where the `Parameter` elements contained within the `EditOps` elements come into play. To make the fields editable, you'll have to change their `ReadOnly` property. Double-click the DataGrid in the Server Behaviors tab. Select one of the simple data fields and click Edit. A dialog box like that shown in Figure 4.13 will appear.

FIGURE 4.13:

Changing a bound data field's `ReadOnly` property

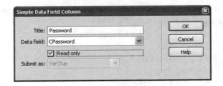

You'll have to change each field you want edited, since the default is for Read Only to be selected. Then, after you close out all the windows, something very cool happens. Look at the `MM:DataSet` element in Code view and you'll see the `EditOps` element and a group of child `Parameter` elements:

```
<EditOps>
<EditOpsTable Name="dbo.ClientInfo" />
  <Parameter Name="CPassword" Type="VarChar" />
  <Parameter Name="ClientName" Type="VarChar" />
  <Parameter Name="CFirstName" Type="VarChar" />
  <!-- possibly several more here, depending on how many editable
  ➥fields you allowed.
  <Parameter Name="CEMail" Type="VarChar" />
  <Parameter Name="Client_ID" Type="Int" IsPrimary="true" /></EditOps>
```

For each item on which you change the `ReadOnly` property, Dreamweaver spits out a `Parameter` element whose name corresponds to the field to be edited. It also changes the `asp:BoundElement`'s `ReadOnly` property to true:

```
<asp:BoundColumn DataField="Client_ID"
   HeaderText="Client ID"
   ReadOnly="true"
   Visible="True"/>
```

Now the page should be fully editable, as shown in Figure 4.14.

FIGURE 4.14:

An editable DataGrid
shown in a browser

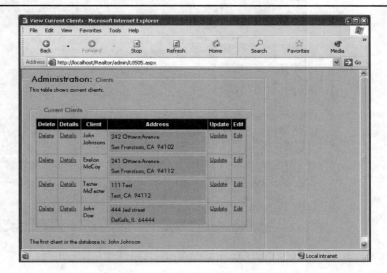

Now that you've seen how to edit a simple data field we can also turn those into editable fields. The concept is the same as when you drop HTML into an `ItemTemplate` (discussed in Chapter 3), only this time you're going to be dropping your code into an `EditItemTemplate`. Again, Dreamweaver makes all of this quite painless.

Let's go back to Listing 4.4 and rename it **Listing0405.axpx** (Listing 4.5). Load it into Dreamweaver and double-click the DataGrid in the Application panel's Server Behaviors tab. Add a new column as you did in the preceding example—an "Edit, update, cancel buttons" column. Again, it's a good idea to move the new column to the top of the list with the arrow buttons so that it's the first thing the user sees.

Next, click on one of the free-form fields and click the Edit button. In the Free Form Column dialog box, notice how the Template field shows more than one option now? Before you added the "Edit, update, cancel buttons" column, that area was grayed out. Click on it and choose EditItemTemplate, as shown in Figure 4.15.

FIGURE 4.15:

Choosing the EditItemTemplate option in the Free Form Column dialog box.

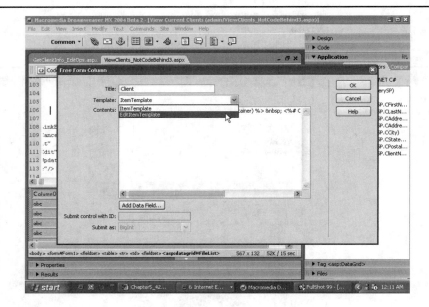

The text window below the Template drop-down list box will show the following text:

```
Replace this text with the contents that should appear
when an item is to be edited.

The DataGrid supports the following controls:
    asp:textbox
    asp:checkbox
    asp:dropdownlist

The id of the control must match the name of the field
that it is bound to.
```

You'll want to clear that text before you do anything, and then add an `asp:textbox` element with an `ID` attribute that matches the field in the database table that you're trying to manipulate.

Don't forget to add `runat="server"`, or the application will throw an error. Then, click Add Data Field, choose the data field you want to display, and insert it into the Contents text box. It's best to insert it well after any other code that appears there. After you've done that, copy and cut it from the field, then add a `Text=` attribute, and paste the data of that field into the text attribute value so it looks like this:

```
text='<%# ClientQuerySP.FieldValue("CFirstName", Container) %>'
```

Note the single quotes around the ASP.NET markup. Create another text box for the last name, so that your finished code looks like this:

```
<asp:textbox id="CFirstName" runat="server" text='<%#
ClientQuerySP.FieldValue("CFirstName", Container) %>' />
<asp:textbox id="CLasttName" runat="server" text='<%#
ClientQuerySP.FieldValue("CLastName", Container) %>' />
```

Next you'll need to bind the values, which you do with the options at the bottom of the Free Form Column dialog box. Enter **CFirstName** into the Submit Control with ID text box. The attribute value must match the name of the field. This will create a `Parameter` element in the `MM:DataSet`'s `EditOps` element. However, there is a small problem. Dreamweaver only accounts for the creation of one parameter per free-form field. So you'll need to hand-code any additional `Parameter` values yourself.

So far, based on the way you completed the Free Form Column's dialog box, Dreamweaver has given you this:

```
<EditOps>
  <EditOpsTable Name="dbo.ClientInfo" />
  <Parameter Name="CFirstName" Type="VarChar" />
  <Parameter Name="Client_ID" Type="Int" IsPrimary="true" />
</EditOps>
```

If you want to add the capability of editing the client's last name, in addition to the client's first name, you'll need to change this code as follows:

```
<EditOps>
  <EditOpsTable Name="dbo.ClientInfo" />
  <Parameter Name="CFirstName" Type="VarChar" />
  <Parameter Name="CLastName" Type="VarChar" />
  <Parameter Name="Client_ID" Type="Int" IsPrimary="true" />
</EditOps>
```

The finished page is shown in Listing 4.5. The application should appear in your browser window as shown in Figures 4.16 and 4.17.

FIGURE 4.16:

An editable DataGrid in a browser before the Edit button is clicked

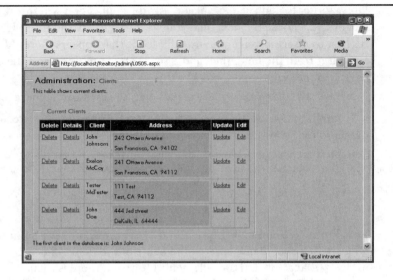

FIGURE 4.17:

An editable DataGrid in a browser after the Edit button is clicked

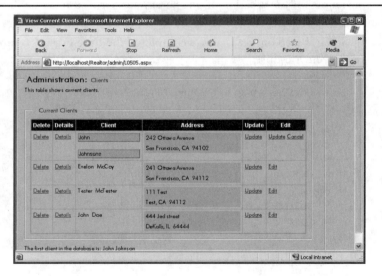

Listing 4.5   **Creating an editable DataGrid using free-form fields**

```
<%@ Page language="c#" AutoEventWireup="false" %>
<%@ Register TagPrefix="MM" Namespace="DreamweaverCtrls" Assembly
➡="DreamweaverCtrls,version=1.0.0.0,publicKeyToken
➡=836f606ede05d46a,culture=neutral" %>
<MM:DataSet
```

```
runat="Server"
id="ClientQuerySP"
IsStoredProcedure="true"
CreateDataSet="true"
ConnectionString='<%# System.Configuration.ConfigurationSettings.AppSettings
➥["MM_CONNECTION_STRING_mdriscollString"] %>'
DatabaseType='<%# System.Configuration.ConfigurationSettings.AppSettings
➥["MM_CONNECTION_DATABASETYPE_mdriscollString"] %>'
CommandText="dbo.ClientQueryNoParams"
Debug="true"
>
  <Parameters>
    <Parameter  Name="@RETURN_VALUE"   Type="Int"   Direction="ReturnValue" />
  </Parameters>
 <EditOps>
    <EditOpsTable Name="dbo.ClientInfo" />
    <Parameter Name="CFirstName" Type="VarChar" />
    <Parameter Name="CLastName" Type="VarChar" />
    <Parameter Name="Client_ID" Type="Int" IsPrimary="true" />
</EditOps>
</MM:DataSet>
<MM:PageBind runat="server" PostBackBind="true" />
<!DOCTYPE HTML PUBLIC "-//W3C//DTD HTML 4.0 Transitional//EN" >
<HTML>
    <HEAD>
        <title>View Current Clients</title>
        <META http-equiv="Content-Type" content="text/html; charset=windows-1252">
        <meta content="C#" name="CODE_LANGUAGE">
        <meta content="JavaScript" name="vs_defaultClientScript">
        <LINK href="admin.css" type="text/css" rel="stylesheet">
        <style>.butClass { BORDER-RIGHT: #d6d3ce 1px solid;
         BORDER-TOP: #d6d3ce 1px solid; BORDER-LEFT:
         #d6d3ce 1px solid; BORDER-BOTTOM: #d6d3ce 1px solid }
    .tdClass { PADDING-LEFT: 3px; PADDING-TOP: 3px }
        </style>
    </HEAD>
    <body topmargin="0" leftmargin="0" bgcolor="#d6d3ce">
        <form runat="server" ID="Form1">

            <!-- %%%%%%%%%%%%% APPLICATION CONTAINER %%%%%%%%%%%%%% -->
            <fieldset style="PADDING-RIGHT: 10px;  PADDING-LEFT: 10px;  PADDING-
BOTTOM: 10px; MARGIN-LEFT: -3px; WIDTH: 440px; PADDING-TOP: 10px;
BACKGROUND-COLOR: #d6d3ce">
                <legend style="FONT-SIZE:13px">
                    <span style="FONT-WEIGHT: 700; FONT-SIZE: 18px; COLOR:
#000000">Administration: </span>
                    Clients</legend>
                <table cellPadding="3" width="75%" border="0">
                    <tr>
                        <td style="WIDTH: 447px">This table shows current clients.
</td>
                    </tr>
```

```
                    <tr valign="top" align="left">
                        <td style="WIDTH: 447px">
                        <!-- ################## COMPONENT ################## -->
        <FIELDSET style="PADDING-RIGHT: 10px; PADDING-LEFT: 10px; PADDING-BOTTOM:
10px; WIDTH: 440px; PADDING-TOP: 10px; BACKGROUND-COLOR: #d6d3ce">
        <LEGEND style="PADDING-RIGHT: 10px; PADDING-LEFT: 10px; FONT-SIZE: 13px;
PADDING-BOTTOM: 10px; PADDING-TOP: 10px">Current
                        Clients</LEGEND>


    <asp:DataGrid AllowPaging="false" AutoGenerateColumns="false"
BorderColor="orange" BorderWidth="2" CellPadding="4" DataKeyField="Client_ID"
DataSource="<%# ClientQuerySP.DefaultView %>" id="FileList" ItemStyle-
HorizontalAlign="Left" ItemStyle-VerticalAlign="Top"  runat="server"
ShowHeader="true" OnUpdateCommand="ClientQuerySP.OnDataGridUpdate"
OnEditCommand="ClientQuerySP.OnDataGridEdit"
OnCancelCommand="ClientQuerySP.OnDataGridCancel"
OnItemDataBound="ClientQuerySP.OnDataGridItemDataBound">
                        <HeaderStyle BorderColor="White" BackColor="black"
ForeColor="White" Font-Bold="True" Font-Name="Arial" Font-Size="9"
HorizontalAlign="Center" />
                        <Columns>
                        <asp:HyperLinkColumn HeaderText="Delete"
DataTextFormatString="Delete" DataNavigateUrlField="Client_ID"
DataNavigateUrlFormatString="DeleteClient.aspx?Client_ID={0}"
DataTextField="Client_ID" ItemStyle-VerticalAlign="Top" ItemStyle-
HorizontalAlign="Left" HeaderStyle-HorizontalAlign="Left" HeaderStyle-
VerticalAlign="Top"></asp:HyperLinkColumn>
                        <asp:HyperLinkColumn HeaderText="Details"
DataTextFormatString="Details" DataNavigateUrlField="Client_ID"
DataNavigateUrlFormatString="ClientDetails_NotCodeBehind.aspx?Client_ID={0}"
DataTextField="Client_ID" ItemStyle-VerticalAlign="Top" ItemStyle-
HorizontalAlign="Left" HeaderStyle-HorizontalAlign="Left" HeaderStyle-
VerticalAlign="Top"></asp:HyperLinkColumn>
                        <asp:TemplateColumn HeaderText="Client"
ItemStyle-HorizontalAlign="Left" ItemStyle-VerticalAlign="Top">
                        <ItemTemplate><%#
ClientQuerySP.FieldValue("CFirstName", Container) %>  <%#
ClientQuerySP.FieldValue("CLastName", Container) %></ItemTemplate>
                        <EditItemTemplate>
                        <asp:textbox runat="server"
id="CFirstName" text='<%# ClientQuerySP.FieldValue("CFirstName", Container) %>'
/>
<br>
                        <asp:textbox runat="server"
id="CLastName" text='<%# ClientQuerySP.FieldValue("CLastName", Container) %>' />
</EditItemTemplate>
                        </asp:TemplateColumn>
                        <asp:TemplateColumn HeaderText="Address"
HeaderStyle-VerticalAlign=Top ItemStyle-VerticalAlign=Top>
                        <ItemTemplate>
```

```
                                             <table width="200" border="0"
bgcolor="#99CCFF">
                                     <tr>
                                     <td><%#
ClientQuerySP.FieldValue("CAddress", Container) %></td>
                                     </tr>
                                     <tr>
                                     <td><%#
ClientQuerySP.FieldValue("CAddress2", Container) %></td>
                                     </tr>
                                     <tr>
                                     <td><%#
ClientQuerySP.FieldValue("CCity", Container) %>, <%#
ClientQuerySP.FieldValue("CStateProv", Container) %>  <%#
ClientQuerySP.FieldValue("CPostalCode", Container) %></td>
                                     </tr>
                                     </table>
                                 </ItemTemplate>
                                 </asp:TemplateColumn>
                                 <asp:HyperLinkColumn HeaderText="Update"
DataNavigateUrlField="Client_ID"
DataNavigateUrlFormatString="UpdateClients.aspx?Client_ID={0}"
DataTextField="Client_ID" DataTextFormatString="Update" ItemStyle-
VerticalAlign="Top" ItemStyle-HorizontalAlign="Left" HeaderStyle-
HorizontalAlign="Left" HeaderStyle-VerticalAlign="Top"></asp:HyperLinkColumn>
                                 <asp:EditCommandColumn
        ButtonType="LinkButton"
        CancelText="Cancel"
        EditText="Edit"
        HeaderText="Edit"
        UpdateText="Update"
        Visible="True"/>
</Columns>
                         </asp:DataGrid>
                         </FIELDSET>
                     </td>
                     <td>
                          
                     </td>
                 </tr>
                 <tr valign="top" align="left">
                     <td style="WIDTH: 447px"><p>The first client in the database
is: <%# ClientQuerySP.FieldValueAtIndex(0, "ClientName", Container) %></p>
</td>
                     <td> </td>
                 </tr>
             </table>
         </fieldset>
     </form>
   </body>
</HTML>
```

The *MM:Insert* Tag

My preference for inserting data using .NET is to use a stored procedure, but the MM:Insert element can offer a quick alternative to stored procedures when you're in a hurry (and it can also be used *with* stored procedures). Sometimes deadlines are such that it can be a little faster to just set up a data-insertion page using Dreamweaver and change it later to a stored-procedure-based application, especially if you are only demonstrating functionality for a client (although if you wish to demonstrate the *speed* of an application, you'd better go with the stored procedure from the beginning). Luckily, you can create an insert using Macromedia's Insert command, and make only minor changes to convert its use to a stored procedure.

The attributes available to this element are the same as those available to the MM:DataSet attribute. However, you won't be able to deduce from the Dreamweaver interface that you can use stored procedures, because there is no GUI for them when using an Insert command. This isn't as big a problem as it may seem, because you can simply build your insert with the GUI using traditional SQL INSERT statements, and then migrate the code to a stored procedure.

Let's see how this works with an example.

Using *MM:Insert* with Basic SQL Statements

We'll begin with a new page. Name the file L0406.aspx. The first thing we'll do is create a new DataSet. We'll need that to work with a list box we are going to use for selecting the client that will be associated with any new listing we create.

Listing 4.6 shows how this DataSet new should look. You should be able from your knowledge of both Dreamweaver and the code underlying its functionality to create your SQL statement just by looking at Listing 4.6. I've highlighted the relevant portions in bold to help you figure it out. Note that the download for Listing 4.6, L0406.aspx, features the entire code listing rather than the pieces we're about to explore, which actually appear in separate listings.

Listing 4.6   **Using MM:Insert with basic SQL (Part 1, the DataSet)**

```
<%@ Page Language="C#" ContentType="text/html" ResponseEncoding="iso-8859-1" %>
<%@ Register TagPrefix="MM" Namespace="DreamweaverCtrls" Assembly
➥="DreamweaverCtrls,version=1.0.0.0,publicKeyToken
➥=836f606ede05d46a,culture=neutral" %>
<MM:DataSet
id="ClientDS"
runat="Server"
IsStoredProcedure="false"
ConnectionString='<%# System.Configuration.ConfigurationSettings.AppSettings
    ➥["MM_CONNECTION_STRING_mdriscollString"] %>'
DatabaseType='<%# System.Configuration.ConfigurationSettings.AppSettings
    ➥["MM_CONNECTION_DATABASETYPE_mdriscollString"] %>'
CommandText='<%# "SELECT Client_ID, ClientName FROM dbo.ClientInfo" %>'
```

```
Debug="true"></MM:DataSet>
<MM:PageBind runat="server" PostBackBind="true" />
```

Listing 4.6 shows how the code will look if you create a DataSet named `ClientDS` using the `mdriscollString` connection we've been employing throughout most of the book. To get the `CommandText` attribute value to look like the bolded code in Listing 4.6, in the Columns list box, select two of the fields shown for the `ClientInfo` table, as shown in Figure 4.18.

FIGURE 4.18:

Selecting columns from the ClientInfo table

Next, we'll go the easy route to creating an insertion, and use Dreamweaver's Record Insertion Form Wizard. This is started by selecting Insert ➤ Application Objects ➤ Insert Record, as shown in Figure 4.19. The Record Insertion Form is the next Dreamweaver goody to make an appearance, as seen in Figure 4.20.

FIGURE 4.19:

Starting Dreamweaver's Record Insertion Form Wizard

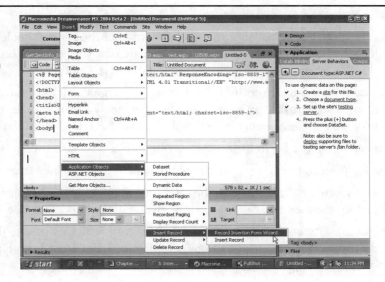

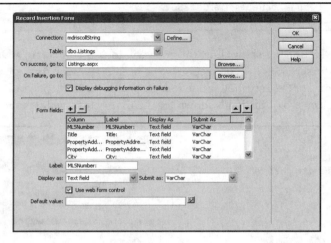

The first field of the Record Insertion Form lets you choose your connection. The next field, Table, is a drop-down list of tables that are available through your connection. The next field lets you name where you want to send users after the insertion of data is successful. This may be to a detail page that shows the data that was just inserted, but it can really be whatever kind of page you wish. The attribute/value pair, which is part of the MM:Insert element, might look like this in Code view:

```
SuccessURL='<%# "Listings.aspx" %>'
```

The next text field lets you choose a "failure" URL, which will send users to a specified page when the insertion fails:

```
FailureURL='<%# "Error.aspx" %>'
```

Underneath that is a check box that specifies whether the system should show a debugging message. You should keep this checked until you are sure your application is working well. If you included a failure URL, however, you should turn this off.

The next part of the Record Insertion Form is the large Form Fields area. Dreamweaver is pretty smart here, in that it can pretty much figure out how to read the data that is already in the table into which you're inserting, as well as the types of fields into which the data will be entered.

Each column in the Form Fields area corresponds to a specific use:

- The Column column refers to a column of data in the database table.
- The Label column refers to how the form field that is used to send data to the column is labeled for the user. You can change it by changing the Label field in this Form Fields area.
- The Display As: column specifies what type of form widget is used to display and then send the data. You can change this by selecting from the drop-down Display As: list, as shown in Figure 4.21.

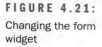

FIGURE 4.21:

Changing the form widget

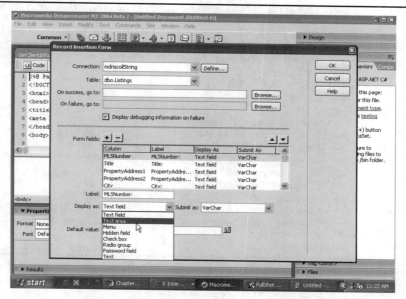

Next to the Display As: text field, you'll see a Submit As: drop-down list box. Use this to change the datatype that will be sent to the field to be updated. Dreamweaver is usually pretty good at determining the correct datatype, but it's not always correct, so you need to keep an eye on things here. Sometimes, for example, you'll need to change a VarChar datatype to Text because Dreamweaver automatically assigns the VarChar datatype to fields that the database assigns as Text datatypes.

Your web form can consist of ASP.NET controls or regular HTML. You make this choice using the "Use web form control" check box. If you check the box, ASP.NET elements will be used to handle the insertion process. The last field in the dialog box is for a default value, which you can either name explicitly or assign a value from a database table by clicking the data (lightning bolt) button next to the text field.

When you're done, your insert element will look something like the `MM:Insert` element shown in Listing 4.7.

Listing 4.7:   **Using `MM:Insert` with basic SQL (Part 2, the `MM:Insert` element)**

```
<MM:Insert runat="server"
CommandText='<%# "INSERT INTO dbo.Listings (MLSNumber, Title, PropertyAddress1,
PropertyAddress2, City, \"State\", PostalCode, DescriptionPlainText,
DescriptionHTML, DescriptionXML, Client_ID, Price, Neighborhood, Status,
StreetOrAve) VALUES (@MLSNumber, @Title, @PropertyAddress1, @PropertyAddress2,
@City, @State, @PostalCode, @DescriptionPlainText, @DescriptionHTML,
@DescriptionXML, @Client_ID, @Price, @Neighborhood, @Status, @StreetOrAve)" %>'
```

```
ConnectionString='<%# System.Configuration.ConfigurationSettings.AppSettings
    ➥["MM_CONNECTION_STRING_mdriscollString"] %>'
DatabaseType='<%# System.Configuration.ConfigurationSettings.AppSettings
    ➥["MM_CONNECTION_DATABASETYPE_mdriscollString"] %>'
Expression='<%# Request.Form["MM_insert"] == "form1" %>'
CreateDataSet="false"
SuccessURL='<%# "Listings.aspx" %>'
Debug="true">
<Parameters>
  <Parameter Name="@MLSNumber" Value='<%#
  ➥ ((Request.Form["MLSNumber"] != null) &&
  ➥ (Request.Form["MLSNumber"].Length > 0)) ?
  ➥ Request.Form["MLSNumber"] : "" %>' Type="VarChar" />
  <Parameter Name="@Client_ID" Value='<%#
  ➥ ((Request.Form["Client_ID"] != null) &&
  ➥ (Request.Form["Client_ID"].Length > 0)) ?
  ➥ Request.Form["Client_ID"] : "" %>' Type="Int" />
<!-- Most parameters removed to save space: see full listing online -->
</Parameters>
</MM:Insert>
```

Note that in the full listing available for download there is a `Parameter` element for each parameter in the SQL INSERT statement:

```
VALUES (@MLSNumber...
```

Most of the `Parameter` elements were removed from Listing 4.7 to save space, so if you're typing in, you'll need to add them in order for the application to work.

The `Value` attribute of each `Parameter` element is generated by Dreamweaver based on the input you entered in the Forms Field area. The Record Insertion Form Wizard also generates all the HTML form widgets you need. Some of these are shown in Listing 4.8, but I took many of them out to save space (you can view all of them in the downloadable file `L0406.aspx`). You can also create your own form fields first, and then use the Insert Record command to map the form fields to table fields.

Listing 4.8   **Using `MM:Insert` with basic SQL (Part 3, the HTML and web controls)**

```
<html>
<head>
<title>Untitled Document</title>
<meta http-equiv="Content-Type" content="text/html; charset=iso-8859-1">
</head>
<body>
<form method="post" name="form1" runat="server">
  <table align="center">
    <tr valign="baseline">
      <td nowrap align="right">MLSNumber:</td>
```

```
      <td>
        <asp:textbox id="MLSNumber" TextMode="SingleLine" Columns="32"
runat="server" />
      </td>
    </tr>
    <tr valign="baseline">
      <td nowrap align="right">Client_ID:</td>
      <td><asp:DropDownList ID="DropDownList"
      DataSource="<%# ClientDS.DefaultView %>" DataTextField="ClientName"
DataValueField="Client_ID" runat="server"></asp:DropDownList>
      </td>
    </tr>
    <tr valign="baseline">
      <td nowrap align="right"> </td>
      <td><input type="submit" value="Insert record"></td>
    </tr>
  </table>
  <input type="hidden" name="MM_insert" value="form1">
</form>
<p> </p>
</body>
</html>
```

The finished page should look like that shown in Figure 4.22.

FIGURE 4.22:

A completed listings
insertion form

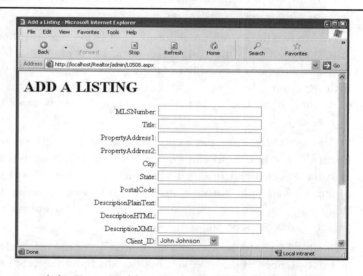

You can see, if you accepted the Form Field names in the Form Insertion Wizard, that they aren't very intuitive to the user or they just seem a little funny—for example, what would a user do with the field labeled DescriptionXML? You can change this kind of label using the

Record Form Insertion Wizard's Label text field when you click each column in the Form Fields area, and you can delete those you don't want using the minus button. However, once you've set up your wizard and clicked OK, form label changes must be done in the code by changing the text next to the `asp:textbox` element (or whatever the widget is):

```
<asp:textbox id=Price Runat="server"> </asp:textbox>
```

If you change the `id` attribute for some reason, you will also need to change the reference in the `Parameter` element, which relies on the `id` attribute to send the form value to the stored procedure. For instance, changing the `id` attribute to `Price2` like so:

```
asp:textbox id=Price2 Runat="server"> </asp:textbox>
```

would force us to change the values in the following `Parameter` elements:

```
    <PARAMETER Type="Int"
Value='<%# ((Request.Form["Price2"] != null) && (Request.Form["Price2"].Length >
0)) ?
    ➥Request.Form["Price2"] : "" %>'
Name="@Price" />
```

Using *MM:Insert* with Stored Procedures

Listings 4.6 through 4.8 showed how you can make a quick-and-dirty insertion form, but chances are you'll eventually want to migrate your insertion forms to a stored procedure because stored procedures are faster.

We can use the stored procedure from Listing 4.3, but there's one catch. Dreamweaver's Stored Procedure command creates `MM:DataSet` elements, but not `MM:Insert` elements. In view of this, your first instinct may be to assume you simply can't use stored procedures with `MM:Insert`, but you can, and the Dreamweaver controls actually support it. You have to do some hand-coding to make it work, however, because the GUI doesn't provide direct support.

We can use the same basic code we got from our efforts with the Record Insertion Form Wizard in our previous examples, and simply change the `MM:Insert` element's `IsStoredProcedure` from its default of false to true. Most likely, the attribute won't be in the original code, since its absence is the same as having the default value. So the first thing that needs to be done is to add an `IsStoredProcedure="true"` attribute/value pair to the `MM:Insert` element.

Listing 4.9 shows how a little manipulation of the original `MM:Insert` element gives us what we need. The other key, besides changing the `IsStoredProcedure` attribute, is giving the `CommandText` attribute a new value. Both of these changes are shown in bold in Listing 4.9.

Listing 4.9   **Using MM: Insert to insert using a stored procedure**

```
        <title>Enter New Listings</title>
        <!-- ############# DREAMWEAVER CONTROLS DLL COMPONENTS ############# -->
        <!-- ######### DREAMWEAVER INSERT COMPONENT -->
        <MM:INSERT id=Insert1 runat="server" IsStoredProcedure="true"
CommandText='<%# "ListingInsertions" %>'
ConnectionString='<%# System.Configuration.ConfigurationSettings.AppSettings
    ➥["MM_CONNECTION_STRING_mdriscollString"] %>'
DatabaseType='<%# System.Configuration.ConfigurationSettings.AppSettings
    ➥["MM_CONNECTION_DATABASETYPE_mdriscollString"] %>'
Expression='<%# Request.Form["MM_insert"] == "form2" %>' CreateDataSet="false"
SuccessURL='<%# "Listings.aspx" %>' Debug="true">
        <PARAMETERS>
            <!-- This will use the same PARAMETER elements as the other Insert,
but with these additions: -->

            <PARAMETER Type="Int"
Value='<%# ((Request.Form["Price"] != null) && (Request.Form["Price"].Length >
0)) ? Request.Form
    ➥["Price"] : "" %>'
Name="@Price" />
            <PARAMETER Type="Text"
Value='<%# ((Request.Form["@Neighborhood"] != null) &&
➥(Request.Form["@Neighborhood"].Length > 0)) ?
➥Request.Form["Neighborhood"] : "" %>'
Name="@Neighborhood" />
            <PARAMETER Type="Text"
Value='<%# ((Request.Form["Status"] != null) &&
➥(Request.Form["Status"].Length > 0)) ? Request.Form["Status"]
➥: "" %>'
Name="@Status" />
        </PARAMETERS>
        </MM:INSERT>
```

If you've done any amount of substantial programming with SQL, your instinct might be to use the following code for the CommandText attribute, since you're executing a stored procedure:

```
CommandText='<%# "exec ListingInsertions" %>'
```

If you do that, though, you'll get a message that the stored procedure is expecting parameters, even though you have Parameter elements inside your MM:Insert element:

```
System.Data.SqlClient.SqlException: Procedure 'ListingInsertions' expects
parameter '@MLSNumber', which was not supplied
```

This occurs because, when you use exec Listing Insertions without the IsStoredProcedure="true" attribute/value pair, the Dreamweaver control doesn't route the parameter information to .NET; therefore, .NET never delivers the expected parameters.

Don't use the `exec` SQL keyword. Instead, use the `IsStoredProcedure="true"` attribute/value pair and then the following:

```
CommandText='<%# "ListingInsertions" %>'
```

As you write out your `Parameter` elements, you don't need to worry whether they are in the same order of appearance as the field values in your stored procedure's SQL `INSERT` statement. You just have to be sure that for each target database table field receiving an insert value, you include a corresponding `Parameter` element.

The other thing you need to consider is that the stored procedure is going to expect parameters for some text fields we're not using yet. Of course, we can simply change the stored procedure, but sometimes we're handed stored procedures from other developers and we don't have that option. I resolved this in Listing 4.9 by adding invisible web controls that send empty strings to the stored procedure. But in that case, you need to be sure the stored procedure will accept an empty string (check with your DBA or, if you have rights to the database, check for yourself). The field can also be set up to be optional. That way, working in tandem with validation controls, you can make sure that fields required by the database simply don't get submitted, because you are using .NET validation controls to prevent the form from being submitted when certain expected fields are not filled in. Or, you or your DBA can set up default values within the stored procedure itself.

The *MM:Update* Element

The `MM:Update` element works very much like the `MM:Insert` element, so instead of drawing out that whole process again for you, I'm going to simply mention that the process for generating the element is nearly the same as the one for generating the `MM:Insert` element. The difference, of course, is that instead of using the Insert Record command you use Dreamweaver's Update Record command.

Let's start our brief examination of this element by revisiting Listing 4.6. We'll delete the `MM:Insert` element by going into the Application panel's Server Behavior tab and clicking the Insert Record behavior, as seen in Figure 4.23. Then, you simply delete it by clicking the minus button. You could also start with a fresh page, and use the Record Update Form Wizard (Insert ➤ Application Objects ➤ Update Record ➤ Record Update Form Wizard).

FIGURE 4.23:

Select the Insert Record behavior and click the minus button to delete it.

In this case, since we already have a form made, we can just resave the file as F0410.aspx and use the Update Record command, which can be found under Insert/Update/Update Record by going to under Insert ➤ Application Objects ➤ Update Record in the main menu or by clicking the plus sign in the Server Behaviors tab. You'll get a dialog box like that shown in Figure 4.24.

FIGURE 4.24:

Using the Update
Record dialog box

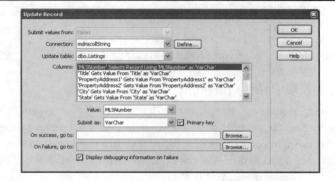

Listing 4.10 shows you a truncated version of the results. You can download the full version from www.sybex.com.

Listing 4.10   **Using Dreamweaver's Update command to create an update**

```
<MM:Update
runat="server"
CommandText='<%# "UPDATE dbo.Listings SET Title=@Title, PropertyAddress1
➥=@PropertyAddress1, PropertyAddress2=@PropertyAddress2, City=@City, \"State\"
➥=@State, PostalCode=@PostalCode, DescriptionPlainText
➥=@DescriptionPlainText, DescriptionHTML=@DescriptionHTML, DescriptionXML
➥=@DescriptionXML, Client_ID=@Client_ID, Price=@Price, Neighborhood
➥=@Neighborhood, Status=@Status, StreetOrAve=@StreetOrAve WHERE MLSNumber
➥=@MLSNumber" %>'
ConnectionString='<%# System.Configuration.ConfigurationSettings.AppSettings
➥["MM_CONNECTION_STRING_mdriscollString"] %>'
DatabaseType='<%# System.Configuration.ConfigurationSettings.AppSettings
➥["MM_CONNECTION_DATABASETYPE_mdriscollString"] %>'
Expression='<%# Request.Form["MM_update"] == "form1" %>'
CreateDataSet="false"
Debug="true"
>
  <Parameters>
    <Parameter Name="@Title" Value='<%# ((Request.Form["Title"]
    ➥!= null) && (Request.Form["Title"].Length > 0)) ?
    ➥Request.Form["Title"] : "" %>' Type="VarChar" />
```

```
<Parameter Name="@PropertyAddress1" Value='<%#
➥((Request.Form["PropertyAddress1"] != null) &&
➥(Request.Form["PropertyAddress1"].Length > 0)) ?
➥Request.Form["PropertyAddress1"] : "" %>' Type="VarChar" />
<!-- Additional Parameter elements here: removed to save trees -->
  </Parameters>
</MM:Update>
```

As you can see, our friend the `Parameter` tag and its child element are back, doing what they did before: passing form values into the database.

The *MM:Delete* Element

Giving your users the power to delete records can be risky because, after all, you're letting people delete records permanently from your database. Nevertheless, there's obviously plenty of reasons to offer this capability. Within the framework of the examples in this chapter, deleting is an important part of any administrative function, so it's an obvious candidate for an admin page. You'll also often want to give users who register a profile on your site a chance to delete parts of their information.

We'll take a brief look here at how to create a simple deletion page. Chapter 7, which explores hand-coding more thoroughly, provides some more-complex examples. Here, we'll focus on how to put together a deletion using Dreamweaver's Delete Record command.

Using the Delete Record Command to Generate *MM:Delete* Elements

When you want to delete a record, often your deletion page will be accessed by another page. Generally, the deleted column is chosen on the first page, and the second page actually carries out the task of deleting data. The first page holds a DataSet containing the table that is acted upon; a form value based on a selection of one of the columns (generally a primary key column) is sent to the second page, where the actual `MM:Delete` element lives and does its work. In this case, we're going to do everything on one page to save space, but the other solution is actually more elegant. You'll see examples of that Chapter 7.

NOTE   Normally DBAs will give users a way out of the deletion process by asking that the delete be confirmed before the actual deletion takes place. Many developers give the appearance of a delete but in fact merely move deleted records to a history or log table. As far as the user knows, the record is deleted.

Before we create a deletion form, we'll need a DataSet from which to choose deletions. In this case, let's make a DataSet from the `Listings` table in the Realtor database. You already know how to create a DataSet, so I'll leave that up to you. You can also use your own table, if you want to follow along using your own application.

Once your DataSet is made, create a conventional HTML table in Dreamweaver using as many columns as you need to hold your data, and two rows: one for headers and the other for your data. From your DataSet in the Bindings tab of the Applications panel you can drag and drop fields into each column of the deletions table. Since you'll want more than one record of data to show up, you need to create a Repeat Region on the row of data you want to display (refer to Chapter 3 if you need to refresh your memory on creating Repeat Regions). The finished table containing the dynamic text from the DataSet should look something like this when you're finished:

```
<form method='POST' name='form1'>
  <table width="100%" border="0" cellpadding="10">
    <tr align="left" valign="top">
      <td>MLS Number</td>
      <td>Title</td>
      <td>Address 1</td>
      <td>City</td>
      <td>State</td>
      <td>Postal<br>
      Code</td>
    </tr>
    <ASP:Repeater runat="server" DataSource='<%# ListingsDS.DefaultView %>'>
      <ItemTemplate>
        <tr align="left" valign="top">

          <td>
<%# ListingsDS.FieldValue("Title", Container) %>
</td>
          <td><%# ListingsDS.FieldValue("PropertyAddress1", Container) %></td>
          <td><%# ListingsDS.FieldValue("City", Container) %></td>
          <td><%# ListingsDS.FieldValue("State", Container) %></td>
          <td><%# ListingsDS.FieldValue("PostalCode", Container) %></td>
        </tr>
      </ItemTemplate>
    </ASP:Repeater>
  </table>
</form>
```

As you can see, creating the data region using Dreamweaver generates an ASP.NET Repeater control. Take note of the highlighted code in the `ASP:Repeater` element. We'll be changing this a bit later.

To begin the process of deleting a record, choose the Delete Record command with Insert ➤ Application Objects ➤ Delete Record or from the Application panel's Server Behaviors tab. You'll see a dialog box like that shown in Figure 4.25.

FIGURE 4.25:

The Delete Record
dialog box

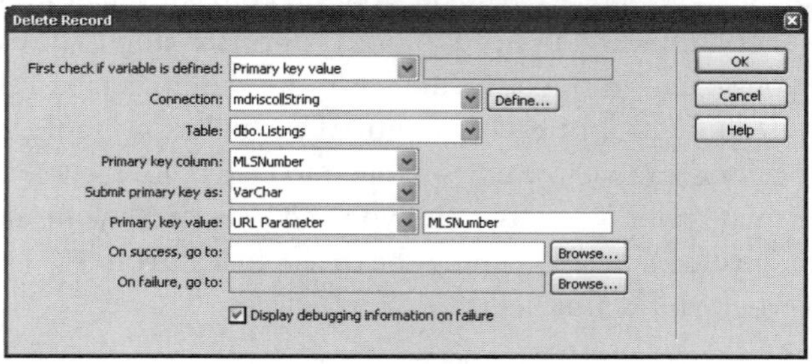

In the "First check if variable is defined" drop-down list, select Primary Key Value. If you want to check a variable other than the variable identifying the record to delete, select the variable and enter its name. In the Connection drop-down, select a connection to the database containing the table on which you want to take action. Then use the Table list to select the database table containing the records to delete.

In the Primary Key Column list, select a key column by to identify the record in the database table. This will correspond to the column that is acting as the table's primary key. Select a datatype using the Submit Primary Key As list. The datatype is the kind of data expected by the column in your database table (`varchar`, `int`, and so on).

The next part of the form is In the Primary Key Value list, where you'll select the variable identifying the record to delete, and then enter its name. In the On Success, Go To text box, enter the location of a page to display after the stored procedure runs successfully, or click the Browse button to find that location. In this case I'm simply redirecting the user back to the same page, so I left the space blank.

In the On Failure, Go To text box, enter or browse to find the location of a page to display if the stored procedure fails. Once again, I've left the page blank. Select the "Display debugging information on failure" check box if you want debugging information when the delete fails. When you enable this option, the Dreamweaver control tells .NET to ignore the On Failure, Go To option (the `FailureURL` attribute).

Click OK, and Dreamweaver adds a server behavior to the page, which lets users delete records in a database table by clicking a Submit button on the form. As you might guess, this server behavior consists of the `MM:Delete` element:

```
<MM:Delete
runat="server"
CommandText='<%# "DELETE FROM dbo.Listings WHERE MLSNumber=@MLSNumber" %>'
ConnectionString='<%# System.Configuration.ConfigurationSettings.AppSettings
➥["MM_CONNECTION_STRING_mdriscollString"] %>'
```

```
DatabaseType='<%# System.Configuration.ConfigurationSettings.AppSettings
➥["MM_CONNECTION_DATABASETYPE_mdriscollString"] %>'
Expression='<%# ((Request.QueryString["MLSNumber"] !
➥= null) && (Request.QueryString["MLSNumber"].Length > 0)) %>'
CreateDataSet="false"
Debug="true"
>
  <Parameters>
    <Parameter Name="@MLSNumber" Value='<%#
    ➥((Request.QueryString["MLSNumber"] != null) &&
    ➥(Request.QueryString["MLSNumber"].Length > 0)) ?
    ➥Request.QueryString["MLSNumber"] : "" %>'
    ➥ Type="VarChar" />
  </Parameters>
</MM:Delete>
```

Rather than creating a form Submit button, let's do something different and use an
`asp:hyperlink` control and hand-code our deletion. Take another look at the Listings table.
The first column of data retrieves values from the `MLSNumber` field using a Dynamic Text
behavior:

```
<td><%# ListingsDS.FieldValue("MLSNumber", Container) %></td>
```

When you click on that behavior in Design view (Figure 4.26) and then look at the Server
Behaviors tab, you'll see the behavior highlighted.

FIGURE 4.26:

The Dynamic Text
behavior

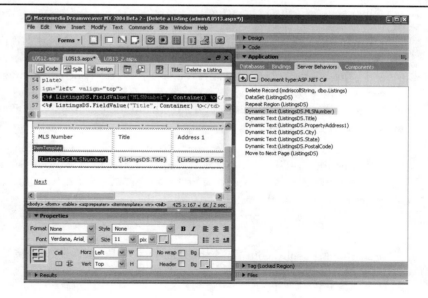

Go into Code view and copy the portion of code highlighted in bold here:

```
<td><%# ListingsDS.FieldValue("MLSNumber", Container) %></td>
```

Next, delete the server behavior by either clicking the minus button on the Server Behaviors tab while the behavior is selected, or by hitting your Delete key.

Now go to Dreamweaver's Insert bar and choose the ASP.NET group, and insert an asp:hyperlink control. A dialog box comes up. In the ID text field, enter **MLSNumber**. In the Navigate URL text field, enter the name of the file we're working with, **L0411.aspx**, and click OK (ignore the rest of the fields). Your control should look like this:

```
<asp:HyperLink ID="MLSNumber" NavigateUrl="L0411.aspx" runat
➥="server"></asp:HyperLink>
```

We need to add a text attribute and change the NavigateURL attribute:

```
<asp:HyperLink ID="MLSNumber" NavigateUrl='<%# "L0411.aspx?
➥MLSNumber="+ListingsDS.FieldValue("MLSNumber", Container) %>'
➥text='<%# ListingsDS.FieldValue("MLSNumber", Container) %>'
   runat="server"></asp:HyperLink>
```

Note the syntax used in the NavigateUrl attribute that starts with a single quote, then the ASP.NET markup indicating bound data. The <% characters followed immediately by a # indicate bound data is being routed to the .NET engine.

NOTE   All data-binding expressions, regardless of where you place them, must be contained between <%# and %> characters.

The string L0411.aspx?MLSNumber= must be in quotes so the .NET engine doesn't interpret its content as C# code and return a parser error. After you close that string with quotes, you add a + character before you paste the <td>...</td> code you highlighted and copied a bit earlier. The + concatenates the string values. The first string is L0411.aspx?MLSNumber=, and the second string is the result evaluated from the ListingsDS.FieldValue("MLSNumber", Container) expression.

One look at the MM:Delete element's Parameter element will tell you why this works. The .NET engine will be looking for a parameter named MLSNumber, which I hard-coded into the NavigateUrl attribute's value. The ListingsDS.FieldValue("MLSNumber", Container) expression returns the MLSNumber when the page is sent to the .NET engine. Therefore, when the hyperlink control is clicked, the row associated with the hyperlinked MLSNumber is deleted.

Listing 4.11 shows our finished Delete Record code, and Figure 4.27 shows how it should appear in the browser.

Listing 4.11   Using the Delete Record command to generate an MM:Delete

```
<%@ Page Language="C#" ContentType="text/html" ResponseEncoding="iso-8859-1" %>
<%@ Register TagPrefix="MM" Namespace="DreamweaverCtrls" Assembly
➥="DreamweaverCtrls,version=1.0.0.0,publicKeyToken
➥=836f606ede05d46a,culture=neutral" %>
<MM:Delete
runat="server"
CommandText='<%# "DELETE FROM dbo.Listings WHERE MLSNumber=@MLSNumber" %>'
ConnectionString='<%# System.Configuration.ConfigurationSettings.AppSettings
➥["MM_CONNECTION_STRING_mdriscollString"] %>'
DatabaseType='<%# System.Configuration.ConfigurationSettings.AppSettings
➥["MM_CONNECTION_DATABASETYPE_mdriscollString"] %>'
Expression='<%# ((Request.QueryString
➥["MLSNumber"] != null) && (Request.QueryString["MLSNumber"].Length > 0)) %>'
CreateDataSet="false"
Debug="true"
>
  <Parameters>
    <Parameter Name="@MLSNumber" Value='<%#
  ➥((Request.QueryString["MLSNumber"] != null) &&
  ➥(Request.QueryString["MLSNumber"].Length > 0)) ?
  ➥Request.QueryString["MLSNumber"] : "" %>'
  ➥Type="VarChar" />
  </Parameters>
</MM:Delete>
<MM:DataSet
id="ListingsDS"
runat="Server"
IsStoredProcedure="false"
ConnectionString='<%# System.Configuration.ConfigurationSettings.AppSettings
➥["MM_CONNECTION_STRING_mdriscollString"] %>'
DatabaseType='<%# System.Configuration.ConfigurationSettings.AppSettings
➥["MM_CONNECTION_DATABASETYPE_mdriscollString"] %>'
CommandText='<%# "SELECT MLSNumber, Title, PropertyAddress1,
➥ City, \"State\", PostalCode FROM dbo.Listings" %>'
Debug="true" PageSize="10" CurrentPage='<%#
➥ ((Request.QueryString["ListingsDS_CurrentPage"] != null) &&
➥ (Request.QueryString["ListingsDS_CurrentPage"].Length > 0))
➥?Int32.Parse(Request.QueryString["ListingsDS_
➥ CurrentPage"]) : 0 %>'
></MM:DataSet>
<MM:PageBind runat="server" PostBackBind="true" />
<!DOCTYPE HTML PUBLIC "-//W3C//DTD HTML 4.01 Transitional//EN" "http:
➥//www.w3.org/TR/html4/loose.dtd">
<html>
<head>
<title>Delete a Listing</title>
<meta http-equiv="Content-Type" content="text/html; charset=iso-8859-1">
```

```
<style type="text/css">
<!--
body {
    font-family: Verdana, Arial, Helvetica, sans-serif;
    font-size: 11px;
}
-->
</style>
</head>
<body>
<h1>DELETE A LISTING</h1>
<form method='POST' name='form1'>
  <table width="100%"  border="0" cellpadding="10">
    <tr align="left" valign="top">
      <td>MLS Number</td>
      <td>Title</td>
      <td>Address 1</td>
      <td>City</td>
      <td>State</td>
      <td>Postal<br>
      Code</td>
    </tr>
    <ASP:Repeater runat="server" DataSource='<%# ListingsDS.DefaultView %>'>
      <ItemTemplate>
        <tr align="left" valign="top">
          <td><asp:HyperLink ID="MLSNumber" NavigateUrl='<%#
➥"LO411.aspx?MLSNumber="+ListingsDS.FieldValue("MLSNumber",
➥Container) %>' text='<%# ListingsDS.FieldValue("MLSNumber",
➥Container) %>' runat="server"></asp:HyperLink></td>
          <td><%# ListingsDS.FieldValue("Title", Container) %></td>
          <td><%# ListingsDS.FieldValue("PropertyAddress1", Container) %></td>
          <td><%# ListingsDS.FieldValue("City", Container) %></td>
          <td><%# ListingsDS.FieldValue("State", Container) %></td>
          <td><%# ListingsDS.FieldValue("PostalCode", Container) %></td>
        </tr>
      </ItemTemplate>
    </ASP:Repeater>
  </table>
</form>
<p> <a href="<%# Request.ServerVariables["SCRIPT_NAME"]
➥%>?ListingsDS_currentPage=<%# ListingsDS.CurrentPage + 1
➥%>">Next</a></p>
</body>
</html>
```

In the tradition of the best "Don't Do This At Home" please notice that there are no routines in Listing 4.11 for alerting the poor user they're about to delete something. You'll find out how to prevent users from doing nasty things in Chapter 6, "Working with Validation Controls."

FIGURE 4.27:

A web page generated from the MM:Delete element

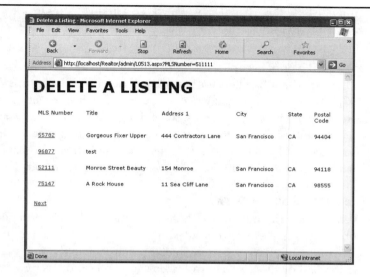

The *MM:PageBind* Element

Normally when you code in .NET sans Dreamweaver, you need to make sure you bind any data you're using. One way to do that is to use the DataBind() method from the DataSet class. With Dreamweaver, you can assume all your data is already bound to the page because the Dreamweaver control handles this for you through the MM:PageBind element. By default, any data from a data set is bound to a page managed by the Dreamweaver control.

ASP.NET and the Event-Driven Environment

When users interact with .NET applications, they initiate event-driven sequences. If you're familiar with the old ASP, you're probably aware that it was a procedural language, which means that things happened in the order you wrote your code. First one thing happened, then another. Sometimes an event was triggered by the fact that something else happened. But you didn't have the kind of event-based model we see with .NET. With .NET, absolutely everything is event based. Nothing can happen unless an event takes place.

The simplest and most obvious event is that the page loads. For that, there is a standard *event handler* called Page_Load() that looks like this:

```
<script runat="server">
protected void Page_Load(Object Src, EventArgs E)
{
  if (!IsPostBack) //do something
}
</script>
```

You don't see these handlers when you're working with Dreamweaver controls because they're written in the source code for the Dreamweaver control before it's compiled; but they're there.

Many kinds of event handlers exist, including another one for pages called `Page_Init()`. There are event handlers for buttons and other .NET controls. You'll find out more about them in Chapter 7. When you develop code for these event handlers, you tell .NET that when, for example, a page loads, some things should be done. Maybe some data gets retrieved; maybe your web page just writes out "bozo" a hundred times. Whatever the case, an event must first occur, and you need to ensure that an event handler for that event exists. In essence, event handlers are functions initiated by user actions or page loading events.

Understanding Postback

Whenever a user interacts with the server, a .NET web form pings the server (signaling the aforementioned event). The advantage of this arrangement is you can do things like mimic Dynamic HTML by returning messages directly to the web page based on some user interaction (although .NET controls won't respond to rollover events). *Postback* occurs when the browser posts information back to the server following some kind of user action.

The default value for the `MM:Postback` element's `PostBackBind` attribute is true, which means that it's assumed data binding will take place regardless of whether or not the user has posted back the form to the server. If you're familiar with .NET programming, this is the same as if you were writing out the following:

```
if (!IsPostBack) //do something
```

This arrangement is necessary because otherwise .NET would wait for a user event to occur before, for example, binding data to a page.

You will occasionally need to override this default behavior, such as when you are using selection controls that are loaded with data from database tables. When you need to prevent this behavior, simply change the value of the `PostBackBind` attribute to false.

Attributes Used by *MM:PageBind*

Aside from the `runat="server"` attribute/value pair, there are only two attributes to the `MM:PageBind` element: `PostBackBind` and `Ignore`. To see exactly how this element can have an effect on your web application, check out Chapter 7, which includes some code demonstrating what happens when the default is turned off.

PostBackBind   This is a Boolean that specifies whether page binding should take place if a postback has or has not occurred. If the value is true, then the page behaves as if a user has initiated activity on the web page that would post back to the server. The default value for `PostBackBind` is true. When you're mixing custom code from code-behind with the Macromedia control, you'll often have to turn this attribute off if you have form fields that are loaded dynamically from a database. However, generally you can keep the default value.

Ignore   When the value for this Boolean-based attribute is set to true, the `MM:PageBind` element is ignored and you can manage all the postback bindings on the page yourself. This is a meaningless attribute in terms of this chapter, where everything is handled by the Dreamweaver control, but as you progress into more complex scenarios (such as those in Chapter 7), you may find yourself needing to wrest control of the page binding process away from the Dreamweaver control. You do this by changing the `Ignore` attribute's default value from false to true.

The *MM:If* Element

Conditional programming is a huge part of ASP.NET. Unfortunately, writing it can be somewhat time-consuming, especially if you're new at development. The `MM:If` element helps with the task by allowing you to simply name a specified condition in the element through its `expression` attribute. Then it generates content based on that `expression`'s evaluating to true, through the use of the element's `ContentsTemplate` child element. Any routines and/or process you want to generate when the statement in the `expression` attribute evaluates to true are placed within the `MM:If` element's `ContentsTemplate`.

To see how this works, return to Listing 4.11 and resave it as `L0412.aspx`. Go to the main menu and choose Insert ➢ Application Objects ➢ Recordset Paging ➢ DataSet Navigation Bar. You'll be presented with a small dialog box labeled Insert DataSet Navigation Bar. Choose your DataSet from the DataSet drop-down list and click OK. The navigation bar will show up in Design view, as shown in Figure 4.28.

FIGURE 4.28:

The Insert DataSet Navigation Bar command inserts an `MM:If` element into the web application

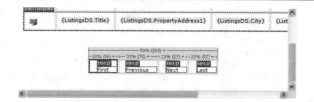

Dreamweaver generates the code shown in Listing 4.12; when rendered to the user's browser, this code results in a records navigation widget like that shown in Figure 4.29. The full code for Listing 4.12 can be downloaded from `www.sybex.com` as `L0412.aspx`.

FIGURE 4.29:

A navigation bar
created using the
MM:If element

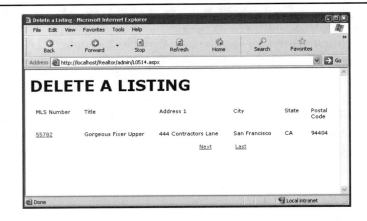

Listing 4.12   **Generating a DataSet navigation bar with an MM:IF element**

```
<table border="0" width="50%" align="center">
    <tr>
      <td width="23%" align="center">
        <MM:If runat="server" Expression='<%#
➡ListingsDS.CurrentPage != 0) %>'>
          <ContentsTemplate> <a href="<%#
➡Request.ServerVariables["SCRIPT_NAME"]
➡%>?ListingsDS_currentPage=0">First</a> </ContentsTemplate>
        </MM:If>
      </td>
      <td width="31%" align="center">
        <MM:If runat="server" Expression='<%#
➡ (ListingsDS.CurrentPage != 0) %>'>
          <ContentsTemplate> <a href="<%#
➡Request.ServerVariables["SCRIPT_NAME"]
➡ %>?ListingsDS_currentPage=<%# ListingsDS.
➡ CurrentPage - 1 %>">Previous</a> </ContentsTemplate>
        </MM:If>
      </td>
      <td width="23%" align="center">
        <MM:If runat="server" Expression='<%#
➡(ListingsDS.CurrentPage < ListingsDS.LastPage) %>'>
          <ContentsTemplate> <a href="<%#
➡Request.ServerVariables["SCRIPT_NAME"]
➡%>?ListingsDS_currentPage=<%# ListingsDS.CurrentPage
➡ + 1 %>">Next</a> </ContentsTemplate>
        </MM:If>
      </td>
      <td width="23%" align="center">
```

```
        <MM:If runat="server" Expression='<%#
➥(ListingsDS.CurrentPage < ListingsDS.LastPage) %>'>
            <ContentsTemplate> <a href="<%#
➥Request.ServerVariables["SCRIPT_NAME"]
➥%>?ListingsDS_currentPage=<%# ListingsDS.LastPage
➥%>">Last</a> </ContentsTemplate>
        </MM:If>
      </td>
    </tr>
</table>
```

To see how the ContentsTemplate element works, simply replace the contents of the ContentsTemplate in the following MM:If element with some straight text, with no data-driven content. In other words, change the section shown in bold here:

```
<MM:If runat="server" Expression='<%# (ListingsDS.CurrentPage <
    ListingsDS.LastPage) %>'>
            <ContentsTemplate> <a href="<%#
➥Request.ServerVariables["SCRIPT_NAME"]
➥%>?ListingsDS_currentPage=<%# ListingsDS.CurrentPage
➥ + 1 %>">Next</a> </ContentsTemplate>
        </MM:If>
```

so that it reads as follows (section in bold):

```
<MM:If runat="server" Expression='<%# (ListingsDS.CurrentPage
➥ < ListingsDS.LastPage) %>'>
            <ContentsTemplate> You're not going anywhere, pal.</ContentsTemplate>
        </MM:If>
```

Load the files into your browser after each change to see the difference.

You can use the MM:If element to create other conditional statements. For example, you could have a message indicating that the user is viewing the first page of a DataSet:

```
<MM:If runat="server"
Expression='<%# (ListingsDS.CurrentPage == 0) %>'>
      <ContentsTemplate>
        <p>
      This is the first page
        </p>
      </ContentsTemplate>
    </MM:If>
```

Of course, you can hand-code this, but it's much easier to insert this behavior from the Server Behaviors tab in the Application panel by clicking the + button and navigating to Show Region, then Show If First Page. This will prompt Dreamweaver to insert the preceding code at the spot where your cursor is at the time you perform the insertion.

Deploying *DreamweaverCtrls.dll*

You need to take the special step of deploying the Dreamweaver control whenever you use it. To do this, select Site in Dreamweaver's main menu and go to Advanced. From the Advanced menu, choose Deploy Supporting Files (see Figure 4.30). A dialog box like that shown in Figure 4.31 will appear.

FIGURE 4.30:

Selecting the Deploy Supporting Files command

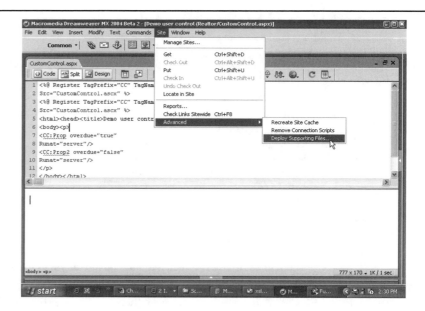

FIGURE 4.31:

The Deploy Supporting Files To Testing Server Dialog Box

It's important that you understand the correlation between your testing server and the remote server, because the Deploy Supporting Files To Testing Server dialog box will ask you to locate the appropriate bin directory. So the question becomes, what is the appropriate bin directory? It all depends on where your application is in relation to the root of your web server. The bottom line is that any page using a Macromedia server tag with an `MM:` `prefix` needs a `bin` directory within the same folder/directory as the page containing it. So if your web page is located in the `hello` directory, the `hello` directory should contain a `bin` folder or directory that in turn contains the `DreamweaverCtrls.dll` file. When you navigate to the appropriate directory, Macromedia will copy the DLL into a `bin` directory on your testing server. Unless your testing server is the same as your remote server, you'll then need to make sure the DLL gets copied to your remote host.

This is not the same process as registering a DLL prior to .NET, when you used a registration utility to register all DLLs to the system. You no longer are required to do that. All you need to do is make sure the DLL is deployed to the correct `bin` directory. From that point on, any `MM:` prefixed tags will work.

If you have trouble deploying for some reason, you can also copy it manually. The original DLL file lives in within a folder structure similar to the following on your computer (taking into account the location of your program files and the actual name of your Dreamweaver application).

```
C:\Program Files\Macromedia\Dreamweaver MX 2004\Configuration
\ServerBehaviors\Shared\ASP.Net\Scripts
```

Wrapping Up

Without the Dreamweaver control, Dreamweaver would be a very nice, reliable, design-focused web development tool. Combine the functionality of its code editor with the Design view, and the fact that in Design view some very clean HTML code can be generated, and you have a pretty worthwhile program, one that many web designers have sworn by for some time. Add the Dreamweaver control, however, and an entire world opens up for you. Using the GUI to manage all the control's functions will save you hours upon hours of coding time. But taking the time to really get comfortable with what's going on under the hood by reading this chapter and working through the examples will save you yet more hours in the long run, because you'll find yourself able to troubleshoot many different kinds of problems.

In the next chapter, we'll take a look at some of the controls that are native to the ASP.NET Framework. Once again, we'll start by seeing how they are accessed using Dreamweaver's GUI, and then we'll take a good look at what's really happening behind the scenes.

Chapter 5

Using Web Server Controls

- The vast world of Web Server controls

- Text and layout controls

- Button and hyperlink controls

- Check boxes and radio controls

- ListBox controls

- Table controls

- Creating a Calendar control in Dreamweaver

There are two major categories of server controls, HTML Server controls and Web Server controls, used in ASP.NET. HTML Server controls are simply HTML elements with a `runat="server"` attribute/value pair that exposes them as objects to an ASP.NET server. Web server controls (also called Web controls) are widgets specifically designed to work exclusively with ASP.NET.

This chapter's focus is on Web Server controls. Once you've grasped their fundamentals, you'll have no problem using HTML Server controls, too, when the need arises.

Dreamweaver is an excellent tool for developing the shells of what you need, but many of your tasks will require some coding by hand. This chapter serves as a gentle introduction to some manual coding techniques you'll need when working with ASP.NET Web Server controls.

NOTE   Some of the listings in this chapter are truncated to save space. You can download the complete listings by clicking the link on the book's page in the catalog at www.sybex.com.

The Vast World of Web Server Controls

ASP.NET is a vast object model comprising numerous classes of objects. One such class of objects is the Web Server Control class, which is derived from the following class hierarchy in the .NET object model:

```
System.Object
    System.Web.UI.Control
        System.Web.UI.WebControls.WebControl
```

Web Server controls are things like buttons, text boxes, selection lists, drop-down menus, and even calendars. They all have a set of common properties and methods you can access programmatically. Beyond that, most of them have at least a few additional properties and methods of their own.

This is the fundamental nature of ASP.NET and, in fact, all things Microsoft. Microsoft is all about objects. Even programs like Word and Excel are full of objects under the hood, which is why so many people can easily write macros for them. All you need do is find out the roles of all these objects and how to use them, and you're halfway to being able to program in ASP.NET. Table 5.1 lists the core properties and methods of the Web Control class. There are actually more, so many more that an entire reference book could be written on them—a very encyclopedic reference, for that matter. Here, we'll stick to the ones you're most likely to use with Dreamweaver. Note that the table indicates that some controls inherit from the `Control` class. This is because the parent class of Web Controls is the `Control` class, so Web Controls inherit most of the properties and methods of that class, in addition to having their own properties and methods.

TABLE 5.1: Public Properties Available to Web Controls

Property	Description
AccessKey	Ever noticed those underlined letters in Microsoft applications' dialog boxes? This property gets or sets this letter, or access key, that allows you to quickly navigate to the Web server control.
Attributes	Gets the collection of attributes that correspond to properties on the control.
BackColor	Gets or sets the background color of the control.
BorderColor	Gets or sets the border color of the control.
BorderStyle	Gets or sets the border style of the server control.
BorderWidth	Gets or sets the border width of the control.
ClientID (inherited from Control)	ASP.NET creates an identifier equivalent to the ID attribute for every control (which is overridden by any you create). This property specifies what that value is so you can use it to refer to the control in your code.
Controls (inherited from Control)	Gets a ControlCollection object that represents the child controls for a specified control in the UI (User Interface) hierarchy.
ControlStyle	Gets the style of the control.
ControlStyleCreated	Gets a value indicating whether a Style object has been created for the ControlStyle property.
CssClass	Gets or sets the Cascading Style Sheet (CSS) class rendered by the control when HTML is generated.
Enabled	Gets or sets a value indicating whether the control is enabled.
EnableViewState (inherited from Control)	Gets or sets a value indicating whether the control persists its view state (the view state remains the same), and the view state of any child controls contained by the control during a browser session.
Font	Gets the font properties associated with the control.
ForeColor	Gets or sets the control's foreground color (typically the color of the text).
Height	Gets or sets the height of the control.
ID (inherited from Control)	Gets or sets the programmatic identifier assigned to the control.
NamingContainer (inherited from Control)	Gets a reference to the control's naming container, which creates a unique namespace for differentiating between server controls that have the same Control.ID property value.
Page (inherited from Control)	Gets a reference to the Page instance that contains the control.
Parent (inherited from Control)	Gets a reference to the control's parent control in the page control hierarchy.
Site (inherited from Control)	Gets information about the website to which the control belongs.
Style	Gets a collection of text attributes that will be rendered as a Style attribute on the outer tag of the control.
TabIndex	Gets or sets the tab index of the control.
TemplateSourceDirectory (inherited from Control)	Gets the virtual directory of the Page or UserControl that contains the current control.

Continued on next page

TABLE 5.1 CONTINUED: Public Properties Available to Web Controls

Property	Description
ToolTip	Gets or sets text displayed when the mouse rolls over the control.
UniqueID (inherited from Control)	Gets the unique identifier for the control.
Visible (inherited from Control)	Gets or sets a value that indicates whether a control is rendered as UI on the page.
Width	Gets or sets the width of the control.

Inserting Web Server Controls Using Dreamweaver

There are two principal ways to access a control's attributes (properties). The first is to simply insert the control from Dreamweaver's Insert bar. As shown in Figure 5.1, be sure to choose ASP.NET from the drop-down menu (which defaults to Common). You won't necessarily be able to access all the properties defined in Table 5.1 from the Dreamweaver interface, but 90 percent of the time what Dreamweaver's GUI offers is enough.

FIGURE 5.1:

The ASP.NET Insert bar in Dreamweaver is shown here at the top of the Dreamweaver Interface.

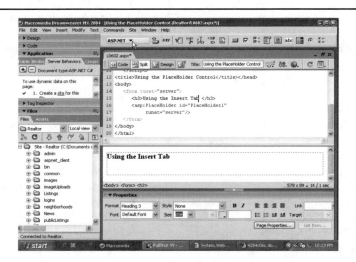

If you don't find the control you want when you roll your mouse over the various ASP.NET icons in the ASP.NET Insert bar, go to the last icon, which looks like this:

This is the second way to add a control. After you've chosen a control, you'll get a dialog box called the Tag Editor, which will present an assortment of different options for the control, depending on which control you've chosen. In Figure 5.2 we've chosen the asp:Label control. You'll find yourself working with the Tag Editor often. If you look at Figure 5.2 you'll see there are five main categories of options. When you click any of them, the options on the right side of the Tag Editor change to reflect options relevant to that category.

FIGURE 5.2:

After you insert a control, the Tag Editor appears.

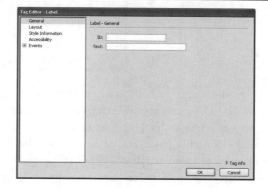

Figure 5.3 shows how these options change when you choose Layout from the options list. Many of these options are intuitive. You'll know what to do simply by looking at them. Others are not so intuitive, but you've got this book, so you're not too worried about that.

FIGURE 5.3:

The Tag Editor options change depending on which option you choose.

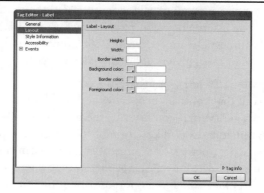

The Tag Editor features comprehensive styling options as well, which you can see in Figure 5.4. Note how in this case, we've chosen the third option, Style Information.

FIGURE 5.4:

Style information
options in the Tag
Editor

FIGURE 5.4:

Style information
options in the Tag
Editor

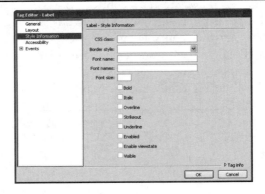

Of course, there's a third way to add a control, and that's to simply start typing it in using Code view. The Dreamweaver interface provides tag completion for most of the ASP.NET control elements. It also displays a list of attributes for that control. This happens when you finish typing a control's name and press the spacebar (and not *until* you press the spacebar). Whenever you need that attributes list, just go into Code view and click on the control, then hit the spacebar, and the attribute list will appear. Double-click the highlighted attribute you want or press Enter, and the attribute shows up in the code, along with double quotes with your cursor in between. Often a group of options will then appear, depending on the type of attribute.

Once you've added a control, you can click on the control within Code view and right-click to obtain a pop-up contextual menu called Edit Tag (the same Tag Editor window that pops up when you insert a new control appears for the ASP.NET control element you wish to edit will show up). In Dreamweaver MX 2004 (but not Dreamweaver MX), you can also click on the control in Design view and right-click to get the same pop-up.

Code view also lets you program a control. As soon as you create your control, you have access to all that control's properties and methods. *Methods* are the object's built-in functions. Think of a car. When you floor it, the car goes really fast. So floor() would be a method that prompts the car to take action of some kind—in this case, to speed off. A really fancy car might have parameters, or arguments, that you can supply to the floor() method, such as "fullSpeed" and "almostFullSpeed", so that when you invoke the method it looks like this: floor("fullspeed"). The important thing to remember is that the method is built in so that you can use it to construct your own function. This process of using other objects and their built-in methods is called *encapsulation*, and it's a key aspect to programming with .NET.

Table 5.2 shows the methods available to the base class of Web Server controls.

TABLE 5.2: Public Methods Available to Web Server Controls

Method	Description
ApplyStyle	Copies any nonblank elements of the specified style to the Web Server control, overwriting any existing style elements of the control.
CopyBaseAttributes	Copies the properties not encapsulated by the Style object from the specified control to the control from which this method is called.
DataBind (inherited from Control)	Binds a data source to a control and to all its child controls.
Dispose (inherited from Control)	Enables a control to perform final clean-up before it is released from memory (for you Java folks, this is similar to garbage clean-up).
Equals (inherited from Object)[no, these need to be capitalized. CW]	Determines whether two object instances are equal.
FindControl (inherited from Control)	Searches the current naming container for a specified control.
GetHashCode (inherited from Object)	Generates a hash function in hashing algorithms and in data structures such as hash tables.
GetType (inherited from Object)	Gets the type of the current instance.
HasControls (inherited from Control)	Determines if the control contains any child controls.
MergeStyle	Copies any nonblank elements of the specified style to the Web Server control, but will not overwrite any existing style elements of the control.
RenderBeginTag	Renders the HTML opening tag of the control into the specified writer, such as an HtmlTextWriter object.
RenderControl (inherited from Control)	Outputs server control content to a provided HtmlTextWriter object and stores tracing information about the control if tracing is enabled.
RenderEndTag	Renders the HTML closing tag of the control into the specified writer such as an HtmlTextWriter object.
ResolveUrl (inherited from Control)	Resolves a relative URL to an absolute URL based on the value passed to the TemplateSourceDirectory property.
ToString (inherited from Object)	Returns a string that represents the current object.

All Web Server controls can be created programmatically or by using Dreamweaver to create an ASP.NET element. For example, to create a Panel control, you create an asp:Panel element. Although the element syntax is not case sensitive (you can write asp:panel or asp:Panel), the syntax used within script tags when you program the controls *is* case sensitive:

```
protected System.Web.UI.WebControls.Label myLabel;
```

WARNING   When creating controls in Dreamweaver, don't forget to surround them with one, and exactly one, form element, with a runat="server" attribute value pair. You can only have one such element per page (which is all you need since you can add as many controls as you want to that one form element).

Getting Information about Controls

This chapter covers the basics of the Web Server Control class of objects, but there's a lot more to them. For instance, each control has its own set of methods unique to it. The Microsoft site has numerous examples to help you once you've finished this chapter. You can access the entire framework of .NET classes at

http://msdn.microsoft.com/library/en-us/cpref/html/cpref_start.asp

If the URL is broken, go to

http://msdn.microsoft.com/netframework/

An invaluable reference, of course, is Google. If you know a method or property name, just enter that name into Google. You'll probably get even better results if you add ASP.NET (preceded by a space). Generally you'll find exactly what you're looking for. You can also go directly to

http://msdn.microsoft.com/library/default.asp?url=/library/en-us/vbcon/html/vbconWebFormsControlsSG.asp.

This includes the library of Web Controls on Microsoft's site.

Another very good resource is www.4guysfromrolla.com.

Text and Layout Controls

When you lay out a page in traditional HTML, you normally use table or div elements to do it. You can still do it that way using ASP.NET, but ASP.NET offers some additional layout options focusing on Web Server controls that are specifically designed to generate HTML-based layout. When you use these controls, ASP.NET reads information about the type of browser that is making a request to your server, and generates the appropriate HTML. If the requesting browser can handle div elements, ASP.NET generates them. If the requesting browser can't handle div elements, ASP.NET generates a more appropriate HTML rendering.

Using the Panel Control

The Panel control is used to host other controls. It's really a layout device, because you can add other controls to it. Think of a Panel control just as you do the HTML div element. In fact, in browsers that support the div element, that's exactly how ASP.NET renders the Panel control.

The Panel control is also good for grouping other controls, as well as (like HTML's `div` element) other HTML elements, because you can nest HTML elements within Panel controls.

Table 5.3 shows the options available to you when you insert a Panel control from Dreamweaver's ASP.NET Insert bar, and how the options presented to you in the resulting dialog box correspond to actual ASP.NET elements generated by Dreamweaver after the insert process is complete. Note that each option corresponds to a tag attribute. This is true with all of the Web Controls you'll work with using Dreamweaver. An example is the option for Back Image URL. When Dreamweaver generates the code from this option, it generates an attribute named `BackImageURL`. There can be no spaces in an element's attribute name, so of course Dreamweaver doesn't generate a `Back Image URL` attribute. It will also add the value you enter into the option field so you'll end up with an element like this:

```
<asp:Panel BackImageURL="myURL.gif" />
```

Note the XML-like syntax of the element, with its closing tag at the end. This is common with all Web Controls that don't contain any actual content. I must stress that this is not XML; it only looks a little like it. Web Controls are not true XML, although you will find tutorials and books that say they are. The `runat=server` attribute value pair, among other things, disqualifies Web Control syntax as XML because ASP.NET will render pages without quotes around the `server` attribute value.

TABLE 5.3: Panel Control/`asp:Panel` Tag Editor Options

Dreamweaver Dialog Box Text Field	Equivalent ASP.NET Element Attribute	Description	Values
ID	ID	Uniquely identifies the element.	A string value you choose.
Back Image URL	`BackImageURL`	Specifies the URL of the background image to display behind the table. If the image is smaller than the table, it's rendered as tiled images.	A string value that represents the location of the image.

When you experiment with this control, view the generated ASP.NET page in your browser and view the source. If you're on a modern browser, you'll see `div` tags instead of `asp:Panel` elements. The `asp:Panel` elements all disappear because they're meant strictly for server consumption; they act as instructions to the server on how to generate HTML.

Using the Label Control

You may have seen web pages that let users do things such as change font sizes. These pages are usually handled by DHTML (Dynamic HTML) scripts, and one serious drawback to them is the issue of browser compatibility. With ASP.NET, you can provide this kind of user-focused functionality (among many other things) on the server side. One way to do that is with the Label control.

Whereas ASP.NET renders Panel controls as `div` elements in browsers that support them, the Label control is treated as a `span` element. You can use the Label control to add text using the Label control's `text` attribute, or you can use it as element content:

```
<asp:Label ID="Label" text="Overidden by element content" runat="server">
➥ <p>Here's a label</p><p>It lives in a Panel.</p></asp:Label>
```

Here, the element content overrides the content in the `text` attribute. The obvious advantage to adding text using element content is that you can add paragraph tags and other HTML elements.

Listing 5.1 shows what a Panel and Label control used together might look like after you've inserted them using Dreamweaver. Dreamweaver generates the appropriate code based on the values you input in the Tag Editor dialog box that appears when you insert the control.

Listing 5.1　　　　**Adding Panel and Label controls to an ASPX page using Dreamweaver**

```
<%@ Page Language="C#" ContentType="text/html" ResponseEncoding="iso-8859-1" %>
<html>
<head>
<title>Panels</title>
<meta http-equiv="Content-Type" content="text/html; charset=iso-8859-1">
<style type="text/css">
<!--
.panel {
   font-family: Verdana, Arial, Helvetica, sans-serif;
   font-size: 10px;
}
-->
</style>
</head>
<body>

<asp:Panel ID="ParentContainer" runat="server"
CssClass="panel"><asp:Label ID="Label"
text="Overidden by element content" runat="server">
<p>Here's a label</p><p>It lives in a
   Panel.</p></asp:Label>
</asp:Panel>
</body>
</html>
```

In Listing 5.1, notice the `CssClass` attribute/value pair highlighted in bold. Now check out the CSS `panel` class definition. When we bind that CSS style to the Panel control named `ParentContainer`, everything contained in that control will inherit the CSS style. This is why the text in Figure 5.5 is in a small sans-serif font. The Label control that resides within the

Panel control inherits the CSS properties from the Panel control. The neat thing is that you can change any of the CSS properties programmatically through user actions, called *events*. That's the beauty of the object model. Each property, such as cssClass, is programmable; it can be changed. For example, by providing an interface allowing users to change the value for cssClass, such as a button, your users can make a page more readable.

FIGURE 5.5:

The Label Control
(inside a Panel
Control) as seen
in a browser

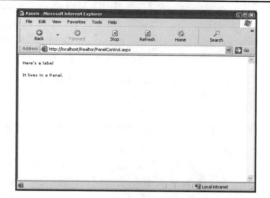

Note that ASP.NET renders the control using div and span elements, as described earlier, when the browser is displayed by the user:

```
<div id="ParentContainer" class="panel">
    <span id="Label"><p>Here's a label</p><p>It lives in a Panel.</p></span>
</div>
```

If you look at Figure 5.6 you can see the relationship between the Panel and Label controls in Listing 5.1 and the HTML that is rendered as output. The Panel control translates to a div element, and the Label control is output as a span element.

FIGURE 5.6:

The Panel control is
output as an HTML
div Element, and the
Label Control is output
as an HTML span
Element.

```
asp:Panel                 ┌─ <div id="ParentContainer" class="panel">
ID="ParentContainer"      │     <span id="Label"> ──────────
                          │        <p>Here's a label</p>
                          │        <p>It lives in a Panel.</p> ├─ asp:Label ID="Label"
                          │     </span>
                          └─ </div>
```

```
<asp:Panel ID="ParentContainer" runat="server"
CssClass="panel">
  <asp:Label ID="Label"
   text="Overidden by element content"
   runat="server">
     <p>Here's a label</p>
     <p>It lives in a Panel.</p>
  </asp:Label>
</asp:Panel>
```

Table 5.4 presents Dreamweaver's Tag Editor options for the Label control and the corresponding attribute/value pairs available to the actual ASP.NET element.

TABLE 5.4: Label Control/asp.Label Tag Editor Options

Dreamweaver Dialog Box Text Field	Equivalent ASP.NET Element Attribute	Description	Values
ID	ID	Uniquely identifies the element.	A string value you choose.
Text	Text	Specifies the text you want your control to display.	Any text value.

Using The PlaceHolder Control to Store Dynamically Created Controls

You can create ASP.NET controls programmatically, or in code. The PlaceHolder control is used to store other ASP.NET controls that are added to a page through code. You'll be learning more about writing your own code in Chapter 7, "Advanced Coding with Dreamweaver MX," but let's look at a typical simple example now, to help illustrate what I'm talking about.

If you create a PlaceHolder control and give it an ID attribute value of PlaceHolder1 to uniquely identify it for ASP.NET's object model, you can then dynamically add a control to it, as shown here:

```
PlaceHolder1.Controls.Add(myControl);
```

In this code fragment, myControl would need to have been created earlier in the code by creating an instance of some Web Server control (or HTML control). Listing 5.2 shows how this is done.

Table 5.5 lists the relevant Dreamweaver choices for the PlaceHolder control in the Tag Editor dialog box, and corresponding attributes in the ASP.NET control.

TABLE 5.5: PlaceHolder Control/asp:PlaceHolder Options

Dreamweaver Dialog Box Text Field	Equivalent ASP.NET Element Attribute	Description	Values
ID	ID	Uniquely identifies the element.	A string value you choose.

Continued on next page

TABLE 5.5 CONTINUED: PlaceHolder Control/asp:PlaceHolder Options

Dreamweaver Dialog Box Text Field	Equivalent ASP.NET Element Attribute	Description	Values
Enable Viewstate	EnableViewState	Specifies whether the control and the controls it stores should persist its view state. If a control's text data comes from a database, you'd want to set this to `false` to reduce server load, since the database data is going to change the view state anyway.	A Boolean `true` or `false`.
Visible	Visible	Specifies whether the control is visible.	A Boolean `true` or `false`.

You can add as many controls as you want into the PlaceHolder control, although in Listing 5.2 I limited it to one.

To begin working with Listing 5.2, create a PlaceHolder control in Dreamweaver by clicking the More Tags icon in the ASP.NET Insert bar. In the Tag Editor, give the ID field the name PlaceHolder1. Now you're ready to write some simple code in Code view. Type in what you see in Listing 5.2, paying special attention to how a new instance of the Button class is created.

Listing 5.2   **Using the PlaceHolder control to store dynamically created ASP.NET controls**

```
<%@ Page Language="C#" %>
<html>
<head>
    <script runat="server">
        void Page_Load(Object sender, EventArgs e)
        {
            Button myButton = new Button();
            myButton.Text = "Button 1";
            PlaceHolder1.Controls.Add(myButton);
        }
    </script>
<title>Using the PlaceHolder Control</title></head>
<body>
    <form runat="server">
        <h3>Using a PlaceHolder Control</h3>
        <asp:PlaceHolder id="PlaceHolder1"
            runat="server"/>
    </form>
</body>
</html>
```

When you create a new object from a class of objects, you have all of that object's properties and methods at your disposal. This is true whether the object is created programmatically, as is the case with the Button control, or by using Dreamweaver to insert a control, as we did here with the PlaceHolder control.

The ASP.NET tab of the Insert bar contains numerous shortcuts to server-side code snippets such as `runat="server"`, bound data tags, and various ASP.NET elements such as the `asp:Button` element. This includes the often-used Page_Load event handler. When you click on the Page_Load icon in the ASP.NET tab of the Insert bar, Dreamweaver inserts a script tag with a `runat="server"` attribute/value pair, and a Page_Load event handler shell script with the correct arguments.

You now have access to all the properties and methods of both the PlaceHolder and Button controls. So you can give the Button a label (my `myButton.Text = "Button 1"`). Then you can add the button to the PlaceHolder control you created (`PlaceHolder1.Controls.Add(myButton)`).

When you're done, your web page should look like that shown in Figure 5.7.

FIGURE 5.7:

A PlaceHolder control storing one Web Server control

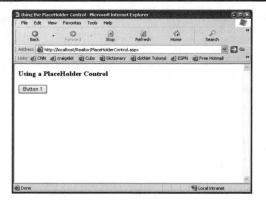

Using TextBox Controls

You've probably worked with text boxes in HTML form elements using the HTML `textarea` element. The TextBox control is similar to these, and can be used as a read-only control for displaying text and as a user input widget on ASP.NET forms.

Table 5.6 shows the relevant Dreamweaver Tag Editor options and corresponding attributes in the `asp.TextBox` control.

TABLE 5.6: TextBox Control/asp:TextBox Tag Editor Options

Dreamweaver Dialog Box Text Field	Equivalent ASP.NET Element Attribute	Description	Values
ID	ID	Uniquely identifies the element.	A string value you choose.
Text	Text	Specifies the text you want your control to display.	Any text value.
Text Mode	TextMode	Specifies how the text should be displayed.	MultiLine, which displays multiple lines and renders a vertical scroll bar.
			Password, which displays as asterisks when a user enters something into the field.
			SingleLine (the default).
Rows	Rows	Used when the TextMode attribute is set to MultiLine, this specifies the number of rows in the text box, which determines the height of the control.	An integer specifying the number of rows the control spans in height.
Columns	Cols	Used when the TextMode attribute is set to MultiLine, this specifies the number of columns in the text box, which determines the width of the control.	An integer specifying the number of columns the control spans in width.
Max Length	MaxLength	Specifies the maximum number of characters allowed in the text box.	An integer specifying the number of allowable characters.
Auto Postback	AutoPostBack	When false (the default), postback to the server doesn't occur until the page is posted by either a button or another web control whose AutoPostBack attribute is set to true. If set to true, changes are posted back to the server as soon as user makes a change to the input.	A Boolean true or false.
Read-only	ReadOnly	Specifies whether you can change the control programmatically.	A Boolean true or false.
Wrap	Wrap	Specifies whether word wrapping takes place. If false, a horizontal scrollbar appears.	A Boolean true or false. Default is true.

Continued on next page

TABLE 5.6 CONTINUED: TextBox Control/asp:TextBox Tag Editor Options

Dreamweaver Dialog Box Text Field	Equivalent ASP.NET Element Attribute	Description	Values
Enable Viewstate	EnableViewState	Specifies whether the control and the controls it stores should persist its view state (the state of the page when it was last processed on the server). If a control's text data comes from a database, you'd want to set this to false to reduce server load, since the database data is going to change the view state anyway.	A Boolean true or false.
Visible	Visible	Specifies whether the control is visible.	A Boolean true or false.

Note that the size of the text box is affected by the way you style it. Consider the following TextBox control, which uses some styling attributes accessed using the Style Information category in Dreamweaver's Tag Editor:

```
<asp:Panel ID="ParentContainer" runat="server" CssClass="panel">
  <asp:TextBox BackColor="#CCCCFF" BorderColor="#0099CC"
  Columns="20" Font-Names="Frutiger, Verdana, Arial,
  Helvetica, sans-serif" Font-Size="10px"
  ForeColor="#333333" ID="TextBox" MaxLength="15"
  Rows="20" runat="server"
Text="Some Default Text" TextMode="MultiLine" />
</asp:Panel></form></body>
```

Now, look at how this is output to HTML using CSS:

```
<textarea name="TextBox" rows="20" cols="20" id="TextBox" style="color:#333333;
  background-color:#CCCCFF;
  border-color:#0099CC;
  font-family:Frutiger,Verdana,Arial,Helvetica,
  sans-serif;font-size:10px;">
    Some Default Text
</textarea>
```

If you change the style in the Tag Editor to, say, a font size of 25px, you'll notice quite a bit of difference in the size of the text box. The text box will grow, as shown in Figures 5.8 and 5.9, to accommodate the new font size even though you're setting the size using the Rows and Columns attributes.

FIGURE 5.8:

Compare this TextBox control with the one in Figure 5.9, which is bigger because a larger font size is used.

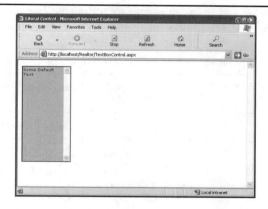

FIGURE 5.9:

The larger text size in this box makes the entire control bigger when the Row and Columns attribute values are set.

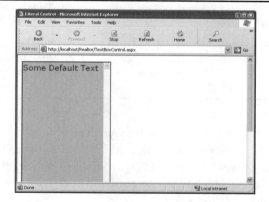

Using the Literal Control

You can use a Literal control to display unstyled text. This is similar to the Label control, except the Label control provides styling characteristics. The only reason to use the Literal control is that you want to work with the control's content dynamically, as when you are changing the text or inserting text from a database.

When you choose this control from Dreamweaver's ASP.NET Insert bar, you'll notice that the left side of the Tag Editor doesn't include the usual styling choices that other controls display. You can cheat, however, by using styling on a Panel control, and then including the Literal control within the Panel control. Or, of course, you can simply use a Label control when you want styling attributes.

Table 5.7 shows the relevant Dreamweaver Tag Editor options for a Literal control, and corresponding attributes for the ASP.NET control.

TABLE 5.7: Literal Control/asp.Literal Tag Editor Options

Dreamweaver Dialog Box Text Field	Equivalent ASP.NET Element Attribute	Description	Values
ID	ID	Uniquely identifies the element.	A string value you choose.
Text	Text	Specifies the text you want your control to display.	Any text value.
Enable Viewstate	EnableViewState	Specifies whether or not the control and the controls it stores should persist its view state. If a control's text data comes from a database, you'd want to set this to false to reduce server load, since the database data is going to change the view state anyway.	A Boolean true or false.
Visible	Visible	Specifies whether the control is visible.	A Boolean true or false.

To see what I mean when I say you can control text programmatically with this control, insert a Literal control in a new ASPX file from the Dreamweaver interface and give it an ID name of LiteralControl. Then insert a Button control and give it the ID attribute chngText. In the Text field, you can enter anything you wish (I entered Change It!!). In Dreamweaver's Tag Editor, expand Events and click onClick, and enter changeIt_Click into the text field on the right.

Click OK, and Dreamweaver will generate the following code (except for the form tags, which you'll need to enter yourself).

```
<form runat="server">
<asp:Literal ID="LiteralControl" runat="server"
Text="This is a Literal Control" />
<div>
<asp:Button ID="chngText" runat="server" Text="Change It!"
 OnClick="changeIt_Click" />
</div>
</form>
</body>
```

TIP   If you create the button first, Dreamweaver will insert the form tag with runat="server", but not if you insert a Web Control that does not process forms directly.

WARNING Make sure that you first include a form tag with a runat="server" attribute/value pair, and that everything you put onto the page is contained in the form. Otherwise, you'll get an error message saying the runat="server" attribute is missing. Also, you must not have more than one form tag with runat="server", or ASP.NET will throw an error.

Next, type in the following code, right under the page directive and before the HTML element:

```
<script runat="server">
protected void changeIt_Click(Object Src, EventArgs E)
{
   LiteralControl.Text="Thank you for changing this text";
}
</script>
```

Save your page as an .aspx file, naming it whatever you wish. When you load it into your browser and click the button, the text in the literal control changes to "Thank you for changing this text."

Button and Hyperlink Controls

You can probably imagine why buttons play a critical role in ASP.NET applications. After all, you've got to click to go somewhere, and usually the thing you click when processing a form is a button of some kind. Of course, there's nothing stopping you from using a regular HTML Submit button. It will work for processing ASP.NET forms when you use the runat="server" attribute/value pair. But web control buttons have a few advantages that come into play when you start to build more complicated code. They offer a couple of events in addition to the usual inherited events associated with most web-page controls:

- The Click event is raised whenever a button control is clicked, and there is no command name bound to that control through the button's CommandName property. You use the EventArgs type in a method argument when this event is raised.

- The Command event is raised when a button is clicked and a command name exists through an assignment via the button's CommandName property. You use the CommandEventArgs type in a method argument when this event is raised.

We'll be exploring these issues momentarily. But first, there are three types of button controls available to you as an ASP.NET developer:

The Button control   This is the standard button. It mimics a Submit button in traditional HTML, except that ASP.NET's event-driven architecture is, of course, fundamentally different in its handling of forms. This button helps you directly manage that process.

The LinkButton control   Using this control is similar to writing a JavaScript link. If you're not familiar with that process, just know that in HTML you can write a link using JavaScript within the `href` attribute—for example, `<a href="javascript:myFunction(this)">`. The LinkButton control matches that functionality, except you don't have to write any of the JavaScript yourself. The LinkButton control handles it all for you, generating a JavaScript-driven link mechanism based on your definition of the control.

The ImageButton control   This control performs the same tasks as a Button control, except its rendering is dictated by an image bitmap assigned through its `ImageUrl` attribute. At runtime, this creates an input element in the HTML output using a `type="image"` attribute/value pair.

Hyperlink controls, though they're not derivative of the Button class (and therefore don't inherit from that class of objects), perform a task somewhat similar to buttons, in that they direct the browser somewhere. They're really just regular hyperlinks on steroids. Their chief advantage is that you can set link properties in server code and/or use data binding to specify a link's URL. This is useful when you're displaying a list of items and you want each item to have a link to a detail page. You'll see more on this technique when we examine the usage of Hyperlink controls.

Using Button Controls

If you've been waiting to do some simple ASP.NET programming, here is where you start getting into the thick of it. To really get a feel for how buttons work, you'll need to roll up your sleeves and get ready to work in Dreamweaver's Code view, so you can write some genuine ASP.NET scripting routines. All the action takes place in the `script` tags, usually within the HTML `head` elements.

WARNING   When writing server-side script within script elements, don't forget the `runat="server"` attribute value pair. Your scripts won't work without it.

Button Control

The Button control posts forms to the server. This control is derived directly from the `System.Web.UI.WebControls.WebControl` class but has some special properties of its own. They're listed in Table 5.8.

TABLE 5.8: Button Control/asp:Button Tag Editor Options

Dreamweaver Dialog Box Text Field	Equivalent ASP.NET Element Attribute	Description	Values
ID	ID	Uniquely identifies the element.	A string value you choose.
Text	Text	This is what the user sees on the face of the button.	A string value you choose.
Command Name	CommandName	Gets or sets the command name associated with the Button control that is passed to the Command event.	A string value representing the name of the command.
Command Argument	CommandArgument	Gets or sets an optional parameter passed to the Command event along with the associated CommandName.	A string value representing the argument of the command.

A Button control can have a use as simple as posting a form to a server. Or it can serve as a centerpiece to more expansive programming operations. An example of this is shown in Listing 5.3. You can assign commands to buttons, and then use the buttons to perform certain tasks that you define with the commands.

TIP You don't actually have to use buttons to post data to a server, believe it or not. You can use the AutoPostBack="true" attribute/value pair in such form widgets as check boxes and radio buttons, and the form gets posted to the server as soon as the user enters a value.

If Listing 5.3 seems intimidating, don't worry, most of the rest of this chapter actually gets easier, because we don't want to get too involved yet in code writing.

Listing 5.3   **Using a CommandName to "bubble up" events to a container**

```
<html>
<head>
    <script language="C#" runat="server">
        void Page_Load(Object Sender, EventArgs e) {
            if (!Page.IsPostBack) {
                ArrayList values = new ArrayList();
                values.Add(new PositionData(
                ➡ "Chuck White", "111 Crawford Street", "$600,000"));
```

```
            values.Add(new PositionData(
            ➥ "John Black", "616 Bailey Blvd", "$300,000"));
            values.Add(new PositionData(
            ➥ "Michael Orange", "112 Citrus Way", "$750,000"));
            repeater1.DataSource = values;
            repeater1.DataBind();
        }
    }

    void Repeater1_ItemCommand(object sender, RepeaterCommandEventArgs e) {
        lbl.Text = "<b>" + e.CommandName
        ➥ + ": " + e.CommandArgument + "</b>";
    }
    public class PositionData {

        private string name;
        private string address;
        private string listingPrice;

        public PositionData(
        ➥ string name,  string address, string listingPrice) {
            this.name = name;
            this.address = address;
            this.listingPrice = listingPrice;
        }

        public string Name {
            get {
                return name;
            }
        }

        public string Address {
            get {
                return address;
            }
        }

        public string ListingPrice {
            get {
                return listingPrice;
            }
        }
    }

    </script>
<title>Buttons!!!</title></head>
<body>
    <h3>A Button Using Commands</h3>
    <p></p>

    <form runat=server>
      <font face="Verdana" size="-1">
```

```
<asp:Repeater id=repeater1
  onitemcommand="Repeater1_ItemCommand"
   runat="server">
     <ItemTemplate>
        <asp:Button id=btnAddress Text="Address"
        CommandName="Address" CommandArgument='<%#
       ➥DataBinder.Eval(Container.DataItem,
         ➥"Address") %>' runat="server" />
          
        <asp:Button id=btnPrice Text="Price"
         CommandName="Price" CommandArgument='<%#
       ➥DataBinder.Eval(Container.DataItem,
         ➥"ListingPrice") %>'
          runat="server" />
          
        <asp:Label id=lblCompany Text='<%#
DataBinder.Eval(Container.DataItem, "Name") %>'
   Font-Bold="true" runat=server />
            <p>
        </ItemTemplate>
     </asp:Repeater>
     <asp:Label id=lbl runat="server" />
   </font>
  </form>
</body>
</html>
```

In studying Listing 5.3, focus most of your attention on the array list's named values (in bold). In ASP.NET, whenever you create an object in code using `script` tags, you have to identify that object. Since we're creating an array list, we need to say so:

```
ArrayList values = new ArrayList();
```

Notice, too, the `Page_Load` event handler. You use this whenever you want something to happen when a page is loaded into the browser. Everything that happens on a .NET page requires some event to trigger it, whether it's a page loading or, as in the next event handler, the reading of a command from a control, in this case a repeater control. This is why I called Listing 5.3 a "bubble events" operation, because the repeater control contains buttons whose command events "bubble up" to the repeater control that contains the buttons.

You then create your own class named `ListingInfo`. Just as you can create an instance of, say, an `ArrayList`, or even a `Button`, programmatically, you can create an instance of a class you create. Our class here basically just consists of some strings made publicly available (available to the entire application).

The binding between the public classes you write and the button commands takes place in the Button control's `CommandArgument` attribute:

```
CommandArgument='<%# DataBinder.Eval(Container.DataItem, "ListingPrice") %>'
```

You've probably spotted another new item, the Container class. Containers are objects that encapsulate and track components. I don't mean visual containers, like panels, but rather logical containment from a programming standpoint. You can refer to specific items in a container, but here's where the massive object model of .NET can foil everything—in order to use these objects, you have to get familiar with the object model, or at least learn how to navigate your way around the classes in order to reference items and subclasses. Unfortunately, there's no shortcut for that, and all you can do is practice.

Luckily, in this chapter we're plunging into some fairly advanced stuff pretty early on, simply for the sake of providing a glimpse into the power of buttons. You can employ this as you wish. If you're ready to take it further, you can. But if you need to get acquainted with Dreamweaver's processes and learn to rely on its code-generation facilities, you can do that here, too.

Figure 5.10 shows how the product of Listing 5.3 should look in a browser after some user interaction.

FIGURE 5.10:

The product of Listing 5.3, rendered in the browser after the user clicks the second Address button

ImageButton Control

The ImageButton control does the same thing as a Button control. The only difference is that it is represented visually by a bitmap image instead of a text label. The properties you can define for this control are shown in Table 5.9.

TABLE 5.9: ImageButton Control/asp:ImageButton Tag Editor Options

Dreamweaver Dialog Box Text Field	Equivalent ASP.NET Element Attribute	Description	Values
ID	ID	Uniquely identifies the element.	A string value you choose.
Image URL	ImageURL	The URL indicating location of the image for the button.	A string value representing the URL of the image.

Continued on next page

TABLE 5.9 CONTINUED: ImageButton Control/asp:ImageButton Tag Editor Options

Dreamweaver Dialog Box Text Field	Equivalent ASP.NET Element Attribute	Description	Values
Alternate Text	AlternateText	Mimics the behavior of the `alt` attribute in an HTML `img` tag, providing alternate text for browsers that don't support images.	A string value to replace the image.
Command Name	CommandName	Gets or sets the command name associated with the Button control that is passed to the Command event.	A string value representing the name of the command.
Command Argument	CommandArgument	Gets or sets an optional parameter passed to the Command event along with the associated CommandName.	A string value representing the argument of the command.

Make sure when you write your code for an ImageButton event handler that you use the right delegate in your method arguments. Most buttons use the `EventArgs` delegate, but for the ImageButton control you must use the `ImageClickEventArgs` delegate, as shown in bold in Listing 5.4.

Listing 5.4   Using an ImageButton control to change text values in a TextBox control

```
<%@ Page Language="C#" ContentType="text/html" ResponseEncoding="iso-8859-1" %>
<html>
<head>
<script runat="server">
  void ClickMe_Click(Object Source, ImageClickEventArgs E)
  {
  TextBox.Text = "Thank you for taking this opportunity
➡to change the default text.";
  }
</script>
<title>Buttons!!</title>
<meta http-equiv="Content-Type" content="text/html;
 charset=iso-8859-1">
<style type="text/css">
<!--
.panel {
    font-family: Verdana, Arial, Helvetica, sans-serif;
    font-size: 10px;
}
-->
</style>
</head>
<body>
<form runat="server">
```

```
<table width="100%" border="0" >
  <tr align="left" valign="top">
    <td width="33%"><asp:TextBox BackColor="#CCCCFF" BorderColor="#0099CC"
Columns="20" Font-Names="Frutiger, Verdana, Arial, Helvetica, sans-serif" Font-
Size="20px" ForeColor="#333333" ID="TextBox" MaxLength="15" Rows="20"
runat="server" Text="Some Default Text" TextMode="MultiLine" /></td>
    <td width="67%"><asp:ImageButton AlternateText="Click Me!" ID="ClickMe"
OnClick="ClickMe_Click" ImageUrl="ClickMe.jpg" runat="server" /></td>
  </tr>
</table>
</form></body>
</html>
```

Notice in Listing 5.4 that there is no page-load event handler because we don't need one. Instead, a click event called ClickMe_Click is included in the script tag. Then it is called using the OnClick event in the ImageButton control's ASP.NET element (in bold in Listing 5.4). Figure 5.11 shows the output of Listing 5.4 in a browser. Figure 5.12 shows the same web page after the user clicks the ImageButton control.

FIGURE 5.11:

The ImageButton control as rendered by a browser

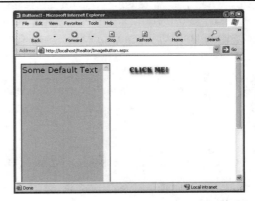

FIGURE 5.12:

When the ImageButton control is clicked by the user, the text in the text field changes.

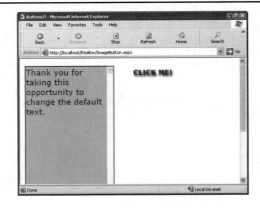

LinkButton Control

A LinkButton control handles business logic on the client side, instead of on the server. It does this by generating JavaScript. The button appears to the user as a hyperlink. Table 5.10 compares the attributes you can enter in Dreamweaver to the actual attribute names of the `asp:LinkButton` element.

TABLE 5.10: LinkButton Control/`asp:LinkButton` Tag Editor Options

Dreamweaver Dialog Box Text Field	Equivalent ASP.NET Element Attribute	Description	Values
ID	ID	Uniquely identifies the element.	A string value you choose.
Text	Text	The text you want to appear in your link.	A string value.
Command Name	CommandName	Gets or sets the command name associated with the Button control that is passed to the Command event.	A string value representing the name of the command.
Command Argument	CommandArgument	Gets or sets an optional parameter passed to the Command event along with the associated CommandName.	A string value representing the argument of the command.

Let's compare the output from a LinkButton control to an ImageButton control, remembering that a regular Button control acts just like an ImageButton except for one thing. The difference between a LinkButton control and other buttons is that the business logic is handled in client-side JavaScript. Look at Listing 5.5. You can see that it's essentially the same as the listing example provided for the ImageButton control in Listing 5.4. The server script, in fact, is exactly the same, except for the EventArgs argument, which replaced the ImageClickEventArgs argument that you use with an ImageButton control.

Listing 5.5   **Using a Link Button to generate client-side DHTML**

```
<%@ Page Language="C#" ContentType="text/html" ResponseEncoding="iso-8859-1" %>
<html>
<head>
<script runat="server">
  void ClickMe_Click(Object Source, EventArgs E) {
  TextBox.Text = "Thank you for taking this
➥ opportunity to change the default text.";
  }

</script>
<title>Buttons!!</title>
<meta http-equiv="Content-Type" content="text/html;
```

```
charset=iso-8859-1">
<style type="text/css">
<!--
.panel {
    font-family: Verdana, Arial, Helvetica, sans-serif;
    font-size: 10px;
}
-->
</style>
</head>
<body>
<form runat="server">
<table width="100%" border="0" >
  <tr align="left" valign="top">
    <td width="33%"><asp:TextBox BackColor="#CCCCFF" BorderColor="#0099CC"
Columns="20" Font-Names="Frutiger, Verdana, Arial, Helvetica, sans-serif" Font-
Size="20px" ForeColor="#333333" ID="TextBox" MaxLength="15" Rows="20"
runat="server" Text="Some Default Text" TextMode="MultiLine" /></td>
    <td width="33%"> <asp:LinkButton ID="ClickMe" runat="server"
OnClick="ClickMe_Click" Text="Click Me!"></asp:LinkButton></td>
  </tr>
</table>
</form></body>
</html>
```

The difference is in the final HTML output. Listing 5.6 shows the output from using the LinkButton control in Listing 5.5.

Listing 5.6   The LinkButton control generates client-side JavaScript

```
<html>
<head>
<title>Buttons!!</title>
<meta http-equiv="Content-Type" content="text/html;
 charset=iso-8859-1">
<style type="text/css">
<!--
.panel {
    font-family: Verdana, Arial, Helvetica, sans-serif;
    font-size: 10px;
}
-->
</style>
</head>
<body>
<form name="_ctl0" method="post" action="LinkButton.aspx" id="_ctl0">
<input type="hidden" name="__EVENTTARGET" value="" />
<input type="hidden" name="__EVENTARGUMENT" value="" />
```

```
<input type="hidden" name="__VIEWSTATE"
value="dDwtMTA4NTQ1MDMwMTs7PldEbgDHM3kONThZ
    ➥EukwVgq5Qw1E" />
<script language="javascript">
<!--
    function __doPostBack(eventTarget, eventArgument) {
        var theform = document._ctl0;
        theform.__EVENTTARGET.value = eventTarget;
        theform.__EVENTARGUMENT.value = eventArgument;
        theform.submit();
    }
// -->
</script>

<table width="100%" border="0" >
  <tr align="left" valign="top">
    <td width="33%"><textarea name="TextBox" rows="20" cols="20" id="TextBox"
style="color:#333333;background-color:#CCCCFF;border-color:#0099CC;font-
family:Frutiger,Verdana,Arial,Helvetica,sans-serif;font-size:20px;">Thank you
for taking this opportunity to change the default text.</textarea></td>
    <td width="33%"> <a id="ClickMe"
href="javascript:__doPostBack('ClickMe','')">Click Me!</a></td>
  </tr>

</table>
</form></body>
</html>
```

On the other hand, when using other button controls, such as ImageButton or Button, the business logic is all handled on the server. Examine the HTML in Listing 5.7 that is generated from Listing 5.4, which featured the ImageButton control. You'll see no client-side JavaScript at all because the text changes when the page is posted back to the server, which then sends the changed page. This means you don't need to worry if JavaScript on the client browser works or not, since it's all handled on the server side.

Listing 5.7   **ImageButton control output containing no client-side logic**

```
<html>
<head>
<title>Buttons!!</title>
<meta http-equiv="Content-Type" content="text/html; charset=iso-8859-1">
<style type="text/css">
<!--
.panel {
    font-family: Verdana, Arial, Helvetica, sans-serif;
    font-size: 10px;
}
-->
```

```
</style>
</head>
<body>
<form name="_ctl0" method="post" action="ImageButton.aspx" id="_ctl0">
<input type="hidden" name="__VIEWSTATE"
value="dDwxMTIONTc4OTg7O2w8Q2xpY2tNZTs+PqaVQ8eo
    ➥NGbTpoIiCAC88p7RD9f2" />
<table width="100%" border="0" >
  <tr align="left" valign="top">
    <td width="33%"><textarea name="TextBox" rows="20" cols="20" id="TextBox"
style="color:#333333;background-color:#CCCCFF;border-color:#0099CC;font-
family:Frutiger,Verdana,Arial,Helvetica,sans-serif;font-size:20px;">Some Default
Text</textarea></td>
    <td width="33%"><input type="image" name="ClickMe" id="ClickMe"
src="/Realtor/ClickMe.jpg" alt="Click Me!" border="0" /></td>
  </tr>
</table>
</form></body>
</html>
```

Using HyperLink Controls

HyperLink controls and the various button controls, although they do similar things, are very different: Button controls post data to the server, and HyperLink controls do not. Instead, they only navigate to a target URL. You can do some cool stuff, of course, such as linking to detail pages from a list of items (in fact, this is probably going to be your most common use for this control).

Table 5.11 serves as your guide for comparing Dreamweaver's Tag Editor fields and the element attributes for the HyperLink control.

TABLE 5.11: HyperLink Control/asp:HyperLink Tag Editor Options

Dreamweaver Dialog Box Text Field	Equivalent ASP.NET Element Attribute	Description	Values
ID	ID	Uniquely identifies the element.	A string value you choose.
Navigate URL	NavigateURL	The target URL.	A string value specifying the URL.
Image URL	ImageURL	You can display an image for the hyperlink instead of text. Use this attribute to specify the URL location of the image you want to display	A string value specifying the URL.

Continued on next page

TABLE 5.11 CONTINUED: HyperLink Control/asp:HyperLink Tag Editor Options

Dreamweaver Dialog Box Text Field	Equivalent ASP.NET Element Attribute	Description	Values
Target	Target	The same as the target attribute in traditional HTML elements, this attribute specifies whether the URL opens in a new window, the same window as the containing web page, or a top or parent window.	_top, _parent, _self, _blank, _new_blank and _new open new windows without any frames; _top renders the content in the current window without any frames; and _parent renders the content in the parent window of the page containing the hyperlink.
Text	Text	This is the text that is surrounded by the link and tells the user where they're going.	A string value.

Rather than show a simple HyperLink control that goes to some static URL, let's look at a more likely scenario—a HyperLink control that links to a URL and requests specific data from a database:

```
<asp:hyperlink ID="UpdateHyperlink"
 NavigateUrl='<%# "UpdateListings.aspx?MLSNumber=" +
➥ ListingsProc.FieldValue("MLSNumber", Container) %>'
  runat="server" Text="Update This Listing">
</asp:hyperlink>
```

Let's see how this works in an application.

The application in this case consists of an administrative page for a realtor who wants to make changes in her listings. Figure 5.13 shows the first step in this process. She edits some fields and then clicks the Update button. From there, she is taken to a "success" page, which indicates that the changes she made were successful (Figure 5.14). This page contains a Hyperlink control ("Update This Listing") that links to the listing she just finished editing. This is made possible by using the control's NavigateUrl attribute, which allows you to interact directly with the database to get the user to the correct listing.

FIGURE 5.13:

Updating this screen takes the user to a "success" page.

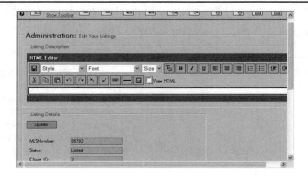

FIGURE 5.14:

The "success" page contains a Hyperlink control that takes the user back to the proper page for further edits.

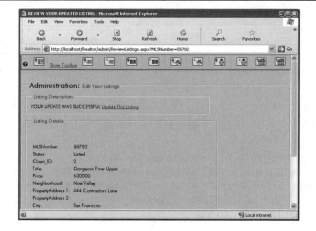

When the user clicks the Hyperlink control, she is then taken to the correct page, as shown in Figure 5.14. In the code, note the attribute value in the `NavigateUrl` attribute:

```
NavigateUrl='<%# "UpdateListings.aspx?MLSNumber=" +
➥ ListingsProc.FieldValue("MLSNumber", Container) %>'
```

You're going to find out more about the nitty-gritty of this particular code in Chapter 7, "Working with Validation Controls." The important thing to remember at this point is that you can use the `NavigateUrl` attribute to create dynamic links and interact with a database to retrieve specific information for a page.

Listing 5.8 shows how this process works. The actual code for this page happens to be quite a bit longer. You can download this code from at `www.sybex.com`. The relevant file is called `ReviewListings.aspx`, which is in the `admin` directory.

Listing 5.8   **Using a Hyperlink control to send a user to a detail page**

```
<%@ Register TagPrefix="MM" Namespace="DreamweaverCtrls"
Assembly="DreamweaverCtrls,version=1.0.0.0,
    ➥publicKeyToken=836f606ede05d46a,culture=neutral" %>
<%@ Page language="c#"  %>
<!DOCTYPE HTML PUBLIC "-//W3C//DTD HTML 4.0 Transitional//EN" >
<HTML>
    <HEAD>
        <title>REVIEW YOUR UPDATED LISTING</title>
            <MM:DATASET id=ListingsProc Debug="true"
            CommandText="ListingQueryImagesAndClientsWithParams"
            DatabaseType='<%#
            ➥System.Configuration.ConfigurationSettings.
            ➥AppSettings["MM_CONNECTION_DATABASETYPE_
            ➥mdriscollString"]%>'
            ConnectionString='<%# System.Configuration.
            ➥ConfigurationSettings.AppSettings
            ➥["MM_CONNECTION_STRING_mdriscollString"]%>'
            CreateDataSet="true" IsStoredProcedure="true"
            runat="Server">
              <PARAMETERS>
                <PARAMETER Direction="ReturnValue"
                Type="Int" Name="@RETURN_VALUE" />
                <PARAMETER Direction="Input" Type="VarChar"
                Name="@MLSNumber"
                Value='<%# ((Request.QueryString["MLSNumber"]
                ➥!= null) &amp;&amp; Request.QueryString
                ➥["MLSNumber"].Length > 0)) ?
                ➥Request.QueryString["MLSNumber"] : "" %>'
              />
            </PARAMETERS>
          </MM:DATASET>
      <MM:PAGEBIND id="Pagebind1" runat="server"
      PostBackBind="false"></MM:PAGEBIND>
    </HEAD>
    <body bgColor="#d6d3ce" leftMargin="0" topMargin="0">
      <form id="Sample" action="ReviewListings.aspx"
      method="post" runat="server">
      <div align="left">YOUR UPDATE WAS SUCCESSFUL
        <asp:hyperlink ID="UpdateHyperlink"
        NavigateUrl='<%# "UpdateListings.aspx?MLSNumber=" +
        ➥ListingsProc.FieldValue("MLSNumber",
        ➥Container) %>'
        runat="server" Text="Update This Listing">
        </asp:hyperlink>
      </div>
<fieldset>
```

```
<legend>Listing Details</legend>
    <table>
      <tr>
        <td>MLSNumber:</td>
        <td>
<%# ListingsProc.FieldValue("MLSNumber", Container) %>
</td>
      </tr>
<tr>
    <!- Additional listing details here ->

    </tr>
    <tr>
  </table>
</fieldset>
</form>
</body>
</HTML>
```

Even though we're covering things like Dreamweaver's DataSet component later in the book (in Chapter 6), let's look at a few things now to start getting used to these concepts. Remember that ASP.NET is all about objects. And, as I've mentioned several times throughout the book, the best architecture features a highly encapsulated design where objects can be dropped in at will.

In this case, even the SQL query is essentially dropped in through a stored procedure called `ListingQueryImagesAndClientsWithParams`. Wow, that's a mouthful. This stored procedure is basically just a SQL query acquiring some information about all the listings in the Realtor database, plus any associated images. (You'll find that the Realtor application, which most of this book is based on, generally contains long stored procedure names to help you identify them. You'll want to use shorter names for your own stored procedures.)

TIP   A good convention when naming stored procedures is to prefix the names with something like usp_, followed by the name: usp_someProcedure. This helps identify them as stored procedures created by you, as opposed to some other source, such as SQL Server itself or another user. In production environments, I like to incorporate my initials, in a cwsp_ prefix. Many development shops will have their own internal conventions that you'll have to follow, of course, but most of them will also have DBAs doing the hard-core SQL development anyway.

You'll see how to create this DataSet control in Chapter 6, but it's useful to examine its operation here. The DataSet control is called `ListingsProc`. Macromedia has a whole slew of properties and methods that are exposed when this object is created. Look through the highlighted code in Listing 5.8 and you can see how often the `ListingsProc` object is used. Pay attention to its use in the `NavigateURL` attribute of the Hyperlink control. That should look familiar to you, because I used it in the HyperLink control example.

As you can see, the key to using this control in this application is the `FieldValue()` method, which you'll find in the `NavigateURL` attribute value and again later, as we iterate through the data to display different columns of data from the database table. The `FieldValue()` method grabs specific columns from the table and displays data from those columns. It finds the specific row you need by associating the request with the `MLSNumber` found in the query string, which is sent through a form field in a previous page. This process is similar to how we use the Hyper-Link control. Here, we check to see if the `MLSNumber` from the same query string (in bold) matches a value in the database table under the `MLSNumber` column. If it does, the URL will navigate to the `UpdateListings.aspx` page and display the appropriate data. Take another look:

```
NavigateUrl='<%# "UpdateListings.aspx?MLSNumber=" +
➥ListingsProc.FieldValue("MLSNumber", Container) %>'
```

Building the string value can be a little tricky, as you can see. Start off with a single quote. Then you can add a double-quote to hold the URL value. Next, you end the quote and concatenate the value of the first string with the value from the `FieldValue()` method, which evaluates to, in this specific case, MLSNumber 55782. So the URL actually resolves to

```
UpdateListings.aspx?MLSNumber=55782
```

Check Boxes and Radio Controls

Check boxes and radio controls have been in use for a long time to get users' choices about things. In ASP.NET, these elements can be used to let users make Boolean selections (true/false or yes/no, for example).

The functionality of the two elements is quite similar, and radio buttons are in fact derived from the CheckBox Control class, which is derived, in turn, from the List Control class.

Using CheckBox Controls

You can use CheckBox controls to grab Booleans from users. Generally, if you want to generate results from user input, you'll probably want to go to CheckBoxList controls because they're easier to program.

Table 5.12 shows the CheckBox control Tag Editor options and the corresponding attribute/value pairs in the `asp:CheckBox` element.

TABLE 5.12: CheckBox Control/asp.CheckBox Tag Editor Options

Dreamweaver Dialog Box Text Field	Equivalent ASP.NET Element Attribute	Description	Values
ID	ID	Uniquely identify the element.	A string value you choose.
Text	Text	The text label for the checkbox.	A string value.
Text Alignment	TextAlign	Specifies whether the label generated by the Text attribute is on the right or the left side of the text box.	Left or Right.
Auto Postback	AutoPostBack	When false (the default), postback to the server doesn't occur until the page is posted by either a button or another control whose AutoPostBack attribute is set to true. If set to true, changes are posted back to the server as soon as user makes a change to the input.	Boolean true or false.
Checked	Checked	Specifies whether the check box is checked. Default value is false.	Boolean true or false.

When you view the CheckBox control using Dreamweaver's Properties panel, you also see an additional choice, besides Checked and Unchecked, that isn't presented in the Tag Editor. Look at Figure 5.15 to see what I'm talking about—it's the Dynamic option. When you choose this option, you get the pop-up menu shown in Figure 5.16.

FIGURE 5.15:

The Properties panel contains a Dynamic option for adding a match against a database value to determine if a check box should be checked.

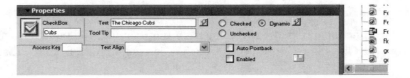

FIGURE 5.16:

Choosing the Dynamic Checked Button reveals a pop-up menu allowing you to access a database.

In the Dynamic Check Box pop-up, there's a little lightning-flash icon beside the Check If text box. Click on this, and you get access to the columns of whatever database tables you've made accessible to your web page. In this brief example, let's assume just one column (CUserName) from the table is available, as shown in Figure 5.17. Select that, and click OK. Then close the Dynamic Check Box dialog box by clicking OK.

FIGURE 5.17:

The Dynamic Data Editor inserts code into the CheckBox control's Checked attribute value according to the choices you make.

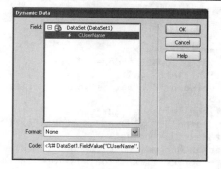

Then you're done, and you'll get a piece of code that looks roughly like this:

```
<asp:CheckBox Checked='<%# (DataSet1.FieldValue("CUserName",
 ➥Container) == Request.QueryString["CUserName"]) ?
 ➥true : false %>' ID="Cubs"  AutoPostBack="false"
  runat="server" OnCheckedChanged="CheckChanged_Click"
   Text='The Chicago Cubs'></asp:CheckBox>
```

Notice in Listing 5.9 that there's an event triggered by the OnClick event of each check box. The event handler, called CheckChanged_Click, contains one basic statement that says if the Yanks check box is checked, the message "Your favorite team is the New York Yankees" will be displayed. As an exercise after you've studied the code, try to add to this listing so that the other check boxes display results when they are checked.

Listing 5.9   **Evaluating check box choices to output messages to the user**

```
<%@ Page Language="C#" ContentType="text/html" ResponseEncoding="iso-8859-1" %>
<html>
<head>
<script runat="server">
  void CheckChanged_Click(Object Source, EventArgs E) {
    if (Yanks.checked)
    {
  message.Text = "Your favorite team is " + Yanks.Text;
  }
  }

</script>
<title>Buttons!!</title>
```

```
<meta http-equiv="Content-Type" content="text/html; charset=iso-8859-1">
<style type="text/css">
<!-
.panel {
    font-family: Verdana, Arial, Helvetica, sans-serif;
    font-size: 10px;
}
->
</style>
</head>
<body>
<form runat="server">
<table width="100%" border="0" >
  <tr align="left" valign="top">
    <td colspan="3">What is your favorite baseball team?</td>
    </tr>
  <tr align="left" valign="top">
    <td width="30%"> <asp:CheckBox ID="Yanks"
    AutoPostBack="true"
   OnCheckedChanged="CheckChanged_Click"
   runat="server" Text="The New York Yankees" /></td>
    <td width="45%"><asp:CheckBox ID="Cubs"
    AutoPostBack="true" runat="server"
   OnCheckedChanged="CheckChanged_Click"
    Text='The Chicago Cubs'></asp:CheckBox></td>
    <td width="25%"><asp:CheckBox ID="Giants"
   AutoPostBack="true" runat="server"
    OnCheckedChanged="CheckChanged_Click"
     Text='The Yomiuri Giants' /></td>
    </tr>
  <tr align="left" valign="top">
    <td colspan="3"><asp:Label ID="message"
    runat="server"></asp:Label> </td>
    </tr>
</table>
</form></body>
</html>
```

In order to enhance this code to produce additional messages for the other check boxes, all you need to do is add additional if statements after the first one completes, like this:

```
    if (Yanks.checked)
    {
message.Text = "Your favorite team is " + Yanks.Text;
    }
    if (Cubs.checked)
    {
message.Text = "Your favorite team is " + Cubs.Text;
    }
```

There are other ways to accomplish this, as you'll see in the next section.

Using RadioButton Controls

Radio controls are derived from CheckBox controls and do pretty much the same thing, except you can use the RadioButton control's GroupName attribute to group radio buttons together and force a user to make only one selection. Radio buttons that share a common group name turn off whenever a different button within the group is clicked.

Table 5.13 shows the properties available to this control.

TABLE 5.13: RadioButton Control/asp:Radio Tag Editor Options

Dreamweaver Dialog Box Text Field	Equivalent ASP.NET Element Attribute	Description	Values
ID	ID	Uniquely identifies the element.	A string value you choose.
Text	Text	The text label for the checkbox	A string value.
Text Alignment	TextAlign	Specifies whether the label generated by the Text attribute is on the right or the left side of the text box.	Left or Right.
Auto Postback	AutoPostBack	When false (the default), postback to the server doesn't occur until the page is posted by either a button or another control whose AutoPostBack attribute is set to true. If set to true, changes are posted back to the server as soon as user makes a change to the input.	Boolean true or false.
Checked	Checked	Specifies whether the check box is checked. Default value is false.	Boolean true or false.
Group Name (accessible only in the Property panel in Dreamweaver 2004)	GroupName	Used to group radio buttons together so that when one is clicked the others are unclicked.	A string value.

Listing 5.10 achieves the same basic functionality as Listing 5.9.

If you want to add to this listing, rather than writing several if statements as I encouraged you to do in the section on CheckBox controls, you can simply write a separate event handler for each RadioButton control. (You can use this method with CheckBox controls, too.)

Listing 5.10 **Writing event handlers for each Radio control**

```
<%@ Page Language="C#" ContentType="text/html" ResponseEncoding="iso-8859-1" %>
<html>
<head>
<script runat="server">
  void CheckChanged_Click(Object Source, EventArgs E)
{
    if (Yanks.Checked)
    {
  message.Text = "Your favorite team is " + Yanks.Text;
  }
  }
    void CheckChanged_Click2(Object Source, EventArgs E)
{
    if (Cubs.Checked)
    {
  message.Text = "Your favorite team is " + Cubs.Text;
  }
  }
    void CheckChanged_Click3(Object Source, EventArgs E)
{
    if (Giants.Checked)
    {
  message.Text = "Your favorite team is " + Giants.Text;
  }
  }
</script>
<title>Radio Buttons!!</title>
<meta http-equiv="Content-Type" content="text/html;
 charset=iso-8859-1">
<style type="text/css">
<!--
.panel {
   font-family: Verdana, Arial, Helvetica, sans-serif;
   font-size: 10px;
}
-->
</style>
</head>
<body>
<form runat="server">
<table width="100%" border="0" >
  <tr align="left" valign="top">
    <td colspan="3">What is your favorite baseball team?</td>
    </tr>
  <tr align="left" valign="top">
    <td width="30%"> <asp:RadioButton OnCheckedChanged="CheckChanged_Click"
  ID="Yanks" runat="server" AutoPostBack="true"
```

```
        Text="The New York Yankees" GroupName="Baseball" /></td>
        <td width="29%"><asp:RadioButton
        OnCheckedChanged="CheckChanged_Click2"
        ID="Cubs" AutoPostBack="true"  runat="server"
        Text='The Chicago Cubs' GroupName="Baseball" /></td>
        <td width="41%"><asp:RadioButton
         OnCheckedChanged="CheckChanged_Click3"
          AutoPostBack="true"  ID="Giants" runat="server"
          Text='The Yomuiri Giants' GroupName="Baseball" /></td>
    </tr>
    <tr align="left" valign="top">
    <td colspan="3"><asp:Label ID="message"
    runat="server"></asp:Label> </td>
    </tr>
</table>
</form></body>
</html>
```

Figure 5.18 shows how these controls are rendered when displayed in a browser using Listing 5.10.

FIGURE 5.18:

Radio buttons displayed using the RadioButton control

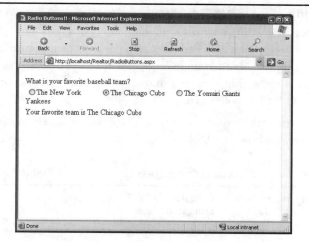

ListBox Controls

When users are interacting with forms on your website, you will often want to present a more compact selection than what check boxes and radio buttons provide. If you are offering a choice from among the 50 U.S. states, for example, you don't want to clutter up your pages with 50 check boxes. So you create a drop-down list from which your users can make selections. This category of widget is called a ListBox control, and it includes the following controls:

- CheckBoxList controls
- RadioButtonList controls
- DropDownList controls
- ListBox controls

These follow the following class hierarchy in .NET:

```
System.Web.UI.WebControls.ListControl
System.Web.UI.WebControls.CheckBoxList
System.Web.UI.WebControls.DropDownList
System.Web.UI.WebControls.ListBox
System.Web.UI.WebControls.RadioButtonList
```

The key to using these controls is understanding how to use the ListItem control, which represents each individual item within any data-bound list control.

Using the ListItem Control

A ListItem control stores individual items in a data-bound control such as a ListBox. Many times you'll want to create ListItem controls programmatically through script, but you can also simply add individual ListItem controls using the `asp:ListItem` element. You have to place them within elements that expect them, such as `asp:CheckBoxList`, `asp:ListBox`, and `asp:RadioButtonList` controls.

ListItem controls have two attributes immediately available through the Dreamweaver Tag Editor, as shown in Table 5.14.

TABLE 5.14: ListItem Control/`asp:ListItem` Tag Editor Options

Dreamweaver Dialog Box Text Field	Equivalent ASP.NET Element Attribute	Description	Values
ID	ID	Uniquely identifies the element.	A string value you choose.
Text	Text	The text for describing the item.	A string value.

There's an important attribute Dreamweaver omits from its Tag Editor interface: the Value attribute, which can be used to distinguish between what you want sent as a form value and what the user actually sees. The Value attribute is very important, particularly when working with a database. If you want to make this distinction, use the Value attribute to indicate what value the form should pass, and use the Text attribute to represent that value to the user. You'll have to insert your ListItem control first, then go into Code view and add the Value attribute manually.

There are three ways you can insert ListItem controls into a web page:

- Loading the values from a database
- Loading them through code using an array
- Using the `asp:ListItem` element

You'll learn how to set up ListItem controls dynamically in the next section. I'll demonstrate first how to set up simple ListItem controls using the `asp:ListItem` element in a CheckBoxList control, and then how to set up ListItem controls dynamically using a RadioListButton control.

Using CheckBoxList and RadioList Controls to Group Controls

The main difference between using CheckBox controls and CheckBoxList controls (and RadioButton vs. RadioButtonList) is that the latter is essentially a *list control*. This makes it easy to program against a selected box, since ASP.NET stores all the items of a list control as part of a collection, which is like an array. You can always access individual members of an array or collection. In this case, you can access a specific member of a group of ListItems in a CheckBoxList control by simply saying, "I want the one(s) checked by the user." You'll see how to do this programmatically in Listing 5.11.

Table 5.2 shows the attributes made available to CheckBoxList and RadioButtonList controls through Dreamweaver's Tag Editor, and their corresponding attributes.

TABLE 5.15: Tag Editor Options for CheckBoxList Control/`asp:CheckBoxList` and RadioButtonList/`asp:RadioButtonList`

Dreamweaver Dialog Box Text Field	Equivalent ASP.NET Element Attribute	Description	Values
ID	ID	Uniquely identify the element.	A string value you choose.
Text Alignment	`TextAlign`	Specifies whether the label generated by the `Text` attribute is on the right or the left side of the text box.	`Left` or `Right`.
Auto Postback	`AutoPostBack`	When `false` (the default), postback to the server doesn't occur until the page is posted by either a button or another control whose `AutoPostBack` attribute is set to `true`. If set to `true`, changes are posted back to the server as soon as user makes a change to the input.	Boolean `true` or `false`.

Continued on next page

TABLE 5.15 CONTINUED: Tag Editor Options for CheckBoxList Control/asp:CheckBoxList and RadioButtonList/asp:RadioButtonList

Dreamweaver Dialog Box Text Field	Equivalent ASP.NET Element Attribute	Description	Values
Data Member	DataMember	Used when there is more than one table in the data source, to identify a specific table to bind to the control.	A string denoting the name of the table.
Data Source	DataSource	A data source that is used to populate the control.	The object that provides the data.
Repeat Columns	RepeatColumns	The number of columns to display before a new row begins.	An integer indicating the number of columns.
Repeat Layout	RepeatLayout	Indicates whether the layout structure is within a layout or the flow of the document.	Flow, Table.
Selected	Selected	Specifies whether an item has been selected. Default is false.	Boolean true or false.

CheckBoxLists and RadioButtonLists are convenient because you can do a lot with little code. For example, you can avoid writing a lot of conditionals (using statements like the if conditional) by using a list control of some kind. Figure 5.19 illustrates how choosing a check box in a CheckBoxList control displays a message related to the choice.

FIGURE 5.19:

When a user makes a selection within the CheckBoxList control, a message is displayed.

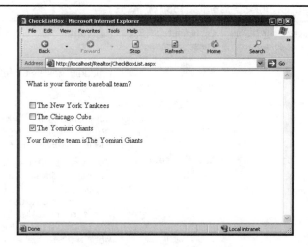

Listing 5.11 shows how to put this together. All it does is create a CheckBoxList control with an event handler; then it defines what happens when the user checks a check box.

Listing 5.11   **Evaluating user selections from a list of check boxes**

```
<%@ Page Language="C#" ContentType="text/html" ResponseEncoding="iso-8859-1" %>
<html>
<head>
<script runat="server">
  void teamsChanged_Click(Object Source, EventArgs E) {
    StringBuilder str = new StringBuilder();
    foreach(ListItem l in teams.Items)
    {
      if (l.Selected == true)
      {
        str.Append("Your favorite team is" + l.Value);
      }
      if (str.Length == 0)
        {
          message.Text = "Your favorite team is not
➥listed?";
        }
        else
        {
        message.Text = str.ToString();
        }
    }
  }
</script>
<title>Buttons!!</title>
<meta http-equiv="Content-Type" content="text/html;
charset=iso-8859-1">
</head>
<body>
<form runat="server">
<table width="100%" border="0" >
  <tr align="left" valign="top">
    <td colspan="3">What is your favorite baseball team?</td>
    </tr>
  <tr align="left" valign="top">
    <td width="30%"> 
    <asp:CheckBoxList AutoPostBack="true" ID="teams"
    runat="server"
    OnSelectedIndexChanged="teamsChanged_Click">
        <asp:listItem ID="Yanks"  runat="server"
        Text="The New York Yankees" />
        <asp:listItem ID="Cubs" runat="server"
        Text='The Chicago Cubs'>
        <img src="cubs.jpg"></asp:listItem>
        <asp:listItem ID="Giants" runat="server"
        Text='The Yomiuri Giants' />
      </asp:CheckBoxList>
```

```
      </tr>
    <tr align="left" valign="top">
      <td colspan="3"><asp:Label ID="message"
      runat="server"></asp:Label> </td>
      </tr>
  </table>
  </form></body>
  </html>
```

Pay special attention first to the `asp:CheckBoxList` element. It has an `ID` attribute of `teams`. As with all things in .NET, this `ID` attribute is important, because it gives you access to all the control's attributes and methods.

Earlier I mentioned that list controls have a collection of items, and that you can always access the individual items in a collection. The following code fragment loops through the collection of items in the `teams` CheckBoxList:

```
    foreach(ListItem l in teams.Items)
```

Here, `l` is a variable that stores an item temporarily as the `foreach` statement loops through the list of items. The `foreach` statement is followed by parentheses, which hold the statements that say what happens for each item. In this case it's pretty simple, but the parentheses could hold a lot of things. Before anything happens, though, a new instance of the `StringBuilder` class called `str` is created. The `StringBuilder` class is similar to the `String` class of objects, except you can't add to strings of characters in a `String` object (although you can simulate adding strings by creating new String objects out of your original—but using `StringBuilder` is much faster).

First, the code checks to see if the item `l` is selected. If it is, we can add to the empty `StringBuilder` object, which we do with this:

```
    str.Append("Your favorite team is" + l.Value);
```

The rest of the script is reasonably self-explanatory.

Populating List Items Dynamically from Databases

You can also populate RadioButtonList and CheckBoxList controls using database information by clicking on the List Items button in the Properties panel. (First, make sure you've already selected the RadioButtonList or CheckBoxList control you wish to edit). Figure 5.20 shows you the List Items dialog box that appears.

FIGURE 5.20:

Use the List Items
dialog box to enter
database values.

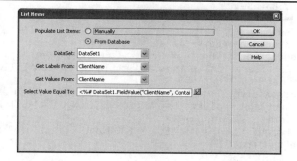

Assuming we make a dataset in Dreamweaver called `DataSet1`, we then enter the fields from which we want to populate the database. This is easy, because the fields that were selected when we created the dataset, chosen by our SQL code, show up in the List Items dialog box, so it's just a matter of choosing them from the drop-down lists. In this instance, I chose the `ClientName` field from a table of client names. This results in a RadioButtonList control that looks like this:

```
<% DataRadio.SelectedIndex =
  ➥DataRadio.Items.IndexOf(DataRadio.Items.
  ➥FindByValue(DataSet1.FieldValue
  ➥("ClientName", null) )); %>
<asp:RadioButtonList  DataTextField="ClientName"
 DataValueField="ClientName" ID="DataRadio"
 runat="server" RepeatColumns="4" RepeatLayout="table"
 DataSource="<%# DataSet1.DefaultView %>"></asp:RadioButtonList>
```

Notice the added piece in bold just above the control. Dreamweaver adds that when you've finished working in the List Items dialog box. Also, notice that Dreamweaver adds some special code to the `DataSource` attribute (also in bold). This identifies the data source from where the data is originating, so that ASP.NET can populate the controls.

Listing 5.12 shows our finished control.

Listing 5.12   **Populating a RadioButtonList control from a database**

```
<%@ Page Language="C#" ContentType="text/html" ResponseEncoding="iso-8859-1" %>
<%@ Register TagPrefix="MM" Namespace="DreamweaverCtrls"
   Assembly="DreamweaverCtrls,version=1.0.0.0,
   ➥publicKeyToken=836f606ede05d46a,culture=neutral" %>
```

```
<MM:DataSet
id="DataSet1"
runat="Server"
IsStoredProcedure="false"
ConnectionString='<%# System.Configuration.
➡ConfigurationSettings.AppSettings["MM_CONNECTION_STRING_
➡ mdriscollString"] %>'
DatabaseType='<%# System.Configuration.Configuration
➡Settings.AppSettings["MM_CONNECTION_DATABASETYPE_
➡mdriscollString"] %>'
CommandText='<%# "SELECT * FROM dbo.ClientInfo" %>'
Debug="true"
></MM:DataSet>
<MM:PageBind runat="server" PostBackBind="true" />
<html>
<head>

<title>Dynamic Radio Buttons</title>
<meta http-equiv="Content-Type" content="text/html;
 charset=iso-8859-1">
</head>
<body>
<form runat="server">
<% DataRadio.SelectedIndex =
DataRadio.Items.IndexOf(DataRadio.Items.FindByValue(
➡DataSet1.FieldValue("ClientName", null) )); %>
<asp:RadioButtonList  DataTextField="ClientName" DataValueField="ClientName"
ID="DataRadio"
    runat="server" RepeatColumns="4" RepeatLayout="table" DataSource="<%#
DataSet1.DefaultView %>"></asp:RadioButtonList>
</form>
</body>
</html>
```

I used a RadioButtonList control here, but you'll find the same general principle works for CheckBoxList controls and ListBox controls, as well. The key is to take advantage of Dreamweaver's built-in facilities for managing data—in this case, selecting the control in Dreamweaver and simply clicking the List Items button in the Properties panel to add your data to your list options.

Using ListBox and DropDownList Controls

The DropDownList control displays single items from a list that drops down when the user clicks it. The user can only select one item at a time, in contrast to a ListBox control where the user can select multiple items. You use both of these in the same way as the RadioButtonList and CheckBoxList controls. In other words, you can populate them from a database or an array, or you can write out each list item individually using the asp:ListItem element.

Table Controls

Dreamweaver supports all of ASP.NET's table controls, which can be used to manage table data dynamically. Table controls are similar to the data controls discussed in Chapter 3, "Working with Databases: An Introduction," except they're not as full featured. Also, they can actually be used in conjunction with data-bound controls because you can put other controls inside them, which you can't do with the data-bound controls.

Working with the Table Control

Many developers have used JavaScript to render tables dynamically by building arrays and filling table cells from those arrays. You can now do the same thing much more easily using a .NET Table control—with the added benefit that you can do it all on the server and not have to worry about whether a user's browser will choke on your extravagant JavaScript code.

Do you prefer working in Design mode? One distinct disadvantage to using the Table control in Dreamweaver in Design mode is that you can't actually work with the control visually. You have to hand code everything. The obvious answer to that, if you need your table to act as an ASP.NET server control that you can work with just like other design elements in Dreamweaver, is to simply create a standard HTML Table control, and give it an attribute/value pair of runat="server". You'll rarely need the dynamic capabilities of a Table control without also wanting to venture into the more complete data-bound controls, so the HTML table control should meet most of your needs when you're simply using tables for layouts. If you don't have any events associated with your table at all, of course, you can simply use the HTML table element.

So, when you want to actually use the Table control as a layout tool, you have to do it by hand in the code editor and then check out your results in the browser. But that's okay, because when you use this control it's probably because you want to build tables programmatically anyway, and the only real way to do that is to get your hands dirty and write some code.

To create a Table control, click on Tag Chooser from the Insert bar. If the Insert bar is in Common mode, expand the ASP.NET Tags folder in the left-hand panel and choose Web Server controls. Double click asp:Table, or click it and then click Insert. The Tag Editor will pop up and present you with three initial property options. Table 5.16 compares these options with their corresponding attributes.

TABLE 5.16: Table Control/asp:Table Tag Editor Options

Dreamweaver Dialog Box Text Field	Equivalent ASP.NET Element Attribute	Description	Values
ID	ID	Uniquely identifies the element.	A string value you choose.
Back Image URL	BackImageURL	Specifies the URL of the background image to display behind the table. If the image is smaller than the table, it's rendered as tiled images.	A string value that represents the location of the image.
Grid Lines	Gridlines (see Warning)	Gets or sets a value that specifies the style of gridline for the Table control.	None, Horizontal, Vertical, Both.

WARNING When you choose Grid Lines in the Tag Editor, Dreamweaver inserts the attribute Gridline (without the s), instead of Gridlines, so you need to correct it by hand for it to work properly.

The Layout options in the Tag Editor will look familiar to anyone who's worked with HTML tables. These options include the usual type of table attributes, such as horizontal alignment (using the HorizontalAlign attribute) and cell padding (using the CellPadding attribute).

When you choose Style Information, the Tag Editor offers several styling options. ASP.NET will render these as CSS styles if the target browser understands CSS. Otherwise, it will use basic HTML to mimic as best it can the look you want to achieve, based on the information you've provided.

```
<asp:Table BorderColor="#CCCCCC" BorderStyle="dashed"
  BorderWidth="1" Font-Name="Verdana" Font-Size="10"
  HorizontalAlign="Left" ID="table" runat="server"
  Width="300">
```

Look at the attribute/value pairs in the preceding code, then compare them to the HTML rendering in the browser by viewing the HTML source. You'll see the following style sheet made for the table:

```
style="border-color:#CCCCCC;border-width:1px;
border-style:Dashed;font-family:Verdana;
font-size:10pt;width:300px;"
```

As with most controls, you can also assign a style sheet by filling in the CSS Stylesheet field in the Tag Editor.

Managing Row Sets

Like data-bound controls, Table controls render to the requesting client's browser as good, old-fashioned HTML tables. The Table control uses the TableRow and TableCell controls to initiate the dynamic rendering of tables. This is in contrast to data-bound controls, which use templates. TableRow and TableCell controls are important because you can access them programmatically to draw your table in your user's web browser, as you'll see in the example code used for this control.

Using the TableRow Control to Set Table Row Properties

Generally, it's likely that you'll use the TableRow control and its relative, the TableCell control, programmatically. Of course you can also, if you want, create them using Dreamweaver by inserting them into the Table control element. Honestly, though, there's not much of a reason to do this, because if you're using tables this way and not creating them dynamically, it's better to use either a regular HTML `table` element or an HTML Table control.

If for some reason you do decide to insert a TableRow control through Dreamweaver, simply choose `asp:TableRow` from the Web Server controls in the Tag Chooser as shown in Figure 5.21.

FIGURE 5.21:

Choosing
`asp:TableRow`
from the Tag
Chooser

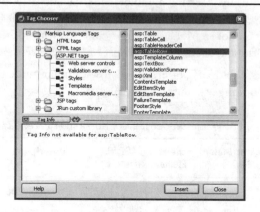

First, make sure your cursor is inside the `asp:TableRow` element, like this (it's in bold in the last line):

```
<asp:Table BorderColor="#CCCCCC" BorderStyle="dashed"
BorderWidth="1" Font-Name="Verdana"
    Font-Size="10" HorizontalAlign="Left"
    ID="table" runat="server"
    Width="300">|</asp:Table>
```

When you're done, your final code should look something like this:

```
<asp:Table BorderColor="#CCCCCC" BorderStyle="dashed"
  BorderWidth="1" Font-Name="Verdana" Font-Size="10"
  HorizontalAlign="Left" ID="table" runat="server"
  Width="300"><asp:TableRow ID="tRow" runat="server">
</asp:TableRow></asp:Table>
```

There's only one field to worry about in the General attributes section of the Tag Editor, and that's the ID field. You'll also find some layout and styling options similar to those in the Table control.

Using the TableCell Control to Set Table Cell Properties

After setting the rows, the TableCell control is the next logical step in the development of the table. The process for inserting this control is the same as for TableRow, only this time, be sure your cursor is in the TableRow element. Then, simply insert the TableCell control from the Insert bar if you're not adding them programmatically.

Using the TableHeaderCell Control to Label Rows

Even if you're creating tables dynamically, you may want to label your columns manually first. You do this by inserting a TableHeaderCell control into your Table control. TableHeaderCell is accessed just like the Table control, by choosing it from the list of Web Server controls in the Tag Chooser. Make sure your cursor is within the asp:Table element, and then choose asp:TableHeaderCell from the list of Web Server controls.

Here's Table 5.17, offering the now-familiar guide to Dreamweaver Tag Editor options and corresponding attribute/value pairs.

TABLE 5.17: TableHeaderCell Control/asp:TableHeaderCell Tag Editor Options

Dreamweaver Dialog Box Text Field	Equivalent ASP.NET Element Attribute	Description	Values
ID	ID	Uniquely identifies the element.	A string value you choose.
Text	Text	Specifies the column header.	A string that acts as a label for the column.
Rowspan	RowSpan	Specifies the number of rows in height the table cell spans.	An integer specifying the number of rows.
Columnspan	ColumnSpan	Specifies the number of columns in width the table cell spans.	An integer specifying the number of columns.

I've mentioned that you can create table cells programmatically; generally, that's why you'd use the Table control in the first place. So let's see how that works in Listing 5.13. Figure 5.22 shows what the code looks like in a browser.

The Table control displaying a directory of files

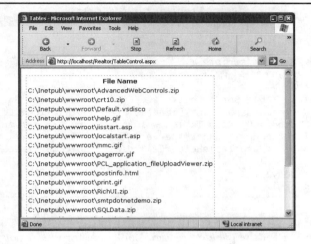

Listing 5.13 **Using the Table control to display a directory's files**

```csharp
<%@ Import Namespace="System.Collections" %>
<%@ Import Namespace="System.IO" %>
<%@ Page Language="C#" ContentType="text/html" ResponseEncoding="iso-8859-1" %>
<html>
<head>
<title>Tables</title>
<meta http-equiv="Content-Type"
content="text/html; charset=iso-8859-1">
<script language="C#" runat="server">
    //create a string to hold the current file name
    public string FileName;
    void Page_Load(Object sender, EventArgs e) {
        if (!IsPostBack)
        {
            //set directory and array
            Directory myDirectory;
            ArrayList values = new ArrayList();
            //get files
            String [] files = Directory.GetFiles("C:\\Inetpub\\wwwroot\\","*");
//iterate through list, replace path info,
//and add to the listbox with the Add method.
            for(int i=0;i<files.Length;i++){
            FileName = files[i];
            values.Add (FileName);
                TableRow rw = new TableRow();
```

```
                TableCell cText = new TableCell();
                Label lbl = new Label();
                lbl.Text = FileName;
                cText.Controls.Add(lbl);
                rw.Cells.Add(cText);
                table.Rows.Add(rw);
                }

        }
    }
      </script>
</head>
<body>
<asp:Table BorderColor="#CCCCCC" BorderStyle="dashed" BorderWidth="1" Font-
Name="Verdana" Font-Size="10" HorizontalAlign="Left" ID="table" runat="server"
Width="300"><asp:TableRow ID="tRow" runat="server"><asp:TableHeaderCell
ID="tHeader1" runat="server" Text="File
Name"></asp:TableHeaderCell></asp:TableRow></asp:Table>

</body>
</html>
```

A public string is declared that is available to the rest of the web page. Then an event handler for the page is created. Look next for the instantiation of a `Directory` object. You may have noticed that there is no instance declared. In other words, we didn't do this:

```
Directory myDirectory = new Directory();
```

This is because a `Directory` is a static class, which means that you don't create a new instance of it, since you won't be destroying it as usual when your program is finished running. Normally, when you create a new instance of an object, the object disappears after a user ends the session (unless you take steps to prevent that). In this case, however, we're accessing files from a directory on the hard drive. If we create a new directory, that directory sticks around and doesn't disappear after the session ends.

Our next step, then, is to get the files from the directory by using the built-in `GetFiles` method, and put them into a string array. Then we loop through the files and store their names in an array list named `values`. After that, the code just iterates through the array and creates new table rows and cells for each item in the array, and dumps a corresponding Label control into each cell.

Creating a Calendar Control in Dreamweaver

The Calendar control is the ultimate fighting machine in the web control category. The plus side of this control is that it is very powerful. On the negative side, harnessing that power can require substantial hand-coding. There are a lot of resources out there for doing so. The first and most obvious place to go is the Macromedia site, which has a gentle introduction to coding the Calendar component using Dreamweaver, at

`www.macromedia.com/devnet/mx/dreamweaver/articles/aspnet_calendar.html`

To create a Calendar control, go to the Insert bar and choose the ASP.NET tab. Expand the ASP.NET Tags folder and click Web Server Controls, which is the second choice from the top. Choose `asp:Calendar` from the list on the right, and click Insert. You'll get a dialog box like the one in Figure 5.23. Give the control a name in the ID text field. You'll notice a large number of fields. You can scan Table 5.18 to compare what these fields mean in relation to the corresponding attribute values in the Calendar Control.

FIGURE 5.23:

The Tag Editor for the Calendar control

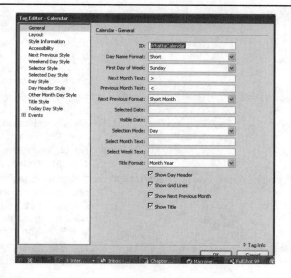

When presented with the Tag Editor dialog box for creating the Calendar control, it helps to understand what each choice or field in the dialog box corresponds to in the code that Dreamweaver generates. It's generally pretty obvious, as you've seen in the tables presented throughout this chapter. Table 5.18 describes each field in the General category of the Calendar control in the Tag Editor, and the corresponding attribute for the control.

WARNING As for other controls, make sure to add a `form` tag to your web page with the `runat="server"` attribute/value pair. If your Calendar control doesn't live within the `form` tag, you'll get an error message that says something like `Control 'IDofControl' of type 'Calendar' must be placed inside a form tag with runat="server"`.

TABLE 5.18: Calendar Control/asp:Calendar Tag Editor Options

Dreamweaver Dialog Box Text Field	Equivalent ASP.NET Element Attribute	Description	Values
ID	ID	Uniquely identifies the element.	A string value you choose.
Day Name Format	DayNameFormat	Formats the day of the week. The default, Short, is the first three letters of the week (e.g. Sun).	Full, Short, FirstLetter, FirstTwoLetters.
First Day of Week	FirstDayOfWeek	Day of week displayed in first column. Default value is default, which displays according to the server's system.	Default, Sunday, Monday, Tuesday, etc.
Next Month Text	NextMonthText	Text label used for navigating to the next month when ShowNextPrevMonth is set to true. The default value is > (which renders as >), but you can use any text you want.	A string value you choose.
Previous Month Text	PrevMonthText	Text label used for navigating to the previous month when ShowNextPrevMonth is set to true. The default value is < (which renders as <), but you can use any text you want.	A string value you choose.
NextPreviousFormat	NextPrevFormat	Determines the format of the next and previous months. When using CustomText, you enter the text you want using the NextMonthText and PrevMonthText attributes.	CustomText, FullMonth, ShortMonth.
Selected Date	SelectedDate	Represents a single date selected when the control is initialized. The value must be a DateTime datatype.	A DateTime value.
Visible Date	VisibleDate	Any date in the month to be displayed. The value must be a DateTime datatype.	A DateTime value.
Selection Mode	SelectionMode	Specifies whether users can select a single day; a single day or a full week; a single day, or full week, or a full month; or nothing. Default value is Day.	Day, DayWeek, DayWeekMonth, None.

Continued on next page

TABLE 5.18 CONTINUED: Calendar Control/asp:Calendar Tag Editor Options

Dreamweaver Dialog Box Text Field	Equivalent ASP.NET Element Attribute	Description	Values
Select Month Text	SelectMonthText	When SelectionMode = "DayWeekMonth", this value acts as text label for the month selection in the selector column. Default is >> (which renders as >>). When label is clicked, the month is selected in the calendar.	A string value you choose.
Select Week Text	SelectWeekText	When SelectionMode = "DayWeekMonth", this value acts as text label for the month selection in the selector column. Default is > (which renders as >). When label is clicked, the week is selected in the calendar.	A string value you choose.
Title Format	TitleFormat	Specifies the formatting at the top of the calendar. Default is MonthYear.	Month, MonthYear.
Show Day Header	ShowDayHeader	Specifies whether days of week are labeled. Default is true.	true, false.
Show Grid Lines	ShowGridLines	Specifies whether gridlines are rendered in the calendar. Default is false.	true, false.
Show Next Previous Month	ShowNextPrevMonth	Specifies whether next- and previous-month navigation labels are visible. Default is true.	true, false.
Show Title	ShowTitle	Specifies whether the title is visible. Default is true. If false, next- and previous-month navigation labels are not visible.	true, false.

You'll also find a dizzying array of styling attributes in the Calendar control's Tag Editor. I suppose you *could* go through each of the dialog boxes available for styling this control, but the minutia is daunting. You're probably better off writing one or more CSS style sheets, and assigning them as needed through the Calendar control's Tag Editor. You do that by assigning a specific class to the appropriate style in the Tag Editor.

For example, if you select Style Information first, as shown in Figure 5.24, you'll see options for styling that involve both CSS styles (you enter the name of your style class there) and other styling information, such as Font Name and Border Style. These are also CSS values. The difference between using the CSS Styles field and the other styling fields is that CSS styles will generate a `class="yourstyle"` attribute/value pair. The other fields will generate inline style sheets (or, in older browsers, things like FONT tags).

FIGURE 5.24:

Style Information options for the Calendar Control in the Tag Editor

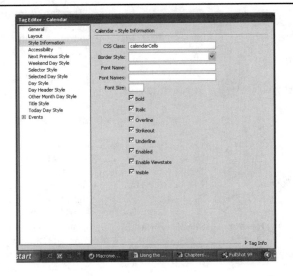

Wrapping Up

Once you begin to get comfortable with programming Web Server controls, you're well on your way to becoming an ASP.NET developer. You have a very powerful tool at your disposal in Dreamweaver. Don't rely on it to do everything for you, however, because as your development tasks become more challenging, the crutch will break and you'll be left without the proper knowledge you need to troubleshoot applications. It's important to use Dreamweaver wisely, and to learn about how ASP.NET's Web Server controls are structured. Watch how Dreamweaver generates code. Ask yourself why it does what it does.

Now that you know how to set up forms in ASP.NET, you'll need to validate them, so that when users enter invalid data, you can catch it before they've done too much work. You do this with Validation controls, and we'll take a look at them in the next chapter.

CHAPTER 6

Working with .NET Validation Controls

- Understanding validation controls

- Comparing values using a CompareValidator control

- The RequiredFieldValidator control

- The RangeValidator control

- The RegularExpressionValidator control

- The ValidationSummary control

Every web developer who has developed forms has encountered the necessity of reminding the user that certain form fields are mandatory or need special characters. Sometimes a form field, such as a password field, needs to be filled twice with the exact same entry; and if a user doesn't do that, you need to generate a reminder of that requirement. This process is called *form validation*, which until recently required scripting on the client or server. Actually, it still does require scripting, but the scripts are generated automatically in ASP.NET using .NET's *validation controls*.

Validation in .NET is handled by an abstract class called the BaseValidator class. Because the BaseValidator class itself inherits from the TextControl base class, the controls we'll be looking at in this chapter are ASP.NET elements, each of which contains a `Text` attribute that is used to display messages about validation problems to the user. These controls are

- The CompareValidator control
- The RequiredFieldValidator control
- The RangeValidator control
- The RegularExpressionValidator control
- The ValidationSummary control

In this chapter we'll take a look at these controls and see how easy it has become to wire up robust validation services by combining Dreamweaver's visual interface tools with .NET's validation controls.

Understanding Validation Controls

When users enter the "wrong" information in a form, the last place they want to hear about it is after they've submitted the form. It's much better, if possible, to give them feedback in real time. At least, you'll want to provide a mechanism through which, if they input information incorrectly, the data they originally inserted in the form will remain there along with the error message telling them what's wrong.

In addition, when data entered into a form goes to a database, it often must be in a certain format so that the right kind of data gets entered into the database.

Maintaining data state in this way is called *persistence*. Persistence is one of the features of .NET validation controls, which help guide the user into entering the right kind of data into a form and keep the entered data. Another feature of validation controls is simple convenience. Validation forms perform tasks that once required scripting, either client-side or through ASP. Now all you need is Dreamweaver and a little knowledge about what to enter in a few fields of Dreamweaver's dialog boxes for creating the controls.

There are five kinds of validation controls in .NET:

The CompareValidator control   Simply compares the value of one input with that of another.

The RequiredFieldValidator control   Ensures that a specific field is filled in by the user.

The RangeValidator control   Allows you to establish a range of permissible values for a field.

The RegularExpressionValidator control   Lets you control what kind of values are entered into a field, such as all numbers or letters, or all lower- or uppercase.

The ValidationSummary control   Lets you provide a summary of all the web page's user errors in one place.

This chapter focuses on using each of the validation controls. We'll start with the two simplest: the CompareValidator control and the RequiredFieldValidator control.

Comparing Values Using a CompareValidator Control

One of the most common form elements you run into on the web involves a registration page that contains two password fields. When registering, many sites expect you to fill them both in, and if your input on one is different from the other, an error is generated. One way to create such a form element is by using the .NET CompareValidator control.

There was a time when the only way to compare fields for validation was to write a lot of script for it, whether the validation took place on the server or on the client. On the server, the script was handled (in the Microsoft world) by ASP, and on the browser client the script was generally handled by JavaScript. The CompareValidator control doesn't really deviate from this arrangement, except that you don't have to write any of the code yourself.

Consider Listing 6.1, which shows the basic CompareValidator at work in a Registration page for a Realtor application. Listing 6.1 is fairly intuitive and simple, so don't worry too much yet about the specifics—although if you're the type who likes to figure things out by just looking, I certainly don't discourage that. (You'll find the complete Realtor application at this book's catalog page at www.sybex.com.)

Listing 6.1   Using the Compare Validator

```
<%@ Page Language="C#" ContentType="text/html" ResponseEncoding="iso-8859-1" %>
<%@ Register TagPrefix="MM" Namespace="DreamweaverCtrls"
➥Assembly="DreamweaverCtrls,version=1.0.0.0,
➥publicKeyToken=836f606ede05d46a,culture=neutral" %>
```

```
<html>
<head>
<title>Register</title>
<meta http-equiv="Content-Type" content="text/html; charset=iso-8859-1">
<link href="home.css" rel="stylesheet" type="text/css">
</head>
<body bgcolor="#000000" leftmargin="0" topmargin="0" marginwidth="0">
<form method="post" name="form2" runat="server">
<table width="100%" border="0" cellspacing="0" cellpadding="0">
  <tr><td>
  <table width="100%" border="0" cellspacing="0"
  cellpadding="10"><tr>
  <td><table width="100%" border="0" cellpadding="5"
  cellspacing="0" bgcolor="#CCCC99">
  <tr><td align="left" valign="top"><table width="100%"
  border="0" cellspacing="0" cellpadding="0">
  <tr><td><table width="100%" border="0" cellspacing="0"
  cellpadding="10"><tr>
  <td align="left" valign="top"><div align="center">
   <h3>Create An Account</h3>
   <p align="left">To register, fill out the form below.
   Most boxes are optional. Boxes with * next to them
   are mandatory. </p></div></td></tr></table></td></tr>
   <tr><td align="left" valign="top"><table width="100%" align="center"
cellpadding="10" bgcolor="#FFFFFF" class="tablebrdr"><tr valign="baseline">
   <td width="37%" align="left" valign="top"> Password
   (must be between 5 and 20 characters <span
   class="red"><strong>and contain at least one number and
letter</strong></span>): </td>
   <td width="15%" align="left" valign="top"><asp:textbox  ID="EnterPassword"
TextMode="Password" Columns="32" runat="server" /> * </td>
   <td width="48%" rowspan="3" align="left" valign="top"><div align="left"><p>
  <asp:comparevalidator ControlToValidate="CPassword"
ControlToCompare="EnterPassword" ErrorMessage="Passwords Must Match!!"
ID="passwordValidatator"  runat="server" Type="String" /></p></div><p> 
</p></td></tr>
   <tr valign="baseline"><td  align="left" valign="top"> Password (must match
above Password):</td>
   <td align="left" valign="top"><asp:textbox  ID="CPassword"
TextMode="Password" Columns="32" runat="server" />*
   </td></tr><tr valign="baseline"><td  align="left" valign="top"> </td>
   <td align="left" valign="top"><input name="submit" type="submit"
value="Create Account"></td></tr>
   </table></td></tr></table></td></tr></table></td></tr>
   </table></td> </tr></table></form></body></html>
```

The highlight of Listing 6.1 is the CompareValidator control, which, as you can see from the following code fragment, consists of an ASP.NET element named `asp:comparevalidator`:

```
<asp:comparevalidator ControlToValidate="CPassword"
ControlToCompare="EnterPassword" ErrorMessage="Passwords Must Match!!"
ID="passwordValidatator"  runat="server" Type="String" />
```

I'll be discussing the role of all those attributes a bit later, but right now let's see what happens to the HTML page when we use this control (and other validation controls, as well). Look at Listing 6.2. This is the HTML file the browser receives (Figure 6.1), which is generated by the ASP.NET engine after it compiles Listing 6.1 and sends a response to the user. The first thing you'll notice is a `form` element. If you look at the `form` element and say, "Hey, I didn't add that `onsubmit` attribute," you're right, you didn't.NET did it when it generated the HTML. The `onsubmit` attribute calls an event handler function that exists in some JavaScript in the HTML:

```
<form name="_ctl0" method="post" action="validator001.aspx"
language="javascript" onsubmit="ValidatorOnSubmit();" id="_ctl0">
```

FIGURE 6.1:

The CompareValidator control lets you create an alert like this one, for use when the characters entered into the two text boxes don't match.

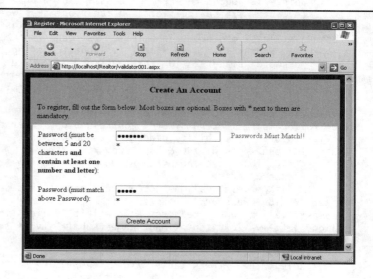

Listing 6.2   **The JavaScript Validation script generated by .NET**

```
<html>
<head>
<title>Register</title>
<meta http-equiv="Content-Type" content="text/html; charset=iso-8859-1">
<link href="home.css" rel="stylesheet" type="text/css">
</head>
<body bgcolor="#000000" leftmargin="0" topmargin="0" marginwidth="0">
<form name="_ctl0" method="post" action="validator001.aspx"
language="javascript" onsubmit="ValidatorOnSubmit();" id="_ctl0">
<input type="hidden" name="__VIEWSTATE"
value="dDwtMzIxMjM5NDA7Oz7IbcXbGuHO6vBZKgo3TNTQRoOGZw==" />
<script language="javascript"
src="/aspnet_client/system_web/1_0_3705_0/WebUIValidation.js"></script>
```

```
<table width="100%" border="0" cellspacing="0" cellpadding="0">
  <tr>
    <td><table width="100%" border="0" cellspacing="0" cellpadding="10"><tr><td>
    <table width="100%" border="0" cellpadding="5" cellspacing="0"
bgcolor="#CCCC99"><tr><td align="left" valign="top">
  <table width="100%" border="0" cellspacing="0" cellpadding="0">
    <tr><td><table width="100%" border="0" cellspacing="0" cellpadding="10"><tr>
    <td align="left" valign="top"><div align="center">
      <h3>Create An Account</h3>
       <p align="left">To register, fill out the form below.
       Most boxes are optional. Boxes with * next to them
       are mandatory. </p></div></td></tr></table></td></tr>
      <tr><td align="left" valign="top"><table width="100%" align="center"
cellpadding="10" bgcolor="#FFFFFF" class="tablebrdr"><tr valign="baseline">
      <td width="37%" align="left" valign="top"> Password
        (must be between 5 and 20 characters <span class="red"><strong>and
contain at least one number and letter</strong></span>): </td>
        <td width="15%" align="left" valign="top"><input name="EnterPassword"
type="password" size="32" id="EnterPassword" />* </td>
        <td width="48%" rowspan="3" align="left" valign="top"><div
align="left"><p><span id="passwordValidatator" controltovalidate="CPassword"
errormessage="Passwords Must Match!!"
evaluationfunction="CompareValidatorEvaluateIsValid"
controltocompare="EnterPassword" controlhookup="EnterPassword"
style="color:Red;visibility:hidden;">Passwords Must
Match!!</span></p></div><p>  </p></td></tr>
        <tr valign="baseline"><td  align="left" valign="top"> Password (must match
above Password):</td>
      <td align="left" valign="top"><input name="CPassword" type="password"
size="32" id="CPassword" />* </td></tr>
        <tr valign="baseline"><td  align="left" valign="top"> </td><td
align="left" valign="top"><input name="submit" type="submit" value="Create
Account"></td></tr>
      </table></td></tr></table></td></tr>
    </table></td> </tr> </table></td></tr></table>
  <input type="hidden" name="MM_insert" value="form2">
<script language="javascript">
<!--
var Page_Validators =  new Array(document.all["passwordValidatator"]);
// -->
</script>

<script language="javascript">
<!--
var Page_ValidationActive = false;
if (typeof(clientInformation) != "undefined" &&
 ➥clientInformation.appName.indexOf("Explorer") != -1)
 ➥{
```

```
if (typeof(Page_ValidationVer) == "undefined")
➥alert("Unable to find script library
➥'/aspnet_client/system_web/1_0_3705_0/WebUIValidation.js'.
➥Try placing this file manually, or reinstall by running
➥'aspnet_regiis -c'.");
➥else if (Page_ValidationVer != "125")
➥ alert("This page uses an incorrect version of
➥ WebUIValidation.js. The page expects version 125.
➥The script library is " + Page_ValidationVer + ".");
 else
     ValidatorOnLoad();
}

function ValidatorOnSubmit() {
    if (Page_ValidationActive) {
        ValidatorCommonOnSubmit();
    }
}
// -->
</script>
</form>
</body>
</html>
```

The script in Listing 6.2 does not exist in our ASP.NET page. It's generated because we used a validation control. This script, in turn, returns a value generated by a function, `ValidatorCommonOnSubmit()`, that is located in an external JavaScript file. Look toward the bottom of Listing 6.2, and you'll see the event handler function that the form is calling:

```
function ValidatorCommonOnSubmit() {
    event.returnValue = !Page_BlockSubmit;
    Page_BlockSubmit = false;
}
```

Notice that .NET also provided an `id` attribute for the form. Generally, it's a good idea to create an `id` attribute/value pair yourself, especially if you're working with code-behind (code that exists on a separate page that your web page refers to; more on this in Chapter 7). This is because all HTML and Web Server controls are objects, but in order for .NET or a client browser to access them, you generally need to name an `id` attribute by which to reference them (I say generally because you can access some collections, such as forms, in other ways).

The element after the `form` element is a hidden input element generated by .NET that maintains state:

```
<input type="hidden" name="__VIEWSTATE"
value="dDwtMzIxMjM5NDA7Oz7IbcXbGuH06vBZKgo3TNTQRoOGZw==" />
```

This kind of element exists in every .NET-generated page. You'll never need to worry about editing or managing this element.

Next, notice the following JavaScript link. This takes us to a JavaScript file that comes as part of the .NET framework:

```
<script language="javascript"
src="/aspnet_client/system_web/1_1_4322/WebUIValidation.js"></script>
```

which is the JavaScript file that defines the function referred to by the script at the bottom of the page:

```
function ValidatorOnSubmit() {
    if (Page_ValidationActive) {
        ValidatorCommonOnSubmit();
    }
}
```

TIP

Sometimes users will get an error message like this: "Unable to find script library '/aspnet_client/system_web/1_0_3705_0/WebUIValidation.js." For some reason, this happens frequently with remote hosting. Don't worry, the file is there; you just have to find it. FTP into the remote site and examine the directory structure under /aspnet _client/system_web. The directory name in bold is the proper directory where ASP.NET expects to find the JavaScript file (it may be different on your machine or on your remote host). The error message will tell you where .NET is expecting to find this file. When it does, create a directory at that location and then locate the one you do have. It should be in a directory similar to that named in bold in the preceding code snippet. Then, copy and paste that JavaScript into your newly created directory. Another reason to make sure you test your applications before they go live!

It's important to remember that the WebUIValidation.js JavaScript file is *not* generated by Dreamweaver. This is strictly .NET material and comes as part of the .NET Framework installation. The reference to the file in the web page sent to users is a result of your creating a validation control. If you don't use a validation control in your ASP.NET page, no script referencing the JavaScript file is generated into the HTML.

You don't have to create client-side scripting for a validation control. You can run it all from the server, by unchecking the Enable Client Script check box in the Dreamweaver Tag Editor dialog box for the validator control you are editing. In the next section, we'll take a closer look at this dialog box.

Creating a CompareValidator Control in Dreamweaver

You can easily see a CompareValidator control in action by creating a new ASP.NET page and adding a couple of password fields to it. Do this through the Dreamweaver interface to yield the following code (note the id attributes in bold):

```
<td><asp:TextBox id="TextBox1"
       runat="server" TextMode="Password"/> </td>
  <td> <asp:TextBox id="TextBox2"
       runat="server" TextMode="Password"/>
```

Next, create a button control.

```
<asp:Button id="Button1"
                  Text="Compare"
                  runat="server"/>
```

To create a CompareValidator control, go to the Insert bar and choose the ASP.NET tab (Figure 6.2). Expand the ASP.NET More Tags Folder icon and click Validation Server Controls, which is the second choice from the top. Choose asp:comparevalidator from the list on the right, and click Insert. You'll get a Tag Editor dialog box like the one in Figure 6.3. Give the control a sensible name in the ID text field, remembering that any programmatic access will be using this name as an object reference.

FIGURE 6.2:

Use the ASP.NET tab in the Insert bar to insert the CompareValidator and other .NET controls.

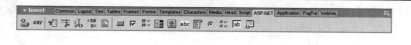

You'll also notice the Enable Client Scripts check box, which is checked by default. It looks like it's grayed out so that you don't have the option to change it, but you can. (Just check the box, and the gray check mark will turn black. Click again to uncheck the box.) Disabling this setting forces validation to occur on the server. Remember, though, that this makes the server work harder. In theory, .NET will create the appropriate client-side JavaScript by doing some browser detection work, so it's probably best to leave this check box alone.

FIGURE 6.3:

The CompareValidator dialog box in Dreamweaver's Tag Editor

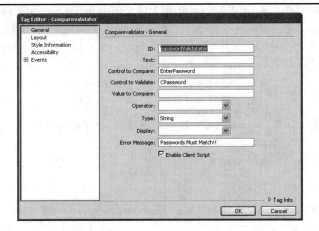

Two important fields in the Tag Editor dialog box are Control To Compare and Control To Validate. This is where the id attributes from the password fields come in handy, because you need to enter them into these fields. Enter **textbox1** into the Control To Compare dialog box, and **textbox2** into the Control To Validate fields. When you do that, you don't need to worry about coding anything to achieve the validation. ASP.NET handles it all for you. To make sure users enter the same data into each password field, choose "Equal" from the Operator drop-down list. From the Type drop-down list, choose "string". The control should look like this:

```
<asp:CompareValidator ControlToCompare="textbox1" ControlToValidate="textbox2"
ErrorMessage="password fields must match" ID="cValidator" Operator="Equal"
runat="server" Type="String" />
```

Did you notice the association between the Tag Editor fields you filled out, and the attribute values generated when Dreamweaver creates the control?

When you're presented with the Tag Editor dialog box for creating the CompareValidator control, it helps to understand what each choice or field in the dialog box corresponds to in the code that Dreamweaver generates. It's generally pretty obvious, but to help you maintain a solid grip on what is happening under the hood, I've included tables that describe the fields and their corresponding attributes. We'll start with the table for the CompareValidator control, which creates an element called asp:comparevalidator. This element consists of the attributes described in Table 6.1.

TABLE 6.1: CompareValidator Control/`asp:comparevalidator` Options

Dreamweaver Dialog Box Text Field	Equivalent ASP.NET Element Attribute	Description
ID	ID	Uniquely identifies the element.
Text	Text	The text that is displayed if validation fails.
Control To Compare	ControlToCompare	The control that the validated control should be compared to.
Control to Validate	ControlToValidate	The control you wish to validate: When the value in this control doesn't match the value of the control named in the ControlToCompare attribute, the validation fails.
Value To Compare	ValueToCompare	An explicit value that the validated control should match.
Operator	Operator	Establishes the basis for the comparison
Type	Type	The datatype of the value being compared.
Display	Display	Indicates whether the display should be dynamic or static. The dynamic option is more powerful because validation occurs in real time, but there is no memory space allocated for the control.
Error Message	ErrorMessage	Generally used with the ValidationSummary control to display an error message.
Enable Client Script	EnableClientScript	A value of true tells ASP.NET to generate JavaScript for validation, and a value of false tells ASP.NET to handle validation on the server.

In the Dreamweaver Tag Editor, all of the validator controls work essentially the same way. In other words, you choose them from the Insert bar (or using the Insert command) and, through a dialog box, provide the appropriate values for the various attributes that are part of the corresponding ASP.NET element for the control you are creating.

TIP   If you choose to use a dynamic display using the Display attribute, ASP.NET doesn't allocate any resources for the control until validation occurs. This can make the control more powerful but is a problem if you're using the control in a table. That's because the table cells used for the control won't be created until the validation occurs, so the objects on your page may bounce around the web page. The graphic designer in me suggests you chose static as the Display attribute value in order to prevent this.

CompareValidator Control Syntax

The syntactical highlights of the `asp:comparevalidator` element are its `ControlToValidate` and `ControlToCompare` attributes.

The `ControlToValidate` attribute contains the same value as the `id` attribute of the control that should be validated. The `ControlToCompare` attribute contains the same value as the `id` attribute of the control against which you are testing the control being validated.

The optional `Operator` attribute determines the type of comparison that should take place. The following values for `Operator` are allowed:

- `Equal`
- `NotEqual`
- `GreaterThan`
- `GreaterThanEqual`
- `LessThan`
- `LessThanEqual`
- `DataTypeCheck`

If no value is specified for the `Operator` attribute, the default value is `Equal`.

When the `Operator` attribute contains a value of `DataTypeCheck`, a comparison of datatypes is made; the datatype of the value entered into the input control being validated is compared to the datatype specified by the `BaseCompareValidator` `Type` attribute. Validation fails if the value cannot be converted to the specified datatype. If the expression resulting from the combination of the various attribute value pairs of the CompareValidator control results returns true, the validation result is valid.

NOTE   Any values within the `ControlToCompare` and `ValueToCompare` attributes are ignored when the `Operator` attribute value is set to `DataTypeCheck`.

Listing 6.3 shows how our control might look if we used a `GreaterThan` value in the Operator attribute when comparing the two text boxes shown in Figure 6.4. (I've removed some of the extraneous HTML from the listing to save some space, but the entire file can be found in the Realtor application at www.sybex.com.)

FIGURE 6.4:

If the integer value entered in the box on the left is not greater than the value entered in the box on the right, an error message appears.

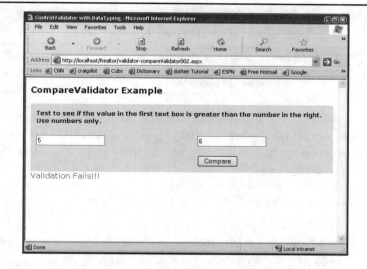

Listing 6.3   **Using `GreaterThan` as the `Operator` attribute in a CompareValidator control**

```
<table bgcolor="#eeeeee" cellpadding=10 style="margin-top:10px">
  <tr align="left" valign="bottom">
    <td colspan="3"><p style="font-size:13px; font-weight:800;">Test to see
        if the value in the first text box is greater than the number in the
        right. Use numbers only.</p>
    </td>
  </tr>
  <tr align="left" valign="top">
    <td> <asp:TextBox id="TextBox1"
                runat="server"/> </td>
    <td align="center" valign="bottom"> <p p style="font-size:13px; font-
weight:800;"> </p>
        <p p style="font-size:13px; font-weight:800;"> </p></td>
    <td> <asp:TextBox id="TextBox2"
                runat="server"/> <p>
        <asp:Button id="Button1"
                Text="Compare"
                runat="server"/>
    </td>
  </tr>
</table>
```

```
<asp:CompareValidator
        ControlToCompare="TextBox2"
        ControlToValidate="TextBox1"
        EnableClientScript="false" ErrorMessage="Validation Fails!!!"
 id="Compare1" Operator="GreaterThan"
        runat="server"
        Type="Integer"/>
```

The two text boxes to be compared are highlighted in bold in Listing 6.3, as is the CompareValidator control that processes the evaluation. Even though this isn't the most robust comparison you might be able to imagine, it's still a significant result for so little code. Because of .NET's inherent postback binding, you don't even need to worry about providing any details for the form element, other than the ubiquitous runat=server attribute/value pair. The key to Listing 6.3 is one simple attribute/value pair:

```
Operator="GreaterThan"
```

This establishes a relationship between the first text box and the second text box.

Most of the possible values for the Operator attribute are self-explanatory. But there's one value in that list we should take a look at: the DataTypeCheck value, which strays a bit off the path from the others. Actually, this value is part of a pretty simple concept. You've just seen how the Operator attribute lets you compare the equality or non-equality of two values. Using the DataTypeCheck value, you can similarly compare datatypes. When you use this value, if the two compared values aren't the same datatypes, the validation fails.

Consider the following CompareValidator control. (You can write it using the DataTypeCheck attribute/value pair, but you'll find it doesn't quite do what you might expect, so it's best to handle it programmatically through script. We'll get to that shortly.)

```
<asp:CompareValidator
   ControlToCompare="TextBox2"
   ControlToValidate="TextBox1"
   EnableClientScript="false"
   ErrorMessage="Validation Fails!!!"
   id="Compare1" Operator="DataTypecheck"
    runat="server"/>
```

Listing 6.4 shows a CompareValidator control using an Operator attribute with a DataTypeCheck value in script. The web page contains two fields, and the user can choose the datatype for the value they enter; they can also change the Operator attribute value programmatically.

Listing 6.4   **Using a CompareValidator control in comparing datatypes in script**

```
<%@ Page Language="C#" ContentType="text/html" ResponseEncoding="iso-8859-1" %>
<%@ Register TagPrefix="MM" Namespace="DreamweaverCtrls"
Assembly="DreamweaverCtrls,version=1.0.0.0,publicKeyToken=836f606ede05d46a,cultu
re=neutral" %>
<html>
<head>
    <script runat="server">
        void Button_Click(Object sender, EventArgs e)
        {
            if (Page.IsValid)
            {
                lblOutput.Text = "Result: Valid!";
            }
            else
            {
                lblOutput.Text = "Result: Not valid!";
            }
        }

        void Match_Ops_Event(Object sender, EventArgs e)
        {
            Compare1.Operator = (ValidationCompareOperator)
➥ListOfOperators.SelectedIndex;
            Compare1.Validate();
        }
        void Match_DataType_Event(Object sender, EventArgs e)
        {
            Compare1.Type = (ValidationDataType)
➥ListOfDataTypes.SelectedIndex;
            Compare1.Validate();
        }
    </script>
</head>
<body style="font-family:Verdana, sans-serif;">
    <form runat=server>
        <h3>CompareValidator Example</h3>
    <table bgcolor="#eeeeee" cellpadding=10 style="margin-top:10px">
      <tr align="left" valign="bottom">
        <td><p style="font-size:13px; font-weight:800;">Enter A Value
          :</p></td>
        <td colspan="3" align="center"><p align="right" style="font-size:13px;
font-weight:800;">Compare
            it to another value you enter here:</p></td>
      </tr>
```

```
<tr align="left" valign="top">
  <td>
    <asp:TextBox id="TextBox1"
              runat="server"/> </td>
  <td align="center" valign="bottom"> <p p style="font-size:13px; font-
weight:800;">Data
      Type</p></td>
  <td align="center" valign="bottom"> <p p style="font-size:13px; font-
weight:800;">Comparison
      Operator:</p></td>
  <td> <asp:TextBox id="TextBox2"
              runat="server"/> <p>
    <asp:Button id="Button1"
            Text="Compare"
            OnClick="Button_Click"
            runat="server"/>
  </td>
</tr>
<tr align="center" valign="top">
  <td align="left" style="font-size: 11px">Use the list boxes at the right
    to further refine your comparisons. </td>
  <td> <asp:listbox ID="ListOfDataTypes"
              OnSelectedIndexChanged="Match_DataType_Event"
              runat="server">
    <asp:listitem selected Value="String" >String</asp:listitem>
    <asp:listitem Value="Integer" >Integer</asp:listitem>
    <asp:listitem Value="Double" >Double</asp:listitem>
    <asp:listitem Value="Date" >Date</asp:listitem>
  </asp:listbox></td>
  <td> <asp:listbox ID="ListOfOperators"
              OnSelectedIndexChanged="Match_Ops_Event"
              runat="server">
    <asp:listitem selected Value="Equal">Equal</asp:listitem>
    <asp:listitem Value="NotEqual">NotEqual</asp:listitem>
    <asp:listitem Value="GreaterThan">GreaterThan</asp:listitem>
    <asp:listitem Value="GreaterThanEqual">GreaterThanEqual</asp:listitem>
    <asp:listitem Value="LessThan">LessThan</asp:listitem>
    <asp:listitem Value="LessThanEqual">LessThanEqual</asp:listitem>
    <asp:listitem Value="DataTypeCheck">DataTypeCheck</asp:listitem>
  </asp:listbox></td>
  <td> </td>
</tr>
</table>

  <asp:CompareValidator id="Compare1"
      ControlToValidate="TextBox1"
      ControlToCompare="TextBox2"
      EnableClientScript="False"
      Type="String"
      runat="server"/>
```

```
    <br>

    <asp:Label id="lblOutput"
         Font-Name="verdana"
         Font-Size="10pt"
         runat="server"/>

  </form>

 </body>
 </html>
```

As you read the explanation of what's happening in Listing 6.4, it will be helpful to refer to Figure 6.5 or, even better, to load the file onto your server to watch its behavior for yourself.

FIGURE 6.5:

You can create comparisons based on both datatype and things such as equality and inequality, using the CompareValidator control.

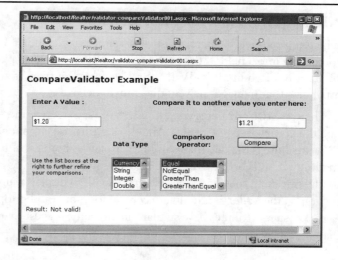

We have to do some of our own coding in this case. In Code view, create a `script` element within the `head` element. It's vital that you use the `runat="server"` attribute value pair, or you'll get an error. The `script` element consists of the object manipulation routines necessary to make the controls behave as expected.

When you're working with validation controls, you can do all sorts of things by simply including statements within an `if` statement that checks to see whether the page is valid:

```
if (Page.IsValid)
    {
        //add statements here
    }
```

In our case, we merely created a text label and gave it an ID of lblOutput, which we then accessed in the code, like so:

```
lblOutput.Text = "Result: Valid!";
```

If the page isn't valid, the lblOutput label's text value is Result: Not valid!. All of this activity is in bold in Listing 6.4.

The next two event handlers, Match_Ops_Event() and Match_DataType_Event(), simply pass the selected value to the ASP.NET processor and validate the CompareValidator control (notice its ID attribute value is Compare1). As noted in the last chapter, when you're working with list boxes, you must tell .NET when a selection has been made before any processing can be done with the selected item.

The RequiredFieldValidator Control

The RequiredFieldValidator control is a simple control that merely demands that a user enter something into a field. If the user doesn't, some text is displayed indicating to the user the error of her ways. RequiredFieldValidator, like other controls, is an element consisting of several attributes that manage the way the control behaves.

There are two attributes you can use to display an error message to the user, the Text attribute and the ErrorMessage attribute. You can actually use either one, or both. If you use both, the Text attribute is the one that is used to display text, unless you change that behavior programmatically. This is because the ErrorMessage attribute actually serves another purpose—it is used to identify and display messages when you wish to display a summary of error messages. (See the section on the ValidationSummary control for more on this topic.) So, although the Text and ErrorMessage attributes have similar functionality, it's best to use the Text attribute unless you plan to display all your messages together in one place.

Creating a RequiredFieldValidator Control

To create a RequiredFieldValidator control, go to the Insert bar and choose the ASP.NET tab (shown earlier in Figure 6.2). Expand the ASP.NET Tags folder and click Validation Server controls, which is the second choice from the top. Choose asp:requiredfieldvalidator from the list on the right. Click Insert, and you'll get a dialog box like the one in Figure 6.6. Give the control a name in the ID field, because, as mentioned, any programmatic access will be using this as an object reference.

FIGURE 6.6:

The RequiredField-
Validator control
dialog box in
Dreamweaver

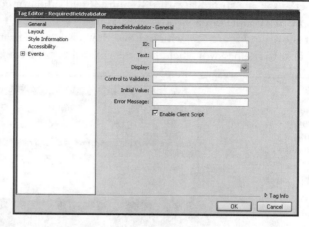

Most of the choices shown in Table 6.2 will be self-explanatory if you've studied the CompareValidator control discussed earlier, but one of the RequiredFieldValidator choices merits some special attention. The Initial Value text field in the dialog box corresponds to the `InitialValue` attribute, which can be used to force a user to change a default value in something like a list box. In many websites, you'll often see something like this within a list box or drop-down menu: – `choose a value` –. Since we don't want that value going into our database, we can use that text as the value in the `InitialValue` attribute. This tells ASP.NET that if the selected item has the same value as the `InitialValue` attribute value, the control should not successfully validate.

TABLE 6.2: RequiredFieldValidator Control/`asp:comparevalidator` Options

Dreamweaver Dialog Box Text Field	Equivalent ASP.NET Element Attribute	Description
ID	ID	Uniquely identifies the element.
Text	Text	The text that is displayed if validation fails.
Display	Display	Indicates whether the display should be `dynamic` or `static`.
Control to Validate	ControlToValidate	The control you wish to validate.
Initial Value	InitialValue	Sets the initial value of the control. This is used for forcing users to actually make a choice from a list box or drop-down list.
Error Message	ErrorMessage	Generally used with the ValidationSummary control to display an error message.
Enable Client Script	EnableClientScript	A value of true tells ASP.NET to generate JavaScript for validation, and a value of false tells ASP.NET to handle validation on the server.

Let's look at a straightforward RequiredFieldValidator control in Listing 6.5, which consists simply of a couple of password fields. When a user doesn't fill in a field, they see a window like that shown in Figure 6.7, which shows the `ErrorMessage` attribute value displayed in a table cell next to the password field that the control is validating.

FIGURE 6.7:

The RequiredField-Validator control displays an error message using either the `Text` or the `ErrorMessage` attribute.

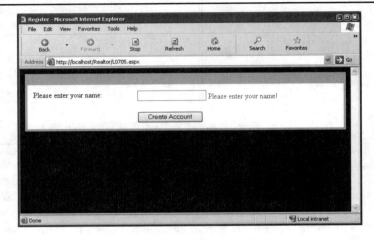

As you can see in Listing 6.5, you don't need to write any actual code to make the RequiredFieldValidator work. Everything is handled by .NET and Dreamweaver. After you enter the appropriate information in the RequiredFieldValidator Tag Editor dialog box, the code is generated and ASP.NET takes it from there.

Listing 6.5   **Using a RequiredFieldValidator**

```
<table width="100%" align="center" cellpadding="10" bgcolor="#FFFFFF"
class="tablebrdr">
    <tr valign="baseline">
        <td width="33%" align="left" valign="top"> Please enter your name: </td>
        <td width="67%" align="left" valign="top">
            <asp:TextBox id="txtName" runat="server" />
            <asp:RequiredFieldValidator id="valTxtName"
            ControlToValidate="txtName"
            ErrorMessage="Please enter your name!"
            runat="server" />
        </td>
    </tr>
    <tr valign="baseline">
        <td  align="left" valign="top"> </td>
        <td align="left" valign="top">
          <input name="submit" type="submit" value="Create Account">
```

```
      </td>
    </tr>
  </table>
```

The RequiredFieldValidator control only needs to know which field you are validating. In this case, it's the `txtName` field, so you'd enter that into the Tag Editor's Control to Validate field when you insert the control using the Dreamweaver interface.

The RangeValidator Control

Sometimes you'll want to be sure a user's entry into a form field falls within some kind of range. The RangeValidator control is another ASP.NET control you can easily program through Dreamweaver. You can compare a user's entry with a range of numbers, dates, or characters.

Creating a RangeValidator Control

To create a RangeValidator control, go to the Insert bar and choose the ASP.NET tab. Expand the ASP.NET Tags folder and click Validation Server Controls, which is the second choice from the top. Choose `asp:rangevalidator` from the list on the right. Click Insert, and you'll get a dialog box like the one in Figure 6.8. Name the control in the ID field.

FIGURE 6.8:

The RangeValidator control dialog box in Dreamweaver

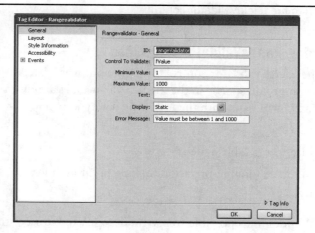

Table 6.3 shows the options available in the RangeFieldValidator dialog box in Dreamweaver and the corresponding attributes created for the `asp:rangevalidator` element.

TABLE 6.3: RangeValidator/asp:rangevalidator Options

Dreamweaver Dialog Box Text Field	Equivalent ASP.NET Element Attribute	Description
ID	ID	Uniquely identifies the element.
Control to Validate	ControlToValidate	The control you wish to validate.
Minimum Value	MinimumValue	On the range scale used for validation, the minimum value allowed.
Maximum Value	MaximumValue	On the range scale used for validation, the maximum value allowed.
Text	Text	The text that is displayed if validation fails.
Display	Display	Indicates whether the display should be dynamic or static.
Error Message	ErrorMessage	Generally used with the ValidationSummary control to display an error message.
Enable Client Script	EnableClientScript	A value of true tells ASP.NET to generate JavaScript for validation, and a value of false tells ASP.NET to handle validation on the server.

WARNING   One quirk about the RangeValidator control is that the validation is successful if the control being validated is empty, unless you've set up that control in conjunction with a RequiredFieldValidator control.

Using RangeValidator Datatypes

The RangeValidator control can figure out what datatype the user enters and compare it with the range you specify in the MinimumValue and MaximumValue attributes. The RangeValidator control will work with the following datatypes:

- String
- Integer (32-bit signed)
- Double (double-precision floating point numbers)
- Date

Although it's possible to use the RangeValidator control to establish ranges for strings of text, you'll probably want to use the RegularExpressionValidator instead for this task, because it gives you a greater range of filtering options. You'll learn about that control in the next section.

Listing 6.6 shows a RangeValidator control created with Dreamweaver.

Listing 6.6 **Creating a RangeValidator control**

```
<table width="100%" align="center" cellpadding="10" bgcolor="#FFFFFF"
class="tablebrdr">
  <tr valign="baseline">
    <td width="37%" align="left" valign="top">
Enter a value</td>
    <td width="15%" align="left" valign="top">
      <asp:textbox Columns="32"   ID="fValue"
       runat="server" TextMode="SingleLine" />
    * </td>
    <td width="48%" rowspan="2" align="left" valign="top">
      <div align="left">
         <p>
            <asp:rangevalidator ControlToValidate="fValue" Display="Static"
ErrorMessage="Value must be between 1 and 1000" ID="rangeValidator"
MaximumValue="1000" MinimumValue="1" runat="server" Type="Integer" /> 
         </p>
      </div>
      </td></tr>
    <tr valign="baseline">
      <td  align="left" valign="top"> </td>
      <td align="left" valign="top"><input name="submit" type="submit"
value="Submit">
      </td>
    </tr>
  </table>
```

The RangeValidator control in Listing 6.6 (see bold lines) uses its MaximumValue and MinimumValue attributes to enforce a range of numbers between 1 and 1,000, inclusive. If the user enters a number that falls outside of that range, the validation fails and an error message is displayed.

Be sure to include a Type="Integer" attribute/value pair, otherwise the control won't work correctly.

WARNING   Although Dreamweaver's Tag Editor includes a Type field on some other validation controls, it doesn't for the RangeValidator control. This is an important omission, one you'll have to compensate for by adding the field manually. To see what I mean, try the same file described just above, *without* the Type="Integer" attribute/value pair. When you enter a number and press the Tab key, the control will give you an error message even if the number you entered falls within the range. This won't happen if you hit the Submit key, but the first time an out-of-range number is entered, the error message persists, even if you change the number to be within the range.

The RegularExpressionValidator Control

In the past, to provide validation on a field that requires certain combinations of letters and/or numbers, you generally had to do a fair amount of programming. ASP.NET borrows a reliable standby from the Perl world by implementing a control that uses *regular expressions*.

Perl is one of the earliest scripting languages to hit the Web, and regular expressions are one of the language's many fine string-manipulation wonders. A regular expression is a series of character sequences that defines what characters are allowed within a certain string. You can, for example, limit a password field to numbers or letters or all caps or all lowercase by creating a regular expression. You can limit the number of characters allowed as input in a field, and even require that a field consist of both letters and numbers. The regular expression is also used for a wide variety of other string-based processes, including search engines; for our purposes here, though, we'll be using it to enforce constraints on fields through validation.

Regular expressions are built using a special sequence of characters shown in Table 6.4 to make up what are called search patterns or pattern matches. If you have a regular expression like this:

    .o.

the dot, or period, on each side of the small letter o indicates that any single character is an acceptable match on either side of the o. So if you created a text field and included .o. as the value of your RegularExpressionValidator control, then a user could input the word for, the word pot, the word word, or anything else with a character on either side of an o. There are many such constructs, as shown in Table 6.4.

TABLE 6.4: Regular Expression Characters Used for Pattern Matching

Character	Description
\	Can indicate a special character, particularly an escape sequence. For example, n matches the character n, but \n matches a newline character.
^	Matches the position at the beginning of the input string.
$	Matches the position at the end of the input string.
*	Matches the preceding character or substring zero or more times. For example, fo* matches f and foo.
+	Matches the preceding character or substring one or more times. For example, fo+ matches fo and foo, but not f.
?	Matches the preceding character or substring zero times or one time.
{n}	Using a non-negative integer inside the { } delimiters specifies the number of times a match should occur. In other words, you replace the n in your code with the number you want to use to indicate that the expression matches exactly n times. For example, o{2} does not match the single o in old, but matches the two os in book.

Continued on next page

TABLE 6.4 CONTINUED: Regular Expression Characters Used for Pattern Matching

Character	Description
{n,}	Specifies how many times a match should occur. For example, {n,} matches at least n times; o{2,} does not match the o in old but matches all the o's in fooooot.
{n,m}	Sets a minimum and maximum number of matches for specific characters so that the input string matches at least n times and at most m times. There must not be a space between the comma and the numbers within the expression. For example, o{1,3} matches the first three o's in foooooot.
?	When this character immediately follows any of the other quantifiers (*, +, ?, {n}, {n,}, {n,m}), the matching pattern matches as little of the searched string as possible. In the string aaaaaaa, the a+? matches a single a, while a+ matches all a's.
.	The period, or dot, is used to match any single character *except* \n. To match any character *including* the \n, use a pattern such as [\s\S].
(pattern)	Using parentheses, you can isolate part of an expression from the rest of the expression. To match parentheses characters themselves ( ), use an escape character: \(or \).
(?:pattern)	You can isolate non-matching patterns using this character sequence, which is useful for combining parts of a pattern with the OR character (|). For example, industr(?:y|ies) is another way of writing this: industry|industries.
(?=pattern)	This is what is called a *positive look ahead,* which means that if any of the options in the pattern on the right side of the equals sign match, then the match is successful. For example, Windows (?=95|98|NT|2000|XP) matches Windows in Windows XP, but not Windows in Windows 3.1.
(?!pattern)	This is a *negative look ahead,* because if any of the options in the pattern on the right side of the equals sign match, then the match is *unsuccessful.* For example, Windows (?=95|98|NT|2000|XP) matches Windows in Windows 3.1, but not Windows in Windows XP.
x|y	This is an OR operator that matches either x or y. For example, good|book matches good or book.
[xyz]	A character set; matches any one of the enclosed characters. For example, [abc] matches the b in boring.
[^xyz]	A negative character set that matches any character not in the brackets. For example, [^abc] matches the s in storing.
[a-z]	A range of characters that matches any character in the specified range. For example, [a-z] matches any lowercase alphabetic character in the range a through z.
[^a-z]	A negative range of characters. Matches any character not in the specified range. For example, [^a-z] matches any character not in the range a through z.
\b	Matches a word boundary, which is the position between a word and a space. For example, or\b matches the or in forlorn but not the or in orb.
\B	Matches a nonword boundary. For example, or\B matches the or in forlorn but not the or in the word or.
\cx	Matches the control character indicated by x. For example, \cM matches a Control-M or carriage return character. The value of x must be in the range of A-Z or a-z. If not, c is assumed to be a literal c character.

Continued on next page

TABLE 6.4 CONTINUED: Regular Expression Characters Used for Pattern Matching

Character	Description
\d	Matches any single-digit character. Equivalent to [0-9].
\D	Matches any nondigit character. Equivalent to [^0-9].
\f	Matches a form-feed character. Equivalent to \x0c and \cL.
\n	Matches a newline character. Equivalent to \x0a and \cJ.
\r	Matches a carriage return character. Equivalent to \x0d and \cM.
\s	Matches any whitespace character, including space, tab, formfeed, and so on. Equivalent to [\f\n\r\t\v].
\S	Matches any nonwhitespace character. Equivalent to [^ \f\n\r\t\v].
\t	Matches a tab character. Equivalent to \x09 and \cI.
\v	Matches a vertical tab character. Equivalent to \x0b and \cK.
\w	Matches any word character, including the underscore. Equivalent to [A-Za-z0-9_].
\W	Matches any nonword character. Equivalent to [^A-Za-z0-9_].
\xn	Matches n, where n is a hexadecimal escape value. Hexadecimal escape values must be exactly two digits long. For example, \x41 matches A, and \x041 is equivalent to \x04 and 1. Generally, this is used for code point references in encodings such as ASCII (code points are hexadecimal numerical representations of characters).
\number	Matches number, where number is a positive integer and acts as a reference back to captured matches. For example, (.)\1 matches two consecutive identical characters.

Using regular expressions takes some practice and some getting used to. Table 6.4 will help, but nothing beats practical use on a regular (no pun intended) basis.

Creating a RegularExpressionValidator Control

To create a RegularExpressionValidator control, go to the Insert bar and choose the ASP.NET tab. Expand the ASP.NET Tags folder and click Validation Server controls, which is the second choice from the top. Choose asp:regularexpressionvalidator from the list on the right. In the Tag Editor (Figure 6.8), enter a name for the control in the ID field.

The main field to watch for and enter data into for this control is the Validation Expression field. This is where you harvest the sequences shown in Table 6.4 to build your expression. Then, when a user enters data into a field that is governed by this control, the RegularExpressionValidator control evaluates whether the entered string matches the pattern you indicated. If it does, the validation succeeds; otherwise it fails.

FIGURE 6.9:

The RegularExpres-
sionValidator control
dialog box in
Dreamweaver

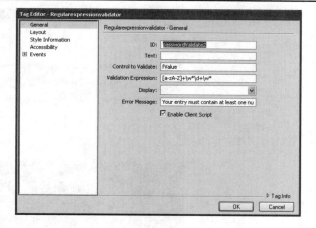

Table 6.5 lists the options Dreamweaver makes available to you for creating the Regular-
ExpressionValidator control.

TABLE 6.5: RegularExpressionValidator Control/asp:regularexpressionvalidator Options

Dreamweaver Dialog Box Text Field	Equivalent ASP.NET Element Attribute	Description
ID	ID	Uniquely identifies the element.
Text	Text	The text that is displayed if validation fails.
Control to Validate	ControlToValidate	The control you wish to validate. If the characters the user enters don't match the pattern specified in the ValidationExpression attribute, the validation fails.
Validation Expression	ValidationExpression	A regular expression that is used to compare against the characters entered by the user.
Display	Display	Indicates whether the display should be dynamic or static.
Error Message	ErrorMessage	Generally used with the ValidationSummary control to display an error message.

The beauty of this control is its simplicity, once you get past the not-so-small hurdle of
learning regular expressions. All you need to do is define your regular expression, and off
you go, as shown in Listing 6.7. This code is for a simple web page with one field that
requires the user to enter at least one letter and one number. Figure 6.10 shows what the
web page looks like after the user fails to accomplish this task.

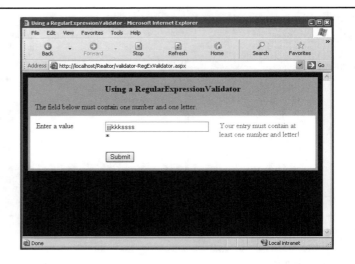

Listing 6.7   Using the RegularExpressionValidator control

```
<table width="100%" align="center" cellpadding="10" bgcolor="#FFFFFF"
class="tablebrdr">
    <tr valign="baseline">
        <td width="37%" align="left" valign="top">
        Enter value</td>
        <td width="15%" align="left" valign="top">
            <asp:textbox Columns="32"  ID="fValue" runat="server"
TextMode="SingleLine" />
                                * </td>
                                <td width="48%" rowspan="3" align="left"
valign="top"><div align="left">
                                    <p>
                                        <asp:regularexpressionvalidator
ErrorMessage="Your entry must contain at least one number and letter!"
ID="passwordValidate2" runat="server" ControlToValidate="fValue"
ValidationExpression="[a-zA-Z]+\w*\d+\w*"/>
                                          </p>
                                    </div>
                                    <p>  </p></td>
                                </tr>
                                <tr valign="baseline">
                                    <td  align="left" valign="top"> Enter another
value:</td>
                                    <td align="left" valign="top">
<asp:textbox  ID="fValue2" TextMode="SingleLine" Columns="32" runat="server" />
                                        * </td>
                                    </tr>
                                    <tr valign="baseline">
                                        <td  align="left" valign="top"> </td>
```

```
                                    <td align="left" valign="top"><input name="submit"
    type="submit" value="Submit">
                                    </td>
                                </tr>
                            </table>
```

The ValidationSummary Control

What better way to end a chapter on validation controls than with a description of the ValidationSummary control? This one lets you summarize all the mistakes your misguided users have made on the page. Your gut feeling about this control might be to avoid it so that you don't beat up on users any more than you have to—but you may want to consider this when you have numerous validations that need to take place. Instead of displaying error messages with each control, you can want to gather up and centralize your users' foibles.

Creating a ValidationSummary Control

To create a ValidationSummary control, go to the Insert bar and choose the ASP.NET tab. Expand the ASP.NET Tags folder and click Validation Server controls, which is the second choice from the top. Choose `asp:validationsummary` from the list on the right.

In the Tag Editor dialog box (Figure 6.11), give the control a name in the ID field. Then you can decide if you want to give the summary some header text. If you do, indicate that text using the Header Text field, which will define the element's `HeaderText` attribute. You can also choose how you want the summary to display error messages, using the Display Mode field.

FIGURE 6.11:

The Validation-Summary control dialog box in Dreamweaver

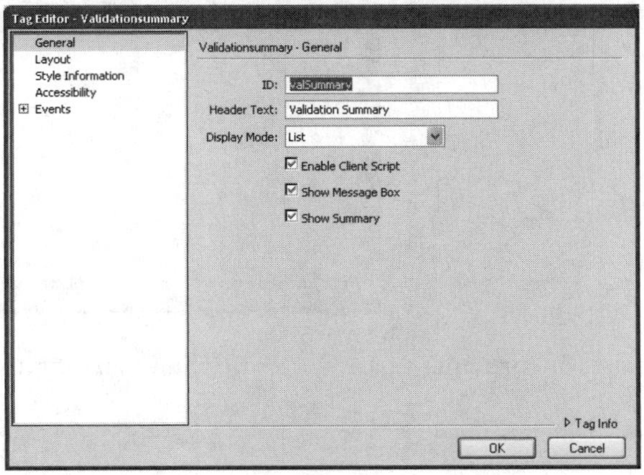

TABLE 6.6: ValidationSummary Control/`asp:validationsummary` Options

Dreamweaver Dialog Box Text Field	Equivalent ASP.NET Element Attribute	Description
ID	ID	Uniquely identifies the element.
Header Text	HeaderText	Used to provide a heading over the summary of error messages.
Display Mode	DisplayMode	Indicates the formatting of the summary: list, bullets, or paragraph format.

Earlier, in the section on the RequiredFieldValidator control, I explained the difference between the `Text` attribute and the `ErrorMessage` attribute. Here in the ValidationSummary control is where that difference comes into play. ASP.NET uses the value in each validation control's `ErrorMessage` attribute to display the errors as part of the summary in the ValidationSummary control. You can display the summary as a bulleted list, paragraphs, or a simple list, using the `DisplayMode` attribute. As you can see in Table 6.6, this attribute is handled through Dreamweaver using the Display Mode drop-down list box in the ValidationSummary Tag Editor dialog box. Figure 6.12 shows a web page displaying a summary from two validation controls and the errors associated with them.

FIGURE 6.12:

The Validation-Summary control displays a summary of all validation errors in one area on the web page.

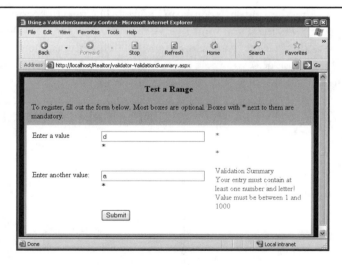

Listing 6.8 presents a basic ValidationSummary control used in a web page.

Listing 6.8   **Using a ValidationSummary control**

```
<table width="100%" align="center" cellpadding="10" bgcolor="#FFFFFF"
class="tablebrdr">
     <tr valign="baseline">
     <td width="37%" align="left" valign="top">
      Enter a value</td>
     <td width="15%" align="left" valign="top">
        <asp:textbox Columns="32"  ID="fValue" runat="server"
TextMode="SingleLine" />
      * </td>
     <td width="48%" rowspan="3" align="left" valign="top">
<div align="left">
                                    <p>
                                      <asp:regularexpressionvalidator
ErrorMessage="Your entry must contain at least one number and letter!"
ID="passwordValidate2" runat="server" ControlToValidate="fValue"
ValidationExpression="[a-zA-Z]+\w*\d+\w*">*</asp:regularexpressionvalidator>
                                          </p>
                                    </div>
                                    <p>
                                      <asp:rangevalidator
ControlToValidate="fValue2" Display="Static" ErrorMessage="Value must be between
1 and 1000" ID="rangeValidator" MaximumValue="J" MinimumValue="A"
runat="server">*</asp:rangevalidator>
                                    </p>
                                    <p>
                                      <asp:validationsummary DisplayMode="List"
HeaderText="Validation Summary" ID="valSummary" runat="server" />
                                          </p></td>
                                </tr>
                                <tr valign="baseline">
                                  <td  align="left" valign="top"> Enter another
value:</td>
                                  <td align="left" valign="top">
<asp:textbox  ID="fValue2" TextMode="SingleLine" Columns="32" runat="server" />
                                      * </td>
                                </tr>
                                <tr valign="baseline">
                                  <td  align="left" valign="top"> </td>
                                  <td align="left" valign="top"><input name="submit"
type="submit" value="Submit">
                                  </td>
                                </tr>
                              </table>
```

In Listing 6.8, there are two validation controls: a RegularExpressionValidator control and a RangeValidator control. Note that instead of using a Text attribute, we use element content instead. The result is the same as using a Text attribute and is another way you can display errors. In this case, we don't want to display an error because it would be redundant. Instead, we display an asterisk to flag the error for the user without giving details, which are provided using the ValidationSummary control instead. You could also pop up a message box to the user listing the errors. Here is the code for displaying a Range Validator control with a simple asterisk and that passes its message to a Validation Summary control:

```
<asp:rangevalidator ControlToValidate="fValue2" Display="Static"
ErrorMessage="Value must be between 1 and 1000" ID="rangeValidator"
MaximumValue="J" MinimumValue="A" runat="server">*</asp:rangevalidator>
```

Wrapping Up

Use validation controls liberally. They're easy to set up and require very little programming expertise. Naturally, once you get comfortable writing code for your web pages, you can write even more powerful validation routines. But an amazing amount of data validation can be done with absolutely no programming. Well-designed form validation is an essential part of good form design, anyway. Since .NET comes with such powerful validation components, there aren't any good reasons for not using them!

These days, since most browsers support JavaScript, it's a good idea to handle your validation on the client side. You can do this by simply leaving off the EnableClientScript attribute, which defaults to true.

CHAPTER 7

Getting Your Hands Dirty: Hand-Coding with Dreamweaver MX

- The Dreamweaver IDE

- Working with script

- The fastest primer ever on C#

- Using code-behind with Dreamweaver MX and .NET

- Event handling

- Building and using custom controls

Most of this book has been devoted to ASPX pages, which are also referred to as *web forms*. There's a good reason for this, since Dreamweaver is so helpful at building them. When web forms are used right, you can cut development costs by extreme percentages using Dreamweaver. This, in turn, leaves open the possibility that you'll have time to do some advanced coding of your own.

In this chapter you'll focus your attention on the code-editing features of Dreamweaver. This will happen not by a comprehensive tour of these features, but instead through a brief introduction into how to actually do some coding. For the most part, I'll leave exploration of Dreamweaver's code editor up to you. You're not paying good money to have a bunch of screenshots with highlighted lines to demonstrate syntax thrown in your face.

This chapter introduces some principles of coding with C#, this book's language of choice. The truth is, coding with VB.NET is not much different from C#, at least from a theoretical standpoint. Most of the differences are syntactical, and if you're an old hand at Visual Basic you'll know what to do. For those of you not familiar with either language, I chose to focus on C# partly because it seems to have a larger code base in the ASP.NET world, and partly because I find it somewhat more intuitive because of its similarity to Java.

After we take a look at the basics behind C# programming, you'll see how to compile programs and use the results of those compilations in custom controls.

The Dreamweaver IDE

Dreamweaver has come a long way from its days as a graphic designer's tool. It still is a great tool for designers, but it has morphed into a very good IDE, as well. Much of the reason for this is Dreamweaver's integration of Homesite, a popular HTML editor that Macromedia acquired when it purchased Allaire. The Homesite interface, including its tag helpers and tag completion tools, has found its way into Dreamweaver (see Figure 7.1). In addition, there is a Tags panel where you can access all of an element's attributes and type in their values. This is located in the same area of the Dreamweaver interface that stores other panels, such as the Server Behaviors tab, the Application panel, and the Code panel.

You can also split the Dreamweaver window and view your web pages in Design and Code views simultaneously. This is a great way to learn how code is written, if that is a weak area for you. As you drop components into Dreamweaver, click on them in Design view and the corresponding code gets highlighted in Code view.

FIGURE 7.1:

The Dreamweaver
Homesite-based Text
Editor helps with
syntax by providing
access to ASP.NET
properties and
methods.

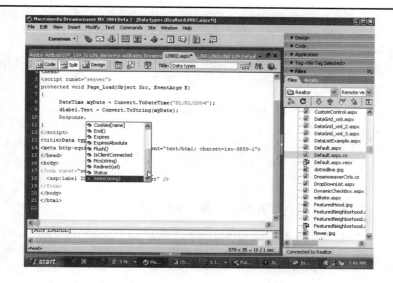

Working with Script

There are two ways to work with scripted code in your ASP.NET web pages. One way is to embed your script using the HTML `script` element. The other way is to use a *code-behind*, which is a separate file containing your script (with a `.cs` extension for C# files or a `.vb` extension for VB.NET files). For now we'll focus on using the `script` element. Code-behind files are covered toward the end of this chapter.

Before you worry about the `script` element, you need to make sure your `Page` directive indicates the proper scripting language for your web page:

```
<%@ Page Language="C#" ContentType="text/html" %>
```

Then you can use a `script` element anywhere in your web page, usually in your `head` element unless you want to execute routines right in your web page.

Don't leave off the `runat="server"` attribute/value pair, or the script will be interpreted on the client browser, not by the server processing your ASP.NET pages:

```
<script runat="server" language="C#" >
protected void Page_Load(Object Src, EventArgs E)
{
 //some code here
}
</script>
```

The `language` attribute is optional, but the `runat="server"` attribute/value pair is most certainly not.

If you omit the `runat="server"` attribute/value pair in your `script` tag, the ASP.NET runtime won't read your script and your application won't run.

Dropping code into your `Page_Load` event means the code in that event handler will be executed when the page loads. You can leave that event handler empty if you want, and create a different event handler to manage all or some other portions of your code. Event handlers are covered in the "Event Handling" section later in this chapter.

The Fastest Primer Ever on C#

Okay, so you probably won't be a world-class guru on C# when you're done reading this section, but you'll have an idea how it works—which is better than nothing, and you'll be able to start writing real applications instead of just HTML on steroids. With some practice, you may even invent something really cool and make millions of dollars on The Next Big Thing. So let's dig in.

When you program with C#, or VB.NET for that matter, you're basically just managing the huge object model that Microsoft developed for ASP.NET. As mentioned elsewhere, ASP.NET consists of a massive library of class objects that you can manipulate. There are three ways to manage the way code is executed in C# to work with this object model:

- Conditional structures, which determine the statements in a group that should and shouldn't be run

- Looping structures, which repeat a set of statements depending on a named set of criteria

- Functions, which are executed upon command from events such as mouse clicks, or from some other code statement when one chunk of code calls another chunk of code into duty

ASP.NET objects consist of numerous properties and methods that will often end up being used by one of these control structures to accomplish some task. Before we look at these control structures, we need to spend a minute or two understanding how C# stores data through variables and other processes.

Storing Data in C#

You already know enough about programming for the Web to understand the importance of your Web application's ability to remember things like usernames and calculated totals for items such as invoices. A web application needs a place to store and manipulate this information. In C# (and other languages such as VB.NET), we use variables to store data for reuse later on.

Understanding Variables

Variables are one of the fundamental building blocks in object-oriented programming, and C# is no exception. Variables are references to specific memory allocations that are given an identifying label by a programmer. Think of them as containers that store a specific byte sequence to represent a string of text, an integer, and many other types of data.

These containers have names. They're also shortcuts. It's a lot easier to write

```
a + b
```

than it is to write

```
"The long winded poet wrote often" + "and wrote badly."
```

It's also easier to simply define something once and then refer to the same thing by name over and over again.

Declaring Variables

To establish the existence of variables, you declare them. In C# and even in VB.NET (I say *even* VB.NET because this wasn't necessary in old Visual Basic), you have to declare what type of variable you're using as part of the declaration. To declare a string variable, you would have something like this:

```
string myStringVariable;
```

The first part of this code declares the datatype, and the second part declares the name of the variable. This variable declaration allocates the memory space needed to store the variable to the identifier, which is the name of the variable. So obviously the name can't clash with an existing variable of the same name, because there's a dependency between the name and the identity of the variable. The variable declaration must always begin with the datatype of the variable, followed by one or more white spaces, followed by the name of the variable, followed by a semicolon (which is always needed to complete a statement in C#).

NOTE   C# is case sensitive, so a variable named `myVar` is different from a variable named `myvar`.

You can also declare more than one variable per line, as long as they're of the same datatype. You separate each variable instance with a comma:

```
string myStringVariable, myStringVariable2, myStringVariable3;
```

You can also declare a variable and assign it a value all at once:

```
string myStringVariable = "Have a nice day";
```

The equals sign here acts as an assignment operator. This isn't the same as an equal; it just means you're assigning a value to the variable. It's like telling the compiler to set the value of the string `myStringVariable` to be "Have a nice day."

You can also declare and assign more than one variable at once:

```
string myStringVariable = "Have a nice day",
myStringVariable2 = "Have an okay day",
myStringVariable3 = "Have a lousy day, and don't let
➥the door hit you on the way out";
```

Developing the code to work with variables can be quite easy when you're working with basic code. Consider the following script, which writes the value of the variable `myStringVariable3` to the browser window:

```
protected void Page_Load(Object Src, EventArgs E)
{
  string myStringVariable = "Have a nice day",
myStringVariable2 = "Have an okay day",
myStringVariable3 = "Have a lousy day, and don't let
➥the door hit you on the way out";

    Response.Write(myStringVariable3);
}
```

In this example, the `Response.Write()` method merely takes the string value of the variable and renders it to the browser window, as shown in Figure 7.2.

FIGURE 7.2:

A web application returning the value of a variable to the browser window

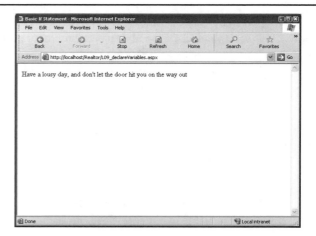

Naming Variables

You should give your variables reasonably obvious names, not only because others may view your code, but because in the mad rush to crank stuff out in the real world we often don't do as much code-commenting as we should.

In C#, variable names must begin with a letter and can't contain a fullstop (period) or a space. You should avoid all symbols except the underscore character, which is acceptable and actually frequently used by some. How you format variables from a case standpoint is up to you, but you should be consistent. If one variable is named `camelCase` and another is named `SclamelCase`, your code won't break, but you'll become the source of dark murmurings at the water cooler. And don't forget that C# is case sensitive.

You also have to avoid using C# keywords, so `int` would be a no-no as a variable name because `int` is used by C# to signify a specific datatype. You could conceivably use a name like `Int`, since keywords in C# start with lowercase letters, but don't do that either because many VB.NET keywords start with uppercase letters and you don't want to confuse VB.NET developers who are working with your code.

Understanding Datatypes

There are two broad categories of datatypes. One category, called *simple types*, consists of values of a fixed length (see Table 7.1 later in this section to see the length ranges for particular datatypes). Simple types are stored in a part of the computer's memory called the *stack*. The other broad category is called a *reference* because only a reference to the data is stored on the stack; the actual data itself is stored in a part of the computer's memory called the *heap*. The heap is used because a reference-type variable may have a variable-length value, which cannot be accommodated in the stack.

Think of stack memory as "local" memory that is directly accessible at all times by the program that is running, and that is dependent on the computer's available memory. In the case of ASP.NET, this means the memory available on the server's computer, not the user's, because the program that is running is the software that runs ASP.NET and serves it to users' browsers (we often refer to these as clients). The memory needed for a simple-type variable is allocated during compilation on the stack.

Using the heap requires access to the operating system and some careful tracking. C#'s predecessor, C++ (some would say Java is really the predecessor to C#, but let's stay out of that war) is famous among fledgling programmers for its *pointers*—references to variables in the heap—because it's so easy to make the kind of mistake with them that causes memory leaks. If you've ever worked with a program that seems to just suck your system dry and then finally causes everything to crash and burn, especially in the old days before multi-threaded operating systems such as Windows 95 or Mac OS pre-X became prevalent, you've probably become a victim of poor heap-allocation. You won't have to worry about the difference between heap and stack very much with ASP.NET because ASP.NET integrates so closely with the operating system anyway, but it's still good to know. The simple types include the numeric datatype, character datatype, and Boolean (true/false) datatypes, Structs (we'll cover those separately), and Enumerations (ditto). The reference types include strings, arrays, classes, objects, and interfaces.

Numeric Datatypes

All numeric datatypes are simple types, so they're stored on the memory stack. There are three numeric datatypes:

- Integer
- Floating point
- Decimal

When storing whole numbers, any three of these can be used. For fraction-based numbers, you need to use either a floating-point type or a decimal.

Table 7.1 lists the kinds of numeric (and other) types available. Notice the difference between *signed* and *unsigned* types. This just means that, in the case of a signed type, the variable can hold negative values (within the ranges specified in Table 7.1), whereas unsigned types cannot hold negative values.

When assigning a value to a numeric-based variable, don't wrap the value in quotes, because the compiler will interpret the value as a string of characters. Write it like this:

```
int myIntVariable = 1;
```

not:

```
int myIntVariable = "1";
```

If you declare an `int` datatype on your variable and wrap its value in quotes, you'll get a message like this:

```
Compiler Error Message: CS0029: Cannot implicitly convert type 'string' to 'int'
```

You can add a suffix to a numeric variable to more explicitly identify its datatype:

```
long myIntVariable = 1125555988761;
```

TABLE 7.1: Numeric Datatypes Used in C#

Name	Description	Suffix (If Applicable)
sbyte	8-bit signed integer with a range of –128 to 127.	
short	16-bit signed integer with a range of –32,768 to 32,767.	
int	32-bit signed integer with a range of –2,147,483,648 to 2,147,483,647.	
long	64-bit signed integer with a range of –9,223,372,036,854,775,808 to 9,223,372,036,854,775,807.	L or l
byte	8-bit unsigned integer ranging from 0 to 255.	
ushort	16-bit unsigned integer with a range of 0 to 32,767.	
uint	32-bit unsigned integer with a range of 0 to 2,147,483,647.	U or u

Continued on next page

TABLE 7.1 CONTINUED: Numeric Datatypes Used in C#

Name	Description	Suffix (If Applicable)
ulong	64-bit unsigned integer with a range of 0 to 9,223,372,036,854,775,807.	UL or ul
double	Double-precision floating-point numbers ranging in value from −1.79769313486231570E+308 through −4.94065645841246544E−324 for negative values, and from 4.94065645841246544E−324 through 1.79769313486231570E+308 for positive values.	D or d
float	Signed 32-bit single-precision floating-point numbers ranging in value from −3.4028235E+38 through −1.401298E−45 for negative values, and from 1.401298E−45 through 3.4028235E+38 for positive values.	F or f
decimal	128-bit integer scaled by a variable power of 10. Scaling is determined by the number of digits to the right of the decimal point, which can range from 0 through 28. With a scale of 0 (no decimal places), the largest possible value is +/−79,228,162,514,264,337,593,543,950,335. With 28 decimal places, the largest value is +/−7.9228162514264337593543950335, and the smallest nonzero value is +/−0.0000000000000000000000000001 (+/−1E−28).	
string	Identifies your variable's content as text consisting of Unicode character sequences. The variable can contain 2 billion characters, so there isn't much of a limit on how big this can be.	
char	Identifies your variable's content as text consisting of Unicode character sequences. This is a fixed-length variable that only holds the value of one character.	
Boolean	These are 16-bit (2-byte) numbers whose only valid values are true or false.	

String Datatypes

Strings are actually stored as Unicode character sequences, which are in fact stored as unsigned 16-bit (2-byte) numbers ranging in value from 0 through 65535. Each number represents a single Unicode character.

Unicode is a universal encoding mechanism that binds each letter of the alphabet in just about any language (but not Cherokee, strangely enough) to a specific number. For example, the string I am bored. would be represented by the following series of Unicode values:

```
\u0049\u0020\u0061\u006d\u0020\u0062\u006f\u0072\u0065\u0064\u002e
```

where the \u sequence acts as a delimiter to each value. The letter I is represented by 0049; and the next character in the string, the apostrophe, is represented in Unicode by the 0020 numerical sequence, and so on. These are hexadecimal numbers, but there are decimal equivalents for each. Since Unicode consists of huge tables of these kinds of mapping sequences, it has gained favor as a way to represent strings of text in modern computer languages.

There are two types of string datatypes: string datatype and char datatype.

A string can contain up to approximately 2 billion Unicode characters; a char datatype variable is a fixed length and can only hold one Unicode sequence. Consequently, char datatypes are stored in the stack memory, and strings are stored on the heap because their length can vary so greatly.

In addition to their size differences, you assign values to string and char types differently. You wrap a string value in double quotes, and a char value in single quotes. The following code fragment outputs the string This is a string! into the browser window.

```
string myString = "This is a string";
char myChar = '!';
Response.Write(myString + myChar);
```

The plus sign *concatenates* the string values, which means you're simply appending one value to the other.

Note that you could also simply assign Unicode values directly to either string or char variables. The following would also output the string This is a string! into the browser window:

```
string myString = "This is a string";
char myChar = '\u0021';
Response.Write(myString + myChar);
```

You can assign empty values to string type variables by simply assigning double quotes with no space in between:

```
string myString = "";
```

Sometimes you need to create newlines or some other special formatting from within your script. To do that, you need to use something called an *escape sequence*, which tells the compiler to temporarily "escape" the literal interpretation of a specified character during the string-parsing process so that the compiler can understand a command you're trying to pass from within the string.

Escape sequences are marked by the backslash character. Table 7.2 shows escape sequences used within string values.

TABLE 7.2: Character Escape Sequences

Escape Sequence	Character
\'	Single quote
\"	Double quote
\\	Backslash
\0	Null

Continued on next page

TABLE 7.2 CONTINUED: Character Escape Sequences

Escape Sequence	Character
\a	Alert
\b	Backspace
\f	Form feed
\n	Newline
\r	Carriage return
\t	Tab
\v	Vertical tab
\u####	A Unicode representation of a character value, where each # represents one single hexadecimal digit

You've already seen one example of an escape sequence, in the demonstration of outputting a Unicode value earlier in this section. Listing 7.1 shows another way to use them.

Listing 7.1 **Using escape sequences in variable string values**

```
<%@ Page Language="C#" ContentType="text/html" ResponseEncoding="iso-8859-1" %>
<!DOCTYPE HTML PUBLIC "-//W3C//DTD HTML 4.01
➥Transitional//EN"
"http://www.w3.org/TR/html4/loose.dtd">
<html>
<head>
<script runat="server">
protected void Page_Load(Object Src, EventArgs E)
{
        string myString = "This is a string\nThis is a new line\n";
    string myString2 = "This is a series of tabs:\t tab
➥\t tab";
    Response.Write("<pre>" + myString + myString2 +
➥"</pre>");
}
</script>
<title>Data types</title>
<meta http-equiv="Content-Type" content="text/html;
charset=iso-8859-1">
</head>
<body>

</body>
</html>
```

Listing 7.1 renders formatted output into the browser as shown in Figure 7.3. Note the use of the HTML pre element in the Response.Write() method, to preserve formatting. This is done because HTML collapses whitespace created by non-HTML means unless you tell the browser you want to preserve the formatting with the pre element.

FIGURE 7.3:

Escape sequences
are used to format
text in the browser.

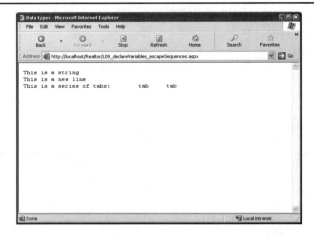

Sometimes, particularly when you're using paths in your string variable definition, you may want to tell the parser to ignore backslashes. You can do this by inserting an @ character before the string and after the = assignment operator:

```
string myString = @"C:\Documents and Settings\Chuck\Start Menu";
```

This will output the string C:\Documents and Settings\Chuck\Start Menu to the browser and will not interpret the backslashes as escape sequences. If you leave off the @ character using that same string, you'll get the following message:

```
Compiler Error Message: CS1009: Unrecognized escape sequence
```

Booleans
A variable using a Boolean value as a datatype can have only one of two values, true or false, and case is important (only lowercase is allowed).

Boolean variables are declared with the bool keyword:

```
bool myBool = true
```

Notice that there are no quotes around the value, as is the case with numeric values.

Object Types
An object type of variable is a reference referring to a pre-existing object through the new keyword. These object types can refer to ASP.NET classes or to custom classes you develop yourself.

Here is an area where it's good to remember the difference between memory allocation types. That's because an object variable, being a reference, has its reference stored in the stack, but the object itself will be allocated to the heap and isn't available until it's *instantiated* with the new keyword. When we say instantiated, we mean that an instance of a class, or object, is created. When a new car rolls off the assembly line, an instance of a car class is created (if you were to make an analogy to the automotive world). You can't use the car until it's off the assembly line, and the go-ahead is given by some guy in a white smock who stamps new onto the car somewhere.

You can also use other datatypes, such as string and int datatypes, as objects; but most of the time you'll create instances of class objects.

One of the nice things about Dreamweaver is that it does a lot of this kind of work for you, but you can always take matters into your own hands if you want. If you look at the source code for the Dreamweaver control, you'll see that it's replete with examples of object instantiations. We can do the same thing if we want to in our own code. For example, we can create an instance of the .NET SqlConnection class, which represents a connection to a SQL Server database:

```
SqlConnection connection = new
SqlConnection(ConfigurationSettings.AppSettings["DSN"]);
```

This declares the variable named connection and assigns its value by instantiating an instance of the SqlConnection class. You can then proceed by declaring yet another variable, the command variable, to pave the way for calling a stored procedure:

```
SqlCommand command = new SqlCommand("UpdateListingInsertions", connection);
command.CommandType = CommandType.StoredProcedure;
```

The immediate question that probably comes to mind is, how does one know what to include in the instantiation statement? In the first example, there was only one parameter (in bold in the first declaration), which appears in parentheses after the class name you're creating:

```
ConfigurationSettings.AppSettings["DSN"]
```

But in the second declaration, there were two parameters (also in bold):

```
"UpdateListingInsertions", connection
```

The easiest way to find class information is to type into Google **MSDN** (the name of Microsoft's developers' website) and the name of the class for which you want information, followed by the word **constructor**. The first link from this Google query will take you directly to the constructor definition for the class, where you can learn about the arguments it takes:

```
MSDN "SqlCommand Constructor"
```

The first link from this result set will take you to Microsoft's developer website (MSDN). On that page you'll see the constructor for the `SqlCommand` class described:

Initializes a new instance of the `SqlCommand` class.

Overload List

Initializes a new instance of the `SqlCommand` class.

Supported by the .NET Compact Framework.

[Visual Basic] `Public Sub New()`

[C#] `public SqlCommand();`

[C++] `public: SqlCommand();`

[JScript] `public function SqlCommand();`

Initializes a new instance of the `SqlCommand` class with the text of the query.

Supported by the .NET Compact Framework.

[Visual Basic] `Public Sub New(String)`

[C#] `public SqlCommand(string);`

[C++] `public: SqlCommand(String*);`

[JScript] `public function SqlCommand(String);`

Initializes a new instance of the `SqlCommand` class with the text of the query and a `SqlConnection`.

Supported by the .NET Compact Framework.

[Visual Basic] `Public Sub New(String, SqlConnection)`

[C#] `public SqlCommand(string, SqlConnection);`

[C++] `public: SqlCommand(String*, SqlConnection*);`

[JScript] `public function SqlCommand(String, SqlConnection);`

Initializes a new instance of the SqlCommand class with the text of the query, a SqlConnection, and the SqlTransaction.

Supported by the .NET Compact Framework.

[Visual Basic] `Public Sub New(String, SqlConnection, SqlTransaction)`

[C#] `public SqlCommand(string, SqlConnection, SqlTransaction);`

[C++] `public: SqlCommand(String*, SqlConnection*, SqlTransaction*);`

[JScript] `public function SqlCommand(String, SqlConnection, SqlTransaction);`

It's fairly safe to say that even at Microsoft there are likely to be few people who know every single property and method available to every class object available in the ASP.NET object model. Not only will ASP.NET push your programming skills, but it will challenge your research skills as well. Having access to a good Internet search engine and learning how to use it effectively can go a long way toward helping you develop in ASP.NET, since any book with a comprehensive reference on this material would be about six feet thick and could contain nothing in the way of tutorials to help you work with .NET objects. The key is simply understanding how these objects are used, not memorizing all of them.

Going back to our second declaration, you may have noticed a second line of code that went unmentioned:

```
command.CommandType = CommandType.StoredProcedure;
```

If you hunt for the `SqlCommand` class definition (**Google/ MSDN "SqlCommand Class"**), you'll notice, first, that the MSDN site isn't listed first; and you have to scroll down to about the third listing in the results page to find the MSDN page containing definitions for this class. When you click on the link for the page, you'll see a link named SqlCommand Members. Click this link and you'll find all the properties and methods associated with this class. Scroll down, and you'll see that one of its properties is named the `CommandType` property. Once again, there's a link to that. When you click the link, you'll see the definition for that property that says, "Gets or sets a value indicating how the `CommandText` property is to be interpreted."

Can you see the similarity between how this works and the way Dreamweaver control elements are generated? Consider the following Dreamweaver control element:

```
<MM:INSERT id=Insert1 runat="server"
 IsStoredProcedure="true"
CommandText='<%# "ListingInsertions" %>'
ConnectionString='<%# System.Configuration.ConfigurationSettings.AppSettings
➡["MM_CONNECTION_STRING_mdriscollString"] %>'
DatabaseType='<%# System.Configuration.ConfigurationSettings.AppSettings
➡["MM_CONNECTION_DATABASETYPE_mdriscollString"] %>'
Expression='<%# Request.Form["MM_insert"] == "form2" %>'
CreateDataSet="false"
SuccessURL='<%# "Listings.aspx" %>' Debug="true">
```

The `IsStoredProcedure="true"` attribute/value pair handles the same task as `CommandType` `.StoredProcedure`; does, and in fact, is used by the Dreamweaver control's source script to pass the value it captures into the commandText property at runtime. You can see this on line 281 of the `DreamweaverCtrls.cs` file:

```
theCommand.CommandType = IsStoredProcedure ?
CommandType.StoredProcedure : CommandType.Text;
```

The reason I mention all of this is that you have two options for code development. You can use the Dreamweaver control for managing much of your code, but on those occasions you wish to write your own, you are taking advantage of the same classes of objects used by the Dreamweaver control. The difference is that it's a lot easier to set those Dreamweaver element attribute values than it is to write the logic for making them work—which is why it can be so advantageous and time-saving to use Dreamweaver controls. Nevertheless, there are times you'll want or need to do your own coding. Those occasions call for an understanding of how the various classes and objects work.

Working with Dates

When your users are working with forms, you'll often be working with dates. Perhaps your users will need to schedule a delivery or book a reservation. Looking at what I've talked about so far, you might wonder, rightly, how dates fit into all of this. They look like numbers on a certain level, but it makes more sense to refer to them as strings—but then how can you do any numerical sorting on a string so that dates appear in sequential order when they need to be?

Luckily, Microsoft's army of programmers has resolved this by supplying us with a special breed of datatype called the `DateTime` datatype. `DateTime`s aren't actually an inherent part of C#. Rather, they reside in a special type of ASP.NET object called a *structure*, which is a set of definitions used to define a custom datatype. Because `DateTime` is accessible via the `System` namespace, it is a native part of .NET. Declaring a variable as a `DateTime` datatype is therefore as easy as calling any other datatype. Well, almost. You actually need to call a method of the

Convert class, which is a member of the System.Object superclass, in order to actually convert a DateTime structure to a string so you can display it in the browser:

```
DateTime myDate = Convert.ToDateTime("01/01/2004");
```

Then, to display it in the browser, you only need to write some kind of routine to do so:

```
Response.Write("New Year's Day is: " + myDate);
```

As you can see, declaring a DateTime variable is just as easy as declaring any other kind of variable, except for the slight syntax difference using the Convert class's ToDateTime() method. However, look what happens when, instead of using a Response.Write() method to write out the date to the browser, we decide to set an asp:Label element's Text value using our myDate variable:

```
dLabel.Text = myDate;
```

We'll get the following compiler error:

```
Compiler Error Message: CS0029: Cannot implicitly convert type 'System.DateTime'
to 'string'
```

This is because the Write() method, which belongs to the HttpResponse class, can write an object out as text output; but you need to convert the object to a string when using it in an ASP.NET web control's Text value (because, after all, you're not using the Write() method in that case).

The way to deal with this is to use another member of the Convert class, the ubiquitous ToString method. This is an important method to remember because it often solves the problem of the error message seen just above. Listing 7.2 shows how this method is used to display the DateTime variable. The relevant code is in bold. The asp:Label element's Text attribute is dynamically given the value of the myDate variable with an assist from the Convert class.

Listing 7.2   **Using the ToString method to convert a DateTime object to a string**

```
<%@ Page Language="C#" ContentType="text/html" ResponseEncoding="iso-8859-1" %>
<html>
<head>
<script runat="server">
protected void Page_Load(Object Src, EventArgs E)
{
  DateTime myDate = Convert.ToDateTime("01/01/2004");
  dLabel.Text = Convert.ToString(myDate);
}
</script>
<title>Data types</title>
<meta http-equiv="Content-Type" content="text/html; charset=iso-8859-1">
</head>
<body>
```

```
<form runat="server">
  <asp:Label ID="dLabel" runat="server" />
</form>
</body>
</html>
```

Understanding Operators

Now that we have our variables, we can do something with them. In order to do that, we will take advantage of operators, which are characters that identify specific operations to be performed on a variable's assigned value, called the *operand*. You've already seen the assignment operator, as represented by an equal sign (=). In the statement that follows, x is the variable, and 1 is the operand:

```
X=1;
```

There are other operators, as well, and you can string them together, which changes the value of the variable on-the-fly:

```
X=1+2
```

Since many operators are mathematical, their order of evaluation matters. The easiest way to deal with this fact is to not worry about it at all and to control the order yourself with parentheses:

```
x=1+3*3/5-4+2/2
```

I don't know about you, but even if I were to memorize Table 7.3, which shows operator precedence, I just don't want to go there. Instead, I want to be sure a calculation does what I want by using parentheses. Each of the two following lines of code will yield two completely different results:

```
int x=1+3*3/5-4+2/2;
int y=((1+3)*3)/(5-4)+(2/2);
```

The first variable, x, will yield a value of 1; and the second variable, y, will yield a value of 13. This is because the parentheses group operators and operands together, calculating their contents before applying the next operator to them.

There is also such a thing as formal operator precedence, as shown in Table 7.3.

TABLE 7.3: Operator Precedence

Type of Operator	Operators
Primary	x.y, f(x), a[x], x++, x--, new, typeof, checked, unchecked
Unary	+, -, !, ~, ++x, --x, (T)x,
Multiplicative	*, /, %
Additive	+, -

Continued on next page

TABLE 7.3 CONTINUED: Operator Precedence

Type of Operator	Operators
Shift	$<<$, $>>$
Relational and type testing	<, >, <=, >=, is, as,
Equality	==, !=,
Logical AND	&
Logical XOR	^
Logical OR	|
Conditional AND	&&
Conditional OR	||
Conditional	? :
Assignment	=, *=, /=, %=, +=, -=, $<<$=, $>>$=, &=, ^=, |=,

You can see from Table 7.3 that there are quite a large number of operators available to C# developers. Many of them are math related; many others are used for testing one value against another using conditional statements, which we'll be taking a look at soon. Other operators, such as ++, are used to increment values; for example, i++ means that a variable named i has its value incremented by 1 (the use of ++ indicates that the increment is always by a value of 1). This operation is often used in looping statements, which are created for repeating a specified number of times until a termination condition stops the processing. The decrement operator, --, does the opposite.

Two other important operators are == (is equal to) and != (is not equal to) and their cousins, the relational operators shown in Table 7.3. These are used in conditional statements such as if(x==7), then do this...

Casting Datatypes
When does 12 divided by 5 equal 2? When you don't cast integer variables. Since calculated integers will remain integers until you do something to change their datatype, the results of calculations performed with them will be rounded off, so that, for example, 5 divided into 12 will equal 2. To change that, you need to *cast* your variables.

Casting is the process by which you convert one kind of datatype into another. To divide 5 into 12 and get a nonrounded result, we cast the variables. To do this, we can set up a new variable, named xy, as float, and then explicitly cast the result of x/y:

```
int x=12;
int y=5;
float xy = (float)x/y;
Response.Write(xy);
```

The datatype of the variable on the left side of the equal sign is placed in parentheses next to the value that needs to be converted. When a cast is attempted on a variable type beyond the range into which the attempted cast is made, doom is the result—there's no error, but data will be lost. You'll wind up with inaccurate results and angry users.

TIP   When passing values to and from forms, your real friend is not casting, it's the Convert class and its many methods, including ToString, ToInt32, and so on. You can view the members of this class at `http://msdn.microsoft.com/library/default.asp?url= /library/en-us/cpref/html/frlrfsystemconvertclasstopic.asp`.

Understanding Arrays

An array is a collection of items grouped together and, like a variable, given a label. Each item in the array can be identified by its position in the array. The position in the array is zero-based, which means the first item in an array is at the 0 position in the array, the second item is at the 1 position, and so on.

The syntax for an array looks like the syntax for a variable, except for a pair of brackets following the name. (The brackets *may* be separated from the name by whitespace, but they don't have to be.)

```
string [] myString
```

Then you have to initialize the array by indicating how many items exist in the array and exactly what is being created. This is accomplished by the new keyword:

```
myString = new String[3];
```

Once you've done that, you can then assign values to each item in the array:

```
myString[0] = "Hello";
myString[1] = "Wonderful";
myString[2] = "World";
```

As I mentioned, arrays consist of zero-based indices, so the first item in the array must be referred to with 0. The following code fragment outputs the string HelloWonderfulWorld into the browser window:

```
string [] myString = new String[3];
myString[0] = "Hello";
myString[1] = "Wonderful";
myString[2] = "World";
Response.Write(myString[0] + myString[1] + myString[2]);
```

Note that you don't need to build these values sequentially, and you don't need to fill every item. You could have omitted one of the items, and the array would have been filled with an empty string. I didn't bother adding any spaces. You can add a space easily enough:

```
Response.Write(myString[0] + " " + myString[1] + " " + myString[2]);
```

You might want to ask, "Wouldn't it be easier to just define your variable like this: myString[0] = "Hello ";? With the extra space?" As simple as this example is, the reason why you *don't* want to do something like that goes to the heart of encapsulation, which involves the reuse of objects. The whole idea of variables and arrays is focused on their reuse. It's better practice to deal with formatting issues within the chunk of code that uses the variable, rather than the form within the variable itself. Of course, there are always exceptions to this, but the central tenet remains true: In encapsulation, choose the best way to define variable values so that you can reference them efficiently with consistent results across a variety of scenarios.

You can also assign your item values within braces right after you instantiate the object that is being created for filling your arrays:

```
string [] myString = new String[] {"Hello", "Wonderful", "World"};
```

Notice that there is no need in this case to name the number of items in parentheses, although it's okay to do so if you wish. The following is perfectly legitimate:

```
string [] myString = new String[3] {"Hello", "Wonderful", "World"};
```

Creating Structures

A structure is like a mini-class. You can use it to define a group of variables, and it can contain groups of data, including methods and properties—all callable in the same way as classes, and instantiated the same way.

Let's look at an easy example to see how they work. We'll create a structure called MLSListings that will simply contain three variables containing the listing number (as a string value), the city the listing is in, and a brief description:

```
struct MLSListing
  {
   public string MLSNumber;
   public string City;
   public string sDescription;
  }
```

As you can see, three different variables are declared. Note the use of the *public* keyword. This makes the variables available outside the scope of our little application, in case we want to make a control later on.

TIP   The public keyword in a variable declaration designates that variable to be outside the scope of the code defining it.

Next, let's make a table consisting of form fields and some labels to pass data into:

```
<table width="100%"  border="0" cellpadding="10">
  <tr>
    <td> </td>
    <td>Your Input</td>
    <td>Your Output</td>
  </tr>
  <tr>
    <td>MLSNumber</td>
    <td><asp:TextBox ID="tbMLSNum" ToolTip="MLS Number" runat="server" /></td>
    <td><asp:Label ID="lMLSNum" runat="server"></asp:Label></td>
  </tr>
  <tr>
    <td>City</td>
    <td><asp:TextBox ID="tbCity" ToolTip="City Listing is located in"
runat="server" /></td>
    <td><asp:Label ID="lCity" runat="server">
    </asp:Label></td>
  </tr>
  <tr>
    <td>Description</td>
    <td><asp:TextBox ID="tbDescription" ToolTip="Short Description"
runat="server" /></td>
    <td><asp:Label ID="lDescription" runat="server"></asp:Label></td>
  </tr>
  <tr>
    <td> </td>
    <td><asp:Button ID="Submit" runat="server" Text="Submit" /></td>
    <td> </td>
  </tr>
</table>
```

Remember, you can use the Dreamweaver interface to bang this code out fast. Just use the ID attribute names shown here in bold for each widget you create.

Next, add the following to your script tag, making sure it is separate from your structure definition:

```
protected void Page_Load(Object Src, EventArgs E)
{
    MLSListing Listing = new MLSListing();
    Listing.MLSNumber = tbMLSNum.Text;
    Listing.City = tbCity.Text;
    Listing.sDescription = tbDescription.Text;
    lDescription.Text = tbDescription.Text;
    lCity.Text = tbCity.Text;
    lMLSNum.Text = tbMLSNum.Text;
}
```

When you defined the structure, you assigned the memory needed for those variables to your stack memory. But when you used the new keyword, you initialized them with empty string values (the initial values for numerical variables would be zero, and for Booleans would be false). Then you assign the values to the variables by sucking the values in from the form. Finally, your labels will display the messages from your newly created variables and the data they received from your form. Your entire script element should now look like this:

```
<script runat="server">
struct MLSListing
  {
      public string MLSNumber;
    public string City;
    public string sDescription;
  }

protected void Page_Load(Object Src, EventArgs E)
{
   MLSListing Listing = new MLSListing();
   Listing.MLSNumber = tbMLSNum.Text;
   Listing.City = tbCity.Text;
   Listing.sDescription = tbDescription.Text;
   lDescription.Text = tbDescription.Text;
   lCity.Text = tbCity.Text;
   lMLSNum.Text = tbMLSNum.Text;
}
</script>
```

You can download the entire code for this example from this book's page at www.sybex.com. The downloadable file is called L07_struct.aspx.

Working with Control Structures

When you're programming in C# (or VB.NET, of course), much of your code relies on the ability to anticipate different scenarios and act accordingly. Something as simple as a user's checking a check box can require your code to process differently based on which box the user checked. We have to watch for and mange two main kinds of events that take place:

- Conditional situations that describe what might happen if something occurs, or if something does not occur

- Repetitive situations that can occur numerous times, stopped only by some kind of termination statement that explicitly tells your code when to stop processing (or, when it's not developed properly, *doesn't* tell your code when to stop processing something, thus repeating into an infinite loop and wrecking your application)

The two main control structures used for handling conditional and looping scenarios are called, amazingly enough, *conditional* (also called *branching*) and *looping* structures.

Using Conditional Structures

When you're developing applications, you don't always want a certain message displayed or a certain calculation performed. Instead, you'll want to provide your web application some means for controlling when something should happen. In other words, *if* such and such occurs, do this, or *else* do something different. So it probably comes as no surprise that the mechanism for controlling this sequence is the *if* statement and its companion, the *switch* statement.

Generally, if the option involves two or three and, maybe, four possibilities, you'll use an if statement. More than three possibilities will generally involve a switch statement, which is generally the same except it has more possibilities and the syntax is slightly different.

The next several sections describe the conditional structures that are available and when they are used. Then we'll take a closer look at two of them, the if statement and the for statement. One of these, if, is an example of a conditional statement, and the other, for, is an example of a looping structure.

NOTE   In the syntax portions of the following descriptions, brackets in the code mean that the enclosed item is an optional part of the syntax. You'll see this especially with braces: [{]. Generally, even though they're optional, you should include braces anyway because they're an accepted programming convention. And it reduces the possibility of introducing bugs into the application.

Using *if* and *if else* Statements

An if statement evaluates an expression and executes a given statement if the evaluation results in a Boolean true. The braces are optional but recommended:

```
if (Boolean expression)
  [{]
    statement(s) to execute
  [}]
```

An if else statement also requires a Boolean true or false test. The general syntax looks like this:

```
if (Boolean expression)
  [{]
statement(s) to execute
  [}]
  else
  [{]
    statement(s) to execute if false
  [}]
```

A common `if` statement is the one Dreamweaver inserts when you click the Page Load icon from the ASP.NET Insert bar, as shown in Figure 7.4. As you can see, Dreamweaver inserts the following code.

FIGURE 7.4:

Inserting a Page Load event handler in Dreamweaver

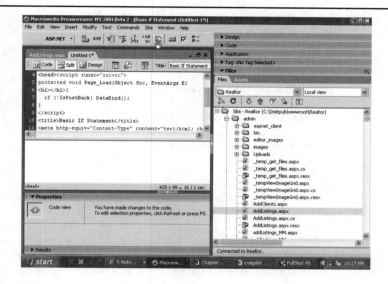

```
{
   if (!IsPostBack) DataBind();
}
```

The following is another example of an `if` statement:

```
<script runat="server">
protected void Page_Load(Object Src, EventArgs E)
{
   int num = 1;
   int num2 = 3;
   if ((num + num2) == 4)
       {
       Response.Write("4");
       }
}
</script>
```

The preceding code would write the string 4 to the browser if it is true that the numbers 1 and 3 added together equal 4.

Notice nothing *else* happens if the Boolean test doesn't succeed. But we can fix that if we want, by using an `else` statement.

if else if else Statements

`if else if` statements are used for multiple `if else` circumstances. There can be any number of `else if` blocks within any `if` block:

```
if (Boolean expression)
  [{]
    statement(s) to execute
  [}]
  else if (Boolean expression)
  [{]
    statement(s) to execute
  [}]
  else if (Boolean expression)
  [{]
    statement(s) to execute
  [}]
  else
  [{]
    statement(s) to execute
  [}]
```

switch Statements

Use `switch` statements when you're overwhelmed with `if else` statements. For me, overwhelmed means about three of them. C# accepts strings, integers, and enumerations in its case expressions. Unlike some other OOP languages, in C# each `case` statement must to be followed by the `break` keyword.

Simply looking at this syntax probably isn't enough to know how to use it if you haven't programmed in similar languages, so jump ahead to the explanation for Listing 7.5 for more on this. The general syntax looks like this:

```
switch(integral or string expression)
  {
    case <expression a>:
      statement(s)
      break;
      .
      .
      .
    case <expression b>:
      statement(s)
      break;
    [default:
      statement(s)]
  }
```

> **WARNING**   Although the `default` case in `switch` statements is optional, some developers maintain that bugs can occur when none of the cases match and you've omitted the `default` case, so it's considered good programming practice to include it.

Using Loops to Manipulate Stored Values

You'll often need to repeat the processing of items. Sometimes it will be to increment values, or you may simply need to display a set of items from a list. These kinds of situations can be managed with loops using iteration statements in C# that terminate based on some condition. There are four basic types of iterative statements:

- `while`
- `do`
- `for`
- `foreach`

while Loops

`while` loops are used when you want a group of statements to be executed for as long as a specified condition is true. *Do not* put a semicolon after the initial `while` expression like this:

```
while (someVariable == "x");
```

or the loop will run forever. The syntax of a `while` loop looks like this:

```
while (Boolean expression)
  [{]
    statement(s) to execute
  [}]
```

do Loops

This is nearly the same as a `while` loop, but it allows you to execute a statement before the loop is initiated:

```
do {
  Statement(s)
} while (Boolean expression);
```

for Loops

When the number of loops is known before the code runs or can be determined programmatically, you can use a `for` loop to iterate through a series of statements. See Listings 7.4 and 7.5 later in the chapter for examples. The syntax for these statements is as follows:

```
for (initializer; Boolean expression; modifier)
  [{]
    statement(s)
  [}]
```

foreach Loops

This is an especially nice type of statement to use for iterating through arrays. If you fast-forward to Listing 7.4, you could iterate through that array like so:

```
{
    string[] sRange = {"100-200K", "200-300K", "300-400K"};
    foreach(string s in sRange)
{
 Response.Write(s + "<br>");
```

This loop would return the following to the browser:

```
100-200K
200-300K
300-400K
```

Here is the syntax for `for` each statements:

```
foreach (type identifier in collection)
   [{]
      statement(s)
   [}]
```

A Little Practice Round with Looping

To get a better idea of how looping works, let's take a brief look at a simple loop in ASP.NET. We'll focus on the `for` keyword, because its usage is quite common in many computer languages, not just in C# and other .NET languages. In fact, one of the most common structures found in any object-oriented programming language is the `for` loop, which generally behaves like the `for` loop in C#:

```
for (int i = 0; i<3; i++)
{
    //do something
}
```

This code simply iterates through a variable named `i`, and as it does so increments its value by 1. Listing 7.3 shows what happens when you plug this kind of code into a web page to work with an array.

Listing 7.3   **Using a basic `for` loop to increment values**

```
<%@ Page Language="C#" ContentType="text/html" ResponseEncoding="iso-8859-1" %>
<html>
<head>
<script runat="server">
protected void Page_Load(Object Src, EventArgs E)
{
    int [] myArray = new int[3];
for (int i = 0; i<3; i++)
{
```

```
Response.Write(Convert.ToString(myArray[i] = myInt + i) +" ");
    }
  }
</script>
<title>Arrays</title>
<meta http-equiv="Content-Type" content="text/html; charset=iso-8859-1">
</head>
<body>

</body>
</html>
```

The highlight of Listing 7.3 is the use of the termination condition in the for loop (in bold). The iteration takes place only while the value of the variable i is less than 3. The variable i starts out with a value of 0 but is incremented until its value reaches 2. The browser then takes the value of the other variable, myInt, and adds to it the incremented variable i for each iteration through that i variable. The output from this listing is the string 10 11 12.

The naming of the i variable is one of the rare occasions where a variable name may not be obvious at first. However, the use of this structure, including the way the variable is named, is so common in the programming world that other programmers will recognize the for loop instantly when they see it.

You also probably noticed in Listing 7.3 the use of the < operator. Take another look at Table 7.3 you'll see two categories of operators that are of special interest to you when developing conditional structures. These are the equality operators and the relational operators. The == operator is very common and is used to test if one value is equal to another. It's important not to confuse it with the = operator, which sets the value of a variable.

Using Loops and Arrays to Populate Web Controls

You can also use a combination of loops and arrays to populate web controls. In Listing 7.4, two arrays are set up to populate an asp:CheckBoxList control. Note the use of the GetLength() method.

What I'd like to do this time is have you research the source of this method. I've been stating throughout much of the book that ASP.NET consists of this massive object model of many, many different classes of objects. If you look at the boldface section of code in Listing 7.4, you should be able to see how the principles introduced in Listing 7.3 are taken one step further. Many times, after all, we won't have a set value for our loop's termination condition. It may have to be determined programmatically. You should be able to tell where the GetLength() method comes from if you look at the object on the left of the fullstop (period) before the method name. Notice that it's the sRange object. All you need to do now is figure out what class that specific object is an instance of.

Listing 7.4   **Using arrays and for loops to populate a web control**

```
<%@ Page Language="C#" ContentType="text/html" ResponseEncoding="iso-8859-1" %>
<html>
<head>
<script runat="server">
protected void Page_Load(Object Src, EventArgs E)
   {
     string[] sRange = {"100-200K", "200-300K", "300-400K"};
     int[] sValueRange = {100, 200, 300};
     int i;
     for (i=0; i < sRange.GetLength(0); i++)
        {
     this.ChckBxList.Items.Add(new ListItem(sRange[i],
     ➡Convert.ToString(sValueRange[i])));
     }
}
</script>
<title>Arrays</title>
<meta http-equiv="Content-Type" content="text/html; charset=iso-8859-1">
</head>
<body>
<form runat="server">
  <asp:CheckBoxList ID="ChckBxList" runat="server"></asp:CheckBoxList>
</form>
</body>
</html>
```

If you determined that the GetLength() method is a member of the Array class based on the fact that sRange is an identifier for an instance of that class, you were right on target. The GetLength() method returns the number of items in a given array, so you know the iterative process must stop repeating before it reaches the last item in the collection, because of the following loop:

```
i=0; i < sRange.GetLength(0); i++
```

The other unfamiliar part of the code may be the Add() method. This is a member of the CheckedListBox.ObjectCollection class and adds an item to the list of objects in the named object—in this case, the asp:CheckListBox (id="ChckBxList") element defined in the HTML portion of the code. The output for Listing 7.4 is shown in Figure 7.5

Using Loops and Switches to Provide Dynamic Feedback

Let's push these concepts just a bit further and see how we can use switches to react to user events. In Listing 7.5, if a user checks a box and submits the page, the application returns a value based on which box the user checked.

FIGURE 7.5:

Using arrays and for
loops to populate a
web control

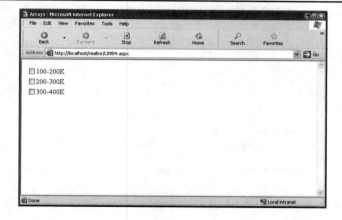

Listing 7.5   **Using loops and switches to manipulate web controls**

```
<%@ Page Language="C#" ContentType="text/html" ResponseEncoding="iso-8859-1" %>
<script runat="server">
protected void Page_Load(Object Src, EventArgs E)
{
    string[] sRange = {"100-200K", "200-300K", "300-400K"};
    int[] sValueRange = {100, 200, 300};
if (!Page.IsPostBack)
{

    int i;
    for (i=0; i < sRange.GetLength(0); i++)
      {
    this.ChckBxList.Items.Add(new ListItem(sRange[i],
    ➡Convert.ToString(sValueRange[i])));
      }
}
  if (Page.IsPostBack)
  {
  switch (ChckBxList.SelectedItem.Value)
{
 case "100":
  sResponse.Text = "100-200";
  break;
 case "200":
  sResponse.Text = "200-300";
  break;
 case "300":
  sResponse.Text = "300-400";
  break;
 default:
```

```
        sResponse.Text = "No ";
        break;
    }
    }
        }
</script>
<title>Using Switch</title>
<meta http-equiv="Content-Type" content="text/html; charset=iso-8859-1">
</head>
<body>
<form runat="server">
    <asp:CheckBoxList ID="ChckBxList" runat="server"></asp:CheckBoxList>
    <p>
    <asp:Button ID="bButton" runat="server" Text="Submit" /> </p>
    <p>
    <asp:Label ID="sResponse" runat="server" /> </p>
</form>
</body>
</html>
```

The first thing to do in order to re-create Listing 7.5 is to create a label for returning the string value of the check box that was selected by the user (actually, a list of check boxes through the asp:CheckBoxList element):

```
<asp:CheckBoxList ID="ChckBxList" runat="server"></asp:CheckBoxList>
    <p>
    <asp:Button ID="bButton" runat="server" Text="Submit" /></p>
    <p>
    <asp:Label ID="sResponse" runat="server" /> </p>
```

We use the Page class's IsPostBack property to find out if the page is being loaded as the result of a form submission. If it isn't, the following code is executed:

```
int i;
    for (i=0; i < sRange.GetLength(0); i++)
        {
    this.ChckBxList.Items.Add(new ListItem(sRange[i],
    ➥Convert.ToString(sValueRange[i])));
        }
```

If the page is loaded as a result of a form submission, the switch statement is executed. The switch statement basically says, "Check the value of the selected check box, and if it equals "100", then write the string 100-200 into the asp:Label element named sResponse." (Actually, I'm not comfortable using the word *name* to refer a control in this way, because sResponse is actually an identifier.)

Using Structured Error Handling to Control Error Messages

Remember earlier when we tried to output a DateTime variable into an asp:Label element? We don't really want these kinds of failures to become public knowledge, so when sites go live they normally won't yield ASP.NET error messages. Of course, you could just turn off debugging in the Web.Config file, and even set up a generic Redirect page there that gives an error message without any specifics. But you can also handle error messages programmatically.

Let's add some code to Listing 7.2 (in bold):

```
try {
DateTime myDate = Convert.ToDateTime("01/01/2004");
dLabel.Text = Convert.ToString(myDate);
}
catch
{
   dLabel.Text = "Format of Date is Not Correct. Please Try Again.";
}
```

Unfortunately, the preceding code fragment won't generate an error (and how often will we say it's unfortunate when we *don't* get an error?), but notice the try and catch keywords. The try keyword basically says, "We're going to try this, and if it doesn't work, catch the exception that occurs and do this other thing instead." This process is called *exception handling*. It's a way to manage the many exceptions that ASP.NET might generate during the life of an application. The structure is pretty simple. You put any code you want to "try" within brackets after the try keyword. Then you add the catch keyword and add the code you want to use as an alternative when something goes wrong.

To see this actually in action, change the content in the try statement to this:

```
try {
   DateTime myDate = Convert.ToDateTime("The first of January,2004");
dLabel.Text = Convert.ToString(myDate);
}
```

The ToDateTime method expects certain kinds of formats for dates, and when it doesn't get them, an exception is thrown. Without the exception-handling routine, your users would get a big ugly message like that shown in Figure 7.6:

```
The string was not recognized as a valid DateTime. There is a unknown word
starting at index 0.
```

FIGURE 7.6:

ASP.NET generates an exception when you supply the wrong format to the `ToDateTime()` method.

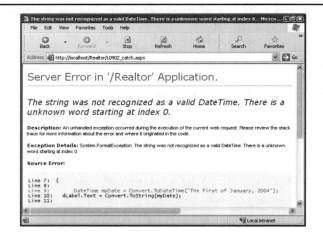

Using Code-Behind with Dreamweaver MX and .NET

One of the drawbacks of the old Active Server Pages model was the difficulty of separating presentation from business logic. In ASP.NET, this is no longer an issue if you don't want it to be. You can remove all the business logic contained in script elements to a completely separate file called the *code-behind* file. When using C#, you simply name the page containing your code with a `.cs` extension. If you're using VB.NET you name the code-behind file with a `.vb` extension.

If you've worked with JavaScript, you may be familiar with the process of linking JavaScript code to your HTML page by way of a file with a `.js` extension. This file contains nothing but JavaScript. Using code-behind is a little like this, except of course the script is processed on the server. You can use any ASP.NET-compatible language for code-behind, including VB.NET and JScript.NET.

When using code-behind, instead of using script tags you create a class that is called by the web page referencing the code-behind file. The easiest way to grasp this is to walk through it, so let's convert Listing 7.5 to a code-behind. The first part of this conversion is shown in Listing 7.6. Pay special attention to the highlighted and commented code.

NOTE   When creating script for code-behind pages, you don't use `script` tags or *any* other HTML elements.

| Listing 7.6 | A code-behind file for Listing 7.7 |

```
using System;
// we need to explictly import any
//classes we might need
using System.Web;
using System.Web.UI;
using System.Web.UI.WebControls;

//Here, we name our class. This is
//where the script tag would go
//if we were developing an ASPX page.
public class switcheroo : Page
    {
//We need to explictly declare any Web Controls we use in our
//code and that appear in the Web Form (aspx) page.
protected System.Web.UI.WebControls.CheckBoxList ChckBxList;
protected System.Web.UI.WebControls.Label sResponse;
//This part of the code should be familiar to you
//since it is also used in script tags
 protected void Page_Load(Object Src, EventArgs E)
{
    string[] sRange = {"100-200K", "200-300K", "300-400K"};
    int[] sValueRange = {100, 200, 300};
if (!Page.IsPostBack)
{
    int i;
    for (i=0; i < sRange.GetLength(0); i++)
        {
this.ChckBxList.Items.Add(new ListItem(sRange[i],
➥Convert.ToString(sValueRange[i])));
}
}
  if (Page.IsPostBack)
  {
  switch (ChckBxList.SelectedItem.Value)
{
 case "100":
  sResponse.Text = "100-200";
  break;
 case "200":
  sResponse.Text = "200-300";
  break;
 case "300":
  sResponse.Text = "300-400";
  break;
 default:
  sResponse.Text = "No ";
```

```
   break;
  }
 }
 }
}
```

As you can see, the code is basically the same in a code-behind page as it is on a web form. It contains the same kind of routines as Listing 7.5. The difference is, you need to instantiate whatever web controls are on the page, because the compiler doesn't yet know about them when it reads the source file for the code-behind.

Notice also in Listing 7.6 that we created a class named `switcheroo`. This class will be inherited by the web form using the code-behind page.

Accessing a Code-Behind Page

In order for the web form to access the code-behind, you need to add an attribute to the `Page` directive in the web form that uses the code-behind, as shown in Listing 7.7.

Listing 7.7   **A web form that accesses a code-behind page**

```
<%@ Page Language="C#" Inherits="switcheroo"
➥Src="L0706.cs" ContentType="text/html"
➥ResponseEncoding="iso-8859-1" %>
<html>
<head>
<title>Using Switch</title>
<meta http-equiv="Content-Type" content="text/html; charset=iso-8859-1">
</head>
<body>
<form runat="server">
  <asp:CheckBoxList ID="ChckBxList" runat="server"></asp:CheckBoxList>
  <p>
    <asp:Button ID="bButton" runat="server" Text="Submit" /> </p>
  <p>
  <asp:Label ID="sResponse" runat="server" /> </p>
</form>
</body>
</html>
```

The web form includes two key attributes (in bold in Listing 7.7) in its `Page` directive to work with your code-behind page. The first is the `Inherits` attribute. This attribute refers to the class that your page is inheriting, which should be defined in your code-behind page. The other important attribute is the `Src` attribute, which consists of the URL of the code-behind file, in this case, `L0706.cs`.

Event Handling

So far everything we've seen has been handled by the Page Load event. This happens through an *event handler*, which is similar to a function except it's triggered by an event (such as a page loading) or a user's click on a button. Whenever you write script, you dictate when something happens by writing everything in an event handler. The Page_Load event handler is the one you've been most exposed to in this book so far, but it's by no means the only event handler that can be used.

Of course, events themselves are nothing new in the world of HTML. DHTML (Dynamic HTML) has relied on them for a long time. You've seen them in action plenty of times, whenever your mouse rolls over an image and the image changes (the famous rollover effect). This kind of dynamic effect occurs because an event called onmouseover was raised. In ASP.NET, the same thing applies. When a user clicks a button, a click event is raised, and you can write a routine in reaction to the event.

You won't see mouse-over events in ASP.NET because events are posted to the server, and you can imagine how draining a whole series of rollover events would be on a server's processing power. But don't worry—there are plenty of events that can occur and to which you can bind processes. Table 7.4 lists these events.

TABLE 7.4: Events That Can Be Added to ASP.NET Web Controls

Event Name	When It Occurs
onLoad	When the control has loaded into the Page object
onUnload	When the control has been unloaded from memory
onClick	When a button or other control is clicked
onCommand	When a button or other control is clicked
onInit	When the control is initialized
onPrerender	Just prior to the rendering of the control in the browser
Disposed	When the control is destroyed
DataBinding	When the control is bound to a data source
SelectIndexChanged	When a list item in a list box, or a check box in a check box list, has been selected
CheckChanged	When a user checks another check box within the check box list control
TextChanged	When text in a text box changes

When an event is handled in your script, it is generally defined with two arguments:

- An object referencing the source that raised the event
- An event object containing data for the event

Normally, the event argument is derived from System.EventArgs, but for control events that generate data, the argument is of a type specific to that control. A Button control, for example, can send a click event and a command event. Click events don't actually generate any real data; they just occur—so the second argument for the event is of type EventArgs. However, a command event sends information about specific commands, so it is derived from the System.Web.UI.WebControls.CommandEventArgs class, which includes information about the command name and other event data.

Let's see how this works with a real example. When you insert an asp:button element using Dreamweaver, you see the usual choices for attributes such as the ID attribute, and so forth, but you can also look at all the available events for the control. In the left-hand panel of the Tag Editor, click Events, and then click the plus sign next to Events to expand the selection. See Figure 7.7.

FIGURE 7.7:

Exploring the events of a Button control in Dreamweaver

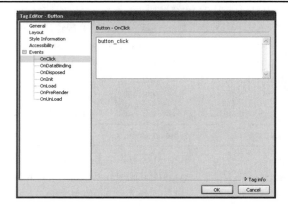

When you enter something into the window on the right, Dreamweaver generates the event into the control, like so:

```
<asp:Button ID="bButton" runat="server" Text="Click Here" OnClick="button_click"
/>
```

Then it's up to you to write the event handler for it. The event handler must have the same name as the value in the OnClick attribute:

```
<script runat="server">
protected void button_click(Object Src, EventArgs E)
{
        DateTime myDate = Convert.ToDateTime("01/01/2004");
        dLabel.Text = Convert.ToString(myDate);
}
</script>
```

You can name the source object and event object anything you want, but be sure to incorporate the keywords `Object` and `EventArgs`, respectively. This is entirely acceptable:

```
protected void button_click(Object x, EventArgs y)
```

However, I would discourage it because it flies in the face of what everyone else does. By convention, the source object is named `Src` and the event object is named `E`, although there doesn't seem to be any solid convention on whether those are in lower-or uppercase.

Building and Using Custom Controls

In Chapter 4 you saw how to develop a simple custom control using the `.ascx` extension in your filename and then accessing that page from your web form (aspx file) using the `Register` directive.

For even more efficient separation of business logic from presentation, you can build your own precompiled DLLs that are just like the Dreamweaver control. The advantage to using these kinds of custom controls is that you don't take quite the performance hit when a web form is first accessed as you do when you don't use compiled controls.

"Performance hit" probably isn't a fair description for what happens when you don't access compiled controls. More accurate is that compiled controls give you greater efficiencies because this level of separation is so new to web development in the Microsoft camp. The reason the efficiencies are greater is that every ASPX page is compiled into an intermediary language called, remarkably enough, the Intermediate Language, which is analogous to the Java world's bytecode that runs on Virtual Machines.

DLLs have been around for a long time in the ASP world, but not for the average web developer—and not for anyone who has to deal with remote hosting services, in older versions of ASP you have to register custom DLLs to the operating system. In ASP.NET, all you have to do is make sure the DLL ends up in the `bin` directory of the target application (in our case, `Realtor`). Because you don't have to ask your host provider to register the DLL for you on their system, you can write it anywhere and simply make sure the proper DLL is uploaded into the proper `bin` directory. This is similar to what is going on in the Java world and in J2EE, the enterprise platform for Java developers, which also relies on a high level of encapsulation through its dependencies on `.jar` files, which play a similar role to .NET DLLs.

To create your own DLLs, you have to venture into the world of compiling, which is not only easy, it's fun. But first, you need to create a source file for your component. For this example, we'll make it an easy one, a small component that generates text strings. Listing 7.8 is downloadable as `L0708.cs`, but the file you really want to download is `tumeric.cs`. That is the file we will later call when we compile the code. You can also download `L0708.cs` and rename it `tumeric.cs` because in addition to having a more user-friendly name, I'll be referring to `tumeric.dll` in these examples, rather than `L0708.dll`.

Listing 7.8   **Creating a .NET assembly source file**

```
namespace Tumeric {
public class Hello {
public string greeting() {
return "Greetings from The Tumeric Partnership";
  }
 }

public class logo {
public string getlogo() {
return "newlogo.gif";
  }
 }
}
```

The first item of interest in Listing 7.8 is the creation of a new namespace called `Tumeric`. This is the beginnings of an *assembly*, which is just a fancy word for a group of classes under one name that can be imported into your web form.

An assembly can consist of numerous custom classes, all of which are made available to the web form importing the namespace that contains them. Both of the classes in Listing 7.8 return simple strings. One will be used to display some text, and the other will be used as the URL of an image control. If you're typing Listing 7.8 in Dreamweaver, save it as `tumeric.cs`. Next, we'll compile it.

Using the .NET Compiler

To compile the `Tumeric` code, you first need to find the compiler on your hard drive. You won't find it if you haven't installed the .NET Framework SDK, so be sure to do that first. The compiler is called `csc.exe`. On my computer it's located here:

```
C:\WINDOWS\Microsoft.NET\Framework\v1.0.3705
```

The last directory named in this path is the .NET version number. Yours may be different; drill down the Microsoft.NET/Framework directories to find it. The name will be very similar, just a different version number, which is how the last directory is named. You can also run a file search for it.

To compile Listing 7.8, you simply open your DOS prompt, change your directory to the directory where `csc.exe` lives, and enter this into the command prompt:

```
csc hello.cs
```

This will generate an `.exe` file, but for ASP.NET applications you'll want to generate DLLs. This requires a somewhat different configuration in your command prompt:

```
csc /target:library hello.cs
```

For additional compiler options, go to

```
http://msdn.microsoft.com/library/default.asp?url=/library/en-us/cscomp/html
/vcrefcsharpcompileroptionsbycategory.asp
```

Creating a Batch File for Compilation

You'll find life gets easier when you create batch files for compiling your code. A batch file is just a bunch of commands strung together in a way similar to what I demonstrated, saved as a text file with a `.bat` extension. The trick, if you're using Notepad, is not to save it as a text file but to make sure you choose All Files from the Save As Type options in the Save dialog box. Otherwise, you'll end up with a filename like `myBatch.bat.txt`, when what you really want is `myBatch.bat`. To avoid another potential gotcha, make sure you don't save your batch file using UTF-8 or Unicode encodings. Choose ANSI as your text encoding. That should be the default, but if it isn't for some reason, change it.

Batch files make life easier because you don't have to fuss with directory paths so much. You can use the `%windir%` alias to locate your Windows directory, and build the path to your `csc.exe` application from there, as shown in Listing 7.9. If you installed the .NET framework, the batch file shown in Listing 7.9 should work on your machine after you make some modifications to it to account for where everything actually is on your computer.

| Listing 7.9 | **Creating a batch file for compiling a custom control** |

```
set indir=C:\Inetpub\wwwroot\Realtor\tumeric.cs
set outdir=C:\Inetpub\wwwroot\Realtor\bin\tumeric.dll

%windir%\Microsoft.NET\Framework\v1.0.3705\csc /t:library /out:%outdir% %indir%

pause
```

The two `set` commands create aliases for the directory locations of the input and the output files. Since the input file is `tumeric.cs` located in my web server's directory, that's the path I used in my batch file. I want to output the DLL into my `bin` directory within the folder of my main application, `Realtor`, so that is how I assign the output file. Then I give the output file a name.

The next line locates the `csc.exe` compiler. If you're compiling VB.NET code, you'll want to change `csc` to `vbc`, and if you're using JavaScript you'll want the JavaScript compiler, which is `jsc`. You can add the `.exe` extension to each of these if you wish, but it's not necessary.

The /t:library command tells the compiler you wish to make a DLL instead of an executable (EXE) file.

In the long run, you may want to compile a large number of your own custom controls. If that's the case, batch files like this are absolutely essential (unless you enjoy the feeling you get when you're pulling hair out of your head). And if you're a real C# wizard, you can even take the original source code from the Dreamweaver Control DLL and tweak it for your own purposes. Just make sure you create a backup of the original Macromedia control if you don't want to end up reinstalling the program.

If you want to start banging out some serious code and you don't want to pay for Microsoft's Visual Studio, you can get an open source IDE for C# .NET here:

```
http://www.icsharpcode.net/OpenSource/SD/Download/
```

or here:

```
http://prdownloads.sourceforge.net/sharpdevelop/094bsetup.exe?download
```

This open-source project is a nice complement to Dreamweaver because it has class browsers, which makes it easy to look up all those classes you need without footing the huge bill you'd normally pay when licensing Visual Studio. It also comes with a compiler that works out of the IDE, which is convenient when your assemblies get larger and more complex.

Accessing Your Custom Control

Next, you'll want to access your custom control. We don't have any elements in our namespace as the Dreamweaver control does, so we don't need to worry about using the Register directive, which you need to do when working with custom controls that have their own namespace-prefixed element names. All you need to be concerned about is importing the namespace:

```
<%@ Import Namespace="Tumeric" %>
```

Next, we'll build a text label for accepting our greeting, and an image control for reading in the text of the URL we defined in the logo class:

```
<asp:Label ID="tLabel" runat="server"></asp:Label>
<p><asp:Image ID="cImage" runat="server" /> </p>
```

By now, hopefully everything is falling together for you and you'll be able to surmise that if we want to use the classes in the namespace we just imported, we'll need to instantiate a new instance of each class:

```
Hello vGreeting = new Hello();
 tLabel.Text = vGreeting.greeting();
 logo tLogo = new logo();
 cImage.ImageUrl = tLogo.getlogo();
```

If you create these controls in Dreamweaver, don't fill in the Text field of the label control or the Image URL field of the image control, because we'll let our script take care of that.

Next, we merely call the methods of each class. Remember that each class returns a text string. Pretty simple stuff. One of these text strings goes into the text label, and the other text string is used as the `ImageUrl` property of our image control.

Listing 7.10 shows us our finished code as we access our control and call its methods.

Listing 7.10   **Accessing a custom control by importing a namespace**

```
<%@ Import Namespace="Tumeric" %>
<%@ Page Language="C#" ContentType="text/html" ResponseEncoding="iso-8859-1" %>

<!DOCTYPE HTML PUBLIC "-//W3C//DTD HTML 4.01
➥Transitional//EN" "http://www.w3.org/TR/html4
➥/loose.dtd">
<html>
<head>
<script runat="server">
protected void Page_Load(Object Src, EventArgs E)
{
 Hello vGreeting = new Hello();
 tLabel.Text = vGreeting.greeting();
 logo tLogo = new logo();
 cImage.ImageUrl = tLogo.getlogo();
}
</script>
<title>Using Custom Controls</title>
<meta http-equiv="Content-Type" content="text/html; charset=iso-8859-1">
</head>
<body>
<asp:Label ID="tLabel" runat="server"></asp:Label>
<p><asp:Image ID="cImage" runat="server" /> </p>
</body>
</html>
```

This is obviously a very simple example. There is no limit to how far you take these concepts, because when you write a control you can write a very complex application.

Wrapping Up

There's a certain logic to saying, "Wow, I can bang stuff out in Dreamweaver in no time compared to using an IDE like Visual Studio or a text editor. Now I should take some of this spare time to create some controls of my own, and conquer the world with them."

The irony with that kind of statement is that even if you're doing some heavy-duty custom coding, Dreamweaver, with its syntax-helping features, can help immensely. In addition, when you're creating web forms for accessing your code, Dreamweaver helps by inserting the web controls you use to interact with them.

But we've only scratched the surface here. In the next chapter, we'll extend these concepts to the world of web services, and then in Chapter 9 we'll build the Realtor application and see how the combination of Dreamweaver's powerful visual-based tools and your new-found coding techniques all come together to build a heavy-duty web application.

CHAPTER 8

Web Services and Dreamweaver MX

- What are web services?

- Creating a web service

- Consuming a web service

So far in this book, you've seen how you can build applications on the Web using Dreamweaver. In other words, web sites no longer exclusively consist of simple, static web pages. Nor are you confined to even "mere" database-driven websites. But wait. There's more. You can now reach out and pull someone else's Java code from another site or computer and make the functions they've built execute on your ASP.NET page, without actually running any Java code or installing a Java Virtual Machine on your own server or your host provider's. For instance, someone can build a Java application or an application in some other computer language, and that application can even be designed for a Unix- or Linux-based operating system, and you can send function calls to it as if it were running on your server.

This is achieved by using the rather intensely hyped technology called Web Services. For all the ballyhoo surrounding Web Services in the trade press and, especially, released through the PR machines of the major software vendors, it may seem that there really isn't all that much going on that a small developer can really tap into yet. But the concept is intriguing, and I'm pretty sure that if you've dismissed Web Services as just so much vaporware, a simple example will demonstrate that Web Services are for real. It demonstrates that the Web Services technology is for real and will really take off when smaller developers, who are the impetus behind many major software advances, get their arms around the concept.

What Are Web Services?

Web services are platform-independent function calls using XML and HTTP as transport/payload mechanisms to disparate software and operating systems. These function calls are accomplished by sending a request to a waiting server somewhere, in the form of an XML file that contains parameters to a named, specific function or group of functions. The machine on the receiving end accepts (or rejects) the request, reads the arguments (parameters) in the XML document, and processes the called function based on the arguments found in the XML document.

It's like making a long-distance call and asking another machine to process some stuff for you: "Hello? Yes, I'd like you to calculate the arithmetic function 2 plus 2. Will you do this for me?" Trust me when I say that I myself could use a service like that. You may need to authenticate the request: "My PIN number is 7345." The machine on the receiving end will honor your request, but you usually will need to make arrangements ahead of time, unless you've done a search for a specific web service and have managed to find one that is public.

Generally, web services are used by trading partners and other businesses and organizations trying to find ways to interact without worrying about whether the machines on each partner's end use the same operating system and/or software environments. The advantage to web services is that you can send the function calls over HTTP or protocol specifically designed for web services called SOAP, wrapped in an XML envelope that can be read by any kind of system (assuming the system has the API for consuming them).

To find a web service, you search the "yellow pages" of web services, called *UDDI registries*. (UDDI stands for *Universal Description, Discovery and Integration*.) This is simply a directory of web services that contains URLs to the web services' descriptions, which are in *WSDL (Web Services Description Language)* documents that these URLs point to. These WSDL documents contain all the information you need to access (or, in Web Services parlance, *consume*) the service.

Dreamweaver has a direct link to the UDDI registry that we'll take a look at shortly.

Consuming a Web Service

Most of the Web Services tutorials and books I've seen tend to show how to build a web service and then how to consume one, but I think it's easier to learn how to build a web service *after* you've consumed one—because by working with someone else's web service, you can get an idea of the benefits of the Web Services technology and a good conceptual command of how web services work.

Dreamweaver provides support for working with Web Services through the Components tab on the Application panel, as shown in Figure 8.1, which shows a web service's methods being browsed in the Web Services browser. On the Components tab, there is a drop-down list with one item, Web Services. When you click the plus button next to Web Services, you have a choice between two methods to add a web service.

FIGURE 8.1:

In the Application panel's Components tab, choose a method for adding a web service.

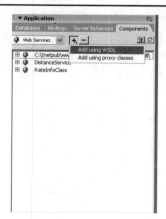

One choice is to select the Add Using WSDL item in the drop-down list, and the other choice is to select Add Using Proxy Classes. In this case, select the first one, Add Using

WSDL. Then another dialog box comes up asking for the location of the WSDL file that describes the web service, as shown in Figure 8.2. Before we get into what all that means, we'll need to find a web service.

FIGURE 8.2:

The Add Using WSDL dialog box

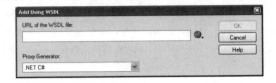

Finding a Web Service

To find a Web Service, the easiest thing to do is go to the "yellow pages" for web services, the UDDI registries. There are currently a few UDDI repositories on the Web. UDDI registries are similar to the traditional phone book in the sense that developers use these repositories to store information about web services they have created. One UDDI repository is hosted by IBM, one is hosted by Microsoft, and another at XMethods.com. You can access all three of these resources directly using the Add Using WSDL dialog box (Figure 8.2). Click the globe button to get a drop-down list of the UDDI resources, as shown in Figure 8.3.

FIGURE 8.3:

Using the Add Using WSDL dialog box to access a UDDI repository

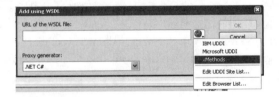

In this case, we'll select XMethods. We'll pick a web service that will calculate the distance between zip codes so that our clients know how far away a listing is from their current home. To do this, choose XMethods from the UDDI drop-down list. Your web browser will open. Scroll down until you see the section titled "The 30 Most Recent Listings," as shown in Figure 8. 4.

FIGURE 8.4:

Browsing the
XMethods UDDI

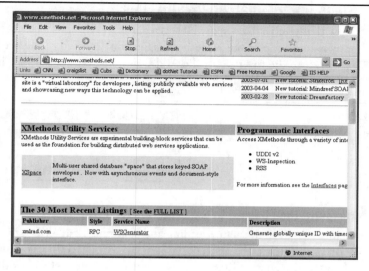

Next to it you'll see a link that says "[See the FULL LIST]." Click on that link. The full
list of web services available on XMethod's UDDI Web page will appear. Look for the ZIP
Distance Calculator from imacination.com. You can find it fast by just searching the web
page from the browser using the keyword distance. Click on the link for that service, and
you should see a page like that shown in Figure 8.5.

FIGURE 8.5:

The Zip Distance
Calculator web service

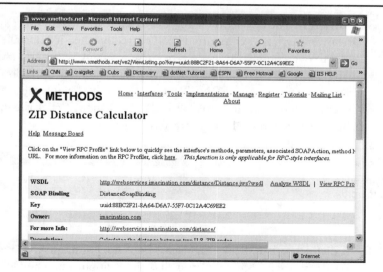

Steps Toward Analyzing WSDL Files

Now that you've located a web service, the next step is to copy the URL for the WSDL shown at the top of the XMethods page you accessed in the preceding section. Then simply paste it into the top field of the Add Using WSDL dialog box, labeled URL of the WSDL File, as shown in Figure 8.6.

FIGURE 8.6:

Pasting the WSDL URL into Dreamweaver's Add Using WSDL dialog box

Handling the "Unable to Generate Proxy" Error

Before we get to the actual reading and analyzing of a WSDL file, I should point out that as soon as you follow the instructions in the previous section, you may get an error message saying, "Unable to Generate Proxy". This happens as soon as you click the Add button. If you get an error message saying "Unable to Generate Proxy," a common occurrence in Dreamweaver, then you may need to build your own DLL from the WSDL, dump it into your local bin directory, and choose the other method of creating a web service: Add Using Proxy Classes instead of Add Using WSDL (from the Add Web Services button in the Components tab of the Applications panel). You'll see how to build your own DLL later in the chapter in the section "Generating a Proxy."

Most often, however, you'll get the "Unable to Generate Proxy" error message because Dreamweaver hasn't configured itself correctly when it is installed on your system. The secret to overcoming this issue is to change the proxy generator. In the Add Using WSDL dialog box, the choices offered in the Proxy Generator drop-down list will be based on the language used in your ASP.NET pages. Since I've been using C# in this book, the Proxy Generator choice defaults to .NET C#. To change it, click the drop-down list and choose Edit Proxy Generator List as shown in Figure 8.7.

FIGURE 8.7:

You may need to change the proxy generator

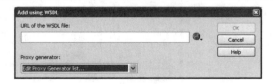

A dialog box like that in Figure 8.8 pops up. Highlight the language you are working in (in this case, we're in .NET C#) and click the Edit button. The Default Proxy Generator dialog box (like that in Figure 8.9) appears.

WARNING You only need to make these changes if you are getting the "Unable to Generate Proxy" error. Do not make proxy generator changes unless you get the error.

FIGURE 8.8:

Choose the language of your ASP.NET pages

FIGURE 8.9:

The Default Proxy Generator dialog box before any changes are made

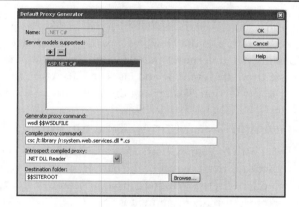

Now I need you to put on your "let's make a batch file" hat again, as you did in Chapter 9. If you look at the text field labeled "Generate proxy command:" it should contain something like this line:

```
wsdl $$WSDLFILE
```

This means that the WSDL tool is going to look for a little program called wsdl.exe. Later in this chapter, in the section "Generating a Proxy," you'll see that we can create a batch file to do the same thing this tool does.

The wsdl you see in the Default Proxy Generator dialog box is a reference to wsdl.exe. What's happening is that Dreamweaver works from batch files, too (actually, it uses XML, but let's keep thinking in terms of batch files to keep things simple). So when you get that "Unable to Generate Proxy" error, there is a good chance that Dreamweaver is simply not finding the wsdl.exe program or the compiler, called csc.exe, which is called from the next field, Compile Proxy Command. You need to help Dreamweaver find it. The easiest way to ensure success is by jumping ahead to the section "Compiling the Web Service Using a Batch

File," near the end of the chapter, testing the batch file, and then copying and pasting the path to `wsdl.exe` from the batch file. In my case, I needed to do this because my copy of `wsdl.exe` was not in a location where Dreamweaver expected it to be. This is what I pasted into the Generate Proxy Command field of the Default Proxy Generator dialog box:

```
"C:\Program Files\Microsoft Visual Studio .NET\FrameworkSDK\Bin\wsdl"
```

WARNING It's important to be sure you don't highlight what was already in that text field and simply write over everything, because it contains additional commands that Dreamweaver needs. Specifically, as shown in Figure 8.9, this field must contain $$WSDLFILE preceded by a space; this is a placeholder telling Dreamweaver where to output the newly created proxy file. So make sure you only highlight wsdl to be overwritten, and then make sure there is a space before $$WSDLFILE.

You can try the WSDL tool when you are finished, but it still may not work. If it doesn't, you need to return to the Default Proxy Generator dialog box and edit the Compile Proxy Command field underneath the Generate Proxy Command field. In this case, you can cut and paste from the batch file you made in Chapter 9; this file is repeated at the end of this chapter in the section "Compiling the Web Service Using a Batch File." The part you need is highlighted in bold in Listing 8.7:

```
%windir%\Microsoft.NET\Framework\v1.0.3705\csc
```

This is the path to your system's C# compiler, so your actual path may be different. The `%windir%` means that the rest of the path is relative to your Windows directory. Most likely, your compiler is in the Windows directory somewhere. It should be in your .NET Framework directory. On my machine it is in the `v1.0.3705` directory (this directory corresponds to the version of .NET running on my machine).

When you paste this line into the Compile Proxy Command text field, highlight only the character string `csc` and be careful not to highlight beyond it, because you want to preserve the spacing in the text field just as you'd want to preserve spacing in a batch file or from a command-line program. Then paste the correct path into the field.

All these changes should look like what you see in Figure 8.10.

FIGURE 8.10:

The Default Proxy Generator dialog box after changes to generate and compile the proxy command

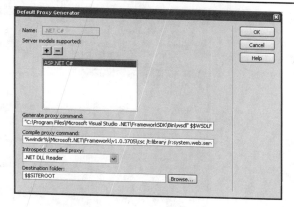

You should now be able to use the Add Using WSDL dialog box to add a web service. If this trick doesn't work, most likely you didn't add a path correctly. If it becomes too frustrating after numerous attempts, you can add a web service using proxy classes as shown later in "Generating a Proxy." After you've generated a proxy class, you can access it by selecting Add Using Proxy Classes in the Components tab. This choice generates the dialog box shown in Figure 8.11. The proxy should be a DLL made from the WSDL.exe tool.

FIGURE 8.11:

Adding a web service using the Add Using Proxy Classes dialog box

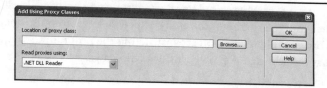

The DLL you use to generate your proxy should live in your application's bin directory. The purpose of this DLL is to translate the functions you are reading on a "foreign" system into classes that .NET can understand. This is made possible by the WSDL file that describes those functions, and by .NET's inherent understanding of what to do with this information.

Analyzing the WSDL

Whether you add a Web Service by WSDL or by proxy, the Components tab will show you a tree of objects belonging to the service, in the web service's window as shown in Figure 8.12.

FIGURE 8.12:

Browsing a web
service in the
Application Panel's
Components tab

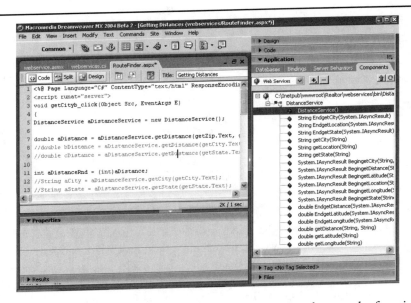

Now let's take a few moments and explore the WSDL file and how it relates to the functions and commands of the web service we are working with. When you use a word processing program such as Microsoft Word, every time you press a letter key you send a command to the program instructing it to render a specific letter into the document. When you choose Save from the File menu, you are instructing the program to save a copy of the file onto your hard drive. And when you play with Word's drawing tools, you are instructing it to do other things.

All this activity is managed through functions that are called as you use the program. You could conceivably, through Web Services, build a word processor that was hosted on your web server and accessed remotely by clients—although it wouldn't be very practical because running something like that over Internet pipes would be ungainly and slow. If you did, though, you would first build the software, and then create a WSDL document to describe all the functions (methods) and properties that are relevant to making the software work remotely.

WSDL is an XML-based vocabulary that describes a web service. The vocabulary contains elements for describing, for example, a specific function. These elements contain the parameters each public function expects. We can assume that a GetService web service would contain a class named `GetService` that served as the main class and returned data to us. We can only assume it because we can't actually see the source code, because it resides on someone else's server; if the WSDL were written correctly, though, we should be in good shape.

Listing 8.1 shows a key portion of the WSDL for the GetDistance Service that we've been working on. This is the portion that defines how to build a class constructor for getting distances between zip codes. You can download the full WSDL file from this book's page at www.sybex.com; look for the DistanceService.wsdl file in the Realtor application, or look at the file named L0801.wsdl.

Listing 8.1   Building a class constructor for getting distances between zip codes

```
<wsdl:operation name="getDistance">
<wsdlsoap:operation soapAction=""/>
<wsdl:input name="getDistanceRequest">
  <wsdlsoap:body encodingStyle="http://schemas.xmlsoap.org/soap/encoding/"
namespace="http://DefaultNamespace" use="encoded"/>
</wsdl:input>
<wsdl:output name="getDistanceResponse">
  <wsdlsoap:body encodingStyle="http://schemas.xmlsoap.org/soap/encoding/"
namespace="http://webservices.imacination.com/distance
➥/Distance.jws" use="encoded"/>
</wsdl:output>
</wsdl:operation>
```

The most important WSDL element, however, is one I haven't even shown you yet. It's the service element, which in this particular case looks like this:

```
<wsdl:service name="DistanceService">
  <wsdl:port binding="impl:DistanceSoapBinding" name="Distance">
  <wsdlsoap:address location="http://webservices.imacination.com/distance
➥/Distance.jws"/>
  </wsdl:port>
</wsdl:service>
```

This simply means that when we build a client for consuming this service, we'll need to create a class constructor for the primary class of the web service, called DistanceService. Think of DistanceService as simply the name of the application that will run when we access the service. We'll be treating this as a class object when we build our service, so we'll need to create a new instance of it.

Remember that since WSDL is simply XML-based markup, it offers no actual business logic of its own. All WSDL does is help systems communicate with each other, but in a standardized way. Like many XML vocabularies, WSDL was cooked up by the W3C, with significant impetus from Microsoft and IBM. When WSDL was introduced, many people panicked. It seemed incomprehensible that anyone could write these documents, because the language is rather complex and the drag on human resources to develop WSDL documents would be tremendous. Luckily, tools quickly emerged that will read source documents containing the code that runs a web service, and convert it into WSDL.

So the good news is that, for now, you don't really have to worry about how to create a WSDL document. You don't even need to worry too much about how to read one, although it can't hurt because it helps you understand what's happening under the hood of web services. All you have to know is how to access a WSDL document and allow a software tool to analyze it and generate code that calls functions with the parameters expected by the web service.

Analyzing by Viewing WSDL Elements

Notice I said that *"for now"* you don't need to worry about WSDL. But in the long run, if you ever get genuinely serious about high-level web services, you'll want to understand WSDL up and down. See this article for more: `www.xml.com/pub/a/ws/2003/07/22/wsdlfirst.html`.

For now, it's enough to know a few basics about WSDL, which uses these elements to describe a web service:

`service` This element gives the name of the web service through its name attribute. This will map to the primary class that you will want in your code, for which you will build a constructor defining a new instance of the class.

`portType` This element describes operations performed by the web service. This element lists the individual operations (or methods or functions, depending on how you want to refer to them).

`message` This element describes messages used by the web service. You'll be interested in these especially in regard to passing information into and out of form fields and other input widgets that communicate with the web services.

`types` This element describes datatypes used by the web service. These will be defined using XML Schema. Sometimes you'll simply see a `types` attribute in, for example, a `message` element's `part` child element, which accomplishes the same task.

`binding` This element describes the communication protocols used by the web service.

By analyzing the WSDL, you can deduce how to build a web client that accesses the methods, or operations, of the web service. However, as I mentioned, there are tools that can help with this. Of course, the software tool you'll be using to analyze WSDL files in the examples in this chapter is the WSDL tool found in Dreamweaver, which, if configured properly, should produce a tree of objects belonging to the web service.

Once a web service has been loaded into Dreamweaver, you can expand the object tree in the Components tab of the Application panel, and literally just drag the appropriate "part" of the web service to your code window.

Building an ASP.NET File for Consuming a Web Service

The next step is to build a client application that can access the web service. This is going to be an ASPX page. You're used to the fundamentals of doing this to some extent already, except that here you're accessing some foreign-looking classes and creating instances of unfamiliar classes. In effect, by adding this web service to your page, you are accessing a new set of classes that aren't documented in the .NET framework because they're not .NET classes. Instead, the WSDL file creates a description of the objects in the web service, and you then drag them into your client application and work with them there.

If you go back to the XMethods page for the Zip Distance Calculator (Figure 8.5), you'll see a link to a page called "Analyze WSDL." When you click it, you'll get the page shown in Figure 8.13.

FIGURE 8.13:

The XMethods WSDL analyzer page for the Zip Distance Calculator

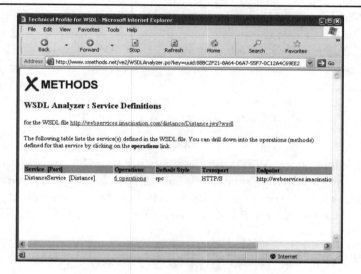

This web page lets you view the operations available from the service. Under "Service [Port]" you'll see the web service name, which is DistanceService. This may be confusing; you may logically have thought the name should be ZipDistanceCalculator, since that's the heading for the page—but that's one of the flaws of Web Services in general. Often, documentation is sparse or even nonexistent, and there are inconsistencies especially in nomenclature. Sometimes you have to muddle through and experiment. If you are involved with a trading partner on a substantial level, there's a better chance the documentation will be much more complete (and at least you can probably shake somebody by the collar if it isn't). If you're trying to access publicly available web services, however, you will often find the documentation isn't very good.

Under "Operations," you'll see a link that says "6 operations." This refers to the six operations, or functions, or methods (whatever you want to call them) that are provided by the web service. Let's look at one of them, and see how to call it from our ASPX page.

Click the link to "6 operations." Another web page will appear, listing each operation. Click the Input message for the getDistance operation. The important piece of information here is the schema datatype under the heading Parts. XML Schemas are rules files that define, among other things, datatypes of specific elements. In this case, you can see that the datatype for the fromZip and toZip elements is string (xsd:string means that the element is an XML Schema string type, where the xsd: is a namespace prefix used to describe schema elements). XML Schema is an essential piece to Web Services, but for the most part you don't need to know much more about it other than how to identify datatypes in web services' functions that you call. Although, like WSDL, as you become more fluent in Web Services, you'll want to learn progressively more about XML Schema.

NOTE If you want to learn more about XML Schema, visit http://www.w3.org/TR/xmlschema-0/ and check out Bonus Chapter 2, "Working with XML."

Now that you've seen the description for the getDistance operation, and you've seen how it looks in the WSDL file, how easy is it to build a constructor for it in Dreamweaver? The answer is that it's ridiculously easy. All you have to do is go to the Components tab and, with DistanceServer's tree expanded, click the DistanceService() node in the tree and drag it to the code window. But don't do that yet. First, we'll need to build an empty event handler, like so:

```
<script runat="server">
void getCityb_click(Object Src, EventArgs E)
{
}
</script>
```

FIGURE 8.14:

Choosing the
`DistanceService()`
method from the tree

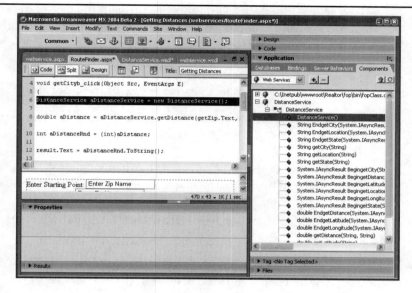

Now, we can drag the `DistanceService()` node from the Components tab over to Dreamweaver's Code view window. Voila! If you look at Figure 8.14 you'll see that Dreamweaver has built a constructor for us! The event handler should now look like this:

```
<script runat="server">
void getCityb_click(Object Src, EventArgs E)
{
DistanceService aDistanceService = new DistanceService();
}
</script>
```

If you read Chapter 9, you may remember my discussion about how classes work in .NET. It's all one big inheritance scheme. The same thing goes for when we're building a Web Services client.

We saw earlier that we want the `getDistance()` operation that's provided by the web service. Whew. Now we have to go back to that WSDL file and find out what datatype the `getDistance()` operation or method is expecting, and what it will return. Or do we?

No, actually all we need to do is browse through the tree of `DistanceService` nodes in Dreamweaver and find the `getDistance()` operation there, and then drag it into our event handler:

```
void getCityb_click(Object Src, EventArgs E)
{
DistanceService aDistanceService = new DistanceService();

double aDistance = aDistanceService.getDistance(/*String*/enter_value_here,
➡/*String*/enter_value_here);
}
```

Dreamweaver comes to the rescue again when it builds the code, and even identifies the datatype returned by the `getDistance()` method for us. It also tells us what datatypes the method is expecting:

```
(/*String*/enter_value_here, /*String*/enter_value_here)
```

It's up to us to replace the placeholder text with actual values.

So let's go to the HTML portion of the code and build a couple of quickie form widgets to accept some user input and send it along to the web service:

```
Enter Starting Point:
<asp:textbox ID="getZip" runat="server" Text="Enter Zip Name" /><br>
Enter End Point:
<asp:textbox ID="getZipEnd" runat="server" Text="Enter Zip Name" /><br>
```

Now all we need to do is replace the placeholder text Dreamweaver dropped in with some real values:

```
double aDistance = aDistanceService.getDistance(getZip.Text, getZipEnd.Text);
```

The first text box is the starting point, represented by a string value representing a zip code; and the second text box is the endpoint, which represents another zip code. When these two values are passed to the web service, it will calculate the distance between the two zip codes and return that distance, in the form of a `double` datatype. Since I don't want a `double` and only want a whole number, I convert that to an integer by creating a new variable to store the integer and doing an explicit cast on the original `double` value:

```
int aDistanceRnd = (int)aDistance;
```

Now we need an ASP.NET widget to display the result:

```
Distance between Zip Codes is:
<asp:label id="result" runat="server"/>
```

Finally, we'll write the code that writes that result to the `result` label:

```
result.Text = aDistanceRnd.ToString();
```

The final result of our efforts is shown in Listing 8.2, and Figure 8.15 shows what the service looks like after a user interacts with it. The real work is performed by the web service. All we are doing is building a client to access that web service.

FIGURE 8.15:

The browser window after a user invokes the DistanceService web service

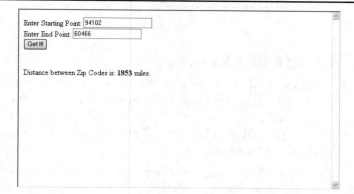

Enter Starting Point: 94102
Enter End Point: 60466
Get It!

Distance between Zip Codes is: 1853 miles.

Listing 8.2   Consuming the DistanceService web service

```
<%@ Page Language="C#" ContentType="text/html" ResponseEncoding="iso-8859-1" %>
<script runat="server">
void getCityb_click(Object Src, EventArgs E)
{
DistanceService aDistanceService = new DistanceService();
double aDistance = aDistanceService.getDistance(getZip.Text, getZipEnd.Text);
int aDistanceRnd = (int)aDistance;
result.Text = aDistanceRnd.ToString();
}
</script>
<html>
<head>
<title>Getting Distances</title>
<meta http-equiv="Content-Type" content="text/html; charset=iso-8859-1">
</head>
<body><form runat="server">
Enter Starting Point:
<asp:textbox ID="getZip" runat="server" Text="Enter Zip Code" /><br>
Enter End Point:
<asp:textbox ID="getZipEnd" runat="server" Text="Enter Zip Code" /><br>
<asp:button ID="getCityb" OnClick="getCityb_click"
 runat="server" Text="Get It!" /><br>
<br>
<br>
```

```
Distance between Zip Codes is:
<b><asp:label id="result" runat="server"/></b> miles.
</form>
</body>
</html>
```

Creating a Web Service

Building a web service is going to be as complex as you wish it to be, since the only limits to what you can create using Web Services are your imagination and/or your time and human resources. We'll take a look at building a simple web service here. To tackle more complex web services, you'll need to either get good at programming (if you aren't already), or find someone else who is good.

The web service we build in this chapter will simply access our Realtor database and return any notes we've written to our client. You wouldn't need a web service for this if everything you are doing is ASP.NET—you could simply build a page for your clients to access (as we've already done) and show any notes there. However, you may want to bind it to some instant messaging service somewhere or to some other non-Web platform. In this case, we'll simply build an ASP.NET page that consumes the service, to reinforce what we learned in the previous sections.

First Step: Building a Stored Procedure

The first thing we'll do is build a stored procedure to return the data. You'll note that this stored procedure returns more than just the notes to the client; I've added some other fields in case you want to try to expand on this on your own. So the stored procedure selects data from the Client_ID, CUserName, ClientName, CFirstName, CLastName, and ClientNote fields in the Clients table. Listing 8.3 shows the stored procedure we'll use.

Listing 8.3　　　**Stored procedure ClientQueryIDandNameAndNotes.sql**

```
CREATE PROCEDURE ClientQueryIDandNameAndNotes
- this is for querying Clients
@Client_ID int
AS
BEGIN
    SET NOCOUNT ON
    DECLARE @IDNumb int
- is there an error, and if so, display it
if @@error <> 0
```

```
return @@error
else
- if no error, set a variable to return the Listings Id as a unique identifier
- NOTE: The column named IDNumb is the identity seed
SELECT @IDNumb = @@IDENTITY
- calculate the expression so it will show in the recordset
SET NOCOUNT OFF
SELECT
    Client_ID,
    CUserName,
    ClientName,
    CFirstName,
    CLastName,
    ClientNote
FROM dbo.ClientInfo
WHERE @Client_ID = Client_ID
    END
GO
```

Building the Web Service Function

Because you're making your web service available to lots of people, possibly including mortal enemies and competitors, you'll want to recall my previous discussion in Chapter 9 about encapsulation. Remember that encapsulation lets you build your applications like containers. So you can actually make the bulk of your application happen in a container nobody sees, then call into that container from the main class of the web service. That way, if you have proprietary code, it's no problem, because the WSDL will not expose the methods in your proprietary code to the rest of the world.

So our Web Service consists of two methods. One of them simply calls the other, unseen method that actually does all the work. The hidden method is actually the one that works with the stored procedure, then returns a value as a result of the stored procedure, which the other, public method then picks up. Both of these methods are special kinds of methods called *web callable methods*, or *web methods* for short. A web method is always declared with the following syntax:

```
[webmethod]
```

Then we declare our actual method:

```
public string Notes(string strGetClientID)
    {
        return getCNote(strGetClientID);
    }
```

To "hide" a method, you use the `private` keyword; and to make a method available as part of the public description of your web service, you use the `public` keyword.

Building the Web Service Step by Step

Let's examine the steps necessary to building your web service.

1. Identify what you're trying to do. In our case, all we're doing is returning a string of data from a database.

2. Create a new page in Dreamweaver, and save it using the .asmx filename extension. This is the extension used for all web services created in ASP.NET. The downloadable file is called NoteService.asmx.

3. Use the WebService directive at the top of your new .asmx page:

   ```
   <%@ WebService Language="C#" Class="GetNotes" %>
   ```

   The class name must match the name of your primary class containing all your web methods. See the highlighted Class="GetNotes" attribute/value pair above, because you'll be naming your primary class GetNotes.

4. Import the appropriate .NET classes:

   ```
   using System.Web.Services;
   using System.Data;
   using System.Data.SqlClient;
   using System.Configuration;
   ```

   As you can see, there is a class for Web Services that inherits classes from the Web class and adds functionality specific to Web Services. You'll need that, along with any other classes that are essential parts of your application. Since we're going to access a database connection string using the web.config file, we'll need ASP.NET's built-in System.Configuration class, and we'll also need database helper classes.

5. Build a shell for your main class, which will contain your application's web methods:

   ```
   [WebService]
   public class GetNotes : System.Web.Services.WebService

   {
   }
   ```

6. So far, your class doesn't do anything. So let's build a private web method within your class that accesses the database and returns a string to the client:

   ```
   [WebService]
   public class GetNotes : System.Web.Services.WebService

   {
     private string getCNote(string strGetClientID)
     {
   ```

```
        SqlConnection connection = new
➥SqlConnection(ConfigurationSettings.AppSettings["DSN"]);
SqlCommand command = new
➥SqlCommand("ClientQueryIDandNameAndNotes", connection);
command.CommandType = CommandType.StoredProcedure;
command.Parameters.Add(new SqlParameter("@Client_ID",
➥SqlDbType.Int));
command.Parameters["@Client_ID"].Direction =
➥ParameterDirection.Input;
➥command.Parameters["@Client_ID"].Value = strGetClientID;
string report;
// Opens the connection
connection.Open();
// executes the stored procedure
SqlDataReader reportObject = command.ExecuteReader();
reportObject.Read();
report = reportObject[5].ToString();
// always call Close when done reading.
 reportObject.Close();
            // Destroys the command object
            command.Dispose() ;
            // Destroys the connection object
            connection.Dispose() ;
        return report;
    }
```

Rather than walk you through each step of the actual application, since it's fairly simple, I've commented out the code so that we can move on to the next step. The two very important pieces to this are the highlighted code at the end, which returns the string obtained from the database, and the strGetClientID parameter that is included in the web method's definition. The web method will be expecting the strGetClientID parameter as a string, so any calling client needs to provide it.

7. Next, go back to the beginning of your .asmx file and add the public method that will be exposed to those consuming your service:

```
[WebMethod]
public string Notes(string strGetClientID)
    {
        return getCNote(strGetClientID);
    }
```

Note that this public method also expects a variable named strGetClientID, which it will then pass to the private getCNote method, since users can't pass parameters directly to private methods. It's sort of like making a hand-off. The public string method Notes() receives an HTTP or SOAP request containing the value for the strGetClientID parameter (or argument) and passes that value to the private getCNote method.

That's all there is to creating a simple web service. Now, we have to prep it for consumption.

Adding a Namespace to Your Web Service

When you save your file, navigate to it using your web browser. You should get a web page like that shown in Figure 8.16. The browser window gives you a warning urging you to change your namespace from the default:

> *This web service is using http://tempuri.org/ as its default namespace.*
>
> *Recommendation: Change the default namespace before the XML Web service is made public.*
>
> *Each XML Web service needs a unique namespace in order for client applications to distinguish it from other services on the Web. http://tempuri.org/ is available for XML Web services that are under development, but published XML Web services should use a more permanent namespace.*

C#

```
[WebService(Namespace="http://microsoft.com/webservices/")]
public class MyWebService {
    // implementation
}
```

FIGURE 8.16:

This page warns you about generic namespaces.

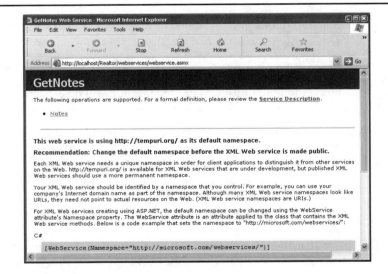

So, let's do that. The warning isn't clear about where exactly the namespace code snippet is supposed to go, but since we know that namespace declarations appear first, before any class declarations on an ASP.NET page, we can make a pretty decent guess that we need to put this at the top of the page. When we do that and resave, we get a browser window like the one shown in Figure 8.17 when we retest our web service's file.

FIGURE 8.17:

When you add a namespace, the warning about default namespaces disappears.

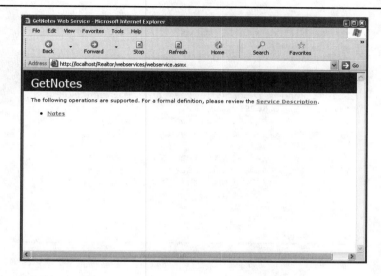

Our final code looks like Listing 8.4.

Listing 8.4   Our finished web service

```
<%@ WebService Language="C#" Class="GetNotes" %>
using System.Web.Services;
using System.Data;
using System.Data.SqlClient;
using System.Configuration;
[WebService(Namespace="http://www.tumeric.net/webservices/")]
public class GetNotes : System.Web.Services.WebService
{
[WebMethod]
public string Notes(string strGetClientID)
  {
      return getCNote(strGetClientID);
  }
private string getCNote(string strGetClientID)
{
```

```
        SqlConnection connection = new
➡SqlConnection(ConfigurationSettings.AppSettings["DSN"]);
SqlCommand command = new
➡SqlCommand("ClientQueryIDandNameAndNotes", connection);
command.CommandType = CommandType.StoredProcedure;
command.Parameters.Add(new SqlParameter("@Client_ID",
➡SqlDbType.Int));
command.Parameters["@Client_ID"].Direction =
➡ParameterDirection.Input;
➡command.Parameters["@Client_ID"].Value = strGetClientID;
string report;
// Opens the connection
connection.Open();
// executes the stored procedure
SqlDataReader reportObject = command.ExecuteReader();
reportObject.Read();
report = reportObject[5].ToString();
// always call Close when done reading.
 reportObject.Close();
            // Destroys the command object
            command.Dispose() ;
            // Destroys the connection object
            connection.Dispose() ;
        return report;
    }
 }
```

Testing the Web Service

You've seen how you can access the .asmx file by navigating to it through your web server. ASP.NET creates a page automatically that provides a description of your web service.

You can actually test the service before unleashing it on the world, and if you try to load the page when your code is not written correctly, the compiler will give you an error message. This is helpful because, after you test the service, you'll have to actually compile the service into a proxy DLL that you install in your bin directory. It's a lot easier to simply reload your browser window and let the ASP.NET engine invoke the C# compiler than it is to keep running from the command line. This is true even if you do have a batch file, because the compiler returns HTML code as part of any error messages, and this code is hard to read in a DOS-like window.

To test the service, go to your NoteService.asmx page on your local server and click the Notes link. You should get a page that looks like Figure 8.18. You can invoke the service from this page by entering a value into the text box. The service will be expecting one of the Client ID numbers that are in the Realtor database's ClientInfo table—specifically, the string supplied via the strGetClientID variable that we created for the service. When ASP.NET built this page, it knew that because it read the WSDL file before it generated the page, and built a text box for passing the `strGetClientID` value. To test the page, you simply type in a real value from the `ClientInfo` table's `Client_ID` column. If you enter a number that doesn't actually exist in the database, you'll get an error message from IIS telling you, "There is a problem with the page you are trying to reach and it cannot be displayed." That's because there's no error handling for this web service (which circumstance you'd likely want to change in a production scenario).

FIGURE 8.18:

The web service test page allows you to invoke the service for testing purposes.

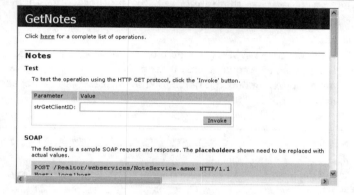

If the test is successful, a new window like Figure 8.19 will pop up.

FIGURE 8.19:

When the test of your web service is successful, ASP.NET returns your data in an XML file.

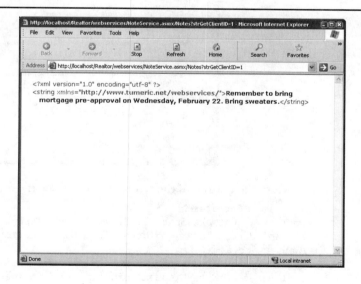

Examining the WSDL File

After you've tested your web service, you can close the results window from the test and examine the WSDL that .NET creates. To do that, go back to the `NoteService.asmx` page and click the "here" link. Or you can delete the highlighted code shown here (but not the rest of the URL) and hit Enter on your keyboard:

```
http://localhost/Realtor/webservices/NoteService.asmx?op=Notes
```

When you click the Service Description link on the resulting page (`NoteServer.asmx`), you get a web page like that in Figure 8.20. In other words, the Service Description link is simply a link to the web service's WSDL file.

> **NOTE**   This section on WSDL requires a bit of knowledge about XML. If you don't know anything about XML, it's probably best to skip this section and go forward to the section on generating a proxy. Although it helps to know WSDL, it isn't a necessity if you want to just keep moving along.

FIGURE 8.20:

The WSDL file produced by clicking the Service Description link in the `NoteService.asmx` page

Scroll down to the bottom of the screen and you'll see the following:

```
<service name="GetNotes">
    <port name="GetNotesSoap" binding="s0:GetNotesSoap">
      <soap:address location="http://localhost/Realtor/webservices
➥/webservice.asmx" />
    </port>
    <port name="GetNotesHttpGet" binding="s0:GetNotesHttpGet">
      <http:address location="http://localhost/Realtor/webservices
```

```
➥/webservice.asmx" />
    </port>
    <port name="GetNotesHttpPost" binding="s0:GetNotesHttpPost">
      <http:address location="http://localhost/Realtor/webservices
➥/webservice.asmx" />
    </port>
  </service>
```

The name in the `name="GetNotes"` attribute/value pair corresponds to the name of your web service and to the name of the class you defined at the top of the `NoteService.asmx` page. It also identifies the location of the page URL for SOAP or HTTP requests.

Next there will be a corresponding element in the WSDL that describes the public operation you developed, called `Notes`:

```
<operation name="Notes">
  <input message="s0:NotesHttpGetIn" />
  <output message="s0:NotesHttpGetOut" />
</operation>
```

You'll see one of these for each binding (in other words, for occasions where a SOAP request is made and for HTTP `GET` and `POST` methods). Generally, you or the tool you use to create WSDL files will also build a series of elements within the `types` element of the WSDL file that provides XML Schema–based datatype information about our operation:

```
<s:element name="Notes">
  <s:complexType>
    <s:sequence>
      <s:element minOccurs="0" maxOccurs="1"
        name="strGetClientID" type="s:string" />
    </s:sequence>
  </s:complexType>
</s:element>
```

Note that there is also a corresponding child element that describes the parameter expected by the function (`name="strGetClientID"`). The previous elements only define the datatype and XML structure of the Notes operation; they don't provide any information about the operation itself, and on its own a system trying out the web service wouldn't know about the expected parameter, `strGetClientID`. The previous code did nothing more than establish that `strGetClientID` is a string. To actually establish that `strGetClientID` is expected as a parameter, the WSDL provides a series of message elements like the following:

```
<message name="NotesSoapIn">
  <part name="parameters" element="s0:Notes" />
</message>
```

This refers to the previously defined `s:element name="Notes"` schema definition, where in turn you'll find the definition for the `strGetClientID` element. If you're not yet thoroughly confused, you should be, and if you are, join the crowd. It's natural to ask, how does the `element="s0:Notes"` attribute value pair correspond to `s:element name="Notes"`? Shouldn't `s:element name="Notes"` be `s:element name=":Notes"` if that's the case?

The answer lies in the rather confusing notion of namespaces. The prefix `s0:` is not the critical piece of the namespace to which the `Notes` element belongs, believe it or not. The critical part to pay attention to is the target namespace in the schema element that houses the `s:element` element (in bold):

```
<s:schema elementFormDefault="qualified"
  targetNamespace="http://www.tumeric.net/webservices/">
   <s:element name="Notes">
    <s:complexType>
      <s:sequence>
        <s:element minOccurs="0" maxOccurs="1"
          name="strGetClientID" type="s:string" />
      </s:sequence>
    </s:complexType>
   </s:element>
```

Now look at the top of the WSDL document and you'll see a namespace declaration:

```
xmlns:s0="http://www.tumeric.net/webservices/"
```

What makes these two instances match from a binding perspective are the namespace nodes, which are represented by the `http://www.tumeric.net/webservices/` URI identifier. In the world of XML namespaces, it looks like the prefix (the part of a namespace element preceding the colon) is important; but actually, it's the namespace itself, represented by the URI, that is the critical part.

This kind of information will make more sense to those of you who know XML pretty well. You don't need to worry much about this level of understanding when you use Dreamweaver to build your web services, but as your web services get more complicated, you may want to wrest control of automated WSDL markup away from tools and roll your own. If that's the case, you'll want to find a decent WSDL tutorial, such as this one:

```
http://www.w3schools.com/wsdl/default.asp
```

By making your own WSDL, you can simply save your WSDL locally on your hard drive, and have Dreamweaver analyze it and create your DLL from that. But since it's unlikely that you'll be able to just jump in and start writing WSDL based on the code you write, we'll let the various tools at your disposal do it for you. In this case, .NET created your WSDL. From that point, you'll need to compile a proxy DLL and dump it into your `bin` folder before people can invoke your web service.

Generating a Proxy

Now that you've tested and (maybe) analyzed your web service, it's time to compile a proxy for it. For this, you'll need to create a batch file, unless you're the kind that enjoys writing and rewriting commands using command-line tools. I'm going to assume you're not and direct you to Listing 8.5, which shows a simple batch file for generating the proxy. This batch file invokes a utility named WSDL.exe that will read your WSDL and generate a C# source file, which you'll then compile with one other batch file.

Listing 8.5   **A batch file for generating a proxy with the WSDL.exe tool**

```
"C:\Program Files\Microsoft Visual Studio
➥.NET\FrameworkSDK\Bin\wsdl" /l:cs
➥/o:C:\Inetpub\wwwroot\Realtor\webservices\NoteService.cs
➥http://localhost/Realtor/webservices/ NoteService.asmx?WSDL
➥ /n:NoteService
➥pause
```

There are some important things to note about this batch file. One is the presence of quotes around the path. This prevents the command-line program (cmd.exe) from expecting something after a space. If you leave off the quotes, the command-line program will expect something after C:\Program and will assume that's the end of the path. Run it without the quotes just to see what I mean.

Another thing to note is the switches. Whenever you see a / character, this indicates to the WSDL.exe program that a new parameter expected by the utility is on its way. So you should have a space followed by a / character before each new parameter.

TIP   To view all the commands you can access from wsdl.exe, you can type in **wsdl /?** (with any appropriate path info before the **wsdl**).

Finally, note that the pause keyword is crucial; if you omit it, the command-line program will literally flicker on your screen and disappear, and the WSDL may or may not get generated. The command-line tool did in fact report its activity to you, but you aren't Superman and you can't read it in time before the program automatically quits. The pause keyword keeps the window open and allows you to see any debugging messages.

When the proxy is created, the WSDL tool should generate screen output like that in Figure 8.21. The final CS file that gets generated should look like Listing 8.6.

FIGURE 8.21:

The WSDL tool reports on the progress of your file-writing activity.

Listing 8.6   **The C# source file for invoking the web service** (NoteService.cs)

```csharp
//————————————————————————————————————
// <autogenerated>
//     This code was generated by a tool.
//     Runtime Version: 1.0.3705.0
//
//     Changes to this file may cause incorrect behavior and will be lost if
//     the code is regenerated.
// </autogenerated>
//————————————————————————————————————


//
// This source code was auto-generated by wsdl, Version=1.0.3705.0.
//
namespace NoteService {
    using System.Diagnostics;
    using System.Xml.Serialization;
    using System;
    using System.Web.Services.Protocols;
    using System.ComponentModel;
    using System.Web.Services;


    /// <remarks/>
    [System.Diagnostics.DebuggerStepThroughAttribute()]
    [System.ComponentModel.DesignerCategoryAttribute("code")]
    [System.Web.Services.WebServiceBindingAttribute(Name=
    ➥"GetNotesSoap", Namespace="http://www.tumeric.net
    ➥/webservices/")]
    public class GetNotes :
    ➥System.Web.Services.Protocols.SoapHttpClientProtocol
{
        /// <remarks/>
        public GetNotes() {
            this.Url = "http://localhost/Realtor/webservices/webservice.asmx";
        }
```

```
        /// <remarks/>
[System.Web.Services.Protocols.SoapDocumentMethodAttribute
➡("http://www.tumeric.net/webservices/Notes",
➡RequestNamespace="http://www.tumeric.net/webservices/",
➡ResponseNamespace="http://www.tumeric.net/webservices/",
➡Use=System.Web.Services.Description.SoapBindingUse.
➡Literal, ParameterStyle=System.Web.Services.Protocols.
➡SoapParameterStyle.Wrapped)]
        public string Notes(string strGetClientID) {
            object[] results = this.Invoke("Notes", new object[] {
                        strGetClientID});
            return ((string)(results[0]));
        }

        /// <remarks/>
        public System.IAsyncResult BeginNotes(string
➡strGetClientID, System.AsyncCallback callback,
➡object asyncState) {
            return this.BeginInvoke("Notes", new object[] {
                        strGetClientID}, callback, asyncState);
        }

        /// <remarks/>
        public string EndNotes(System.IAsyncResult asyncResult)
        {
            object[] results = this.EndInvoke(asyncResult);
            return ((string)(results[0]));
        }
    }
}
```

Compiling the Web Service Using a Batch File

Finally, we need to create a batch file for compiling the DLL. Aim the DLL into your bin directory. Place it into the web server's root bin directory or, if you've made a web application (using the Virtual Directory wizard in IIS) you can put it into the bin directory of the application that houses the web service. Listing 8.7 shows a basic batch file that does the trick. Your path names may differ, so you'll have to account for that.

Listing 8.7   Compiling the web service using a batch file

```
set indir=C:\Inetpub\wwwroot\Realtor\webservices\webservices.cs
set outdir=C:\Inetpub\wwwroot\Realtor\webservices\bin\webservices.dll

%windir%\Microsoft.NET\Framework\v1.0.3705\csc /t:library /out:%outdir% %indir%

pause
```

Consuming the Notes Service

Since we've used a pretty simple example of creating a web service, I'm going to leave the consumption of this web service to you as an exercise. You'll have no trouble figuring it out if you apply the principles set forth when we built a consumer for the DistanceService earlier in the chapter. You can find a finished version of a file that consumes the Get Notes service in the Realtor application, in a file named `NoteService.aspx`.

Wrapping Up

The widespread use of Web Services is right around the corner. A lot of trading partners are already using the technology, and it's only a matter of time before you'll find it necessary and/or desirable to start using it yourself.

The key to understanding web services is to simply remember that you are essentially extending the class-based ASP.NET object model to the rest of the world. You now have access to a potentially limitless object model created by other people and, of course, yourself. This means your applications can do things over the Internet that nobody could have imagined 5 years ago.

Remember the key to making web services work for other people: Document your code carefully. You'll also need to follow the usual script when it comes to customized code-based content and make sure you have compiled the business logic of any application you build into a DLL, which is then dropped into your `bin` directory. You will then be on your way to exposing the world to your first set of web services.

CHAPTER 9

Putting It All Together: The Realtor Application

- An overview of the Realtor application

- Developing the administrative area

- Developing the public access area

- Building the registration and login area

- Exploring the Realtor application

Most of this book has taken samples from a website named Realtor, designed for use by a real estate professional. The site consists of a public access area where the realtor can show current listings and news, an administrative area that allows the realtor to make changes in the site, and a login area where the realtor's customers can log in and view information specific to them. The site is rather large, and since writing and examining the entire site would take an entire book, I thought I'd focus on an overview and allow you to peruse the source code on your own. Of course, to do this, you'll need to download the file for the site, which is called `Realtor.zip`. Be sure to look at the Read Me file for instructions on how to install the site on your server.

In this chapter, we'll examine the various pieces that go together to make the Realtor site. I'll also give you a tour of a couple of specific areas in greater detail to help you on your way to studying the rest of the site on your own. Exploring the many files made available to you through the Realtor application will be an essential part of understanding how you can use Dreamweaver MX as an important, time-saving tool in building powerful ASP.NET web applications.

An Overview of the Realtor Application

The Realtor Application consists of three main areas:

- One is an administrative area that allows the owner of the site to perform administrative tasks, such as adding to the database and managing accounts, creating and editing newsletters, and adding, updating, and deleting listings.

- The second area is a login area for clients. Here the realtor can personalize communications with individual clients.

- The third area is the public access area, in which property listings and other information are presented to the general public.

Developing the Administrative Area

The Administrative area consists of the following core features:

- An area that manages clients
- An area that manages listings
- An area that manages newsletters

The one thing you don't want to happen is for someone other than the owner of the website to access the administrative area, so the login page for this area should be airtight. With older versions of Active Server Pages, making a reasonably secure administrative area required more programming than is needed today. ASP.NET includes a class called the FormsAuthenticationTicket class that essentially encapsulates all the routines needed to build an authentication page. You use this class to build a login page that allows the website owner to perform administrative functions. We'll take a look at that first, since it's such an important piece to the puzzle.

First Things First: Building the Login Page

Imagine being able to build a login page that tracks users throughout their session and returns them to a login page automatically once the session expires. That part is easy to envision, but now imagine using about 15 lines of code to do it. That's what the FormsAuthenticationTicket class offers you. It's really just a matter of creating an instance of the class, as shown in Listing 9.1.

Listing 9.1 **The login code-behind page (`logon.aspx.cs`)**

```
using System;
using System.Configuration;
using System.Collections;
using System.ComponentModel;
using System.Data.SqlClient;
using System.Web.Security;

using System.Data;
using System.Drawing;
using System.Web;
using System.Web.SessionState;
using System.Web.UI;
using System.Web.UI.WebControls;
using System.Web.UI.HtmlControls;

namespace admin
{
    /// <summary>
    /// Summary description for logon.
    /// </summary>
    public class logon : System.Web.UI.Page
    {
        protected System.Web.UI.WebControls.RequiredFieldValidator vUserName;
        protected System.Web.UI.WebControls.RequiredFieldValidator vUserPass;
        protected System.Web.UI.WebControls.CheckBox chkPersistCookie;
        protected System.Web.UI.WebControls.Label lblMsg;
        protected System.Web.UI.HtmlControls.HtmlInputText txtUserName;
        protected System.Web.UI.HtmlControls.HtmlInputText txtUserPass;
        protected System.Web.UI.HtmlControls.HtmlInputButton cmdLogin;
```

```
        private bool ValidateUser(string uid, string passwd)
        {
            SqlConnection cnn;
            SqlCommand cmd;
            SqlDataReader dr;
            cnn = new SqlConnection(ConfigurationSettings.AppSettings["DSN"]);
            cmd = new SqlCommand("Select * from admin where
        ➥username='" + uid + "'",cnn);
//You really won't want a SELECT all statement here
//This is just to save space
            cnn.Open();
            dr = cmd.ExecuteReader();
            while (dr.Read())
            {

                if (string.Compare(dr["password"].ToString(),passwd,false)==0)
                {
                    cnn.Close();
                    return true;
                }
            }
            cnn.Close();
            return false;
        }

        private void cmdLogin_ServerClick(object sender, System.EventArgs e)
        {
            if (ValidateUser(txtUserName.Value,txtUserPass.Value) )
            {
                FormsAuthenticationTicket tkt;
                string cookiestr;
                HttpCookie ck;
                tkt = new FormsAuthenticationTicket(1,
                        ➥txtUserName.Value, DateTime.Now,
                        ➥DateTime.Now.AddMinutes(30),
                        ➥chkPersistCookie.Checked,
                        ➥"your custom data");
                cookiestr = FormsAuthentication.Encrypt(tkt);
                ck = new
                        ➥HttpCookie(FormsAuthentication.
                        ➥FormsCookieName, cookiestr);
                if (chkPersistCookie.Checked)
                        ➥ck.Expires=tkt.Expiration;
                Response.Cookies.Add(ck);
                string strRedirect;
                strRedirect = Request["ReturnUrl"];
                if (strRedirect==null)
                  strRedirect = "default.aspx";
                Response.Redirect(strRedirect, true);
            }
            else
                Response.Redirect("logon.aspx", true);
        }
```

```
    private void Page_Load(object sender, System.EventArgs e)
    {
        // Put user code to initialize the page here
    }

    #region Web Form Designer generated code
    override protected void OnInit(EventArgs e)
    {
        //
        InitializeComponent();
        base.OnInit(e);
    }

    private void InitializeComponent()
    {
        this.Load += new System.EventHandler(this.Page_Load);
        this.cmdLogin.ServerClick += new
         System.EventHandler(
         ➥this.cmdLogin_ServerClick);
    }
    #endregion
    }
}
```

Listing 9.1 is a code-behind page that falls within the admin namespace. Each key area of the Realtor application consists of a namespace, and you should create a virtual directory in IIS with a name that corresponds to each namespace. So your administrative area should be in a virtual directory named admin, and all the web forms and pages should be in the admin namespace, as highlighted in Listing 9.1.

The first thing you'll probably notice is new in Listing 9.1 is a series of variable declarations like the following:

```
protected System.Web.UI.HtmlControls.HtmlInputButton cmdLogin;
```

When you embed your script in a web form, you don't need to explicitly declare web and HTML controls as variables because the script engine knows about them already; but when running code-behind, you do. So you have to declare a variable for each server control you use.

The next thing that happens is that a Boolean function is declared:

```
private bool ValidateUser(string uid, string passwd)
```

This function returns a Boolean value based on certain conditions; namely, that a password field value matches one found in the database:

```
if (string.Compare(dr["password"].ToString(),passwd,false)==0)
        {
            cnn.Close();
            return true;
        }
```

The `if` statement uses a string comparison method to match against the database. The highlighted `false` keyword in the argument denotes whether the comparison should ignore the case. Since you're dealing with passwords, you will want them to be case-sensitive, so the third argument should be `false`. If there's a match in the database through the `if` statement for the `password` field, the Boolean `ValidateUser()` function returns true, and you can use this returned value later in the code.

In fact, you use it in a form handler named `cmdLogin_ServerClick`, which is the event handler for the login button.

Note to Advanced Users: Using Session Variables with *FormsAuthenticationTicket*

If you're using Session variables to store information about the logged-in user, the Session variables and forms authentication don't expire at the same time, which causes some problems in managing overall user sessions. The answer is to create a base class that inherits from `System.Web.UI.Page`. Add a virtual `Page_Load` handler with the normal `Object sender`, `EventArgs e` parameters, and include in that handler what you need to validate the form login (such as a way to check if the `FormsAuthenticationTicket` has expired), and perform a redirection to the login form if the session is invalidated. Make this class the base class for your other web forms pages and include a `base.Page_Load(sender, e);` call in the `Page_Load` event handler.

For example, your base class would look like this:

```
public class BaseForm : System.Web.UI.Page
{
protected virtual void Page_Load(object sender, EventArgs e)
{
//Refresh the expiration on the user's authentication ticket
try
{
FormsAuthenticationTicket authTicket =
((FormsIdentity)this.Page.User.Identity).Ticket;
if(authTicket.Expired)
{
Response.Redirect("login.aspx?action=SessionExpired", true);
}
authTicket = FormsAuthentication.RenewTicketIfOld(authTicket);
//Validate the session
if("test to see if the session is valid")
{
```

Continued on next page

```
            Response.Redirect("login.aspx?action=SessionExpired", true);
            }
            }
            catch(Exception AuthorizationException)
            {
            Trace.Write(AuthorizationException.Message);
            Response.Redirect("login.aspx?action=InvalidSessionID", true);
            }
            }
            }
```

Then your actual web forms page, from a strictly generic standpoint, would look like this:

```
            WebForms page:
            public class MyPage : BaseForm
            {
            //....
            protected override void Page_Load(Object sender, EventArgs e)
            {
            base.Page_Load(sender, e);
            // prepare the page's state
            }
            ....
            }
```

The login button's event handler instantiates a new instance of `FormsAuthenticationTicket` and takes advantage of that class's built-in properties and methods.

For more information on how to work with forms authentication, visit the Macromedia site and read this article:

```
http://www.macromedia.com/devnet/mx/dreamweaver/articles/forms_a
thentication.html
```

This is an especially good article if you want to run forms authentication from a Dreamweaver DataSet object, which, as you can see, I did not do in this case. (I thought it was easier this way, and I wanted to precompile my code-behind into the `admin` DLL to make it run faster.)

Building the Login Web Form

The next step is to build a login page, which is simply a web form that provides an interface for logging in. This is shown in Listing 9.2. I removed some of the extraneous code, but you can view all of it in the file `logon.aspx` in the Realtor application.

Listing 9.2   **The Logon ASPX page (`logon.aspx`)**

```
<%@ Page language="c#" Codebehind="logon.aspx.cs" AutoEventWireup
➥="false" Inherits="admin.logon" %>
<!DOCTYPE HTML PUBLIC "-//W3C//DTD HTML 4.0 Transitional//EN" >
<HTML>
    <HEAD>
        <title>Logon Page</title>

        <LINK href="admin.css" type="text/css" rel="stylesheet">
        <script language="JavaScript" src="admin.js"></script>
    </HEAD>
    <body topmargin="0" leftmargin="0" bgcolor="#d6d3ce">

        <form id="logon" method="post" runat="server">
            <table>
                <tr>
                <td>User Name:</td>
                    <td>
                        <input id="txtUserName" type="text"
                          name="txtUserName" runat="server">
                    </td>
                    <td>
    <ASP:REQUIREDFIELDVALIDATOR id="vUserName" runat="server" ErrorMessage="*"
Display="Static"
    ControlToValidate="txtUserName">
    </ASP:REQUIREDFIELDVALIDATOR>
                    </td>
                </tr>
                <tr>
                    <td>Password:</td>
                    <td>
    <input id="txtUserPass" type="password" name="txtUserPass"
    runat="server"></td><td>
    <ASP:REQUIREDFIELDVALIDATOR id="vUserPass"
     runat="server" ErrorMessage="*" Display="Static"
     ControlToValidate="txtUserPass">
    </ASP:REQUIREDFIELDVALIDATOR></td>
                </tr>
                <tr>
                    <td>Persistent Cookie:</td>
                    <td>
                        <ASP:CHECKBOX id="chkPersistCookie"
                          runat="server" autopostback="false">
                        </ASP:CHECKBOX>
                    </td>
                    <td></td>
                </tr>
            </table>
        <input id="cmdLogin" type="submit" value="Logon"
```

```
      name="cmdLogin" runat="server">
          <asp:label id="lblMsg" runat="server" Font-Size="10"
      Font-Name="Verdana" ForeColor="red"></asp:label>
        </form>
      </body>
    </HTML>
```

Listing 9.2 is fairly self-explanatory, using simple form fields to pass values to the validator in the script file and using field validators to make sure users enter a value. In this case, all that happens is that a red asterisk appears when the user doesn't fill in one of the required fields.

Editing the *Web.config* File for Forms Authentication

Once your forms authentication code and web form are finished, you'll need to go into the `Web.config` file to tell the web server that the `admin` application is a protected area. To do this, you add the following element to the `Web.config` file:

```
<authentication mode="Forms">
  <forms name=".ASPXFORMSDEMO" loginUrl="logon.aspx"
protection="All" path="/" timeout="30" />
  </authentication>
```

As long as this element is a child of the `system.web` element it can live anywhere in the `Web.config` file. When you set up your configuration this way, whenever a user attempts to access a page in the `admin` directory, even if they happen to know the URL that they want, they'll be redirected to `logon.aspx` if they haven't yet logged on.

Building the Administrative Area

Now that you've put together your login area, you can start building some administrative tools for your website owner. These are tools only the website owner can access.

You can start by building some administrative functions, such as web pages for the realtor to add listings, clients, and so forth. For the Realtor application, I relied heavily on stored procedures, although I added a few pages using SELECT statements directly in the web page just to make sure you could see examples of both techniques.

Table 9.1 shows some of the files that are used for the administrative area, and their roles. The table lists filenames, their purpose, and any supporting files (not all will necessarily be listed). The table doesn't show every supporting file. For a complete list, you'll need to simply peek inside the `admin` directory within the Realtor directory to see what's there.

In the case of supporting files with `.sql` extensions, the files aren't actually embedded or linked in any way, but instead can be used to create a stored procedure that matches the name of one used in the application. Additionally, most of them use `admin.js`, a JavaScript file for managing the HTML editor that is a part of many of the pages, and `admin.css`, a stylesheet.

If a page has as one of its supporting files a file with a `.cs` extension, this means it's a code-behind page. Note that some of these pages were compiled with another IDE to ease the batch compilation process. You can download a free IDE at

`http://www.icsharpcode.net/OpenSource/SD/Download/`

In the Realtor application's admin directory you'll find alternatives for some of the examples; these alternatives use strictly Macromedia controls instead of compiled code-behind pages, or they use a combination of code-behind and Macromedia controls with an emphasis on the Macromedia controls. These usually have names containing MM, such as `addListings_MM.aspx`.

TABLE 9.1: Example Files Used by the Administrative Area of the Realtor Application

File Name	Purpose	Supporting Files
`AddClients.aspx`	Inserts new clients into database.	`ClientQueryNoParams.sql`
`AddListings.aspx`	Adds new listings into database.	`AddListings.aspx.cs`
`AddNeighborhoodNews.aspx`	Allows website administrator to add articles.	`AddNeighborhoodNews.aspx.cs`
`addNews.aspx`	Allows website administrator to add news articles.	`addNews.aspx.cs`
`ClientDetails.aspx`	Allows administrator to view details on each client.	`ClientDetails.aspx.cs,` `ClientQuery.sql`
`CodeShell.txt`	A template of sorts, to help construct code-behind pages.	N/A
`ColorPicker.aspx`	A helper application used by the HTML editor to choose colors.	`ColorPicker.aspx.cs`
`DeleteClient.aspx`	Deletes clients from the database.	`DeleteClient.aspx.cs,` `DeleteClient.sql`
`DeleteImage.aspx`	Deletes images from the database.	`DeleteImage.aspx.cs,` `DeleteImage.sql`
`DeleteListing.aspx`	Deletes listings from the database.	`DeleteListing.aspx.cs,` `DeleteListing.sql`
`DeleteNews.aspx`	Deletes news articles from the database.	`DeleteNews.aspx.cs`

Continued on next page

TABLE 9.1 CONTINUED: Example Files Used by the Administrative Area of the Realtor Application

File Name	Purpose	Supporting Files
`Listings.aspx`	Reviews, updates and deletes listings.	`Listings.aspx.cs`, `Listing-QueryImagesAndClients.sql`
`logon.aspx`	Logs users into the system.	`logon.aspx.cs`, `web.config` (for authentication),
`News.aspx`	Provides a grid view of currently running stories.	`News.aspx.cs`
`ReviewListings.aspx`	This is the page returned after a listing has been updated.	`ListingQueryImagesAnd-ClientsWithParams.sql`
`UpdateClients.aspx`	Updates client information	None
`UpdateNeighborhoodNews.aspx`	Updates website articles	`UpdateNeighborhoodNews.aspx.cs`, `NeighborhoodNews-QueryWithParams.sql`
`UpdateNews.aspx`	Updates newsletter	`UpdateNews.aspx.cs`,
`UploadImage.aspx`	Updates images associated with listings	`UploadImage.aspx.cs`

Building a Client Listings Administrative Tool

Let's walk through one area of the administrative application, the area that adds and updates listings.

When a website administrator logs in, they sees a general administration area that contains links to various areas of the admin site, as shown in Figure 9.1. The administrator clicks the Add Listings link to navigate to a page containing a form for adding listings, as shown in Figure 9.2.

FIGURE 9.1:

The administrative area's home page

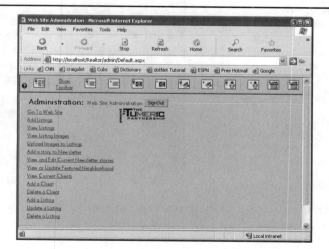

FIGURE 9.2:

A form for adding listings

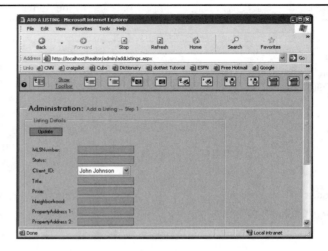

Once the form is filled out and the administrator clicks the Update button, the page updates to indicate that the Listing has updated successfully (Figure 9.3). A number of pages throughout the administrative area work like this form. Some of them report user-friendly errors if the administrative task isn't successful, and others report SQL-Server errors. You'll need to test and/or look at the code for various pages to see which have user-friendly errors. I included both kinds of code so that you could compare the differences and make alterations yourself.

FIGURE 9.3:

When the listings are successfully added, the page reflects the successful change.

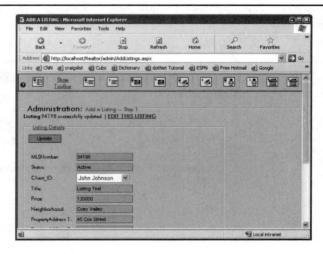

If the insertion was not successful, an error message appears, as shown in Figure 9.4.

FIGURE 9.4:

The page displays an error message when the administrator's update isn't successful.

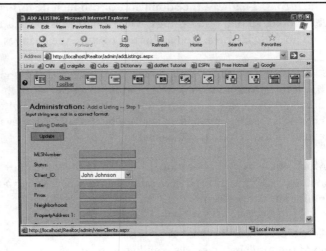

Assuming the listing insertion succeeded, the administrator can then click the "EDIT THIS LISTING" link (see Figure 9.3) in the resulting page. Note the URL in the browser's status bar when you do a mouseover. It will be something like this:

```
UpdateListings.aspx?MLSNumber=87765
```

The web page then takes the administrator to a page for working with that particular listing, as shown in Figure 9.5.

FIGURE 9.5:

The administrator is taken to a page for updating a listing based on the ID number of the created listing.

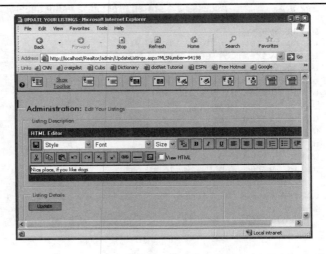

On the `UpdateListings.aspx` page you'll see an HTML editor. This is based on an open-source DLL that allows the administrator to provide HTML code for the description of the listing. That way, the administrator can include formatted statements such as **Must See!** in bold, among other things. The administrator needs to click the little floppy-disk Save icon before clicking the Update button to store the changes from the HTML editor.

NOTE   There is an alternative way to use an HTML editor, but it has the drawback of relying on the Internet Explorer object model and will not work in Netscape, Safari, or other browsers. I'm referring here to a client-side HTML editor that can be found in the addNews.aspx file; it relies extensively on the admin.js JavaScript file for its functionality and uses the IFRAME HTML element.

Much of the admin application is built along the same lines as these pages that handle listings. You'll see many variations on the same theme, which will expose you to different methods for handling similar problems.

Accessing Stored Procedures Using Custom Code

One of the fundamental tasks you'll want to eventually master is running some code-behind pages using custom code and stored procedures.

If you go back to Chapter 4, "Working with the Dreamweaver Custom Control," you'll recall a discussion about using the Parameter element in a Dreamweaver control that can be used with stored procedures. You can accomplish essentially the same thing using script, as shown in Listing 9.3. Note the listing segments highlighted in bold.

Listing 9.3   **Accessing a stored procedure using code-behind (AddListings.aspx.cs)**

```
using System;
using System.Configuration;
using System.Collections;
using System.ComponentModel;
using System.Data;
using System.Data.SqlClient;
using System.Drawing;
using System.Web;
using System.Web.SessionState;
using System.Web.UI;
using System.Web.UI.WebControls;
using System.Web.UI.HtmlControls;

namespace admin
{
    public class AddListings : System.Web.UI.Page

    {
        protected System.Web.UI.WebControls.Label Label1;
        protected System.Web.UI.WebControls.Label report;
```

```csharp
        protected System.Web.UI.WebControls.DropDownList Client_ID;
//You need to declare ALL of your WebControls
//Not all of them are shown here so that
//Space could be saved
DescriptionPlainText;
        protected System.Web.UI.WebControls.Panel reportPanel;
        protected System.Web.UI.WebControls.Button Update;

        protected System.Web.UI.WebControls.Button UpdateButton2;
        protected System.Web.UI.WebControls.Panel Panel1;
        protected System.Web.UI.WebControls.TextBox DescriptionXML;

        public void onclick_Update(object sender,
        ➥System.EventArgs e)
        {
            string sql="ListingInsertions";
            SqlConnection connection = new
                ➥SqlConnection(ConfigurationSettings.
                ➥AppSettings["DSN"]);
            SqlCommand command = new SqlCommand(sql, connection);
            command.CommandType = CommandType.StoredProcedure;
            //add the parameters
            command.Parameters.Add(new SqlParameter
                ➥("@MLSNumber", SqlDbType.VarChar, 50, "input"));
            command.Parameters["@MLSNumber"].Value =
                ➥MLSNumber.Text;
            command.Parameters.Add(new SqlParameter("@Title",
                ➥SqlDbType.VarChar, 50, "input"));
            command.Parameters["@Title"].Value = Title.Text;
//Add a command.Parameters method for EACH field in
//the database stored procedure expecting a parameter.
//Some have been left off here. Download the file to see all.

            try
            {
                // Open the connection
                connection.Open();

                // execute the stored procedure
                command.ExecuteNonQuery() ;

                // get the confirmation on the screen
                report.Text = "<b>Listing</b> " +
                        ➥command.Parameters["@MLSNumber"].Value +
                        ➥" successfully updated. | <a
                        ➥href='UpdateListings.aspx?MLSNumber=" +
                        ➥command.Parameters["@MLSNumber"].Value + "'>
                        ➥<b>EDIT THIS LISTING</b>" ;

            }
            catch(Exception ex)
            {
```

```
        // catch the error message and put it in the string "msg"
        string msg = ex.Message ;

            //show the error message on the screen

            report.Text = msg;

        }
        finally
        {

            // Destroy the command object
            command.Dispose() ;

            // Destroy the connection object
            connection.Dispose() ;
        }

    }

}
```

The following code fragment from Listing 9.3 achieves the same thing as the `Parameter` element we used in Chapter 4:

```
command.Parameters.Add(new SqlParameter
➥("@MLSNumber", SqlDbType.VarChar, 50, "input"));
```

Once again, we need to find a way to pass parameter values to the stored procedure. Dreamweaver handles all of this kind of coding for us in the Dreamweaver Control, but if we want, we can do it ourselves as shown in Listing 9.3.

Listing 9.4, truncated to remove extraneous code to save space, shows the general outline for a web form that takes advantage of the functionality in Listing 9.3. Note that the code-behind refers to the actual filename found in the Realtor application, and not to a file named `L0903.cs`.

Listing 9.4   **A web form for accessing a stored procedure (`AddListings.aspx`)**

```
<%@ Register TagPrefix="MM" Namespace="DreamweaverCtrls" Assembly
➥="DreamweaverCtrls,version=1.0.0.0,publicKeyToken
➥=836f606ede05d46a,culture=neutral" %>
<%@ Page language="c#" Codebehind="AddListings.aspx.cs" AutoEventWireup
➥="true" Inherits="admin.AddListings" %>
<!DOCTYPE HTML PUBLIC "-//W3C//DTD HTML 4.0 Transitional//EN" >
<HTML>
    <HEAD>
        <title>ADD A LISTING</title>
        <script language="JavaScript" src="admin.js"></script>
        <LINK href="admin.css" type="text/css" rel="stylesheet">
        <MM:DATASET id=ClientsDS runat="Server"
```

```
        CommandText='<%# "SELECT Client_ID, ClientName
        ➥FROM dbo.ClientInfo" %>'
        ➥ConnectionString='<%# System.Configuration.ConfigurationSettings.
➥AppSettings["MM_CONNECTION_STRING_mdriscollString"] %>'
➥DatabaseType='<%# System.Configuration.ConfigurationSettings.
➥AppSettings["MM_CONNECTION_DATABASETYPE_mdriscollString"] %>'
➥Debug="true" IsStoredProcedure="false">
    </MM:DATASET>
    <MM:PAGEBIND id="Pagebind1" runat="server"
    PostBackBind="false"></MM:PAGEBIND>
  </HEAD>
<body bgColor="#d6d3ce" leftMargin="0" topMargin="0">
   <!-- ###########  HELP BLOCK DELETED TO SAVE SPACE ########### -->

   <form id="Sample" action="UpdateListings.aspx" method="post" runat
   ➥="server">

<!-- skin based on fieldset element deleted to save space -->
<!-- UPDATE CONTAINER -->
   <div style="PADDING-RIGHT: 3px; PADDING-LEFT: 3px; PADDING-
   ➥BOTTOM: 3px; PADDING-TOP: 3px">
   <table>
     <tr>
       <td>MLSNumber:</td>
       <td>
         <asp:textbox id=MLSNumber Runat="server" />
       </td>
     </tr>
     <tr>
       <td>Status:</td>
       <td>
         <asp:textbox id=Status Runat="server" />
       </td>
     </tr>
     <tr>
      <td>Client_ID:</td>
      <td>
        <% Client_ID.SelectedIndex =
        ➥Client_ID.Items.IndexOf(Client_ID.Items.
        ➥FindByValue (ClientsDS.FieldValue
        ➥("Client_ID", null) )); %>
<asp:dropdownlist id="Client_ID" runat="server"
 DataSource="<%# ClientsDS.DefaultView %>"
 DataTextField="ClientName" DataValueField="Client_ID">
</asp:dropdownlist>
   </tr>
<!-- Additional TR elements here
    Deleted to save space -->
</table>
 <asp:Panel ID="Panel1" Runat="server"
  CssClass="button" Height="36px">
```

```
        <asp:Button id="UpdateButton2" onclick="onclick_Update"
          Runat="server" Text="Update" Width="75px">
        </asp:Button>
      </asp:Panel>
  </div>
  </form>
    </body>
  </HTML>
```

Developing the Public Access Area

The public access area features a home page, some listings, newsletters, and some current articles about the realtor's business. Figure 9.6 shows you the home page.

FIGURE 9.6:

The Realtor
application's
public access area
home page

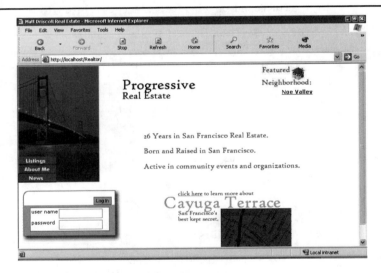

The home page is represented by the `Default.aspx` file that lives in the Realtor root folder. It doesn't contain any special features that are related to .NET architecture, so we'll move on.

Building the Public Entry Page

The home page is like any other home page on the planet, but the next page past that, `main.aspx`, does many things. Users access `main.aspx` whenever they click on an appropriate link on the home page. These links live mostly in the Flash movie in the upper-left part of the web page.

I designed `main.aspx` to be more of an instructional page than a solution you'd want to try yourself (it's a little too fat and will load slowly on some machines). I really consider `main.aspx` the gateway to the rest of the public areas. If you were to mimic this page, you'd want to put some of its pieces into their own page. But `main.aspx` shows how you can use ASP.NET to mimic Dynamic HTML and incorporate a lot of functionality on one screen.

The key to `main.aspx` is the menu bar at the top. When the user clicks a menu item, the face of the page changes accordingly, as shown in Figures 9.7 and 9.8.

FIGURE 9.7:

When the Listings menu item is clicked, the website visitor sees current listings.

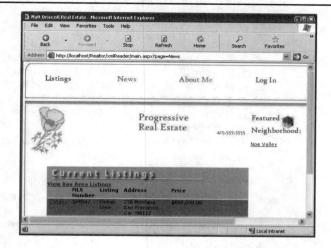

FIGURE 9.8:

When the About Me menu item is clicked, the website visitor sees information about the realtor.

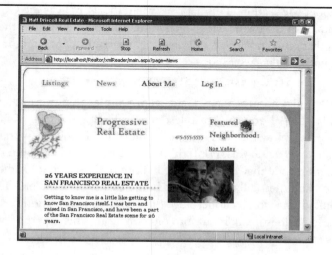

As much as I like working with XML, I still prefer storing data in SQL-based databases using stored procedures because they're so fast. Many books featuring .NET will suggest that you write your content management system using XML, but if you have access to a high-performance database, I think you're still better off going that route.

That said, in this case I use some XML to display the text about the realtor that the user sees after clicking the About Me button. This is accomplished with this simple ASP.NET control:

```
<asp:label ID="txtXmlTextReader" runat="server" />
```

The management of the XML takes place in the `main.aspx.cs` file's `AboutButton_OnClick` event handler:

```
XPathDocument doc = new XPathDocument(Server.MapPath("about.xml"));
        XslTransform trans = new XslTransform();
        trans.Load(Server.MapPath("about.xsl"));

        StringWriter sw2 = new StringWriter();
        XmlTextWriter xmlWriter =
        ➥new XmlTextWriter(sw2); //Write to StringWriter
        xmlWriter.Formatting = Formatting.Indented;
        xmlWriter.Indentation = 4;
        trans.Transform(doc,null,xmlWriter);
        this.txtXmlTextReader.Text = sw2.ToString();
        sw2.Close();
        xmlWriter.Close();
```

The XML documents will also load if the Flash file in the main page directs users to the About Me section. This happens when the user clicks the Go Button that appears in the Flash movie on the main page, which in turn happens only after the *first* clicks the About Me button in that same movie. The Flash sends a variable, `page`, and the `Page_Load` event handler picks it up using a `QueryString`:

```
else if(Request.QueryString["page"] == "About")
```

You'll see in the `Page_Load` event handler that there is another exact duplicate of the XML/XSLT routine I just described, which is also called in the `AboutButton_OnClick` event handler. Now that you know a bit more about how C# works, start thinking about how you can improve on this. Hint: think *functions*. It would be better to remove the XML transformation code that appears twice in both of those event handlers, and create a separate function and then call that function in the two event handlers. Try doing that as an exercise. The bulk of the work is done, since the XML transformation code is already developed. All you need to do is break it out into one function. This is part of what I have referred to previously as encapsulation.

The `main.aspx.cs` code page hides and displays parts of the interface based on what is called for when the user clicks a particular link.

Building the Registration and Login Area

When users log in, they're taken to a private area on the site that can contain any kind of personalized information the administrator deems useful. In the Realtor site, I kept things to a minimum, so all that's seen are a personalized greeting, notes from the Realtor to the client, and a calendar (using the ASP.NET Calendar control). See Figure 9.9.

FIGURE 9.9:

Clients can have their own personal space on the site.

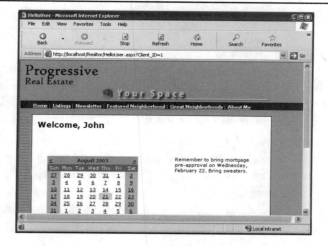

The Calendar control is a fairly interesting control from Microsoft that comes as part of the ASP.NET Framework. It offers powerful data-driven control similar to the DataGrid. The actual code to create the Calendar control is minimal:

```
<asp:Calendar id="Calendar1" runat="server">
  <TodayDayStyle BackColor="PaleTurquoise"></TodayDayStyle>
  <SelectorStyle BackColor="SlateGray"></SelectorStyle>
   <DayHeaderStyle ForeColor="White" BackColor
  ➥="CornflowerBlue"></DayHeaderStyle>
     <WeekendDayStyle BackColor="LightBlue"></WeekendDayStyle>
</asp:Calendar>
```

Once you've figured out DataGrids, you can apply many of the same principles to Calendar controls and write data-driven applications. That way, when a user clicks on a date in the control, a specific event could be displayed to the user—perhaps a reminder of something, or some other alert, or, since this is a real-estate site, simply the closing date of a home sale.

Exploring the Realtor Site

The Realtor site is quite extensive. However, it's far from perfect. I intentionally made certain parts of it somewhat inefficient to challenge you to come up with better code. There are also instances of pages with similar functionality that take very different approaches to the same problems. The reason for this is so you can explore the various avenues you can take with .NET. Different approaches will be better for different people.

Look for areas in which SELECT statements take place directly in the web forms, and where these would work better as stored procedures. Then, create some stored procedures and replace the less efficient, non-stored-procedure pages with pages that do use stored procedures.

There are other areas throughout the site in which you can improve the code. Look for ways to do so. For example, are there any multiple if statements that could be better served with switch statements?

If you're having trouble compiling using namespaces, just forget about them for now and build all your code-behind pages without namespaces. If you have to, forget about even compiling the pages, and just use event handlers in your code-behind files without worrying about assemblies and namespaces and DLLs.

If necessary, don't use code-behind at all; simply embed your script in script tags in the web form. Ultimately, code-behind and compilation will be your friends, but they can take some getting used to. The idea here is to get a handle on how C# works, so focus on that if you're new to this language.

Hopefully, if you study the code in Realtor, you'll be able to figure out most of how it works based on what you've read in this book. If not, take it slow. Take apart a .cs page and embed its event handlers in your web form's script, and try running your pages without code-behind at all. Of course, first you'll have to take out the codebehind attribute from the @Page directive.

Wrapping Up

The best way to familiarize yourself with Dreamweaver's ways of writing code and how you can develop your own handwritten code is to explore the Realtor application in Dreamweaver. Simply create a new site in Dreamweaver, expand the compressed file into a directory named Realtor, and make that directory the root of your site.

Then go through the files and see how things are pieced together. You'll find a lot more in the application than what I've described in this chapter or even the book as a whole. You should be able to find some code that needs to be optimized. You'll also find a few surprises, such as an image-uploading web form that allows site administrators to upload images associated with their listings.

In many ways, even though the book is filled with examples based on the Realtor application, there are many features in Realtor that are "undocumented." As you become familiar with the application and with coding in Dreamweaver, you'll find ways to improve many pieces of the application. You may want to think about how to do some things differently, such as building an XML-based navigation bar, or an XML-based blog site.

To me, the most interesting feature about the Realtor application is that it reflects my discovery of Dreamweaver as a legitimate application environment. I began the Realtor site as a real project for a real company (no puns intended) shortly after the .NET Framework was introduced. I began the project using Microsoft's Visual Studio, and this fact is reflected in the project files for that program that you'll see sprinkled throughout the site. About midway through the project, I discovered that I could cut my development time by as much as 50 to 75 percent using Dreamweaver. My only regret about the discovery was not making it sooner. Luckily, you won't have to wait. You have this book. So start exploring, and watch your development time get shaved in the process.

Appendix A

Errors Using Dreamweaver MX and ASP.NET

This brief appendix lists a few common errors you may run into while building applications using Dreamweaver MX and ASP.NET. The section titled "Troubleshooting Runtime Errors" includes portions of errors the C# compiler will show you, followed by an explanation of how to fix the problem.

Customizing Error Pages

To customize the default ASP.NET error page, you need to change the default configuration settings of the application by editing the Web.config file. The customError element's mode attribute is used to indicate whether an ASP.NET error message is displayed. The mode attribute can take the following three values: Off, On, or RemoteOnly. By default, the mode value is set to RemoteOnly.

- Off: ASP.NET uses its default error page for both local and remote users when an error is generated:

    ```
    <customErrors mode="Off" />
    ```

- On: ASP.NET uses a user-defined custom error page instead of its default error page for both local and remote users:

    ```
    <customErrors defaultRedirect="error.aspx" mode="On" />
    ```

If you don't specify a custom error page in the Web.config file, ASP.NET shows an error page describing how to enable remote viewing of errors:

- RemoteOnly: ASP.NET displays an error page to local users only:

    ```
    <customErrors defaultRedirect="error.htm" mode="RemoteOnly" />
    ```

On remote requests, ASP.NET will first check the configuration settings for the custom error page and show an IIS error if there is no custom error defined in the Web.config file.

Configuration Issues with Dreamweaver and .NET

The following are some issues and errors that are related to core configuration issues. These can include your FTP configuration, or the way your IIS is set up.

Unsuccessful URL Test or FTP Connection

If you can't connect to your web server using a Test URL button on the Site Definition panel, test to make sure your web server is actually running. In the Internet Information Services snap-in, right-click your Default Web Site and make sure Start isn't grayed out. (If it is not grayed out, Stop should be.) If Start is not grayed out, navigate to it with your mouse and release the mouse when Start is highlighted to start IIS.

If your FTP connection isn't working, check to see whether you entered the FTP host server name or IP address correctly. If you are working with a host provider and they assigned you a domain name, it might not be registered with the Internet's Domain Name Servers yet, so you will need to enter the IP number of your server instead of the domain name.

Dreamweaver's Nefarious "Waiting For Server" Message

One of the more detested messages developers receive when working with FTP in Dreamweaver is the "Waiting For Server" message they get on a site they have all ready set up. The quick solution: Go into your site editor and click the Advanced tab. Look in the Category window for Remote Info. Under the text field for Password is a checkbox for Passive FTP. Check that box and click Test to try out your server. It should successfully complete the connection.

So the obvious question is, what is Passive FTP?

FTP works in two channels—command and data. The command channel and, therefore the login password, is what gets encrypted. The data channel remains wide open.

FTP has two modes of operation, active and passive. In active mode, your machine contacts the server's command port and sends the command PORT 1027. The server then sends an acknowledge message (ACK if you look in the Results Panel and click the FTP Log tab) back to Dreamweaver's FTP command port. Next, the server initiates a connection on its local data port to the data port the client specified earlier. Then the client sends back another ACK command. In other words, the server needs to shake hands with the client. This can be a problem if you're working from behind a firewall.

The FTP client in Dreamweaver doesn't actually connect to the data port of the server. Instead, it tells the server what port it is listening on, and the server responds by connecting to that port. If you have a firewall, your firewall will notice an outside system initiating a connection and, usually, especially if you are working with default settings, will block the connection.

In passive FTP, the client and server communicate using the aforementioned command channel and the server tells the client which port to use for the data channel on the server. The first port contacts the server on port 21, but instead of then issuing a PORT command and allowing the server to connect back to its data port, Dreamweaver FTP will issue the PASV command, which cues the server to open a random unprivileged port ($P > 1024$) and return a PORT P command back to the client. The client then initiates the connection from port N+1 to port P on the server to transfer data. That's the key to remember if you are working behind the firewall—the client in effect initiates the connections, rather than listening for connections only to have a firewall intervene to block the communication between server and client.

Human-Readable ASPX Files Appear in the Browser or No Documents Are Served

You might take a few things for granted when working locally and deploying files to a remote hosting service, but they are important to keep in mind, especially if, when you deploy to your remote production server and nothing works, you don't know what's wrong because you know your files are correct.

By far the most common problem with working with a remote hosting service is that after you've deployed the files, you discover that ASP.NET simply doesn't work. When you test the site on the remote host, you find that either the pages you are requesting don't get served or they get served as HTML pages displaying all your ASPX code. Generally the reason for this is that the remote hosting service has not yet enabled ASP.NET for your site. Usually a simple help ticket asking them to enable ASP.NET will do the job. On your own machine or server, of course, you have to be sure you have installed the .NET Framework. IIS won't serve ASP.NET pages without it.

Of course, one other reason for not seeing a generated page from ASP.NET is if you are viewing a page from your hard drive, which means that your web page hasn't been served to you by any process. You'll need to view the website from a live web server, whether it's a testing server, staging server, or production.

403 Forbidden: Execute Access Forbidden

The error "403 Forbidden: Execute Access Forbidden" occurs when you forget to assign directory permissions to ASP.NET, which is installed when you install the .NET framework as a user but isn't granted any permissions until you grant them. If you get this message while working with a host provider, let them know so they can assign permissions to ASP.NET. If you get this message while working locally, either ask your administrator to grant permissions to ASP.NET, or if you are an administrator, do this yourself through Windows Explorer by navigating to the appropriate directory and right-clicking to bring up the Properties dialog box. Click the Security tab and then the Add... button. Type in **ASPNET** (without any period between ASP and NET) in the text field labeled `Enter the object names to select`, then click OK.

DreamweaverCtrls Not Found

`File or assembly name DreamweaverCtrls, or one of its dependencies, was not found.`

You won't get this error when first testing your connection and server unless you decide to immediately try a simple Dreamweaver-driven ASP.NET page, but it's such a basic issue that you should know about it before starting to build applications. When you build .NET applications using Dreamweaver's RAD tools, Dreamweaver relies on a special Dynamic Link

Library (DLL) named `DreamweaverCtrls.dll` that you need to deploy to your server using `Site/Deploy Supporting Files…`. This is because Dreamweaver's server controls rely on the compiled code within `DreamweaverCtrls.dll` to do their magic. One of the nice things about .NET is that you don't need to register DLLs anymore. .NET web applications will always look for DLLs in the root directory's bin directory.

By default, Dreamweaver MX deploys the `DreamweaverCtrls.dll` into the bin directory at the root level of your site. If you then create a virtual directory, ASP.NET will look for the control in the bin directory within the virtual directory you created, if there is one. If there isn't a bin directory or if the bin directory doesn't contain the `DreamweaverCtrls.dll`, you'll get an error message indicating that the system can't find the assembly.

The solution is to either add a redirect in the `web.config` file residing in the root directory's bin directory, or create a bin directory in the virtual directory you've just created and copy the `DreamweaverCtrls.dll` into it.

Unable to find script library

```
Unable to find script library
'/aspnet_client/system_web/1_0_3705_288/WebUIValidation.js'. Try placing this
file manually, or reinstall by running 'aspnet_regiis -c'.
```

You may get an error message similar to this one, although some of the particulars, such as the directory name after `system_web`, might be different. The solution is to look for the script that the system can't find (in this case `WebUIValidation.js`) and manually create a directory and path exactly like that described in the message. It's likely that you already have a directory named `aspnet_client` and one named `system_web`, and that all you have to do is create a directory named, in this case, `1_0_3705_288`, or whatever the message tells you is missing. Then manually add the `WebUIValidation.js` file to the newly created directory.

Troubleshooting Runtime Errors

The following is a list of common errors that can occur during the course of developing and, particularly, testing your web applications.

Browser Tries to Download an ASP.NET File

A true newbie error, this occurs when you aren't accessing an ASP.NET file, such as one with an aspx extension, through a web server. If you are running the file on your local machine, you can't double-click it. You have to run it from your local host like this:

```
http://localhost/site.
```

You're Unable to Create a Web Application on a LAN That Uses a Proxy Server

When developing on a local LAN that uses a proxy or firewall to access the Internet, you may need to set your connection options to "Bypass proxy for local addresses." Perform the following steps to set this up:

1. In the Tools menu, select Options.

2. Under the Projects node, select Web Settings.

3. In the Options dialog box, click Connection Settings.

4. In the Internet Properties dialog box, select the Connections tab and click LAN Settings.

5. In the LAN Settings dialog box, select "Bypass proxy server for local addresses."

6. Click OK to close all open dialog boxes.

System.IndexOutOfRangeException

```
Exception Details: System.IndexOutOfRangeException: Password
```

This exception is thrown when an attempt is made to access an array element with an index that is outside the bounds of the array. What this means, in this particular case, is that you attempted to access a field in the database that doesn't exist. The answer, as you might guess, is to make sure that the field you are accessing does indeed exist.

For example, consider this code fragment:

```
if
(string.Compare(dr["Password"].ToString(),passwd,false)==0)
```

If there is no field in the database named `Password`, you'd get the error. This is the kind of typo that is easy to make. Assuming the actual field is named `CPassword`, the problem is corrected by changing the field name to `CPassword`:

```
if
(string.Compare(dr["CPassword"].ToString(),passwd,false)==0)
```

SQL Errors Show Up on Return Pages

Often, you'll get an error like this showing up just above the rest of your page:

```
System.FormatException: The string was not recognized as a valid DateTime. There
is a unknown word starting at index 0.
```

The exact wording isn't what's important; it's the fact that your page is returning an error that your users can see. Be sure to set the `debug` attribute in your Dreamweaver control tag to `false`. Setting it to `true`, of course, is a nice way to debug potential problems before you go live. After you've tested your code and gone into production, however, you'll want to prevent these kinds of messages from appearing.

Page.IsValid cannot be called before validation has taken place

You can get this message when you haven't properly handled server validation in your server code:

```
Page.IsValid cannot be called before validation has taken place. It should be
queried in the event handler for a control with CausesValidation=True or after a
call to Page.Validate.
```

The simplest solution when receiving this error is to simply start off with the Page object's Validate() method. You can just add that to the beginning of the event handler:

```
void Page_Load(Object Sender, EventArgs e) {
    Validate();
    if (Page.IsValid){
...
    }
}
```

Chances are you'll want something more robust, but you get the point.

In this book I've pretty much focused on page load events, but as you tinker, you may use some other page-related events. In that case, you'll need to know in what order they fire. It's actually pretty intuitive:

```
Page_Init
Page_Load
Page_PreRender
```

If you build a custom control that might need to be initialized before the page loads, for example, you'd want to call it from the Page_Init event handler, instead of the Page_Load event handler.

Empty Values for Dreamweaver Elements

```
System.Exception: This page has a MM:DataSet, MM:Insert, MM:Update or
MM:Delete
tag with a null or empty value for the ConnectionString and DatabaseType
attributes.
```

You can get this message when obtaining values for application settings from the Web.config file, and that file is missing from the server or the server can't find it for some reason. You should also check to be sure that the add element's key attribute has been configured for the database connection you are working with. For example:

```
<appSettings>
    <add key="DSN"
  value="server=(local);uid=sybex;pwd=dreamweavermx;
  ➥Database=Realtor"/>
</appSettings>
```

You can find more information on this at:

`http://www.musikstationen.net/musikkatalogen/`

'System.Data.DataRowView' does not contain a property with the name undefined

```
DataBinder.Eval: 'System.Data.DataRowView' does not contain a
property with the name undefined.
Exception Details: System.Web.HttpException: DataBinder.Eval:
  'System.Data.DataRowView' does not contain a property with the name
undefined.
```

You can get this error when working with DataGrids, particularly after you've made changes in Code view, such as when you're editing `EditItemTemplate` elements. Check the DataGrid's `DataKeyField` attribute and make sure its value isn't `undefined`. Dreamweaver will change the value to `undefined` if you've hand-edited the code for an `EditItemTemplate` and then attempt to edit through the user interface. Change the value back to the primary key of the table to which the DataGrid's datasource is bound.

Identifier expected, 'checked' is a keyword

```
Compiler Error Message: CS1041: Identifier expected, 'checked' is a keyword
```

This error occurs if you don't use the `checked` property correctly with a check box. It should be capitalized:

```
if (myCheckBox.Checked) ...
```

not

```
if (myCheckBox.checked)...
```

Array Initializer Error

```
Compiler Error Message: CS0622: Can only use array initializer expressions
to assign to array types. Try using a new expression instead.
Source Error:
Line 6:   protected void Page_Load(Object Src, EventArgs E)
Line 7:   {
Line 8:      string sRange = {"100-200K", "200-300K", "300-400K"};
Line 9:      string sValueRange = {"100", "200", "300"};
Line 10:     int i;
```

This error happens when you forget to add the brackets for an array yet appear to be attempting to work with one. This is easily fixed by simply adding the brackets:

```
String[] sRange = {"100-200K", "200-300K", "300-400K"};
```

The type or namespace name 'xxxxx' could not be found

One of the more common errors, this is usually resolved by finding out what class the named entity belongs to and importing it into your code. Consider the following error:

```
Compiler Error Message: CS0246: The type or namespace name
'Exception' could not be found (are you missing a using directive or an assembly
reference?)
```

The solution in this example is to make sure you include the System class (using System) in your code. System.Web or System.Web.UI is not enough, because those classes alone don't inherit the needed Exception class.

You can also get this error when you use HTML controls that you are trying to access programmatically on the server and you forget to include the runat="server" attribute.

This error also frequently occurs when you cut server controls out of Dreamweaver and paste them back into the document, even if it's the same document. So this:

```
<td><input id="txtUserName" type="text" name="txtUserName" runat="server">
```

becomes this:

```
<td><input id="txtUserName4" type="text" name="txtUserName" runat="server">
```

Note the ID attribute. To fix it, just change the ID attribute back to what it was originally.

For more help with this error message, you might also wish to refer to Microsoft's site (Q304656):

```
http://support.microsoft.com/default.aspx?scid=kb;EN-US;Q304656
```

'TextBox' cannot have children of type 'DataBoundLiteralControl'

```
Exception Details: System.Web.HttpException: 'TextBox' cannot have children of
type 'DataBoundLiteralControl'.

Source Error:


Line 152:            Visible="True">
Line 153:                        <ItemTemplate>
Line 154:                          <asp:textbox runat="server" id
                                  ="CXSLTPresentation" width="200" height
                                  ="200"> <%# Code.FieldValue
                                  ("CXSLT", Container) %> </asp:textbox>
Line 155:                          </ItemTemplate>
Line 156:                        <EditItemTemplate>
```

You get this error if you do something like the following (note the missing single quote):

```
<asp:textbox runat="server" id="CXSLTPresentation"
width="200" height="200">
<%# Code.FieldValue("CXSLT", Container) %>
</asp:textbox>
```

Fix it with this (by adding a single quote character):

```
<asp:textbox runat="server" id="CXSLTPresentation"
width="200" height="200" text =
'<%# Code.FieldValue("CXSLT", Container) %>' />
```

allowDefinition='MachineToApplication' Error

```
Parser Error Message: It is an error to use a section registered as
allowDefinition='MachineToApplication' beyond application level. This error
can be caused by a virtual directory not being configured as an application
in IIS.
Source Error:
Line 21:     <trace enabled="true"/>
Line 23:      <authentication mode="Forms">
Line 24:       <forms name=".ASPXFORMS" loginUrl="Default.aspx"
Line 25:     protection="All" path="/" timeout="30" />
```

This error may seem self-explanatory, but the thing to note here is to make sure that if the file you are accessing is within a subdirectory of the application, that subdirectory also needs to be configured as an application.

Dreamweaver Sets Quotes Improperly on the Hyperlink Control

Some versions of Dreamweaver don't correctly set quotes on the asp:hyperlink element's NavigateURL attribute when using the visual interface and data-bound values. The code for this element should look something like this:

```
<asp:hyperlink ID="UpdateHyperlink" NavigateUrl='<%#
➡ "UpdateListings.aspx?MLSNumber=" +
➡ ListingsProc.FieldValue("MLSNumber", Container) %>'
runat="server" Text="Update This Listing">
</asp:hyperlink>
```

not all code paths return a value

```
Compiler Error Message: CS0161: 'GetNotes.getCNote(string)': not all code
paths return a value

Line 20:
Line 21:
Line 22: private string getCNote(string strGetClientID)
Line 23:    {
Line 24: SqlConnection connection = new SqlConnection
(ConfigurationSettings.AppSettings["DSN"]);
```

In this example (`webservice.asmx` from Chapter 10), we forgot to write the last line, `return report`. In other words, we forgot to return the string.

Macromedia's Error Website

Macromedia provides a website that describes common errors experienced when using Dreamweaver MX and ASP.NET. It can be found at either of the following URLs:

```
http://sdc.shockwave.com/support/dreamweaver/ts/documents/asp_net_common
_errors.htm#two
http://www.macromedia.com/support/dreamweaver/ts/documents/asp_net_common
_errors.htm
```

Index

Note to the Reader: Throughout this index **boldfaced** page numbers indicate primary discussions of a topic. *Italicized* page numbers indicate illustrations.

D

E

S

X

Z

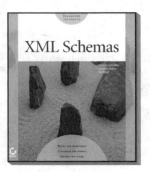